LENIN

COLLECTED WORKS

40

THE RUSSIAN EDITION WAS PRINTED
IN ACCORDANCE WITH A DECISION
OF THE NINTH CONGRESS OF THE R.C.P.(B.)
AND THE SECOND CONGRESS OF SOVIETS
OF THE U.S.S.R.

ИНСТИТУТ МАРКСИЗМА-ЛЕНИНИЗМА при ЦК КПСС

В. И. ЛЕНИН

СОЧИНЕНИЯ

Издание четвертое

ГОСУДАРСТВЕННОЕ ИЗДАТЕЛЬСТВО
ПОЛИТИЧЕСКОЙ ЛИТЕРАТУРЫ
МОСКВА

V. I. LENIN

COLLECTED WORKS

VOLUME
40
Notebooks on the Agrarian Question
1900–1916

PROGRESS PUBLISHERS
MOSCOW

TRANSLATED FROM THE RUSSIAN
BY YURI SDOBNIKOV

First   printing 1968
Second   printing 1974
Third   printing 1976
Fourth   printing 1980

Printed in the Union of Soviet Socialist Republics

Л $\dfrac{10102\text{---}214}{014(01)\text{---}82}$ без объявл.

CONTENTS

II

CRITIQUE OF BOURGEOIS LITERATURE
AND ANALYSIS OF MASSIVE AGRARIAN STATISTICS
1900-1903

III

MATERIAL FOR A STUDY OF THE CAPITALIST ECONOMY
OF EUROPE AND THE UNITED STATES
1910-1916

ILLUSTRATIONS

PREFACE

The present volume contains Lenin's *Notebooks on the Agrarian Question*, which is preparatory material for his works analysing capitalist agriculture in Western Europe, Russia and the United States, and criticising bourgeois and petty-bourgeois theories, and reformism and revisionism in the agrarian question.

The material in this volume relates to the period from 1900 to 1916. In the new conditions, with capitalism at its highest and final stage—the stage of imperialism—Lenin worked out and substantiated the agrarian programme and agrarian policy of the revolutionary proletarian party, and took Marxist theory on the agrarian question a step forward in its view of classes and the class struggle in the countryside, the alliance of the working class and the peasantry under the leadership of the proletariat, and their joint struggle against the landowners and capitalists, for democracy and socialism. The success of the revolution depended on whom the peasantry would follow, for in many European countries it constituted the majority or a sizable section of the population. In order to win over the peasantry, as an ally of the proletariat in the coming revolution, it was necessary to expose the hostile parties which claimed leadership of the peasantry, and their ideologists.

In the new epoch, these questions became especially pressing and acquired international significance. That is why bourgeois economists, reformists and revisionists fiercely attacked Marxism. It was subjected to criticism by bourgeois apologists, the ideologists of petty-bourgeois parties, and opportunists among the Social-Democrats. They all rejected Marx's theory of ground-rent,

and the law of concentration of production in agriculture,
and denied the advantages of large- over small-scale production; they insisted that agriculture developed according
to special laws, and was subject to the inexorable "law of
diminishing returns". They said it was not human labour
and the implements of labour, but the elemental forces of
nature that were decisive in agriculture. These "critics
of Marx" juggled with the facts and statistics, in an effort
to show that the small-scale peasant economy was "stable"
and had advantages over large-scale capitalist production.

Lenin's great historical service in working out the agrarian question lies in the fact that he defended Marx's revolutionary teaching against the attacks of his "critics", and
further developed it in application to the new historical
conditions and in connection with the working out of the programme, strategy and tactics of the revolutionary proletarian
party of the new type; he proved the possibility, and the
necessity, of an alliance between the working class and the
peasantry under the leadership of the proletariat at the
various stages of the revolution, and showed the conditions
in which this could be realised.

It was of tremendous importance to produce a theoretical
elaboration of the agrarian question so as to determine
the correct relations between the working class and the
various groups of peasantry as the revolutionary struggle
went forward. Under capitalism, the peasantry breaks up into
different class groups, with differing and antithetical interests; the "erosion" of the middle peasantry yields a numer-
ically small but economically powerful rich peasant (kulak)
top section at one pole, and a mass of poor peasants, rural
proletarians and semi-proletarians, at the other. Lenin
revealed the dual nature of the peasant as a petty commodity producer—the dual nature of his economic and
political interests: the basic interests of the toiler suffering
from exploitation by the landowner and the kulak, which
makes him look to the proletariat for support, and the
interests of the owner, which determine his gravitation
towards the bourgeoisie, his political instability and vacilla-
tion between it and the working class. Lenin emphasised
the need for an alliance between the working class and the
peasantry, with the leading role belonging to the proletariat,

as a prerequisite for winning the dictatorship of the proletariat and building socialism through a joint effort by the
workers and peasants

*   *   *

The *first* part of the volume contains the plans and outlines of Lenin's writings on the agrarian question, the main
being the preparatory materials for "The Agrarian Question
and the 'Critics of Marx'" (see present edition, Vols. 5
and 13). The variants of the plan for this work give a good
idea of how Lenin mapped out the main line and the concrete points for his critique of reformist bourgeois theories
and of revisionism. Lenin defined a programme for processing
the relevant reliable material from numerous sources to
refute the arguments of the "critics of Marx" concerning
the dubious "law of diminishing returns" and the Malthusian explanation of the root causes of the working man's
plight, and to ward off their attacks on the Marxist theory
of ground-rent, etc.

In preparing "The Agrarian Question and the 'Critics of
Marx'" and his lectures on the agrarian question, Lenin
made a thorough study of the most important sources, and
utilised European agrarian statistics to give Marxist
agrarian theory a sound basis. He verified, analysed and
summed up a mass of statistical data, and drew up tables
giving an insight into the deep-going causes, nature and
social significance of economic processes. Lenin's analysis
of agrarian statistics shows their tremendous importance
as a tool in cognising economic laws, exposing the contradictions of capitalism, and subjecting it and its apologists
to scientific criticism.

The writings in the first part of the volume show the
direct connection between Lenin's theoretical inquiry,
his elaboration of Marxist agrarian theory and the practical
revolutionary struggle of the working class.

The preparatory materials for his lectures on the "Marxist
Views of the Agrarian Question in Europe and Russia",
and on "The Agrarian Programme of the Socialist-Revolutionaries and of the Social-Democrats", both included in
this volume, are a reflection of an important stage of Lenin's
struggle against the petty-bourgeois party of Socialist-

Revolutionaries and opportunists within the Social-Democratic movement, in working out and substantiating a truly
revolutionary agrarian programme and tactics for the
Marxist working-class party in Russia.

Russia was then on the threshold of her bourgeois-democratic revolution. In Russia, capitalism had grown into
imperialism, while considerable survivals of serfdom still
remained in the country's economy and the political system
as a whole. The landed estates were the main relics of pre-
capitalist relations in the economy; the peasant allotment
land tenure, adapted to the landowners' corvée system,
was also shackled with relics of serfdom. These tended
to slow down the development of the productive forces
both in Russia's industry and agriculture, widen the technical and economic gap separating her from the leading
capitalist countries of the West, and create the conditions
for indentured forms of exploitation of the working class
and the peasantry. That is why the agrarian question was
basic to the bourgeois-democratic revolution in Russia and
determined its specific features.

Lenin laid special emphasis on the importance of theory
in working out the Party programme: "In order to make
a comparison of the programmes and to assess them, it is necessary to examine the *principles*, the theory, from which the
programme flows" (see p. 53). Lenin's theoretical analysis
of the economic nature of the peasant economy enabled
him to determine correctly the community or the distinction
of class interests between the proletariat and the various
sections of the peasantry in the bourgeois-democratic revolution, and to map out the Party's policy towards the
peasantry. The main task of the agrarian programme during
the bourgeois-democratic revolution was to formulate the
demands that would secure the peasantry as the proletariat's
ally in the struggle against tsarism and the landowners. "The
meaning of our agrarian programme: the Russian proletariat (including the rural) must support the peasantry
in the struggle against serfdom" (see p. 62). Lenin subjected
the agrarian programme of the Socialist-Revolutionaries
to withering criticism and proved that their theoretical
unscrupulousness and eclecticism had induced them to say
nothing of the historical task of the period—destruction of the

relicts of serfdom—to deny the stratification of the peasantry along class lines, and the class struggle in the countryside, to invent all manner of projects for "socialisation of land", "equalisation", etc.

While Lenin aimed his criticism against the Socialist-Revolutionaries, he also exposed the anti-Marxist stand on the agrarian issue in Russia and the peasantry taken by P. P. Maslov, A. S. Martynov, D. B. Ryazanov and other Mensheviks-to-be, who denied that the peasantry had a revolutionary role to play, and who regarded it as a solid reactionary mass. By contrast, Lenin emphasised the dual nature of Narodism: the democratic side, inasmuch as they waged a struggle against the relicts of serfdom, and the utopian and reactionary side, expressive of the urge on the part of the petty bourgeois to perpetuate his small farm. In this context, Lenin pointed to the need to take account of the two sides of Narodism in evaluating its historical importance.

The first part ends with two plans for "The Peasantry and Social-Democracy" (see pp. 69-70). These plans warrant the assumption that Lenin had the intention of writing a special work on the subject to sum up his studies of agrarian relations and the experience gained by socialist parties abroad in working out agrarian programmes, and to substantiate the R.S.D.L.P.'s policy towards the peasantry. With his usual insight, he points to the "practical importance of the agrarian question in the possibly near future" (see p. 70), and notes the specific nature of class relations in the Russian countryside, and the need for the rural proletariat to fight on two flanks: against the landowners and the relicts of serfdom, and against the bourgeoisie. Lenin marked out the guiding principles which were to serve the Marxist party as a beacon in the intricate conditions of the class struggle in the countryside: "Together with the peasant bourgeoisie against the landowners. Together with the urban proletariat against the peasant bourgeoisie" (see p. 69).

The writings in the *second* part of the present volume are a reflection of his critical processing of a great mass of facts and statistical data from bourgeois and petty-bourgeois agrarian works and official sources. Of special

interest in this part is the material on the study and processing of the results of special statistical inquiries into
the state of agriculture, especially the peasant economy,
in a number of European countries.

Lenin gives a model of scientific analysis of agrarian
relations, application of the Marxist method in processing
social and economic statistics, and critical use of bourgeois
sources and writings. Lenin adduces reliable data to refute
the assertions of bourgeois economists, reformists and revisionists, and shows that in agriculture as well large-scale
capitalist production is more effective than small-scale
production and tends inevitably to supplant it, that small
peasant farms are being expropriated by big capital, and
that the toiling peasantry is being ruined and proletarised.
That is the *general law* governing the development of agriculture on capitalist lines, although it may *differ in form*
from country to country.

In his critical remarks on the works of S. Bulgakov,
F. Hertz, M. Hecht, E. David, and K. Klawki, Lenin refutes
the bourgeois reformist theories which extol small farming
and assert that it is "superior" to large-scale production.
He exposes the tricks used by bourgeois and petty-bourgeois
economists to minimise the earnings of the big farms and
exaggerate those of the small. Lenin counters the false eulo-
gies to the "viability" of the small farms—due allegedly
to the small farmer's industry, thrift and hardiness, by
showing that small-scale production in agriculture is sus-
tained by the back-breaking toil and poor nutrition of the
small farmer, the dissipation of his vital forces, the deterio-
ration of his livestock, and the waste of the soil's productive
forces.

Lenin has some particularly sharp words for the reformists
and revisionists who "fool others by styling themselves
socialists", and put more into prettifying capitalist reality
than the bourgeois apologists themselves. Lenin makes
a detailed analysis of E. David's *Socialism and Agriculture*—
the main revisionist work on the agrarian question—and
shows it to be a collection of bourgeois falsehood and bias
wrapped up in "socialist" terminology.

At the same time, Lenin takes pains to sift and examine
any genuine scientific data and correct observations and

conclusions which he finds in bourgeois sources and writings. He makes the following extract from O. Pringsheim's article: "Modern large-scale agricultural production should be compared with the *manufacture* (in the *Marxian sense*)" (see p. 108), and repeatedly makes such comparisons in his works (see present edition, Vol. 5, p. 141 and Vol. 22, p. 99). On F. Maurice's book, *Agriculture and the Social Question. Agricultural and Agrarian France*, Lenin makes this remark: "The author has the wildest ideas of the most primitive anarchism. There are some interesting factual remarks" (see p. 173).

Lenin devotes special attention to an analysis of statistics on the agrarian system in Denmark, which the apologists of capitalism liked to present as the "ideal" country of small-scale peasant production. He exposes the trickery of bourgeois economists and revisionists and demonstrates the *capitalist* nature of the country's agrarian system. The basic fact which bourgeois political economists and revisionists try to hush up is that the bulk of the land and the livestock in Denmark is in the hands of landowners running farms on capitalist lines (see p. 225 and pp. 376-82). "The basis of Danish agriculture is large-scale and medium *capitalist* farming. All the talk about a 'peasant country' and 'small-scale farming' is sheer bourgeois apologetics, a distortion of the facts by various titled and untitled ideologists of capital" (see present edition, Vol. 13, p. 196). Lenin castigates the "socialists" who try to obscure the fact that production is being concentrated and that the petty producer is being ousted by the big producer, and the fact that the prosperity of capitalist agriculture in Denmark is based on the *massive proletarisation* of the rural population.

The *third* part of the volume contains material for a study of the capitalist agriculture of Europe and the United States from 1910 to 1916, including the material relating to Lenin's *New Data on the Laws Governing the Development of Capitalism in Agriculture. Part One. Capitalism and Agriculture in the United States of America*.

In this work, Lenin stresses that the United States, "a leading country of modern capitalism", was of especial interest for the study of the social and economic structure of agriculture, and of the forms and laws of its development

in modern capitalist conditions. "In America, agricultural
capitalism is more *clear-cut*, the division of labour is more
crystallised; there are *fewer* bonds with the Middle Ages,
with the soil-bound labourer; ground-rent is not so burdensome; there is less intermixing of commercial agriculture
and subsistence farming" (see p. 420). The important thing
is that the United States is unrivalled in the vastness of
territory and diversity of relationships, showing the greatest
spectrum of shades and forms of capitalist agriculture.

Bourgeois economists, reformists and revisionists distort
the facts in an effort to prove that the U.S. farm economy
is a model of the "non-capitalist evolution" of farming, where
the "small family farm" is allegedly supplanting large-
scale production, where most farms are "family-labour
farms", etc. N. Himmer, who gave his views in an article
on the results of the U.S. Census of 1910, epitomises those
who believe that agriculture in capitalist society develops
along non-capitalist lines. Lenin makes this note: "Himmer
as a *collection* of bourgeois views. *In this respect,*
his short article is worth volumes" (see p. 408). The opponents
of Marxism based their conclusions on facts and figures,
major and minor, which were isolated from "the general
context of politico-economic relations". On the strength
of massive data provided by the U.S. censuses, Lenin gives
"a complete picture of capitalism in American agriculture"
(present edition, Vol. 22, p. 18). Lenin notes that through
their agricultural censuses, bourgeois statisticians collect
"an immense wealth of complete information on each enterprise as a unit" but because of incorrect tabulation and
grouping it is reduced in value and spoiled; the net result
is meaningless columns of figures, a kind of statistical
"game of digits".

Lenin goes on to work the massive data of agricultural
statistics into tables on scientific principles for grouping
farms. The summary table compiled by Lenin (pp. 440-41)
is a remarkable example of the use of socio-economic statistics as an instrument of social cognition. He brings out
the contradictions and trends in the capitalist development
of U.S. agriculture through a three-way grouping of farms:
by income, that is, the value of the product, by acreage,
and by specialisation (principal source of income).

Lenin's analysis of the great volume of facts and massive agrarian statistics proves that U.S. agriculture is developing the capitalist way. Evidence of this is the general increase in the employment of hired labour, the growth in the number of wage workers, the decline in the number of independent farm owners, the erosion of the middle groups and the consolidation of the groups at both ends of the farm spectrum, and the growth of big capitalist farms and the displacement of the small. Lenin says that capitalism in U.S. agriculture tends to grow both through the faster development of the large-acreage farms in extensive areas, and through the establishment of farms with much larger operations on smaller tracts in the intensive areas. There is growing concentration of production in agriculture, and the expropriation and displacement of small farmers, which means a decline in the proportion of owners.

In his book, Lenin shows the plight of the small and tenant farmers, especially Negroes, who are most ruthlessly oppressed. "For the 'emancipated' Negroes, the American South is a kind of prison where they are hemmed in, isolated and deprived of fresh air" (present edition, Vol. 22, p. 27). Lenin notes the remarkable similarity between the economic status of the Negroes in America and that of the one-time serfs in the heart of agricultural Russia.

An indicator of the ruin of small farmers in the United States is the growth in the number of mortgaged farms, which "means that the actual control over them is transferred to the capitalists". Most farmers who fall into the clutches of finance capital are further impoverished. "Those who control the banks, *directly* control one-third of America's farms, and indirectly dominate the lot" (ibid., pp. 92, 100).

Lenin's study of the general laws governing the capitalist development of agriculture and the forms they assumed in the various countries shed a strong light on the whole process of displacement of small-scale by large-scale production. This complex and painful process involves not only the direct expropriation of toiling peasants and farmers by big capital, but also the "ruin of the small farmers and a worsening of conditions on their farms, a process that may go on for years and decades" (Vol. 22, p. 70), which may assume a variety of forms, such as the small farmer's overwork or malnutrition, heavy debt, worse feed and poorer care of livestock, poorer husbandry, technical stagnation, etc.

Lenin analysed the capitalist agriculture of Europe and the United States decades ago. Since then, considerable changes have taken place in the agriculture of the capitalist countries. However, the objective laws governing capitalist development are inexorable. The development of capitalist agriculture fully bears out the Marxist-Leninist agrarian theory, and its characteristic of classes and the class struggle in the countryside. The Programme of the Communist Party of the Soviet Union emphasises that the agriculture of the capitalist countries is characterised by a further deepening of the contradictions inherent in the bourgeois system, namely, the growing concentration of production, and ever greater expropriation of small farmers and peasants. The monopolies have occupied dominant positions in agriculture as well. Millions of farmers and peasants are being ruined and driven off the soil.

In the decades since Lenin made his analysis, there have been major changes in the technical equipment of agricultural production. But, as in the time of Marx and Lenin, the machine not only raises the productivity of human labour but also leads to a further aggravation of the contradictions in capitalist agriculture.

The mechanisation of production on the large capitalist farms is accompanied by intensification of labour, worsening of working conditions, displacement of hired labour and growing unemployment. At the same time, there is increasing ruin of small peasants and farmers, who are unable to buy and make rational use of modern machinery, and who are saddled with debts and taxes; the small and middle farmers, who are supplanted by the large farms, become tenants, or wage workers; and the dispossessed tenant farmers are driven off the land. This is borne out by the massive statistics furnished by agricultural censuses in the United States, Canada, France, the Federal Republic of Germany and other capitalist countries.

But in the teeth of these facts present-day bourgeois economists, reformists and revisionists of every stripe keep coming up with the theories long since refuted by

Marxism-Leninism and upset by practice itself—asserting that under capitalism the small farm is "stable", that it offers "advantages" over the large farm, and that under capitalism the toiling peasant can enjoy a life of prosperity.

Modern reformists and revisionists try to revive the old theories of the "non-capitalist evolution of agriculture" through the co-operatives. However, the marketing co-operatives extolled by the bourgeoisie and their "socialist" servitors fail to save the small farmers from privation and ruin. Modern reality fully bears out Lenin's analysis of co-operatives under capitalism. Lenin adduced concrete facts on associations for the marketing of dairy produce in a number of capitalist countries to show that these consist mainly of large (capitalist) farms, and that very few small farmers take part in them (see pp. 207, 209-10). In the capitalist countries today, co-operative societies, which are under the control of banks and monopolies, are also used mainly by capitalist farmers and not by the small farmers.

Lenin's critique of bourgeois reformist and revisionist views on the agrarian question is just as important today as a brilliant example of the Party approach in science, and of irreconcilable struggle against a hostile ideology, bourgeois apologetics, and modern reformism and revisionism. With capitalism plunged in a general crisis, and class contradictions becoming more acute, the bourgeoisie and its ideologists have been trying very hard to win over the peasantry, by resorting to social demagogy, propounding reformist ideas of harmonised class interests, and promising the small farmer better conditions under capitalism. Lenin's guiding statements on the agrarian question teach the Communist and Workers' Parties of the capitalist and colonial countries to take correct decisions on the working-class attitude towards the peasantry as an ally in the revolutionary struggle against capitalism and colonialism, for democracy and socialism.

Lenin stressed that, in contrast to those bourgeois pundits who sow illusions among the small peasants about the possibility of achieving prosperity under capitalism, the Marxist evaluation of the true position of the peasantry in the capitalist countries "inevitably leads to the recognition of the small peasantry's blind alley and hopeless position (hopeless, outside the revolutionary struggle of the proletariat against the entire capitalist system)" (present edition, Vol. 5, p. 190).

The historic example of the Soviet Union and other socialist countries has shown the peasants of the world the advantages of the socialist way of farming; they are coming to realise that only the establishment of truly popular power and producers' co-operatives can rid the peasants of poverty and exploitation, and assure them of a life of prosperity and culture. The experience of the U.S.S.R. and the People's Democracies has toppled the theories spread by the servants of the bourgeoisie which say that the peasantry is basically hostile to socialism. There is now practical proof of the correctness of the Marxist-Leninist proposition that the peasant economy must and can be remodelled on socialist lines, and that the toiling peasants can be successfully involved in the construction of socialism and communism.

* * *

The bulk of the material contained in the present volume was first published from 1932 to 1938, in *Lenin Miscellanies XIX, XXXI* and *XXXII*. Seven writings were first published in the Fourth Russian edition, among them: remarks on E. Seignouret's book, *Essays on Social and Agricultural Economics*; a manuscript containing an analysis of data from the *Agricultural Statistics of France*; remarks on G. Fischer's *The Social Importance of Machinery in Agriculture*; a manuscript containing extracts from *Hand and Machine Labor*; and remarks on E. Jordi's *Electric Motor in Agriculture*.

The publishers have retained Lenin's arrangement of the material, his marks in the margin and underlinings in the text. The underlinings are indicated by type variations: a single underlining by *italics*, a double underlining by *s p a c e d   i t a l i c s*, three lines by **heavy Roman type**, and four lines by **s p a c e d   h e a v y   R o m a n   t y p e**. A wavy underlining is indicated by *__heavy italics__*, if double—by *__s p a c e d   h e a v y   i t a l i c s__*.

In the Fourth Russian edition the entire text of this volume was verified once again with Lenin's manuscripts and sources.

All statistical data were checked again, but no corrections were made where the totals or percentages do not tally, because they are the result of Lenin's rounding off the figures from the sources.

The present volume contains footnote references to Lenin's "The Agrarian Question and the 'Critics of Marx'" and *New Data on the Laws Governing the Development of Capitalism in Agriculture*. This has been done to show the connection between the preparatory material and the finished works, and to give an idea of how Lenin made use of his notes.

Institute of Marxism-Leninism under the C.P.S.U. Central Committee

I

PLANS AND OUTLINES OF WORKS ON THE AGRARIAN QUESTION

PLAN OF
"THE AGRARIAN QUESTION
AND THE 'CRITICS OF MARX'"[1]

FIRST VARIANT

Perhaps the following division:

A. Some of Bulgakov's general propositions and "theories"
B. Factual data against the critics
   M. Hecht *
   Baden Inquiry (connect with Winzer) **
   "Solid peasantry"
   K. Klawki ***
   The Condition of the Peasants[2]
   (Hertz ****, 15) Baudrillart[3]
   French statistics. (Souchon and Maurice) *****
   German statistics ****** (connect with co-operatives)
   Belgium (Vandervelde, Chłapowski *******?).
C. Class struggle *o r* co-operation?
   Distortion of Engels.[4]
   Overall data on employers and wage workers. Capitalist system.
   Böttger.[5] [Bulgakov's greater consistency]
D. Russian agrarian programme in No. 3 of *Iskra*[6].

----

  * See pp. 116-25.—*Ed.*
  ** Wine grower. See pp. 180-85.—*Ed.*
  *** See pp. 138-59.—*Ed.*
  **** See pp. 96-106.—*Ed.*
  ***** See pp. 170-77.— *Ed*
  ****** See pp. 189-217.—*Ed.*
  ******* See pp. 178-79.—*Ed.*

SECOND VARIANT

A. Bulgakov on the law of diminishing returns
(cf. Maslov, who is not quite right[7]).
A. Bulgakov on big and small farms.
((To B?)) Bulgakov on co-operation and individualism in agriculture.
B. Baden data (in connection with Hecht).
B. Baudrillart....
B. *The Condition of the Peasants*....
C) ... Böttger....
C) ⌈ Distortion of Engels and Marx.
            ("The Peasant Question")
B. | Moritz Hecht.
B) | Co-operatives. (Cf. German statistics on dairy farms)
C) ⟨ *Overall data on rural labourers and rural employers.*
D) | Russian agrarian programme in No. 3 of *Iskra*.
B. ⌊ K. Klawki.
B. French data on holders and proletariat in agriculture.
(To A?) Electric power in agriculture

> Pringsheim*
> Mack[8]
> Kautsky[9]

THIRD VARIANT

CRITICS IN THE AGRARIAN QUESTION

A)
   1. Introduction. Breach in orthodox Marxism (Chernov No. 4, 127[10]).
I 2. General methods of the critics' "theory" Bulgakov: law of diminishing returns (cf. Maslov)
   3. Bulgakov's own data in refutation of it.
   4. Theory of rent (cf. Maslov).
   5. Malthusianism: cf. Ireland.[11]

---

* See pp. 107-10.— *Ed.*

II   6. Hertz   (+Bulgakov).   Agricultural   machinery, large- and small-scale production (Bulgakov δ* Hertz: ε**). Con—Bulgakov I, 240, II, 115, 133.
7. Hertz. "Definition of capitalism" (and Chernov)
8. —mortgages (and Chernov). Cf. Bulgakov on savings banks II,375.
9. —Engels on America[12] (Idem Chernov).
Bulgakov II, 433 (cf. I, 49)
Electric power in agriculture (Pringsheim, Mack, K. Kautsky).

III   10. Chernov. Kautsky is annihilated (A—6 Chernov[13]). Ibidem Kautsky on usury, Kautsky on the distinguishing characteristics of the proletariat. Voroshilov
11. Voroshilov   about   N.—on   and   others.   (A—1
Chernov[13])
12.   "   "form and content" of capitalism

B)) IV   1. M. Hecht (Blondel,[14] Hertz, David, Chernov).
2. K. Klawki (against Auhagen) (Bulgakov)

V   3. The Condition of the Peasants (Quotations from Hertz and Bulgakov)[15]
4. Baden Inquiry
5. Conclusions   on   "solid   peasantry"   (Bulgakov ε.*** Hertz—p. 6 N.B. Hertz δ.**** Chernov on petty-bourgeois peasantry. Chernov No. 7, 163; No. 10, 240).

VI   6. Baudrillart (Hertz p. 15 et al., Bulgakov II, 282)
7. Souchon and Maurice.

VII   8. French statistics. (Property and farm operations, cf. Hertz: "no proletarisation at all" p. 59. Employers and labourers; establishments with hired labour).

VIII 9. German statistics. Latifundia. (Cf. Hertz and Bulgakov).
9 bis. German statistics....***** (Cf. Bulgakov II,106).

———————

* See p. 87.—Ed.
** See p. 104.—Ed.
*** See p. 87.—Ed.
**** See p. 104.—Ed.
***** Several words illegible.—Ed.

10. German statistics. Industrialisation of rural indus-
    try (Bulgakov and Hertz, p. 88).
11. German statistics. *Co-operatives.*
    Cf. Baden data on the Winzer.

IX 12. Belgium. (Vandervelde, Chłapowski).

C)) X 1. Overall data on employers and labourers.
    (*Capitalist* system)
2. Nonsense about "peasantry".
3. Distortion of Engels ("The Peasant Question").
    (Hertz, Chernov.)
4. Bulgakov (more consistent).
5. Class struggle *or* co-operation.
6. *Böttger.*

D)) XI   Russian agrarian programme and No. 3 of *Iskra.*
    Iskra's approach to the question.
    Objections of 2a3b [16]
    The *pros* and *cons.*

FOURTH VARIANT

CRITICS IN THE AGRARIAN QUESTION

I

1. **Introduction.** Agrarian question—"breach" (first one)
   in orthodox Marxism. (Chernov No. 4, 127; No..*8, 204*).
2. **General** theoretical propositions and reasoning of critics
   (Bulgakov, Hertz and Chernov). *Bulgakov: law of diminishing returns* (cf. Maslov). Bulgakov's phrases: I, 2,
   13, 17, 18, 20, 21 (29-30 especially), 34, 35, 64
   and many others. (Cf. K. Kautsky versus Brentano. No
   wonder Bulgakov is delighted with Brentano. I, 116.)
3. Refutation of this law with Bulgakov's own data: in
   Britain: I, 242, 260; in *Germany*: II, 132-33. In France
   II, 211.
4. Theory of *rent.* (Cf. Maslov.) Bulgakov I, 92, *105.
   111-13.*
5. *Malthusianism.* Bulgakov I, 214,
   255. II, 41 etc. II, 212 (France
   N.B.)—cf. II, 159.
   Especially II,
   221, et seq. 223, 237 and 233, *249,*   Bulgakov about
   265 N.B. (and 261). Ireland II,   Hertz I, 139
   351, 384.   ("remarkable").

II

6. Bulgakov + Hertz. *Agricultural machinery* Bulgakov I, 43-51. Hertz pp. 40, 60-65. *Reactionary attitude towards agricultural machinery*: Hertz, 65; Bulgakov I, 51-52; II, 103.

   Machines in Britain: I, 252

   Con on machines. Hertz 36 (America); 43-44; 15 (latifundia), 124 (steam plough). Bulgakov I, 240; II, 115, 133.

   (Hertz 67: higher yields from steam plough.)

7. Bulgakov + Hertz. *Large- and small-scale production.* Bulgakov I, 142, 154; II, 135; 280 (Cf. 282-83).

   Con — Bulgakov. In Britain: I, 311, 316, 318-19. Small-scale production was >damaged.

   Con—Bulgakov I, *239-40*. Hertz 52, 81. (Machines on small farms). Con 74 (small farms >labour); 89-90 (peasant's labour rent); 91-92 (collateral employment).

   I, 333 (in Britain—? their (small farms') unviability has not been proved?).

   Bulgakov II, 247 (small farms< rich in capital).

   France II, 188-89. (Reduction in the number of medium farms — Bulgakov's dodges) II, 213 (small farms "in the vanguard"??). Ireland II, 359-60.

8. Hertz: *"definition of capitalism"* (p. 10)—and Chernov No. 4, 133.

9. Hertz (and Bulgakov in *Nachalo*[17]?)—*mortgages*. Hertz 24, 26, 28. (*Chernov* No. 10, 216-17). Kautsky's reply.

10. "Engels's mistake" (Hertz 31; Chernov No. 8, 203). Cf. Bulgakov I, 49 and II, 433 ("naïveté").
    Cf. *Electric power* in agriculture (Pringsheim, Mack, K. Kautsky).

III

11. Chernov—"*Form and content* of capitalism": No. 6, 209; No 8, 228.

12. Chernov about *Russian* Marxists: No. 4, 139; No. 4, 141; No. 8, 238; No. 10, 213; No. 11, 241 and No. 7, 166 (who are their comrades?) eulogises Nikolai—on and Kablukov: No. 10, 237

Distortion of *Marxism: International*: No. 5, 35. Marx on agriculture No. 6, 216, *231* and many others. Engels on Belgium, No. 10, 234.

The journal *Nachalo* I, pp. 7 and 13.

13. Chernov. Kautsky is "annihilated": "have even failed to grasp what Marx says" (No. 7, 169)—idem in the collection *At the Glorious Post* on usury, on the distinguishing characteristics of the proletariat.

Voroshilov: No. 8, 229. (Cf. K. Kautsky).

IV

14. *M. Hecht* (Blondel, p. 27, Hertz 68, 79; Chernov No. 8, 206. David).

15. *K. Klawki* (Bulgakov I, 58). A couple of words about Auhagen. Hertz 70 and Bulgakov I, 58. (Cf. Hertz 66; crops in Prussia and Southern Germany.)

16. *The Condition of the Peasants.* (Quotations by Bulgakov and Hertz.)

V

17. *Baden Inquiry* (Hertz's especially; and Bulgakov passim: references 68, *79* especially II, 272).

18. VII Conclusions on the "*solid peasantry*" (Bulgakov II, *138* N.B. and 456), on the peasant's attitude to the worker (Bulgakov II, 288; Hertz 4-15; 9. Hertz, *6* (with 1-2 hired labourers) and 5. Chernov No. 7, 163 ("petty-

Bulgakov II, 289 ("peasantophobia"). Bulgakov II, 176 ("the French peasantry split up into the proletariat and the proprietors") Bulgakov II, 118

bourgeois"); No. 10, 240 (peasant = working man)).

("solid peasants +technically advanced big ones").

VI

19. *Baudrillart* (Hertz, 15 et seq., *56-58*; Bulgakov II, 282).

> Cf. Bulgakov II, 208
> from Baudrillart, Vol. 1

Souchon and Maurice. (Cf. Bulgakov II, 280 on hired labourers on small farms.)

Souchon on the need of big and small farms. Cf. Bulgakov I, 338 (Britain: verdict of history — for small farms) Cf. Rentengüter.[18]

VII

20. *French* statistics. Distribution of rural population. Hertz 55; Bulgakov II, 195-97 and Hertz 59 and *60*: (no pauperisation). Employers and workers (cf. Bulgakov II, 191).
Establishments with hired labourers.

Hertz p. 55 and p. 140 on the migration of peasant hired labourers from the North to the South of France. (Cf. Bulgakov II, 191.)

VIII

21. *German* statistics.
Acreage statistics.
Fewer labourers owning land (Bulgakov II, 106).
Latifundia. (Cf. Hertz 15; Bulgakov II, 126, 190, 363.)
Industrialisation (Bulgakov II, 116; Hertz 88).

—Bulgakov II, 260
> illusion that the big farm is vehicle of progress.
—Hertz 21, 89 ("The chief task of socialism").

Co-operatives (cf. Baden data on the Winzers). Hertz 120.

IX

22. *Belgium.* (Vandervelde. Subsidiary earnings. Chłapowski. The state of small-scale production. Collateral earnings.)

X

23. Overall data on owners and labourers in European agriculture (*Capitalist* system). (Cf. Maurice on concentration. Hertz 82 and 55 (!).)

Cf. Bulgakov II, 455 ("the grain problem > terrible than the social one")

24. Nonsense about the concept of "peasantry". (Cf. Russian statistics. Its advantages.)

25. Distortion of Engels ("The Peasant Question") on the question of co-operatives. Hertz 122 (Chernov No. 5, 42; No. 7, 157).

26. Bulgakov > consistent (II, 287, 266, 288). Hertz on *socialism*: pp. 7, 14, 10, 72-73, 123, 76, 93, 105.
    On socialism: Bulgakov II, 289, *456, 266* [denial of class struggle: cf. also Bulgakov I, 303 *and* 301.—Britain].

Antithesis of town and country. *Hertz 76*

Bulgakov in *Nachalo.*

27. Class struggle *or* co-operation. Hertz 21, 89. ("The chief task of socialism".) (Cf. *Chernov.* Non-capitalist evolution No. 5, 47; No. 10, 229, 243-44.)

Class struggle or adaptation to the *interests* of the big and petty bourgeoisie.

Chernov in the collection *At the Glorious Post 195,* 185, 188, 196.

(Is the money economy the best way? Hertz 20.)
[Bulgakov versus socialism, see § 26.]
Bulgakov II, 255 (in favour of vegetable plots: cf. II, 105. Agrarian.

Idem on corn taxes.
II, 141-48).

28. Böttger (Cf. K. Kautsky) (Quoted by Chernov No.)
XI
29. Russian agrarian programme and No. 3 of *Iskra*.
   Approach
   $\begin{cases} 1) & \text{class struggle} \\ 2) & \text{its two forms} \end{cases}$
30. Objections of 2a3b ("cut-off lands").
   The *pros* and *cons*.

Written in June-September 1901

First published in 1932   Printed from the original
in *Lenin Miscellany XIX*

CONTENTS
OF "THE AGRARIAN QUESTION
AND THE 'CRITICS OF MARX'"

Written in June-September 1901

First published in 1932
in *Lenin Miscellany XIX*

Printed from the original

CONTENTS OF CHAPTERS V-IX
OF "THE AGRARIAN QUESTION
AND THE 'CRITICS OF MARX'"[19]

*) rapid silent reading—
about half an hour

120 pages ≧ about 2 hours[20]

Written before February 1906

First published in 1938
in *Lenin Miscellany XXXI*

Printed from the original

MARXIST VIEWS OF THE AGRARIAN QUESTION IN EUROPE AND RUSSIA [21]

OUTLINE OF LECTURES

FIRST VARIANT

MARXIST VIEWS OF THE AGRARIAN QUESTION IN EUROPE AND RUSSIA

A. *General Theory of the Agrarian Question.*

1. *Growth of commercial agriculture.*—Phases of process.—Formation of market: towns.—Peasant-industrialist (*Capital,* II, 2?).[22]—Remnants of natural economy.—Degree of peasant's subordination to market.—Free competition in agriculture. For how long?

N.B. (Decline of natural peasant household industries
K. *Kautsky* and *Engels.*[23]   )
    Need of money (Usurers. *Taxes*).

2. *Law of diminishing returns.* Ricardo—Marx (Bulgakov and Maslov lately).

3. *Theory of rent.* Ricardo—Marx: differential and absolute rent. (Maslov's mistake.)

3a. *Separation of town from country* (cf. Bulgakov and Hertz. *Zarya* No. 2-3.[24] Nossig*).

4. *Present agricultural crisis.* (Parvus.)
    Inflation and consolidation of rent. Burden of rent.

---

* See pp. 263-64.—*Ed.*

5.　The *"mission"* of capital in agriculture
　　　1) separation of landownership from production
　　　2) socialisation
　　　3) rationalisation

B.　**Small-Scale Production in Agriculture** (*1-4*—one
　　　lecture; *5-6,* another).

1.　*Technical superiority of large-scale production.* Statistics.
　　Machines. (Large-scale *economy* and large-scale *land-ownership.*)

2.　*Displacement, proletarisation of the peasantry.* Flight
　　to towns.—Handicraft industries.—Collateral em-
　　ployment.

3.　*Worsening of draught animals.* German statistics.
　　Use of cow as draught animal.

　　Additio n. Baudrillart, Souchon, Chłapowski

4.　*Co-operatives.* German statistics.[25] (Hertz, David, etc.)

5.　*Comparison of profitability of big and small　　 man*
　　farms. Klawki,* **Stumpfe**. Cf. Hecht, *The* 　 cattle
　　Condition of the Peasants. 　　　　　　　　 land

6.　*South-German Inquiries.* Baden, Bavaria, **Württem-
　　berg.**[26]

C.　**Statements of Principles by Marxists in the West.**

┌──┐
│　　Transfer to end? of Section IV (D)
│　　*The Agrarian Programme of*
│　　*West-European and Russian*
│　　*Social-Democrats*
└──┘

1.　*Marx and Engels in the 1840s.* The *Communist Man-
　　ifesto.—Neue Rheinische Zeitung*[27]—Marx on American
　　agriculture in the 1840s.[28]

2.　*Resolutions of the International,*[29] Engels in 1874, his
　　programme.[30]

3.　*The agrarian debates of 1895.*[31] Engels in *Die Neue
　　Zeit* on the French and German programmes.

　　N.B.　**Social-Democrats in the Countryside.** (*Böttger*
　　Hugo.)

---

* See pp. 138-59.—*Ed.*

4.   *K. Kautsky in Soziale Revolution.*
      [A § from D to this point? Principles of the Russian
      agrarian programme.] *

D.   **The Agrarian Question in Russia.**

To D. Russia's agricultural decline. Stagnation.
        Famines. **Collapse or transition to capitalism?**

Narod- nik the- ories	1. *Commune.* Fiscal nature ig- nored. Isolation ignored. 2. *People's production.* Cherny- shevsky—.... (V. V., N.—on). 3. *No soil for capitalism.* No internal market. Decline.	Flight from "people's pro- duction" in the central areas to the capital and the border areas.	N.B.

4.   Historical significance of Narodnik theories.
5.   *Disintegration of the peasantry.* Overall data. Results.
      Meaning (=petty bourgeoisie)
6.   *Class struggle in the countryside.* Formation of an
      agricultural proletariat. Transition from the corvée system
      to the capitalist economy.
7.   Growth of commercial and capitalist farming.
8.   *Struggle against the relicts of serfdom.* Freedom of
      movement (Maslov).[32] Withdrawal from commune.
      Freedom to alienate land.
9.   Agrarian programme of the Social-Democrats. "Cut-
      off lands".

_____

Essay II[33] (*agrarian statistics*)
1.   Hecht   +*Bavarian* Inquiry
2.   (Auhagen) Klawki   +*Württemberg* Inquiry
3.   *The Condition of the Peasants* +*Stumpfe*
4.   Baden Inquiry.
5.   German agrarian statistics
         small-scale economy
         latifundia
         middle peasantry. Worsening of animals.
6.   Livestock. Industries.

_____

* Section C crossed out in MS.— *Ed.*

7. Dairy farming (tobacco-growing, wine-growing).
8. Co-operatives.
9. Rural population by status.

———

A. 1 dessiatine—80 poods.   Rent 34
   40 rubles of invested
   capital + 8 rubles of
   profit =48 rubles ÷ 80 =   60 kopeks 51.$_2$ r. (64 k.) 3.$_2$ r.
B. 1 dessiatine—75 poods.
   40 rubles of invested
   capital, + 8 rubles of
   profit=48 rubles ÷ 75=   64 kopeks 48 r. (64 k.)
A)   — 64 r.   16 r.
B)   — 60 r.   12 r.
C) 1 dessiatine—60 poods.
   40 rubles of invested
   capital + 8 rubles of
   profit=48 ÷ 60=   80 kopeks 48 r.

Written before February 10 (23).
          1903
   First published in 1932   Printed from the original
in *Lenin Miscellany XIX*

———

SECOND VARIANT

MARXIST VIEWS OF THE AGRARIAN QUESTION IN EUROPE AND RUSSIA

A. *General Theory of the Agrarian Question.*
(One lecture for A)
1. Theory implies *capitalist* agriculture = commodity production + wage labour.
Growth of commercial agriculture: formation of market towns (in Europe and in Russia)
industrial development (Parvus)
international grain trade.
Forms of commercial agriculture:
its areas
specialisation
industries

example of concentration of dairy farming on farms with up to 2 hectares: p. 103 of the article*

David, p. 152, note: "On the whole, it is small-scale production that is prospering in vegetable- and fruit-growing as well as in agriculture. According to 1895 industrial statistics, of 32,540 fruit and vegetable farms,
40 per cent had an acreage of less than 20 ares,

N.B.

David (and K. Kautsky) on market-gardening

---

* See present edition, Vol. 5, p. 212.— *Ed.*

25 per cent from 20 to 50 ares,
and 'only' 6 per cent more
than 2 hectares."
Degree of the peasant's subordination to the market

{ need in money { percentage of cash budget.
Usurers. Taxes.
Decline of patriarchal household industries
(K. Kautsky and Engels)
Peasant = half industrialist and half merchant
(*Capital*, III, 2, 346,[35] *Development of Capitalism, 100**)

Formation of a class of *farmers* and a class of *agricultural hired labourers* is the start of the process (K. Kautsky. P. 27.[36] *Capital*, III, 2, 332.[37] *Development of Capitalism* 118**)

diverse forms of agricultural wage labour (*Develop-
ment of Capitalism* 120***)

cf. article pp. 68-70 on the "depend-ent" and "inde-pendent" nature of small farmers****

(non) influence of the form of landownership (*Develop-ment of Capitalism* 242*****) N.B.

fragmentation, *par-cellisation of* peas-ant holdings.

2. *Theory of rent.*

Marx's theory of value. Rent can come only from *surplus value*, that is from surplus profit.

Profit (=surplus value: *Capital*). Average profit. (K. Kautsky, 67.)

Surplus profit comes from the *diffe-rences in fertility*
Differential Rent I.

Differential rent

The price of grain is determined by the worst production

{ limited quantity of land }
{ growth of market }

Differential Rent II: additional investment (expenditure) of capital into the land.

---

* See present edition, Vol. 3, pp. 155-56.—*Ed.*
** Ibid., p. 176.—*Ed.*
*** Ibid., pp. 178-79.—*Ed.*
**** Ibid., Vol. 5, pp. 195-96.—*Ed.*
***** Ibid., Vol. 3, pp. 323-24.—*Ed.*

Differential Rent **grows** in a mass of (most) combinations.
Differential Rent originates from capitalist *enter-prise* on the land
    it comes from the difference in the quantity of *produce*.
Monopoly of private ownership of land   Absolute
                                                                    rent
    —*Absolute rent*
    or = monopoly price
(absolute rent) = or = from the **lowest** composition of
    agricultural capital
Absolute rent does not come from   Price
    capitalist *enterprise* on the land   of land
    but from the private *owner-ship* of land
— it does not originate from the
    quantity of produce, but is a
    tribute
A tribute fixed in the *price of land*.
Price of land = capitalised rent. Removal of capital from
    agriculture
    Fixing of high prices.
3. *Role of rent and capitalism in agriculture.*
Rent prevents grain prices from   Role
    falling (*Parvus*)   of rent

cf. *Capital*, III, 2, ?[38]

Rent *takes away* all agricultural improvements
    all profits over and above the average.
(Nationalisation of land would do away with absolute
    rent.)
Agrarian crisis does away with *absolute* rent.
    { competition between lands without rent }
    {   and lands with rent.   }
Two *forms* of levying rent:
    the **farmer system** (K. Kautsky, 85)   Forms of
    the **mortgage system** (K. Kautsky   levying rent
    87-89. *Development of Capitalism,*
    442 *)

---

* See present edition, Vol. 3, p 555 — *Ed.*

Both processes =
  (1) separation of the landowner from agriculture. In this context, deal with the role of capitalism in agriculture.
  (2) rationalisation of agriculture (competition)
  (3) its socialisation
  (4) elimination of indenture and labour service.
4. [3]. *Law of diminishing returns.*
    Ricardo   (and   West).   *Marx's   correction.*
    Zarya No. 2-3, p.*
    Bulgakov: the difficult problem of grain production. Refutation. *Zarya* No. 2-3, p.**
    Maslov
con: on the one hand, against Bulgakov
    on the other, admission of>productivity of extensive farming. Maslov pp. *72*, 83 et al. Especially *72*.
    Con—Marx III, 2, 210 [39]   *Extract*
    (*Development of Capitalism*, 186   *from Marx*
    and *187***)   *on R. Jones* [40]
"concentrate all agriculture on 1 dessiatine"
    Maslov, pp. 79 and 110 (without "the law" there would have been no differential rent)
    p. 86 (incontrovertible fact of diminishing returns)
    Con—p. *114* (there are different cases!)
Maslov p. *72*. Economists denying "the law" labour under a misunderstanding.
    110: productivity of labour may grow, but "the law" remains. (No proof!)
    130-31: con Marx (denial of absolute rent).
N.B. *109*: "he does not explain competition by the level of rent but vice versa".=Meaning of *Maslov*'s mistake. *Obscures tribute (rent) by means of ostensibly natural causes, as the cost of producing grain.*
5. *Contradictions of agricultural capitalism*: rationalisation of agriculture—and plunder of the soil
    Meaning of separation of town from country (Bulgakov and Hertz and Chernov and *Zarya* No. 2-3, p.****)
    Nossig, p. 103: **extracts**
_____
   * See present edition, Vol. 5, p. 110.—*Ed.*
  ** Ibid., pp. 114-19.—*Ed.*
 *** See present edition, Vol. 3, pp. 257-59.—*Ed.*
**** See present edition, Vol. 5, pp. 146-59.—*Ed.*

Elimination of indenture—and the debasement of the agricultural hired labourer and small peasant.

Development of the productive forces—and the growth of *tribute*, the rent, which prevents the lowering of prices and investment of capital into agriculture.

Superiority of the big farm (as capitalism develops).

To A. 1) K. Kautsky. 2) *Development of Capitalism*; 3) *Zarya* (2-3) 4) Maslov 5) Parvus 6) Extracts from Nossig.

B.   Small- and large-scale production in agriculture. (Two lectures for B.)*

1. The approach to the question as an *isolated* one is incorrect

⎛ everything within the framework of capitalism. ⎞
⎜ The important thing is not the displacement ⎟
⎜ of small-scale farming but the *wholesale* ⎟
⎝ capitalist transformation of agriculture. ⎠

2. Technical superiority of large-scale production. Machines. *Zarya No. 2-3*** (objections of Bulgakov, Hertz, David, etc.)

Commercial cost-cutting
        machines
(α) fertilisers
        drainage

‖ α ⎰ division of labour
‖ α ⎱ co-operatives

(β) buildings
        implements
(γ) marketing and purchasing

3. Diverse forms of *displacement* and *decline* of small farms: household industries
                        outside seasonal work
                        wage labour
                        worsening of nutrition
                        more work

---

* Points 1, 2 and 3 of Section B in the manuscript are crossed out in plain pencil by means of two vertical lines, apparently in the process of an editorial reading.— *Ed.*

** See present edition, Vol. 5, pp. 130-46.— *Ed.*

worsening of animals
          "   " land (plunder)
debts
             etc.

4. *Detailed studies.*
   (2nd agrarian article)

Hecht	N.B.	
Auhagen	+*Bavarian*	N.B.
Klawki	+Württem-	+Baudrillart
The Condition of the	berg	+Souchon
Peasants		
Baden Inquiry	+Stumpfe	+Chłapowski
	N.B.	N.B.

{ Result: (1) man
           (2) cattle
           (3) land }

5. **Overall data of German agrarian statistics:**
   (1) small farms
   (2) latifundia
   (3) medium farms. Worsening of animals
   Distribution of animals. Industries.
   Dairy farming (tobacco-growing, wine-growing)
6. — *Co-operatives*
7. —Loss of land and proletarisation.
   Distribution of *rural population*
   by land holdings.

C. *The Agrarian Question in Russia*
   (1 Lecture for C).

1. Old views = Narodism   *Essence*
   Peasantry = "people's produc-   *of Narodism*
   tion" (not petty bourgeoisie)
   Commune = rudiments of communism (not fiscal)
   no soil for capitalism: no internal market, peasantry is the
   greatest antagonist, no class
   struggle in agriculture.
2. This is a whole world outlook,   { *"agrarian*
   starting from Herzen and end-   *democracy".*
   ing with N.—on.[41] A vast   Its historical mean-
   stretch of social thinking.   ing }

|| *Its historical mean-
ing: idealisation* of
the struggle against serfdom and
its relicts ("Agrarische Demokratie") Marx } *survivals
among Social-
ist - Revolu-
tionaries*
Elements of *democracy*
+ utopian socialism
+ petty-bourgeois reforms
+ reactionary nature of the
petty bourgeois.
Separate wheat from *chaff.*

3. Central question: *disintegration* of peasantry, its
transformation into *petty
bourgeoisie, class
struggle in the coun-
tryside.*

*disintegra-
tion of
peasantry*
(the mistake
of the Davids)

Disintegration of peasantry.
Ways of studying it (*inside* commune).
Principal symptoms of it: *Development of Capitalism,
81*
(14 symptoms, 2– and 12+)*
Analysis of each symptom with a few examples.
(*Extract* from Maslov on the buying of land by
peasants.)
Con— *Vikhlyaev* p. *108.*[42] Loss of horses, "statics" and
"dynamics".
Conclusions = *petty bourgeoisie.* (*Development of Capitalism, 115,* §2**)
Overall results from data of horse census (*Development
of Capitalism,* 92***).
Areas of disintegration: *South of Russia, dairy*
farming, Amur (Maslov 324), *Orenburg* (Maslov 325),
Siberian butter-making.
(there is disintegration wherever the peasant is in
a better position
internal tendencies to disintegration)

---

* See present edition, Vol. 3, p. 129.— *Ed.*
** Ibid., pp. 172-73.— *Ed.*
*** Ibid., p. 144.— *Ed.*

> The agrarian system of Russia. There would be no need for an agrarian programme, if it were a question of capitalism alone. (Engels. Böttger.) But—the *relicts of serfdom.*

Delays in disintegration:

N.B.
- labour service
- high taxes
- no freedom of movement— (Maslov on commune: *extract*).
- usurer's capital

4. Transition from the corvée system to the capitalist economy.

relicts
of
serfdom

$\left(\begin{array}{c}\text{trans-}\\\text{itional}\\\text{system}\end{array}\right)$ Labour service system. (*Development of Capitalism*, 133, 135*) cut-off lands, etc.

Class of hired labourers in agriculture: **3.5** million **at least.**

5. *Migration of workers* in Russia as summarised development of capitalism *fleeing from people's production* (*Development of Capitalism, 466-469*).**

Migration
of workers
in Russia

Hence, the essence of the present moment in the economic evolution (and the whole history) of Russia.

= *Elimination of the relicts of serfdom*
= freedom of capitalist development
= freedom of proletariat's class struggle

---

* See present edition, Vol. 3, pp. 197-98, 199-200.— *Ed.*
** Ibid., pp. 585-88.— *Ed.*

{ A totally diffe-rent agrarian question (than in Europe) } { Stagnation, famines. Decline? *or* freedom for capitalism? } ||| Essence of our agrarian programme

There is the nucleus of *Narodism,* its *revolutionary*-democratic nucleus

Rich peasantry already there

Diverse forms of hired labour

> 10 million
> Development
> of Capitalism,
> 462*

— elimination of the relics of serfdom will formalise and enhance its power
— higher living standards will expand the internal market, and develop *industry*
— development of the *proletariat and the class struggle for socialism.*

||| *Failure of the Socialist-Revolutionaries and the Ryazanovs to understand the agrarian programme*
Rudin's theses**
"Moderate nature" of cut-off lands.
Empty talk: co-operation + socialisation + expropriation—it is *neither* agrarian *nor* a programme

Written before February 10 (23), 1903

First published in 1932
in *Lenin Miscellany XIX*

Printed from the original

---

* See present edition, Vol. 3, p. 581.— *Ed.*
** See p. 61.— *Ed.*

THE AGRARIAN PROGRAMME
OF THE SOCIALIST-REVOLUTIONARIES
AND OF THE SOCIAL-DEMOCRATS [43]

OUTLINE OF LECTURE

FIRST VARIANT

THE AGRARIAN PROGRAMME
OF THE SOCIALIST-REVOLUTIONARIES [44]
AND OF THE SOCIAL-DEMOCRATS .

In order to make a comparison of the programmes and to assess them, it is necessary to examine the *principles*, the theory, from which the programme flows.

A) Attitude of the S.R.s to the Narodniks.[45]

1. S.R.s are neither for nor against.
2. *Rudin*[46] *29*: "valuable legacy" ("the purified"!?)
3. *Rudin* denies differentiation. *Rudin 21.* (!)
4. Bashful concealment of Narodism.
5. And failure to understand its *historical* significance (the initial form of democracy "**agrarische Demokratie**").
6. Deviation: the orthodox, the dogmatists start from Russian relations and data, whereas the "heirs" of the Narodniks have *nothing* to say about this, but then they travel all over Belgium + Italy.

"Already land in some parts of Russia is flowing from *cap-ital to* labour" *No. 8,* p. 8 [47]

Revolutsionnaya Rossiya No. 11, pp. 8-9: David and K. Kautsky and Guesde and Jaurès and Belgium and Italy!! Trying to *draw in* the peasant. *Into what?*

B) Failure to Understand the Whole of the Historical and Economic Evolution of Russia.

1. Sitting between two stools, between the Narodniks and Marxism.

Vestnik Russkoi Revolutsii No. 1 "the creative side" of capitalism. !!!
(quotation in *Zarya* No. 1, editorial.)

Revolutsionnaya Rossiya No. 12, 6: the peasant— "*servant and master*" lives a life based on the "*law* of *labour*"
The class struggle in the countryside (*Revolutsionnaya Rossiya* No. 11).
"We do not agree that the peasantry belongs" to the *petty-bourgeois* sections. !
(A centre of Narodism and Marxism!)
"*family*" and "*bourgeois-capitalist*" economies

2. Failure to understand the total *change* of the two structures of life in Russia (the patriarchal structure based on serfdom and the capitalist)
See:
3. Are there any relicts of serfdom? Is there a task to develop capitalism?
No: *Revolutsionnaya Rossiya* No. 8, p. 4. Yes: *Revolutsionnaya Rossiya, No. 15, 6.*
"The 1861 reforms have *cleared* the way (!) and given full (!!!) scope to the development of capitalism." !!

Revolutsionnaya Rossiya No. 11, p. 9: "they failed to see that the creative role of capitalism in agriculture gives way to the destructive one", "the *disorganising*" one. !

Revolutsionnaya Rossiya No. 15, 6: if the peasantry is demanding an "equalisation of land" there are only two ways: (1) transfer to *individual* ownership or (2) to *collective* ownership, *socialisation.*

4. Cut-off lands—indenture. Let's assume that's so (*Rudin 14*). "But not **widely comprehensive**" *Rudin 14* (!)

"This fails to give a *broad*!!
provision of land" (Rudin *14*).
"Give" more; *promise* more!!
 5. Mr. Rudin's two theses (17)
(α) Allotment of land will help the
    peasant to fight capitalism!
(β) it will slow down the capital-
    isation of large-scale farming,
    (a   process!!)   which   is
    grinding   slow   as   it   is
    Perhaps+thesis (γ) the "blunt-
    ing" of the class struggle (17).

Don't   analyse!   What
for?   What   does   the
peasant   want?   "*addi-
tion   of   land*'   !!
Revolutsionnaya   Rossiya
No. 8, p. *7?*
we do not count on the
well-to-do peasants, for
this is the start of the
socialist movement
Revolutsionnaya   Rossiya
No. 13, p. 5: "no doubt"
that the peasant move-
ment is not socialist.
But from half-socialist
ideas the propagandist
may arrive at "*purely
socialist conclusions*".

The poor versus
the   rich,   whereas
Ilyin   speaks   of
the   merger   of   the
bourgeois   and   the
proletarian   ele-
ments in the move-
ment

C. Failure to Understand the Class Struggle and Efforts to Obscure It.

 1. The peasantry will not stop
at the cut-off lands. Rudin *18*.
 2. The peasantry—"*labour*"
principle
 (and not class struggle?)
Rudin *18*.
 3. What will happen *after*
the cut-off lands? Consequent on
the cut-off lands? (Class struggle.)

Half-socialist   programme of the peasants.
*Revolutsionnaya   Ros-
siya* No. 8, p. 3/1.
"Labour principle"

*Hence:**
E. Failure to Understand the Russian Revolution.

1. Is it bourgeois *o r* democratic? *Revolutsionnaya Rossiya No. 8,* p. *3/2* and "Revolutionary Adventurism". Sowing illusions.

2. Vulgar socialism: private property must not be defended. *Revolutsionnaya Rossiya* No. 13, pp. *5* and *6. Revolutsionnaya Rossiya* No. 15, 6.

(Socialists—vehicles of the bourgeois spirit!)

Con *Marx* in 1848. ⌇⌇⌇

3. The peasant's equality ("*To All the Russian Peasantry*", p. *28, § 1*).[48]—and denial of the right to dispose of the land.

4. Freedom of movement—and the commune "*To A l l the R u s s i a n P e a s a n t r y*", p. *28, § 1.*

(**Maslov's** data)

F. The Social-Democratic Agrarian Programme

		Martynov
1. Unfeasible?	We vouch	"Fearful for Martynov" Rudin 26.
2. Its **principles**	(α) Serfdom »→	nov" Rudin 26.
	(β) Class struggle	*Quote from Martynov.*[49]
	(γ) Socialism.	

3. Its meaning = *the rural proletariat must help the rich and well-to-do peasant to fight serfdom.*

Rudin "not all the peasants are hostile to the old*) regime" 15-16.

Against: **quote from Engelhardt**[50]

5. What are we going to tell the peasant?

Agrarian system (10:1$\frac{1}{2}$—2—6$\frac{1}{2}$)[51]

(!) *) *Revolutsionnaya Rossiya No. 8,* p. *7, 1: "petty-bourgeois sections" "always in general" "hold on to the existing order"* (Sic!)

---

* Lenin indicated a switch of points by means of a bracket in blue pencil, but failed to alter the alphabetical order of the points. They are given as indicated.— *Ed.*

4. The question of reviewing the peasant reform has been raised by all the progressive (= liberal) intelligentsia of Russia.

| Quote from V. V. | [52]

Hence:

Cf. *Ireland.*

{ 1) agrarian non-capitalist struggle.
2) buying out now.
3) the Narodniks draw a comparison between Russia and Ireland. }

D. *Vulgarised Petty-Bourgeois "Criticism"*

Narodism+Bourgeois

1. Between the orthodox and the critics (*Vestnik Russkoi Revolutsii No. 2,* p. 57). The small is growing.

Unprincipled attacks (wails) against the "*dogmatists*" etc. *Revolutsionnaya Rossiya No. 8* passim.

2. "New Way to Socialism" *Revolutsionnaya Rossiya.*

3. Game: distortion of Engels (extracts). *Revolutsionnaya Rossiya No. 14,* p. 6 and Rudin *21.*

Engels supplemented by Böttger: *Engels's prediction is coming true.*

4. Attitude to the small peasant on the part of *our programme* and the whole *working-class*=Social-Democratic socialism.

5. Co-operatives. *Revolutsionnaya Rossiya* No. 8, p. 11 ("all possible types").

in general!

(Levitsky)

Bourgeois and socialist co-operatives

German and Russian data!

German
Rocquigny [53]
Russian

G. *Unprincipled Stand of the Socialist-Revolutionaries.*

1. Man without convictions—party without principles.

2. Rudin *16*: "the future will clarify".

3. Ibid: "try to prevail upon the farm hand" (!!)

4. *No programme!* Con—Rudin, *4*

Revolutsionnaya Rossiya also boasts in *No. 11, p. 6* ("Our programme has been put forward") (?)

Thus,

H. *"Universal men"*
We have seen the co-opera-
tives,
    but about
Socialisation.

Four meanings:
1) = nationalisation.
Revolutsionnaya Rossiya No. 8,
p. 11.
    (economic association et al.).
2) = socialist revolution ("To
All the Russian Peasantry")
p. 31, §12. (minimum?)
3) = commune. Popular anarchy

"Fellows, there's more
land to be had!"
Revolutsionnaya Rossiya
No. 8, p. 7.

stressing this to be a ⎫
    minimum! |
socialisation = i.e., |
"transfer to the owner-   ⎬
ship of society and the |
use of the working |
            people"   ⎭
Revolutsionnaya Rossiya
No. 8, pp. 4, 2.

"The peasantry proclaims the equalisation principle."

"We are free from idealisation", **but** it is easier to start
from the "traditions of communal management". "Supersti-
tious hostility to the communal principle."

!! *"Colossal organisation of the communal peasantry"*
    No. 8, p. 9
    no other class is so impelled to political struggle. Ibidem,
    p. 8
    use on labour and equal lines to be "implemented to the
    end" No. 8, p. 8.

            (Equalisation?
        between communes?)
4. = "Dutch meaning" *Revolutsionnaya Rossiya No. 15,*
p. 8, "the Dutch *type* is most suitable" *), i.e., *communalisa-*
tion.

(petty-bourgeois triviality)
"Universal men" indeed!

Written before February 18
(March 3), 1903

First published in 1932
in *Lenin Miscellany* XIX   Printed from the original

---

*) Dutch: "extension of the commune's rights in taxing,
buying out and expropriating land" *Revolutsionnaya Rossiya*
No. 15, 7.

SECOND VARIANT

THE AGRARIAN PROGRAMME OF THE SOCIALIST-REVOLUTIONARIES AND OF THE SOCIAL-DEMOCRATS

Three main themes: I. The Basic Principles of an Agrarian Programme. II. The Agrarian Programme of the Social-Democrats. III. The Agrarian Programme of the Socialist-Revolutionaries.

I. *The Basic Principles of an Agrarian Programme* (= the views of Russian socialists of the agrarian question in Russia).

1. *Narodism* = the Σ of the old socialist views of the *agrarian question*. The *whole* history of Russian socialist thinking on the agrarian question is a history of Narodism and *its struggle against Marxism*.

2. *S.R.s neither here nor there.*

On the one hand—the "creative" side of capitalism (*Vestnik Russkoi Revolutsii*   No. 1, *p. 2*)

   not saying: "We are Narodist Socialists".

On the other hand— *"they do not recognise the petty-bourgeois nature of the peasantry"* (*Revolutsionnaya Rossiya No. 11, p. 7*)

   "family and bourgeois-capitalist economies" *ibidem*

   R u d i n   (21)   *denies*   the   *"differentiation"* (Rudin 21) "already *land in some parts"* "*is flowing from capital to labour*" (*Revolutsionnaya Rossiya* No. 8, p. 8)

   the peasant—"*law of labour*", "**servant and master**" (*Revolutsionnaya Rossiya* No. 12, 6).

3. *Equivocation.* War on the "dogmatists", the orthodox, and at the same time avoidance of a straightforward stand on questions of Russian socialism, and travel all over Belgium + Italy!

Between the "**critics**" and the "orthodox"

David and K. Kautsky ⎱
Jaurès and Guesde   ⎰ etc. etc.

Compare *Vestnik Russkoi Revolutsii No. 2, p. 57*; (K. Kautsky and "critics").

4. *"Game"*: quotations from **Engels.** "Agreeing" with Liebknecht, and with Marx and with Engels!!

Revolutsionnaya Rossiya No. 14, p. 7, quotations from Engels (idem Rudin briefly 21)

(total distortion of Engels)

Extracts from Engels.

Engels supplemented by Böttger. (The prediction is coming true.)

1

> 5. An instance of confusion in Russian issues: **are there any relicts of serfdom?** *No: Revolutsionnaya Rossiya No. 8, p. 4.*
>
> | Full scope given!!! |
>
> *Yes,* not juridical but economic. *Revolutsionnaya Rossiya* No. *15, 6.*
> {No straightforward answer!! No principle at all!!} In the event, our agrarian programme or the "cut-off lands" *cannot* be understood!!

Nothing can be understood without clarifying your attitude to the relicts of serfdom and to the *whole* "change", all the post-reform economic evolution.

6. Socialists can *never* stand up for private *property*: "socialists" are "vehicles" of the "bourgeois spirit". *Revolutsionnaya Rossiya* No. *13, 5* and *6, No. 15, 6.*

they have adopted the "slogans of the bourgeois camp", etc.

"introduction of the bourgeois spirit" into the programme. *Revolutsionnaya Rossiya No. 15, p. 7.*

(vulgar socialism)

Con—Marx in 1848*

---

* In the MS., Point 6 is crossed out in plain pencil.— *Ed.*

extracts

7. Failure to understand (1) relics of serfdom
                             (2) historical significance of small *private free* property leads to total incomprehension of the cut-off lands.

Instead of assessing the *historical* significance they make an assessment in general in the sense of *provision*. *Rudin 14*: it involves indenture, etc., but not *"widely comprehensive"*!! (there is no "broad land provision") *(Rudin 14)*

good wishes instead of a *conclusion* from the evolution: either "allotment of land" to peasants as their private property, or the "organisation" of equalised peasant land tenure.	*Revolutsionnaya Rossiya No. 15, 6*

8. *Rudin's* "Theses" (p. 17)

2
      (1) *Allotment* of land will help to fight capitalism
      (2) it will slow down the capitalisation of privately owned farms, which is *grinding slow as it is*
      (3) it will blunt the class struggle.

9. They will not stop at the cut-off lands (Rudin 18). Of course, not. **What then?** The class struggle or the "labour" principle (Rudin 18)??

II. *The Agrarian Programme of the Social-Democrats.*

1. *Unfeasible*? We vouch—(in what sense).

2. Its **principles**
      (1) relics of serfdom—cf. *Martynov, p. 34.*

3

         Rudin, 26 "fearful for Martynov"

      (2) class struggle
      (3) socialist revolution of the proletariat.

3. The *land issue is being seen in the cut-off lands, where-as that is* **only** *a way of formulating the struggle against serfdom, of eliminating the relicts of serfdom.*

4. The question of reviewing the "1861 reform" has been *raised* by all the progressive (= liberal = bourgeois-demo-cratic) thinking in Russia.

Quotation from V. V.

4

5. The **meaning** of our agrarian programme: the Russian proletariat (including the rural) must support the peasantry in the struggle against serfdom.

Rudin 15-16: "*not all the peasants are hostile to the old regime*".

Cf. *Revolutsionnaya Rossiya* No. 8, p. 7: "petty-bourgeois sections" "always in general" "hold on to the existing order".

5

6. *What are we going to tell the peasant*? The "peasantry's" agrarian system
Con Engelhardt
The Socialist Party and the immediate task = *start* of the class struggle for socialism.

III. *The Agrarian Programme of the Socialist-Revolutionaries.*

1. Man without convictions = party without theory

2. Rudin *16*: "the future will clarify": "We must go out both to the worker and to the peasant"

3. **No programme.** Con—*Rudin 4* and *Revolutsionnaya Rossiya* No. 11, p. 6.
("our programme has been put forward")

4. *Reactionary* silence on the historic tasks of the moment—and invention of benevolent, confused wishes of "sociali-sation".

the peasant's equality "*To All the Russian Peasantry*", **p. 28, § 1**
—and no right to dispose of the land

freedom of movement—and no withdrawal from the commune.   (***Maslov's data***)

5. *Co-operatives: Revolutsionnaya*
    Rossiya No. 8, p. 11   { German }
                                                  { Russian }
                                                  { Rocquigny }

6. **Socialisation**

    1) = nationalisation. *Revolutsionnaya Rossiya*
          No. 8, p. 11. Talks on land, 15

(one in) 2) = socialist revolution. *"To All the*
(four   ) *Russian Peasantry"*, p. 31, § 12.
(parts) 3) = commune. *"Colossal organisa-*
            tion of the communal peasant-
            ry" No. 8, p. 9.

    +--+
    | "easier to start from" "communal |
    | traditions", etc. |
    +--+

    "equalisation principle to be implemented to
    the end" No. 8, p. 8.
    (although we are free from "idealisation"!)

    4) *Dutch* herring
    "extension of the commune's rights in taxing,
    buying out and expropriating land". *Revo-*
    lutsionnaya Rossiya No. 15, p. 7 "The
    Dutch type is most suitable."
    Revolutsionnaya Rossiya No. 15, p. 8.
    Universal men!!

Written before February 18
(March 3), 1903

First published in 1932
in *Lenin Miscellany XIX*

Printed from the original

PLANS AND OUTLINES OF CONCLUDING SPEECH

PRELIMINARY PLAN

α Inadequacy of cut-off lands. Nevzorov 3.
                                    Chernov 11.
   easements. Nevzorov 6
   contradictions between Lenin and Ilyin. Nevzorov 2
   beyond cut-off lands: confusion (Chernov 1) #

to α "unfeasibility" {Chernov 10 no}
   class struggle within commune (Chernov 2). Liberal
   kulaks still there: Chernov 3

β {commune. Nevzorov 5
   {collective responsibility. Nevzorov 4

γ   K. Kautsky and Engels. (Chernov 8) (and Chernov 16)
|| {repetition of predictions about differentiation,
   {proletarisation (Chernov 17)
   {the orthodox and the critics. No concentration (Cher-
|| {nov 18)

δ   co-operatives (4-6 Chernov)

ε   socialisation (7 Chernov)

ζ   *implanting of petty bourgeoisie*. Chernov 9 and
               {Nevzorov 1 *prodding on*}
                     Chernov 12 (*Russkoye Bogatstvo*)[54]

η   Plekhanov (Chernov 13. Nevzorov 7)

ϑ   *No. 1* of *Narodnaya Volya* (Chernov 14)
               Böttger (Chernov 15)

ι   Narodism = a tag (Chernov 19)

SUMMARY OF PRELIMINARY PLAN

I 1—3 ι	I 6—ζ
I 4—γ	I 7—9 nil #

$$\text{I } 5\text{—nil and } \alpha \qquad\qquad \text{II}^1\text{—ad } \alpha$$
$$\qquad\qquad\qquad\qquad\qquad \text{II } 2\text{—6 nil}$$
$$\text{III}^{1\text{-}2}\, 3\text{— } = \qquad\qquad \text{III } 5\delta$$
$$\text{III } 4 \text{ nil} \qquad\qquad\qquad \text{III } 6\varepsilon$$

Nevzorov β

RESUMÉ OF LECTURE

1. *Between Narodism and Marxism.*
    ("Gofstetter")
    Narodism is a "tag" (Mr. Vladimirov)   ⎫
    Kablukov, N.—on (Mr. Vla-   ⎬   "family
    dimirov)   economy"?
    (*Karyshev's* and *Vikh-*   ⎭   *Nil!*
    lyaev's "classical studies"
2. *Between the orthodox and the critics.*
    Quotation from Engels (Mr. Vladimi-   ⎫
    rov)   ⎬ + *Böttger*
    and K. Kautsky (Mr. Vladimirov)   ⎭
    Kautsky's "reservations": "not all is correct", etc.!!
    Repetition of *predictions* (Mr. Vladimirov)—
    No concentration, "*we do not believe in concentration*".
    (Minimum programme)
    "*There can be no difference of principle between an agrarian programme and a labour programme*" (Nevzorov)
3. **Are there any relicts of serfdom?**
    Yes and no. Nil.
    cut-off lands not everywhere (Mr. Vladimirov).
    Poltava gubernia
    three types of cut-off lands (Nevzorov)
    easements (Nevzorov)
    Lenin con Ilyin. (Nevzorov)
    labour services are not maintained chiefly by cut-off lands (Nevzorov)
4. *Marx on small property.*
    (1) *implanting of petty bourgeoisie* (Mr. Vladimirov).
    (2) not our business to *prod on* (Nevzorov and quotation from K. Kautsky)

{promotion of technical progress}
(3) Nevzorov. (Marx against Marx)
　　Lenin against
5. *What lies beyond the elimination of relics of serfdom? The class struggle or the labour principle? Nil?*

Our agrarian programme
6. Mr. Vladimirov: "No one said **unfeasible**."

Sic *Rudin, 13-14*

⌐*Russkiye Vedomosti* = bourgeoisie.
Quotations from V. V., from *Russkiye Vedomosti* on *agricultural conference.*[55]
7. *The principles of an agrarian programme. No one has said a word.*
8. Have these principles changed?
Plekhanov and the 1886 programme.
⎧Plekhanov and nationalisation
⎨Plekhanov and expropriation
⎩Marx and expropriation + mortgage
　　　　　　　　　　　　+ producers' associations.
⌐Plekhanov said there: "*The most likely thing is that the lands will pass to the peasant bourgeoisie*" (as Engels believed)....
{Plekhanov—extreme weakness of character}
9. *The meaning of our agrarian programme* = the Russian proletariat must support the peasantry. *Nil.*

Socialist-Revolutionary Agrarian Programme
10. *Reactionary. Collective responsibility* and the *commune. "I disagree in principle"* (Nevzorov). *Equality of rights but no withdrawal from the commune.* Nil.
⌐Class struggle within the commune? (Mr. Vladimirov). "For that reason" extension of communal land ownership.
11. *Co-operatives.* **Mr. Vladimirov.** *Two trends* (Where? in *Revolutsionnaya Rossiya* or *Iskra*?)

12. *Socialisation.* 4 meanings. ((Small communes = domination of the rural bourgeoisie.))

PLAN OF LECTURE RESUMÉ

finale: root of mistake
failed to understand the difficulty
our agrarian system
resumé

RESUMÉ OF LECTURE

a)   The root of Nevzorov's mistake is the effort to correct Plekhanov, without having understood him. The root of the S.R.s' mistake lies *deeper*: it is a confusion of the *democratic* and the *socialist* tasks, of the *democratic* and the *socialist* elements, of the democratic and the socialist *content* of the movement. This confusion is the result of the entire social nature of the Socialist-Revolutionary movement. Socialist-Revolutionarism = an attempt on the part of the petty-bourgeois intelligentsia to obscure the working-class movement = radical, revolutionary petty-bourgeois democracy. Like · the liberal democrats, they tend to *confuse* the democratic and the socialist tasks, and also to confuse the issue of the autocracy and the question of the agrarian programme.

b)   The S.R.s and Nevzorov have absolutely failed to understand the *difficulty* in drawing up an agrarian programme. Theirs applies to everything, and can be used anywhere, hence: nowhere. Sd* China and Abyssinia. Sr* Peru and Uruguay. It is *neither a programme nor an agrarian one.* It does not reflect anything; it does not define the ***moment*** (the historical moment: cf. 3 conditions of the programme), it fails to *provide guidance* for the present, current struggle.

c)   Our agrarian system. No answer
Four horizontal strata [big + peasant bourgeoisie $1^1/_2$ ($6^1/_2$ out of 14) + middle peasantry 2 (4 out of 14) + rural semi-proletariat and proletariat $6^1/_2$ millions

---

* These abbreviations have not been deciphered — *Ed.*

$(3^1/_2$ out of $14)^{56}$]. If that were all, there would be no
need for an agrarian programme. But there are also the
vertical partitions = commune, collective responsibility, cut-off lands, labour services, indenture. It is
impossible to liberate the rural semi-proletarian and
proletarian for the struggle, without also delivering
the rural bourgeoisie of labour services.

d) Resumé of the differences between the S.R. and the
S.D. agrarian programmes: 1) *truth* (semi-serfdom +
class struggle + capitalist evolution) + 2) *untruth* (member of a trade union, "colossal organisation of the communal peasantry", balanced extension of socialisation,
etc.).

A policy expounding untruths = a policy of revolutionary adventurism.

Written between February 18
(March 3) and February 21
(March 6), 1903

First published in 1932
in *Lenin Miscellany XIX*   Printed from the original

THE PEASANTRY AND SOCIAL-DEMOCRACY [57]

The Peasantry and Social-Democracy.
Marxist Theory and the Social-Democratic Programme.

{
1. The agrarian question with West-European Social-Democracy. David, etc.
2.   ,,   ,, in Russia: the old Narodniks, the Liberals and the Socialist-Revolutionaries. Practical significance during reforms.
}

3. *Large-*   *and*   *small-scale*   *production*
Auhagen
Klawki, etc.
  Conclusions concerning the **maintenance of labourers, livestock and land**

  Denmark.

4. **Co-operatives.** DAVID, etc.   French reactionaries
                                 Rocquigny
                                 Holtz
                                 Buchenberger.

5. Specifics of Russia.
  Together with the peasant bourgeoisie against the landowners.
  Together with the urban proletariat against the peasant bourgeoisie.

6. The importance of Social-Democratic agitation among the peasants, especially in the epoch of political revival. Development of the peasants' class-consciousness, and of democratic and Social-Democratic thinking.

---

1. Theory of Marxism (α) on the condition, evolution and role of the peasantry—and (β) the Social-Democratic programme. Closely bound up.

2. Urgency of the peasant question. The agrarian programmes of the Social-Democratic parties: the French
(petty-bourgeois nature. Criticism by Engels), the German (1895. Breslau), the opportunist and revolutionary
wings of the *Russian*. (Critics. **"David."**) (Bulgakov)....

3. The *Russian* agrarian programme of the Social-Democrats, their special distinction from the *Narodniks* and
the *Socialist-Revolutionaries*.

4. The principles of the Marxist theory concerning the
peasantry (cf. *Development of Capitalism*, quotations from Marx)
1) the role of large-scale production; 2) the petty-
bourgeois nature of the peasant; 3) his past and future +
{Souchon. Add K. Kautsky's *The Social Revolution*.

5. Large- and small-scale production in agriculture....
From the *Manuscript*: *Hecht*, Auhagen, Klawki,
Baden, German statistics, Stumpfe.

6. Conclusion: the importance of the maintenance of
labourers, livestock, land.

7. Add: Huschke, Haggard, Baudrillart, Lecouteux, *Prussian Inquiry*, Bavarian and Hessen Inquiries, Hubach.

8. Indebtedness. *Prussian statistics*.

9. Co-operatives. General approach to the question. Rocquigny, Holtz, Buchenberger, Haggard. Statistical
data: *German* and *Russian* (public lease). *Denmark*.

10. Conclusions concerning the West.

11. Russia's specific features.... On two flanks.
The peasant bourgeoisie and the rural proletariat.
Relicts of *serfdom* and the struggle against the bour-
geoisie.

12. Together with the peasant bourgeoisie against ⎤ Tie in
                 the landowners, etc. ⎬ with
Together with the urban proletariat against ⎢ cut-off
                   the bourgeoisie ⎦ lands

13. The practical importance of the agrarian question in
the possibly near future. Exposure of the class antagonism in the countryside. Democratic and Social-
Democratic agitation and propaganda.

Written not before September 1904

   First published in 1938   Printed from the original
in *Lenin Miscellany XXXII*

II

CRITIQUE OF
BOURGEOIS LITERATURE
AND ANALYSIS OF MASSIVE
AGRARIAN STATISTICS
1900-1903

CRITICAL REMARKS
ON S. BULGAKOV'S BOOK,
CAPITALISM AND AGRICULTURE,
VOLS. I AND II, PUBLISHED IN 1900 [58]

Bulgakov

I. *"From the author"* "essay on the theory (?) of agrarian development in connection with the general development of capitalism" — "slavishly dependent on the material"....

1. Chapter I, § 1: "Law of diminishing returns"....

2. Note: "In industry man wields (!?) the forces of nature", but in agriculture *adapts himself* (?)

13. Note. Marx denies this law, but accepts Ricardo's theory of rent, which is based on it (??). (III, 2, 277?) [59]

16. "Increasing difficulties of existence"....

17. — "An evident truth", which needs merely to be stated (?) — although agrarian progress temporarily nullifies the tendency indicated by this law.

18. The law of diminishing returns is of *universal significance—the social question is essentially bound up with it.*

20. *The agrarian crisis* is a direct consequence of the law of diminishing returns (?)

21. In agriculture, man is a "slave" to the laws of nature, in industry, he is master ("basic distinction").

25. Agriculture does not obtain the benefits latent in co-operation.

26-27. Marx's unhappy example (on co-operation)....

29-30. "Absolutely inapplicable to agriculture"

$$\left(\text{the law} \ll \frac{v}{c} \right) \quad \text{[Skvortsov] idem } 52.$$

31. Holds forth on trifles—about machines....

32. "*Particular case* of law of diminishing returns" — $\gg$ labour with intensification of agriculture.

34. "The despotism of nature"... labour $\ll$ its productivity....

35. "The economy of low wages"... "the economy of high wages is not applicable in agriculture".

37. Anyone will do for agriculture: the Russian no < than the Englishman.

38. — ..."even centaurs"... Con II 433

43. The *agricultural m a c h i n e* does not revolutionise production, does not create confidence or precision of work ... in the hands of Mother Nature.... (Empty phrase!)

44. The machine cannot convert the worker into its adjunct.

45. "The plough stops at the will of the driver"... (sic!)

46. "The role of the machine is not exceptional" (distortion and rubbish).

48. "I am sufficiently free from the Marxist prejudice" that any machine means progress.... Sometimes agricultural machines are reactionary (!!)

49. "Naïve" comparison between American and European agricultural machines.

50. Development of agriculture tends to narrow down the field of application of machinery....

51. "It makes no difference from the technical standpoint" whether labour is manual or machine

51 and 52. **The usefulness of the thresher is doubtful (!!)**....

55. A loaf defies telling who produced it ...Mother Nature is above such distinctions....

59-60. Small farms also make use of machines: they hire them!

64. In agriculture, there are two elements beyond human control: the forces of nature (!!) and the social forces (!!)

67. Backhaus welcomes the division of labour in agriculture (Bulgakov — con).

76. The decisive instance is the theory of cognition (in the question of value).

82. The price of grain is determined *not* by the last application of labour and capital, but by the average.

87. Marx adds nothing to Ricardo (on differential rent)   —absolute rent is a specific instance of differential rent.

90. "The limited productivity of the land"

92. "Grain has no value" (!)

95-96. Marx's *unhappy* example of the waterfall — Marx's fetishism ... (idem 105)

98. Agricultural capital takes no part in determining the rate of profit.

104. Petitio principii=*a b s o l u t e r e n t*....

105. Rent is "not a material thing" but a "*c o n c e p t*".

106. The concept of value is an "*aerial bridge*" (?)

107. Marx's theory of rent: obscure, contradictory, nothing new, etc.

111. "Pursuing their own path", "by their own efforts" ("have failed to find a material definition of rent").

113. Rent is not surplus-value—it is paid out of *n o n - a g r i c u l t u r a l* labour. (Bulgakov has forgotten the history of rent)....

116. Brentano's "remarkable" *Agrarpolitik*....

120. There is no **"English rent"** in other countries. —Agricultural profit is divided between the landowner, the farmer and the labourer. {defeats himself}

125. Rent (in a landed estate)—not an English one??

131. "In Britain grain is more expensive than on the continent" (?).
139. "The mystical law of concentration" is "a Marxist prejudice"
     ..."Hertz's remarkable work"....
142. "The peasant economy is not going down at all"....
143. Marx vs. Marx: the dualism of the politician and the researcher.
146-147. Marx "obscures"—according to the law of culture, the peasant's requirements are growing....
148. Bulgakov himself keeps comparing the peasant with *capital*....
154. The peasant economy—"the most profitable *for society*".

---

176. Hasbach: "The industry and thrift" of the small owner.
214. "Pre-capitalist overpopulation"....
237-238. The progress of English agriculture from 1846 to 1877.
239. The growth of bigger farms
     ..."not the result of conflict between small- and large-scale production"??...
239-240. Once farming is run on capitalist lines, it is indisputable that within certain limits the large is superior to the small (!!! N.B. !!)
242-243. *Tendency to concentration 1851-1861-1871 until 1880* ... in Britain....
246. The scourge of competition strained all the productive skill ... but this did not refute the law of diminishing returns....
251. Under a pastoral economy the capital per area unit increases (> capital-intensive)....
252. Growth in the number of agricultural machines

$$1855—1861—1871—1880$$

55   236
1,205 2,160 4,222 [60]

252. Reduction in the number of agricultural labourers ... 1851-1871 (and 1881-1891).

255. What explanation? *Overpopulation in the preceding period.*

(+also the consolidation of land holdings)
(+also the introduction of farming) (!!)
(machines)

260. Marx (and *Hasbach*) regards this as confirming the law of concentration, the growth of $\frac{c}{v}$. (Bulgakov con!)

262. English population by occupations 1851-1881.

268. *Basic cause of the crisis:* the law of diminishing returns....

273. Per-acre productivity in Britain is not ≤.
— Dairy farming, vegetable gardening, etc., have been *developing.*

279. Rent has suffered most of all (from the crisis)....

293. The labourer's wages and welfare are *growing....*

301. The agricultural labourers' movement has never been socialist.

303: "Large-scale production in agriculture has no positive social consequences" (there is not even a rudimentary trade union movement among agricultural labourers) (?).

306. Small farmers < stable.

308-309. Distribution of farms and area in Britain *1880-1885-1895.*

311. The crisis most severely affected the *small farmers....*

312. **Engels's "fantastic construction".**

313: Many small holders were ruined at the beginning of the 19th century.... ⌡

316. The condition of the yeomen is *worse than that of the labourers....* ⌡

318-319. *Small* holders have suffered >, their condition is
320-321. worse than that of the labourers, it is terribly hard....

325. Efforts to create a small peasantry. Small Holdings Act[61] 1892.

328 and *331.* Small Holdings Act was not widely applied. Small Holdings Act was of no practical importance.

333. Bulgakov's conclusions: > ruin of small farms *does not prove* (!!!) their unviability.... (!!)
338. "The final result": restoration of the **peasantry.** "A verdict against the capitalist organisation of agriculture."

II*

12. Three-field system prevailed from the 9th to the first third of the 19th century.
17. Insts[62] are diminishing....
30. *Communist Manifesto* gives a *wrong* picture of reality ("prophecy").
41. Prussia of the 1840s — **general overpopulation.**
44. Progress of German agriculture 1800-1850 (> than in 1,000 years) ??... "direct outcome of the growth of population" and "natural consumption"
45. Emancipation of peasants is the basis of capitalist agriculture.
46. Progress in agriculture is seen mainly on the *big* farms (that is, the *exchange* farms).
49. The crisis of the 1830s — capitalist baptism.
50. *Small farms were being ruined....*
56. *Big farms grow faster than small ones.*
57. 1852 and 1858. Distribution of farms and area.
62. A mass of small farms have been ruined... (since 1802)
63. "Flourishing of the large-scale economy" (distillation)....
76. Growth in the soil's productivity and technical progress — — — mainly in the *large-scale economy*... ("apparently")
79. Quarter century of agricultural improvement — nil for the agricultural labourers.
80. ..."*fatal feature*": lack of economy of high wages
89. *Growth* of rentals 1849-1869-1898....

* Vol. II of the summarised book.— *Ed.*

89-90. The peasant economy was the first to feel the brunt of the crisis. It soon turned out that it was most destructive for the *large-scale economy.*

103. The steam thresher was undoubtedly an evil for the labourers. This is also pointed out by Holtz; *a utopian idea*: to limit its use.

102. The number of Insts ≪ with an increase of free labourers.

104. Labourers *p r e f e r* >free status.

103. *"Capitalist reorganisation of the labourers' old condition"* !!

105. It is *u t o p i a n* to set up wage labourers with land allotments. Cf. II 255.

106. Own farm is the ideal of all agricultural labourers....

106. Reduction in the number of *Insts.* 1882-1895
number of labourers with land   –   N.B.
  "   "   "   without   "   +

106. Growth in the number of persons (agricultural labourers) for whom agriculture is a *side line....*

114. Number of agricultural machines in 1882 and 1895 by types.

116-117. Number of farms combined with industries... (figures interesting but obscure)....

117. "The crisis *has not deprived* the economy of the possibility of progress."

115. Large-scale farming is always more capital-intensive than small-scale, and, therefore, *n a - t u r a l l y* gives preference to the mechanical factors of production over live labour (!!)... ((the understating of the superiority of the big farms is interesting!))

115-116. "The reference to the supplanting of labourers by machines is quite groundless."

116. On the strength of what has been said the condition of the big farms is *critical* (!)...

118. *To hold its ground, large-scale production m u s t* ! show *progress*: income is derived only by those ! farms which are up to the technical standard.

119. With small farms, the price of land is *higher*— ergo, **big farms give way to small ones.**

119. Tendency: disintegration of the big farms into small ones ... and good luck!!

120. 1882 and 1895 statistics: *supplanting of big farms and in rather considerable proportions.* (!!?)

126. Middle peasant farming has grown stronger at the expense of the parcels and the big farms (5-20 hectares).

126. The growth of *latifundia* is a sign of decline (for intensiveness must lead to disintegration!!!)...

127. The increase (?) in farm employees. (?).

131. The growth of agricultural production, | especially of the area under *root crops* and || N.B. *beet root*

132-133. Prussian agriculture is developing, and the rural population? ∓+4·5 % (135)

133. "*Unremitting* and *even dissipating* labour on their own farms" (N.B.)

135. Increase in the number of machines *not only* on the big but also on the medium-big farms.

135. Increase in artificial fertilisers (note).

135-136. How is progress possible when prices are falling? (contrary to normal conditions *)....

136. Germany owes her current progress above all to *peasant farming* ... (!!)....

138. Policy: to establish a *solid* peasantry ("The way German Social-Democracy must take!!") "*Possibility of establishing independent farms*"....

141. There is no denying the beneficial effect of the *corn tariffs*

143. —"the tariffs *cannot evoke unconditional censure*".

144. *Hóltz* is right: labourers (!!) as well as producers.

145. ..."compromise" is the only way.

148. The technical progress of large-scale farming || is highly doubtful, its historical role is played out (!)

---

159. France at the end of the 18th century: "*A natural-economy overpopulation.*"

---

* The word "conditions" is not in the MS., and has been inserted according to the meaning.— *Ed.*

168. Growth in the urban and industrial population of France.

171. *Area under large-scale farming in the 19th century was relatively larger than* in the 18th....

172-173. Distribution of côtes foncières* 1884 (*2 types of data*).

173-174. *"Absolute fantasy"* ("stemming from his prejudice") Marx's assertion (1850) concerning the indebtedness of the French peasant.

174. ≫Growing *number of côtes*

> Con Souchon, p. 87, since '83 ≪   **

176. "The peasantry is divided into a proletariat and small holders" (after the revolution).

179. *"Hands are rare"*=employers *are finding wages high* (Vicomte d'Avenel).

181. The *market* is the power behind progress in France. Which class? (? *big capitalists+ peasant owners.*)

185. In France, there is an especial growth in the *area under root crops* and in the cattle population.

187. Rural population, 1882 and 1892.

188. *Distribution of farms*, 1882 and 1892.

190. Conclusion: "strengthening of peasant farms" and *"latifundia degeneration"* (!).

191. "Statistical sages" say ≫ under-1-hectare farms owing to increase in workers. *Con*: in these departments > peasant farms.

193. *There are fewer farms than plots. "Of course,*
?(!!) there is *no* reason to assume that many big estates are concentrated in the hands of one individual ... *there are only 2¹/₂ per cent of them"*

193. In wine-growing < 1 hectare may take up *all* the working time.

194. *Growth* in the number of farms with *managers* (*patently capitalist*)
Decline in the number of *day-labourer* farmers.

195. —refutation of "the fantastic assertion".

---

* An individual land holding in a commune in France.— *Ed.*
** See p. 171.— *Ed.*

195. *Growth in leases* (*"undoubtedly, small ones"*)?
196. Reduction in the number of agricultural labourers.
207. French farm labourer is being *transformed* (??) into a *peasant*.
210. France owes her progress to small-scale farming (??)
211. ‖ Despite the progress of French agriculture, the rural population has dwindled....
212. *Agricultural machines* (? Answer: "excess population disappearing")
213. *"We have seen* that small-scale farming is ahead" (!!)

213 and 215. Eulogy of peasant farming.

214. There has been no concentration: the third estate bought its lands before the revolution.... "The expropriation of a section of the peasantry"....

---

217. Population is limited by the means of subsistence....
218. Bulgakov "long" tended to underestimate Malthus ("invaluable work")
220. Population increase tends to stimulate the transition to new economic forms.
221. ...Some of the poverty "undoubtedly" springs from "absolute overpopulation"....
221. Overpopulation used to be more common in the past (?)...
223. Overpopulation is not a social but "merely" an "economic" theory.
223. opop="special problem" (opop=overpopulation)
224. "Neo-Malthusianism", deliberate adaptation of the birth-rate....
225. Dühring (Lange): capacity of territory.
229. Capitalism is inevitable with a higher density of population... (Struve (Lange))

231. "The old political economy." Verelendungs-theorie,* etc.
233. *"Emptiness"* of Marx's concept of station-ary overpopulation ....
237. "The peasants are not so hard hit by the crisis."
237. *"Rural* overpopulation".…
247. Peasant farming, having least capital at its disposal, is *naturally less stable* (but this has nothing to do with the question of its viability).
249. "Keeping within the territory's capacity" is the main negative condition of prosperity.
251. …One way… of thinning out the population (cf. *note*).
253. Artisan-farmers in Germany.
255. *Development of vegetable plots (among industrial workers) should be welcomed* (!!) Cf. II 105
259. A kulak section, starvation leases, etc., tend to grow on the basis of overpopulation (!!)
259. N.B.: Who takes over from the ruined peasants? *The peasants themselves.*
260. "Illusions" on the part of "conservative Marxists" that large-scale production is a vehicle of pro-gress.
261. "Boundless lust".…
263. …"Depravity rather than increase in the poor population".…
265. The problem of population is the main difficulty
N.B.: of collectivism.…
266. Individual landownership is the supreme com-mandment.
271. The fatal indebtedness of the peasantry is a myth.…
272. Indebtedness. Figures. Not high on peasant farms.
280. Kautsky's "fantasy", "pathetic effort to stretch a point" to prove that small farms furnish hired labour for big ones.
(There is no interlocking of big and small farms)

---

* Theory of impoverishment.— *Ed.*

280. Chronic Marxist prejudice that the peasantry is incapable of technical progress.
[Tables prove nothing]

282. Progress of peasant farming: *The Condition of the Peasants* $\left(\begin{array}{l} \text{I } 72, 276 \\ \text{II } 222 \end{array}\right)$

282-283. Peasant farming is *naturally* > labour-intensive than large-scale farming....

284-285. Peasant co-operatives ("and the big farms, of course").

287. *It is short-sighted and utopian to regard the peasant association as a step forward to socialism* ("Hertz is too closely tied to the opinion of his party") ·
"Narrowness" of collectives....

288. Socialisation in industry
individualism in agriculture $(!)$
The "slogan" of democratic development.

288. *The peasant is no less a working man than the proletarian....*

289. Against "peasantophobia"....
"*There is no room* in the villages *for the class struggle*"..."no educational influence of this struggle"... (bis)....

290. The peasant has fewer political interests, as compared with the townsman....

---

311. Ireland—overpopulation.

323. Two views of Ireland: the Malthusian, and that of agrarian relations.

324. Bulgakov: some of the evil is the fault of landlordism....

331. Middlemen,[63] *like the kulaks*, are not an inevitable concomitant of peasant farming.

339. Leasehold interest is of subordinate significance....

340. Against Manuilov.

346. Dispossession of land would have occurred even without the landlords, in virtue of overpopulation.

351. The famine of 1846 was beneficial. There is no reason for connecting evictions and emigration (*table proves the opposite*).

352. "Diminution of the population is, the cause of Irish progress"....
358. Growth in potato patches (up to 1 hectare: held by rural labourers, among others) in Ireland.
357. In Ireland there is no reduction of area under crop (thanks to peasant farming!)
359. *Farms* in Ireland by size (and *362*) (*consolidation*).
360. *Capitalist agriculture* is developing in Ireland.
361. In time of crisis capitalist agriculture in Ireland tends to regress (??)
  1) farmer capital $<$ (! by $0._{08}$%!)
  2) "fragmentary evidence".
363. "Latifundia degeneration" (!)
$$\left.\begin{cases} 30\text{-}200 \text{ acres } - \\ 200 \text{ and } > \text{acres } + \end{cases}\right\}$$
365. *Marx* is "tendentious" about Ireland, gives "a chaotic heap of figures"....
369-370. Progress used to come from capitalist farming, and latterly $>$ from the peasants (!!)...
371. Development of co-operatives in Ireland.
375. "*Welfare is spreading widely among the lower orders*" (loan and savings banks)....
379. Marx's "tendentious distortion of reality"....
380. Now there is overpopulation once again.
384. History of Ireland: importance of the population adapting itself to the capacity of the territory....

---

385. Law of diminishing returns is the scourge of mankind....
386. Marx gave Wakefield an unfair and biased assessment.
393. —in Wakefield's assessment, Marx is an *economic reactionary*. ("The idea of putting capitalism in place of the savage does not deserve condemnation.")
396. North American population by occupations....
398-399. American industry 1850-1860-1870-1880-1890....

412. Millionaires and *paupers* have made their appearance in America.
414. Farm area 1850-1890 (≥)
422-423. Division of labour in American agriculture (rapaciousness).
425. Crisis in the Eastern States.
429. Dairy farming and market gardening in the Eastern States.
433: "Naïveté" about machine farming in North America.
435-436. *Distribution of farms*
438. No concentration (con the "overjoyed Marxists").
445. In 1896 I "did not deny" Zusammenbruchstheorie*... ("I would have made deletions").
449. The growing prevalence of the internal market.
454. Urban civilisation *would have come up against* the *law of diminishing returns.*
(!) 455. *The grain problem is > terrible than the social one.*
456. Marx is quite wrong about agriculture.
456. N.B. ‖ *It is not true that capitalism leads to collectivism.*
456. *Solid peasant* farming is supplanting large-scale farming ("democratic tide").
457. Marx's prediction—"*short-sightedness* turned to ridicule by history", "the *self-conceit* of scientific socialism".
457. ... *"over-estimation of social cognition" ....*
* 458. "Sorcery and fraud" — — — — ignoramus.

Written in June-September 1901

First published in 1932
in *Lenin Miscellany XIX*

Printed from the original

---

* The collapse theory.— *Ed.*

PLAN OF OBJECTIONS TO BULGAKOV'S BOOK

Note especially

α) law of diminishing returns;
β) theory of rent;
γ) refutation of α in Britain, Germany, France, Ireland and America;
δ) on agricultural machines;
ε) "solid peasantry" and the agrarian on the question of labourers (vegetable plots), machines and taxes; "latifundia degeneration"
II, 126, 190, 363 (con—Hertz 15*)
(Ad ε: cf. II 375)
ζ) complete break with socialism. II. 287, 266, 288
— co-operatives
— class struggle   II 289
— capitalism does not lead to collectivism.   II 456

Written in June-September 1901

First published in 1932
in *Lenin Miscellany XIX*

Printed from the original

---

* See p. 98.— *Ed.*

CRITICAL REMARKS ON THE WORKS
OF S. BULGAKOV AND F. BENSING

Once again Mr. Bulgakov *garbles* a quotation in the grossest manner in Note 2, on p. 273 of Vol. II. The third column of his table does not apply to the "big farms", as he declares in the heading, but *to all farms in general (Untersuchungen,* etc.* S. 573, Anhang. III).

The last but one column of Mr. Bulgakov's table shows not the percentage of indebtedness of the "medium farms" (as Mr. Bulgakov says) but the average size of the *holding* (sic!) in *small-scale farming.* (L. c., Anhang, V, S. 575.) The last column shows not the percentage of indebtedness of the "small farms", but the average size of *holding* in *large-scale* farming (ibidem). It is incredible, but a fact that Mr. Bulgakov has managed to *confuse* the tables of the original he quotes and has "mixed up" the data on size of holdings and the data on the percentage of indebtedness.

The actual figures:

$843._{10}$	24	$643._{20}$	24	$485._{06}$	23
	$35._{13}\%$		$26._{80}\%$		$21._{09}\%$

(average % of indebtedness)

*Kleinbetrieb***		*Mittelbetrieb****		*Grossbetrieb*****
$35._{13}$	—	$26._{80}$	—	$21._{09}$

---

* Untersuchungen der wirtschaftlichen Verhältnisse in 24 Gemeinden des Königreichs Bayern (Study of Economic Conditions in 24 Communities of the Bavarian Kingdom).—*Ed.*

** Small farms.—*Ed.*

*** Medium farms.—*Ed.*

**** Large farms.—*Ed.*

Once again: this is how Mr. Bulgakov quotes.

He refers to p. 77 of Bensing, where Bensing says that agricultural machines* have a *smaller* part to play in raising productivity than industrial machines.

But this is Bensing's introduction to a *chapter* whose *result*, **p. 99,** gives a considerable increase in production owing to agricultural machines.

Mr. Bulgakov quotes Bensing. I 32, 48, *44*

Bensing 4: Marx—Gegner der Maschinen in der Industrie**

Insert on Bensing in § on machines***:

1) Bensing's bourgeois attitude to agricultural machines (adopted by Bulgakov) is well illustrated by a *similar* attitude to machines in industry.

(p. 4. Marx—Gegner der Maschinen (cf. 1-2)

p. 5. Marx "dreht" distorts the beneficial effect of machines.

p. 11. Marx "allerhand Unheil nachsagt"****... to agricultural machines.

Bensing's standpoint is that of the bourgeois and the entrepreneur

female and child labour—*n i l* (pp. *13-14*)!!

2) Higher productivity of agricultural machines

α) special inquiry

β) a comparison of literary data p. *99* (results)

$\left\{ \begin{array}{l} 81,078=117._4\% \\ 69,040=100\% \end{array} \right\}$ reduction of costs, p. *167* (results).

3) Bulgakov quotes Bensing p. 42, but says nothing about this being Bensing's illustration of the importance of machines: p. *45.*

Bensing on *electricity*: pp. 127 and 102.

N.B. also about *Feldbahnen****** pp. 127-29.

Can Bensing's calculations (pp. 145 et seq.) be used to determine $\frac{c}{v}$ and modify it?

Estate=*310* hectares (240 hectares of fields+70 hectares of meadow).

It is better to take the even not-too-exact figures of Bensing himself, p. 171.

---

* The word "machines" has been inserted by the editors.—*Ed.*
** Opponent of machines in industry.—*Ed.*
*** See present edition, Vol. 5, pp. 130-34.—*Ed.*
**** Predicts all sorts of misfortunes.—*Ed.*
***** Field supply railways.—*Ed.*

Fall I*.

ν** $= 1 + 2 = 3$ Lfd Nummer***
(pp. 147-48, table)

Mk
$= 2,400 = 2$ persons
$+ 9,700 = 17$ persons
$17,525 = 13,294$ work- | 5,242 men |
ing days | 8,052 women |

m** $= 10$ (Abgaben +
Lasten) + Reinertrag**** $= 300$
$+$
$\dfrac{425}{725}$ Mk

$v = 29,625$
c** $= 38,690$ ⧣ 19 persons and
$m = \dfrac{725}{\quad}$ *13,294* working
W** $= 69,040$ days

$c = 4+5+6+7+8+9+11+12+13$ Lfd. Nr.
c here $=$ annual wear and tear of c.
All $c = 57,000+14,000+150,000+$ (part of 35,500)
(namely $35,000 - 29,625$)

4,470
11,699
1,464
6,660
2,800
1,000
6,035
1,900
2,662
$\overline{38,690}$ Mk ⧣

Mk
Capital: 57,000 livestock
14,000 dead stock
150,000 buildings
35,500 working capital

256,500

Fall II.

Mk	ν Mk	Mk		
$-$ 1,776	29,625	$-$ 1,776 $=$ 1,184 working days	$-$	13,294
832.5	1,446	330 $=$ 220 ,, ,,		964
$\overline{943.5}$	$\overline{28,179}$	$\overline{1,446 = 964}$		$\overline{12,330}$

Hence: *19 persons +
12,330 working days*

---

* Case One.— *Ed.*
** c—constant capital (the cost of the means of production);
v—variable capital (the cost of labour-power); m—surplus-value;
W—value of the gross product.— *Ed.*
*** Serial number.— *Ed.*
**** (Taxes+duties)+net income.— *Ed.*

m 300 taxes
    1,368.$_5$ Reinertrag
    ‾‾‾‾‾‾‾‾‾
    1,668.$_5$

c 38,690
 + 502.$_5$ (new machinery)
  ‾‾‾‾‾‾‾‾   ($^1/_4$.2,010)
  39,192.$_5$

$c = 39,192._5$
$v = 28,179$
$m = 1,668._5$
‾‾‾‾‾‾‾‾‾‾‾‾
$W = 69.040._0$

Capital
57,000

16,010 $\left\{ + \begin{array}{c} 14,000 \\ 2,010 \\ \hline 16,010 \end{array} \right.$

150,000
35,500?*)
‾‾‾‾‾‾‾‾‾
258,510

Fall III A. v $\quad \underline{\quad 28,179}$
           92
      ‾‾‾‾‾‾‾‾
      $v = 28,087$

$\left. \begin{array}{l} 546 \text{ Mk} = 439 \text{ working} \quad \text{days} \\ 454 \text{ Mk} = 304 \quad \text{”} \quad\quad \text{”} \\ \hline 92 \text{ Mk} \quad \overline{135} \text{ working days} \end{array} \right\}$ $\left\{ \begin{array}{r} - \quad 12,330 \\ 135 \\ \hline 12,195 \end{array} \right\}$

Hence: *19* persons +
12,195 working days

$c = 39,192._5$
 +   362.$_5$($^1/_4 \times 1,450$)
  ‾‾‾‾‾‾‾‾‾
  39,555

$m = $ 300 taxes
     4,878 Reinertrag
     ‾‾‾‾‾‾‾‾‾
     5,178

Mk
$c = 39,555$
$v = 28,087$
$m = \ 5,178$
‾‾‾‾‾‾‾‾‾‾‾
$W = 72,820$

Capital
57,000   Mk

17,460 $\left\{ + \begin{array}{c} 16,010 \\ 1,450 \\ \hline 17,460 \end{array} \right.$

150,000
35,500
‾‾‾‾‾‾‾‾‾

---

*)? The author assumed the circulating capital $=^1/_2$ live-stock + dead stock $57 + 14 = 71$ thousand. $71 \div 2 = 35._5$; consequently, here too he should have taken $57 + 16._{01} = 73._{01}$ $73._{01} \div 2 = 36,505$ Mk.

Fall III B.

$$\begin{array}{r} v \ 28,087 \\ - 1,482._5 \\ \hline 26,604._5 \end{array}$$

$$\left\{\begin{array}{l} 1,523 \text{ Mk} = 1,269 \text{ working days} \\ 40._5 = 27 " " \\ \hline 1,482._5 1,242 \text{ working days} \end{array}\right.$$

$c 39,555$
$+ 150 \ \{^1/_4 \times 600\}$

$c = 39,705$
$v = 26,604._5$
$m = 6,510._5 \ \{300 + 6,210._5\}$

$$\left\{\begin{array}{l} 12,195 \\ 1,242 \\ \hline 10,953 \end{array}\right.$$

Hence: *19* persons and
10,953 working days

$W = 72,820$

Capital. Dead stock
$+ \ 17,460$
600
$\overline{18,060}$

Fall III   C.

$$\begin{array}{r} v \ 26,604._5 \\ - 418._5 \\ \hline 26,186._0 \end{array}$$

$$\left\{\begin{array}{l} 486 \text{ Mk} = 360 \text{ working days} \\ 67._5 = 45 " " \\ \hline 418._5 = 315 " " \end{array}\right.$$

$c = 39,705$
$+ 400 \ \{^1/_4 \times 1,200 + 100\}$

$c = 40,105$
$v = 26,186$
$m = 6,529 \ \ (300 + 6,229)$

$$\left\{\begin{array}{l} 10,953 \\ - 315 \\ \hline 10,638 \end{array}\right.$$

Hence: *19* persons+
10,638 working days

$W = 72,820$

Capital. Dead stock
$18,060$
$+ 1,200$
$\overline{19,260}$

Fall III D.

$$\begin{array}{r} v \ 26,186 \\ - 2,320._5 \\ \hline 23,865._5 \end{array}$$

$$\left\{\begin{array}{l} 2,616 \text{ Mk} = 2,024 \text{ working days} \\ 295._5 \text{ Mk} = 197 " " \\ \hline 2,320._5 1,827 \end{array}\right.$$

$c = 40,105$
$+ 400 \ (^1/_4 \times 1,600)$

$c = 40,505$
$v = 23,865._5$
$m = 8,449._5 (300 + 8,149._5)$

$$\left\{\begin{array}{l} 10,638 \\ - 1,827 \\ \hline 8,811 \end{array}\right\}$$

Hence: *19* persons +
8,811 working days

$W = 72,820$

Capital. Dead stock
$19,260$
$+ 1,600$
$\overline{20,860}$

Fall III E.

$$v = 23,865._5 \quad \left\{ \begin{array}{l} 2,100 \text{ Mk} = 1,400 \text{ working days} \\ \\ 630 \text{ Mk} = 420 \quad \text{''} \quad \text{''} \end{array} \right. \quad c = \begin{array}{l} 40,505 \\ + \\ 861 \quad (735+126) \end{array}$$

1,470

$$v = 22,395._5 \quad \left. \begin{array}{l} -1,470 \text{ Mk} = 980 \text{ working days} \\ + \; 215 \text{ Mk*}) = 140 \quad \text{''} \quad \text{''} \end{array} \right\} \quad \begin{array}{l} 41,366 \\ - \\ \quad 215\text{*}) \end{array}$$
\+ 215

22,610._5
8,811
—

$\quad\quad c = 41,151$
$\quad\quad v = 22,610._5$

980

$\quad\quad m = 14,476._5 \; (300+14,176._5)$

7,831
+

$\quad\quad W = 78,238$

140

Capital.
Dead stock
20,860
(machine *hired*)
(steam thresher)

7,971   Hence: *19* persons + *7,971* days

Fall III F.

$$v = 22,610._5 \quad \left\{ \begin{array}{l} 1,890 \text{ Mk} = 1,575 \text{ working days} \\ 855 \quad\quad 690 \quad \text{''} \quad \text{''} \end{array} \right. \quad c = \begin{array}{l} +41,151 \\ 250 \quad (^{1}/_{4} \times 1,000) \end{array}$$
1,035

21,575._5 $\left. \begin{array}{l} 1,035 \text{ Mk} = 885 \text{ working days} \end{array} \right\}$ $c = 41,401$
$v = 21,575._5$
$m = 14,781._5 \; (300 + 14,481._5)$

$$\left. \begin{array}{l} 7,971 \\ - \\ 885 \\ \hline 7,086 \end{array} \right\} \quad \begin{array}{l} \text{Hence: } 19 \text{ persons +} \\ 7,086 \text{ working days} \end{array}$$

$W = 77,758._0$

dead stock
20,860

1,000

21,860

---

*) These 215 Mk (=about $^{1}/_{4}$ of 861) I tentatively charge to *v* from the cost of the *hired* machine. (thresher). [The same thing in Fall IV with the steam plough.]

Fall IV

$c = 38{,}786$
$v = 23{,}465._5$
$m = 18{,}826._5$

dead stock   21,860
                 + 10,000   Feldbahn

                 31,860

$W = 81{,}078._0$ (steam plough *hired*)

Hence = *17* persons and *9,096* working days

(introduction of the steam plough (one only) and the Feldbahn) changes the quantity of the livestock and the permanent labourers.

19 persons
2 (Ochsenmeister und
   Pferdeknecht)*
      — 1,250 Mk

Day labourers
— *700* days (at 1.50 = 1,050 Mk)●
Hence, minus *2,300* Mk

17 persons

Reduction of the livestock:

— 7 horses	4,200	
— 18 oxen	8,100	

                  — *12,300* Mk

Maintenance of dead stock:
   before = 24,866 Mk
   now   = 20,981 Mk

   − 3,885 Mk

i.e., a reduction of v by 2,300 Mk (2 permanent labourers + 700 days)

" " " " c " 16,185 $\left\{ \begin{matrix} 12{,}300 \\ + \\ 3{,}885 \end{matrix} \right\}$

Meanwhile, c increases by *1,000* ($^1/_{10} \times 10{,}000$ Feldbahn) $+ ^3/_4$ (on my assumption) of the cost of hiring the Dampfflug, i.e., $^3/_4 \times 16{,}760 = 4{,}190 \times 3 = 12{,}570$, i.e., by 13,570

Sum total reduction of c is $16{,}185 - 13{,}570 = \mathbf{2{,}615}$ v is reduced by 2,300 Mk, but is, on the other hand, increased by $^1/_4 \times 16{,}760 = 4{,}190$, at 1.5 Mk = c. 2,800 working days

---

* Labourer tending oxen and labourer tending horses — *Ed*

Hence v has increased by *1,890* Mk {$\equiv 2$ permanent labourers $\pm 2,100$ working days.}

c =	41,401	v = 21,575.5	m = 300
	2,615	+ 1,890	18,526.5
c =	38,786	23,465.5	18,826.5
v =	23,465.5		
m =	18,826.5		
W =	81,078.0		

Written in June-September 1901

  First published in 1932
in *Lenin Miscellany XIX*

Printed from the original

CRITICAL ANALYSIS OF F. HERTZ'S BOOK, *THE AGRARIAN QUESTIONS IN RELATION TO SOCIALISM**

Hertz

VI. Typical approach (lack of historical view, tendency to ramble and delve into detail)

Russian translation 17.

1. K. Kautsky has "no doubt" *impeccably* cleared up two questions: *on rural labourers*
   on large-scale agriculture
   Alias—the *"peasant question"*.

2. According to Hertz, K. Kautsky has two important points:

   N.B. { 1) in agriculture the interests of wage labourers are superior to the interests of the owners.
   2) the peasant is an antagonist of the labourer.

3. In Austria.
   $8^{1}/_{2}$ million active in agriculture.
   $4^{1}/_{4}$ million rural labourers.
   Hertz believes that 0.8 million rural labourers are de facto co-heirs.

4. "Wortspiel"** by Kautsky: the peasant-entrepreneur (cf. Chernov).

5. The peasant's alternate transformation (in K. Kautsky) into a labourer and an entrepreneur.

---

* Hertz, F., *Die agrarischen Fragen im Verhältnis zum Sozialismus*. Wien, 1899.— *Ed.*
** Word juggling.— *Ed.*

6. *Note 15.* Hertz also regards holders with 1-2
! {labourers as Kleinbetrieb or peasant farm.
6. There is no *class antagonism* between the labourers and the small peasants.
7. Demands must be "immediately attainable" —
communal ownership of land (K. Kautsky) does
not meet the requirement.
9. Not every peasant with subsidiary employment
is already a proletarian [*very stupid*].
"Help" is not exploitation.
10. "Definition" of capitalism [forgot all about commodity production and wage labour!!]
10. Real definition of capitalism: production under
the domination of capital (!! that's all!!).
"Genetic" definition
10. *Note 25.* "The economic usefulness of the capitalist
is still being debated." (Sic!)
11. "Extremely false" — "*die*" *Agrarfrage* (!)
11. Britain: now "a model for everyone", now "we are
not Britain" (con — Bernstein).
12. "Normal" capitalism. (?!)
The most important thing: the fact that capitalist
exploitation is not connected with progress *towards capitalist large-scale production.*
12. Agriculture in Russia. Nikolai — on.
12-13. Large landed estates have not made for progress
in Russian agriculture?
13. New peasantry (according to P.S.[64]).
14. *Also* — gilt *Nicolai — on* (??)* "Nowhere does the
new mode of production supplant the old."
14. In Russia, capital does not go on to a *juridical*
possession of the means of production, being
satisfied with ≥ share of the products.
Sic! ((Socialism will possibly take a similar stand in
respect of capitalism?
15. Latifundia in Austria are not as common as
K. Kautsky believes (although there are model
farms) (*and nothing more*).
15. Baudrillart's *excellent* works.

---

* Consequently, Nikolai — on remains in force (??). — *Ed.*

16. The Middle Ages bequeathed a great many pecu-
liarities. *K. Kautsky* is **totally unhistorical** in
his summing-up conclusions [Where? What? When?]

17. Austrian Alps: in 1867 (idem *1887*) the same
economy as in the Middle Ages.

18. Colossal growth of debt.

20. Hertz agrees with Engels that the peasant must be
rescued from "the vegetative life" of the patriarchal natural economy, but is the money economy
the *best* way? (Sic!)

20-21. Peasants ruined in the Alps, the rich buying up
peasant lands (for hunting). That is not a case
of large-scale production displacing the small.

21. The transforming effect of capitalism in the Alps
is a complete fiasco!

(!!) 21. Hence K. Kautsky is wrong on the educative role
of capitalism: *parcel leaseholds are designed to
supplant large-scale production altogether.*

21. Accordingly, the "main task of socialism" is *to
sustain the co-operatives!!!*

22. Concentration of mortgages. Mortgages are not
always
1) large farms owe > than small ones.

24. Small depositors in mortgage banks. Cf. figures.
{ Enormous % of holders}
{ and small % of capital. }

26. Savings banks in Austria..1'd *

28. Russian savings banks, 65.5% workers, etc.

28. This tendency is not one of centralisation but of
decentralisation (*!*).

29. Small artisans and workers are expropriating the
landowners. *Bernstein is quite right about agriculture: a growing number of holders* (*!!!*).

31. Engels's mistake about America (displacement
of small farmers by big ones).

33-34. In the Eastern United States of America, land
prices have dropped, but the progress of agricultural production continues, and K. Kautsky is
quite wrong. [Cf. Bulgakov II, 435-436.]

* Not deciphered.— *Ed.*

36. +America: *absence of parcels* allows the > use of machines.

36. The Americans take pride in the fact that they do not have such a *low-standing peasantry as Europe does.*

39. The modern Grossbetriebe should also be compared with the modern Kleinbetriebe Chernov .

40. There is a terrible waste of labour-power under the parcel economy in Europe: neither the large nor the small farms have any "absolute" superiority.

43. The fatalism of European peasants. An American would take a limitation of credit worthiness as an affront.

44. "dire misery" of the European peasant.

45. Characteristic headline: *"Socialist* Attacks on Small-Scale Production."

47-48. Countries according to crop yields: Britain, Belgium, Denmark, Holland, Sweden, France.
[4 countries with small-scale cropping surpass France!]

in % of farms!!

49. In large-scale production, the wheat crop is *only* 0.$_{49}$ hectolitre higher. [Yes, at a rough estimate!]

50. Growth in crop yields in France in the 19th century.

51. Decline in crop yields in Britain.

52. The growth in the number of agricultural machines in France is evidence (51) that the *Kleinbetrieb* does not shun science.

52. Growth in the number of holders (???)

53. Rural handicraft industry—*none* in France (we see nothing)?? [Souchon] (Maurice, p. 294).

53. *Distortion.* Parcel farms decline in **area** (on the question of the growth of wage labour!!)

54. Hypocritical over "normal" development.

55. Kautsky's assertion (about wage labour among

small peasants) "total zerfällt"*—data 1862-1882-1892 (Bulgakov) on the decline in the number of **day labourers** with land.

55. *An exclamation mark over the fact that Gross-betrieb is already > 40 hectares*!

56. K. Kautsky's quotation about the French peasantry has been taken from a reactionary, romantically-minded lady. Foville has refuted....

56-58. *Baudrillart....*

59. The consumption of meat in the countryside is *much* < than in the towns (although it is growing faster!)

59. K. Kautsky's assumption (on the consumption of meat).

59. *Pauperisierung der französischen Bauern keineswegs stattfindet* (!!)**

60. The state of France is the "*goal*" of all other countries (!)

60. Is there an *absolut* überlegener Betrieb***?

61. K. Kautsky should have said: Grossbetrieb *may* be superior to Kleinbetrieb.

— K. Kautsky does not give any figures for *crop yields* on Grossbetrieb and Kleinbetrieb.

61. "*Feuilleton method*"... (of Kautsky's).

62. Examines the arguments for Grossbetrieb
Buildings
Machines (co-operatives)
Credit (something he does not examine).

62-63. David in *Sozialistische Monatshefte*.

63. Steam plough: not possible everywhere
— excellent results on heavy soils
— but *not*—on light soils.

64. Describes in detail where the steam plough cannot be used.

65. It is absurd to say, he adds, that the steam plough is better *under any conditions* (? who? where?).

65. Threshing in winter: labour (!) cheap (N.B.).

65. Once again (bis) *absolut* (!!) (swindler!)

65-69. *Incomes.*

* Does not hold water.— *Ed.*
** There is no pauperisation of the peasants in France at all.— *Ed.*
*** A farm with absolute superiority.— *Ed.*

66. — East-Elbe—and *South* (!!) *Germany*: and so on (comic)
67. Higher yields following the introduction of the steam plough.
68. —and in South Germany (Baden) even higher!!!
68-69. *M. Hecht**)—first-rate.
70-71. Auhagen. (Cf. K. Kautsky.)
72. Marx. Contrasts cash income with agriculture (!!!) K. Kautsky does not even touch upon the question.
72-73. Nachklang naturrechtlichen etc.* (communal land-ownership).
73-74. Chewing on an inexpressible commonplace

$$\left(\frac{w-k}{t} \right) ** \text{ with praise for Wagner (!)}—$$

74. Accordingly, *rough method*—simply compares gross incomes.
74. *Kleinbetrieb* uses relatively $>$ labour than *Grossbetrieb*.
76. The bulk of the peasantry still using the most primitive implements.
76. Abolition of the antithesis between *t o w n a n d c o u n t r y* (Hauptwunsch alter Utopisten*** and *Communist Manifesto*), but *"we do not believe"*....
76-77. *The Condition of the Peasants* (Kutzleb??) [see separate sheet. Cf. *B u l g a k o v* II 282] *in part the same references!!*
79. *"First-rate"*—Moritz Hecht....
80. Stumpfe on peasant livestock farming.
81. Small holders *widely* (?) *use* agricultural machines (?)
82. *Grossbetrieb in Europe not$>$ than $^1/_3$ of the area.* [*"Cannot treble production"*]

---

*) Remember to note à propos M. Hecht intensified (and *age-old*) use of urban waste, sewage, etc., **as fertiliser.**

---

* Echo of natural right, etc.— *Ed.*
** A formula used by Hertz to denote productivity, where w—value of gross product, k—costs of production, and t—time of production.— *Ed.*
*** The main dream of the old utopians.— *Ed.*

83. The *Grossbetrieb* has had the worst of the crisis.
84-85. *Engels* is wrong in expecting overseas competition to intensify.
87. Kautsky's "trick" (data on artificial wine).
87-88. Kautsky's groundless hopes for the industrialisation of agriculture: the displacement is insignificant. The merger of agriculture with industries often goes through the co-operatives.
88. **"If" Grossbetrieb has "really" combined large-scale** industry and large-scale agricultural production. ("If"!?!)
88. 1) No concentration.
   2) Growing number of independent holders.
   3)   "   " of all holders.
   4) Superiority of large-scale over small-scale production is relative.
89. 5) Two trends in development:
          towards a growth of *medium* production;
          towards parcel farms.
   6) *Parcel leaseholds*—the ultimate goal of capitalist agriculture.
   7) Capitalism fails to create any economic or psychological premises for socialist large-scale production.
   8) *"The main task of socialism"* is to organise
!! small-scale production through co-operatives.
89. The small peasant as well as the small tenant is not a capitalist, but a worker.
89-90. Labour rent of the small peasant drops to subsistence minimum—(!!N.B.)
90. *The price of land*—the main cause.
91. The small holder buys land and pays his debts through *subsidiary employment* ((work for a wage...!))....
92. //The contemporary peasant question is a transmut-
N.B. ((ed form of the unemployment problem. (Hertz
    \fails to make both ends meet.)
92. For Kautsky the agrarian question is everywhere the same.
93. What will a socialist state do with its employees in agriculture? (Very clever!)

95. In agriculture, the lever of economic self-interest
|| (Selbstinteresse) is indispensable. [Russian trans-
lation p. 227.]

! ! !   ⌜socialist!⌝

103. Terrible *nonsense on the content* of the modern
right of ownership, etc.

104. —division on the basis of property [pure scholas-
ticism!]

105. —and all of this just to say that it's no use
|| waiting for a social revolution. We are in it.
|| Property will not be transformed "all at once".

111. The peasants are "entering socialism": the co-
operatives....

112. Every year, about *1,500* agricultural co-operatives arise.
— *1,050,000* farmers have united in a purchasing society ("*con*" K. Kautsky!!).
Kautsky is absolutely wrong....
In Austria (Hohenbruck) dairy farm co-operatives
have less than 1 cow per farmer. [Cf. Germany!!]

112. **The co-operatives mostly benefit the small and**
Sic!   **the smallest holders.**

113. Kautsky's objection *"Absolut unhaltbar".*— *Ko-
misch** (?) on sale of milk. The peasants receive
cash.

113. How "weak" the exploitation of the rural
labourers by the co-operatives is! Hundreds
of peasants have 2 or 3 labourers (!?). Associations
graded:

118. ...Disqualifizierung minderwertiger Produkte.**
...regulations by dairy co-operatives on the maintenance of cattle, etc.

119. The co-operatives have started to build elevators
with strict sorting of grain.

120. Wine-makers' co-operatives: fully Grossbetrieb....

121. The poor are saved from ruin: their **vineyards** are
!! || bought from them **and leased back on**

---

* Absolutely groundless.— Absurd.— *Ed.*
** Rejection of low-grade products.— *Ed.*

          instalments! They open their own wine-cellars....

          ...what more does Kautsky want?...

122. Engels also speaks about co-operatives.

123. The *failures* of socialist co-operatives. *N.B.*

123. Centralised farming is !! "*absolutely* impossible".

  124. That is for the small ones, whereas the big ones

!!!!   are *socialised*! It pays to use the steam plough, etc.

129. The reactionaries also favour co-operatives.

PLANS OF OBJECTIONS TO F. HERTZ'S BOOK

1

α   "Definition of capitalism" (p. 10)!

β   *Mortgages* (pp. 24, 26, 28)
          (Decentralisation)

γ   Engels's mistake about America (p. 31)

δ   Proprietary interests in agriculture (pp. 2, 3).
    The peasant entrepreneur.
    ("Wortspiel") (p. 4) (p. 5) and p. *89.*
    ‖Kleinbetrieb—and *farms* with *1-2 hired labourers* (p. 6, Note 15)
       There is no class antagonism between the Kleinbetrieb and the hired labourers (p. 6).
    On *subsidiary employment* (p. 9)

ε   ‖The big farm has no *absolute* superiority (p. 40) (p. 60)
    ‖(60-65)
      Threshers: labour cheap in winter: p. *65*
      Crop yields in France p. 49.
      The Kleinbetrieb does not shun machines p. *52* (indiscriminate figures on France). Cf. 81 (widely??)
      On the sale of milk: p. 113.

ζ   *M. Hecht*: *68* and *79* et al. ("first-rate")
    Crop yields in East-Elbe and South Germany (66)
            Auhagen: 70-71.

ϑ   Higher crop yields following the introduction of the steam plough (67)
      124: advantages of the steam plough!

There are model farms among the latifundia in Austria: *p. 15* (con Bulgakov)

Con! America: absence of parcels allows greater use of machines; no peasantry of such low standing (p. 36) and *43. 44.*

Con. Kleinbetrieb uses relatively more labour (74). Most peasants have primitive implements.

The peasant's labour rent: pp. *89-90* (!!)

Small farmer resorts to collateral employment: *91* cf. *92.*

× Growth in the number of holders in France 52 (??)
In France there is no rural industry 53 (??)
Distortion on parcel farms (reduction in number) 53.
Refutation of Kautsky's assertion on wage labour among small peasants 55.

λ Hertz on N.—on etc. (p. 12).
(Cf. Chernov)
Is the money economy the best way? (p. 20)
Parcel leaseholds—the goal of capitalism: p. 21.
Industrialisation of production: Kautsky's groundless hopes (87-88)

σ Demands must be immediately attainable—con social ownership of land (p. 7).
p. 10: the economic usefulness of capitalism is still being debated.
p. 14. Perhaps socialism takes the same attitude towards capitalism as Russian capitalism does to the patriarchal economy.

Only a greater share!

Nachklang naturrechtlichen views: pp. 72-73.
Abolition of the antithesis between town and country: p. 76.
In agriculture, the lever of self-interest is indispensable: 95.
What socialism will do with the employees: 93.
On social revolution: 105.
123: Centralised farming is *absolutely* impossible (!!).

τ   "The main task of socialism" is to sustain the co-operatives (p. 21) and p. *89.*
    124:   Co-operatives *for the small ones,* !!
and socialisation for the big ones.
    Wine-growers' co-operatives 120   –
    Co-operatives: "entering" socialism (111).
    Number of members in co-operatives (112)
    Dairy co-operatives (112)
To τ Engels on co-operatives
        distortion 122.

2

α   "theory"
β   mortgages
γ   Engels on America
δ   on the peasantry and versus the proletariat
ε   large- and small-scale production
ζ   Hecht, Auhagen, etc.
ϑ   admission of superiority of the large
ι   admission of overwork in Kleinbetrieb
ϰ   Hertz on French data
λ   Hertz and Narodism
=
σ   — attitude to socialism
τ   — co-operatives

Written in June-September 1901

First published in 1932
in *Lenin Miscellany XIX*

Printed from the original

ANALYSIS OF DATA
FROM O. PRINGSHEIM'S ARTICLE,
"AGRICULTURAL MANUFACTURE AND ELECTRIFIED AGRICULTURE" [65]

Dr. Otto Pringsheim (in Breslau), "Landwirtschaftliche Manufaktur und elektrische Landwirtschaft". [Braun's Archiv, XV (1900), S. 406-418.]

The author starts by pointing out that he will try to characterise "the forms which agricultural production assumes in the capitalist epoch" (406). Until now "the question of agrarian morphology" has hardly been dealt with. (Farms were classified into large and small in a stereotyped way, superficially, only by the area under cultivation—407.)

Is there not in agriculture an analogy with the capitalist household industry (the middle link between the handicrafts and large-scale industry)?—In Dutch tobacco-growing, in beetroot production (dependence on the sugar refineries, control over their crops, etc.—408). (Consequently: much weaker than in industry—409.)

Let us take a look at a typical specimen of the modern large-scale agricultural enterprise: an East-Elbe estate of 200-400 hectares

  the prevalence of isolated manual labour
               and simple co-operation
  small division of labour
               not permanent (reapers and binders)
               permanent (in stock raising).

Machines*) are used sporadically (as in the industrial manufacture. Cf. *Das Kapital,* I[3], 335, 349[66])—p. 410. No system of machines (410).

Modern large-scale agricultural production should be compared with the *manufacture* (in the *Marxian sense*) (410).

N.B. | Marketing in agriculture is not so much on a world as on a local scale (411). And the size of the unit is not big: very few with a turnover of 100,000 marks, whereas in industry this was surpassed long ago (411).

[This indication is very important!] The exception proves the rule [Benkendorf's estate in Saxony, 2,626 hectares, of which 375 is cultivated by steam plough; livestock—123 draught horses + 70 pairs of oxen + 300 milch cows + 100 fattened bull-calves + 3,600 fattened lambs. A sugar refinery and a distillery, etc., 13 employees, etc. Outlays *1¹/₂-2 million* marks a year.—Böckelmann in Atzendorf: 3,320 hectares, own steam plough + (99 horses, 610 oxen), sugar refinery, etc.: Mitteilungen der deutschen Landwirtschaftsgesellschaft. 1899, Stück 17**)].****

On the whole, the nature of the large-scale agricultural enterprise is not like that in industry, and it will be easily proved that the middle peasants are not below this level.

But while the Davids and Hertzes, the Oppenheimers and Weisengrüns predicted the early end of large-scale agricultural production, there started a technical revolution which should apparently lead to a strengthening of the positions of large-scale agricultural production and take it to a higher stage of development.... 412.

---

*) *Backhaus, Agrarstatistische Untersuchungen über den preussischen Osten im Vergleich zum Westen,* 1898. *F. Bensing, Der Einfluss der landwirtschaftlichen Maschinen auf Volks- und Privatwirtschaft,** 1898.

) On Benkendorf also see Thiel's *Landwirtschaftliche Jahrbücher,* 1887 (16. Jahrgang), S. 981.*

* *A Comparative Agrarian Statistical Study of East and West Prussia.*—*Ed.*

** *The Influence of Agricultural Machinery on the National and Private Economy.*—*Ed.*

*** *Agricultural Yearbooks,* 1887, 16th year of publication, p. 981.—*Ed.*

**** Material of the German Agricultural Society, 1889, Part 17.—*Ed.*

Electrical Machines

advantages of electrical machines
—for milking
—farm supply railways
—threshers
—plough, etc., etc.

This means opening up the possibility of the machine system in agriculture.... What could not be achieved by steam power will certainly be achieved by electrical machines, namely, the advancement of agriculture from the old manufacture stage to modern large-scale production (414).*

Sinell, Jahrbuch der Deutschen Landwirtschaftsgesellschaft, Band 14.

Benno Martiny, Arbeiten der deutschen Landwirtschaftsgesellschaft, Heft 37.

Technische Rundschau, 1899, No. 43 (Electrical supply tracks).

Adolf Seufferheld, Die Anwendung der Elektrizität im landwirtschaftlichen Betriebe, aus eigener Erfahrung mitgeteilt, Stuttgart 1899.

P. Mack, Der Aufschwung u.s.w. 1900**

Electricity will sharpen the competition between the big and small farms (the co-operatives will not make up for the advantages of large-scale production).... Writers who, like Hertz, in treating of competition between small- and large-scale production in agriculture ignored electrical engineering, must start their investigation all over again (415).***

Growing industrialisation of the countryside. Coalescence of industry and agriculture (cf. *Mack*):
—countryside drawing closer to town
—introduction of more educated workers (416)
—night work (examples in Bohemia and Saxony) (p. 417).
A reference to Russia in note (p. 417)—V. Ilyin, p. 166****
—introduction of female and child labour, etc.

"The prospects for agriculture in the 20th century are truly brilliant" (417). *Max Delbrück,* "Die deutsche Land-

---

* See present edition, Vol. 5, p. 144.—*Ed.*

** Sinell, *Yearbook of the German Agricultural Society,* Vol. 14; Benno Martiny, *Transactions of the German Agricultural Society,* Part 37; *Technical Survey;* Adolf Seufferheld, *Report from Personal Experience on the Use of Electricity in Agricultural Production;* P. Mack, *Boosting, etc.—Ed.*

*** See present edition, Vol. 5, p. 142.—*Ed.*

**** Ibid., Vol. 3, p. 235.—*Ed.*

wirtschaft an der Jahrhundertswende" (*Preussische Jahrbü-cher*, 1900, Februar)* predicts a doubling of crop yields in grain production, a trebling of potato crops, and an eightfold increase in the whole of production by the end of the 20th century over the beginning of the 19th century.

Lemström's study of the influence of electricity on the growth of plants also opens up unexpected prospects (418).

Written in June-September 1901

First published in 1938
in *Lenin Miscellany XXXI*   Printed from the original

---

* Max Delbrück, "German Agriculture at the Turn of the Century" (*Prussian Yearbooks*, 1900, February).— *Ed.*

CRITICAL REMARKS ON E. DAVID'S ARTICLE, "THE PEASANT BARBARIANS"

David's short article, "Bäuerliche Barbaren" (*Sozialistische Monatshefte*, 1899, No. 2, III. Jahrgang, S. 62-71) is a typical example of the outrageous approach to the small peasant concept. David gives a description according to Hecht (Moritz Hecht, *Three Villages in the Hard of Baden*, Leipzig, 1895) of three villages near Karlsruhe, lying within 4 to 14 kilometres. In one village (Hagsfeld) the majority are workers who go to work in Karlsruhe, in the second (Blankenloch), they are a small minority, and in the third (Friedrichsthal), all are farmers.

They have holdings of 1 to 3 hectares *) (only one has 9 hectares, and 18—4 to 6 hectares), and lease from $\frac{1}{2}$ to 1 hectare. Twenty-nine are landless.

Price of hectare

$4._2$-$4._4$ thousand marks.		Grow *tobacco*, 45% of farmland (area under crop) in Friedrichsthal (1,140 souls)
$4._8$-$5._0$ "	"	Raise *corn* (wheat), 47% of farmland (area under crop) in Blankenloch (1,684 souls)
9.-10. "	"	Grow *potatoes*, 42% of farmland (area under crop) in Hagsfeld.
	(p. 67)	

---

*) "Holdings everywhere are *small and dwarf peasant farms*":

Hagsfeld	"average"	$2._0$ hectares	
Blankenloch	"	$2._5$ "	
Friedrichsthal	"	$1._8$ "	(!!)

Income (from tobacco)—up to 1,800 marks (gross, 690 net) per hectare.*) Crop yields are everywhere *much* higher than the *average for Germany* (p. 67)

Potatoes: 150-160 double centners per hectare (87.$_8$ for German   Reich)
Rye and
  wheat: 20-23   „   „   „   „   (10-13 „   „   „)
Hay: 50-60   „   „   „   „   (28.$_6$ „   „   „)

Living standard is high (clothes, food, dwellings, etc.), for instance, consumption of sugar in the three villages is 17 kg per head (only 8.2 kg for German Reich!), etc.

David is jubilant: There's your "backward small peasants!" he says about these "still really and truly small holders" (p. 66). This only shows him up as a real and true petty bourgeois, because his is a most eloquent example of the *bourgeois village*, a visual example of the worthlessness of area statistics. These are nothing but rich tobacco-planters and suburban peasants—and suburban workers with plots of land!

From the outset, E. David attacks the theory of underconsumption and overwork (62) ("superhuman work and inhuman way of life").

And, ridiculing orthodox Marxism, etc. (63), E. David says:

"I should subsequently like to contrast the *backward* small peasant described by Kautsky with a portrait of the *modern* small peasant. In fact, such a type does exist; but he is so different, as man and farmer, from the semi-barbarian beggar we find in Kautsky's book, that anyone wishing to engage in practical land agitation will find it very useful to have a closer look at him as well" (63).

Before that E. David "retells" Kautsky as follows: Agriculture has become "one of the most revolutionary, if not the most revolutionary of modern industries", but small peasant farming is "the most irrational economy one can imagine". (No reference to *Agrarfrage*.)

---

*) 1,825.$_{60}$ marks per hectare. And this holder has 2.$_5$ hectares plus milch cows and pigs (dairy farm near Karlsruhe) (p. 67). "Let the reader calculate the total income of this (!!) 'backward small peasant'" (67).

"Comrade Kautsky starts from the premise that small peasant farming *cannot* be rational at all; that the successes of agricultural science and engineering virtually do not exist for it at all. Modern machinery, chemical fertilisers, soil improvement, rational crop rotation, improvement of seed and livestock, organisation of marketing and credit— all of this he imagines to be the privilege of capitalist large-scale agriculture from whose table, it is true, some small crumbs do fall to the small peasants, but these are quite insufficient to raise small farming to the economic and technical productivity which is characteristic of large-scale farming" (63).

(A specimen of "vulgarising" Marxism!)

Statistics of income from crops: in the south-western states (small farming) it is higher than in East Prussia (large-scale farming).

That the soil is better in the south-west is only a *part* of the explanation.

Even if the rye and hay crops in Saxony are lower than in Hessen (the wheat crop is higher), this goes best to show how *backward* the concept of the general *backwardness* of peasant farming is (64).

Of course, machines are not *as* (not *equally*) accessible to small farming, but

1) machines do not play such a role in agriculture
2) the most important machines are also "accessible" (zugänglich) to small farming.

"Concerning steam and other threshing machines this is admitted even by Kautsky; their application is becoming ever more widespread on the small farms as well. But Kautsky is wrong when he says that 'apart from the thresher, the use of machinery in small farming is hardly in evidence'.

"Of the machines included in the count during the 1895 farm census, there is above all the seed drill, which is accessible to *all,* at any rate, to farms of 5 to 20 hectares, and smaller farms as well, insofar as they have an even area under crop. It is true that the *percentage* of small farms already using it is still insignificant, but if we look at the high *absolute* figures and the *progress* between 1882 and

1895, we shall have a positive answer to the question of *whether or not* they can be used everywhere. This is borne out by the following survey. Seeders were used by *:

	Number of farms:			
	1882	1895		
Under 2 ha	4,807	14,949	(214) +	10,142
2-5	4,760	13,639	(551)	8,879
5-20	15,980	52,003	(3,252)	36,023
	25,547	80,591	(4,017)	55,044
20-100	22,975	61,943	(12,091)	38,968
> 100	15,320	26,931	(12,565)	11,611 (p. 65)

"The assertion that apart from the thresher, the use of machinery in small farming is hardly in evidence, is refuted by these figures, for the *seed drill*, at any rate."

and in the note there is a reference to *The Condition of the Peasants*, I, 106, to the effect that in the Weimar district, the "*seed drill* is common among the richer (!!) and is already making its way into the 30- or 40-acre farms".

$\left(\begin{array}{l}\text{Let's note that } 28._5 \text{ ha} = 100 \quad \text{Weimar acres} \\ \text{about} \qquad\qquad 9._5 \text{ ha} = 30\text{-}40 \qquad " \qquad\qquad "\end{array}\right)$

"Nor can it be said that the *reaper* is absolutely beyond the reach of small farming. In 1895, it was already in use on 6,746 farms of 5 to 20 ha" (p. 65).

Then comes a quotation from a Frankfort-on-the-Main factory catalogue: 20-25-30-60 pfennigs for $^1/_2$ day's use of a machine: seeder (60 pfennigs), harrow (25 pfennigs), etc.

"But the *other achievements* of modern agriculture have penetrated into small peasant farming to a much greater extent than the machines. To give a visual picture of this I shall quote in somewhat greater detail one of the most fundamental (!!!) and interesting (!) monographs on the condition of the peasantry which have appeared in the recent period"... **Hecht** (66) **

in these three villages:

"Holdings everywhere are *small and dwarf peasant farms*" (E. David's italics).

---

* Under the 1882 census, the count dealt only with seeders; and in 1895 broadcast sowers and seed drills were classified under separate heads. Consequently, the 1882 figures should be compared with the total number of machines of both types in 1895; the relatively smaller number of farms using the broadcast sowers, the less important type, is given in brackets after the total figure (E. David's note).

** See present edition, Vol. 5, p. 160.—*Ed.*

"What has been said must cast doubt on Kautsky's assertion which is presented to us as a generally recognised truth: 'that in contrast to large-scale farming peasant farming rests *not on a higher productivity* but on *more modest requirements*'" (68).

For all *labour*-intensive crops, small farming is undoubtedly more rational (68).

Good dwellings, "clean room" ... carpets, lamps, photographs, mirrors, gold rings, postage stamps, etc. (69)

"Our Hard peasants are already at the pure *money economy* stage and—oh, miracle!—this has *not* ruined them. (¡
In defiance of Kautsky's prophecies! In fact, they are having it very well indeed, and any cash surplus—and they often have one—is instantly deposited in savings (¡
banks to earn interest" (68).

"I have quoted this study, based as it is on serious data, at such length because it gives an excellent characteristic of every aspect of the *most modern* type of West-German small peasantry" (70) ... that even the urban reader will understand....

"For it should not be imagined that Hecht's facts are exceptional cases, without any importance for the *general condition* and the *future* of small-scale farming" (70)

In *Mombach* (near Mainz), where E. David lives, the peasants are no worse off than the Hard peasants. They raise lettuce, asparagus, peas, etc.

E. David objects to Kautsky's taking "a few pictures of poverty" from the Rhön mountains, Spessart, upper Taunus,ᵒ etc., and drawing *general* conclusions (71). His, David's, picture will help to find a *general correct average* (71) (my italics).

The condition of the peasants is now on the whole *better* than before. E. David quotes *The Condition of the Peasants*, I, 270—(last paragraph, first sentence: "*That welfare in general*" up to "*proves*")—and puts it in *italics*.

———————

(*David* says *not a word* about hired labour among the Hard peasants. *Not a word either* about overwork (after other work).)

Written in June-September 1901
    First published in 1932   Printed from the original
    in *Lenin Miscellany XIX*

ANALYSIS OF DATA FROM M. HECHT'S BOOK,
THREE VILLAGES IN THE HARD OF BADEN[67]

Hecht

1. 4-14 kilometres from Karlsruhe.

			workers
	Hagsfeld	1,273 inhabitants	350
2,957	Blankenloch	1,684 "	103
	Friedrichsthal	1,140 "	11

Total = 4,097

3. Lumbering in winter.
7. Density of population

	Hags-feld	(Friedrichs-thal)	(Blanken-loch)
per hectare	$3._2$	$4._5$	$2._3$
Baden	$1._{04}$		
Germany	$0._{83}$		

Total land

Friedrichsthal	258 hectares
Hagsfeld	397 "
Blankenloch	736 "

Total = 1,391

Distribution of land:		Friedrichs-thal	Hags-feld	Blan-kenloch
p. 7: Farm consists of 5-7 persons	9 hectares	—	—	1
	6-8 "	—	6	—
	5 "	—	3	2
	4 "	—	6	4
	2 "	43%	?	55%
under	2 "	the rest		
	landless—8		14	7

Freedom of division

8. Additional lease of $1/2$-1 hectare.
9. Heavy exodus (to America) in the 1830s and 1850s
10. Today the formation of a middle estate
      (in place of the former poor)

11. Extensive and subsistence farming—18th century.

Poverty of the population, *emigration* | to the towns and to America |

12. *Hagsfeld*—into an industrial township
    Blankenloch and *Friedrichsthal*—*specialisation* of
    agriculture, money economy. *The farmer has become
    merchant and entrepreneur.*
15. In *Hagsfeld*, farming is a *side line.*
15-16. —Only nine families are engaged in farming alone.
    —The Hagsfeld peasant has become a factory worker.
    The wives farm: they even have their linen washed
    in town.

6-17. *The price of land* Hagsfeld   4.$_2$-4.$_4$ thousand
                                                          marks
    cf. Baden   Blankenloch   4.$_8$-5
    2 thousand marks Friedrichsthal 9 -10

17. Only specialisation gives an effectively high income.
    Potatoes for the aristocratic board.
    "Seed potatoes."
17. "Virtuosity" in developing potato grades

18. Potatoes 120 double centners × 4 = 480 marks per
hectare
Carrots   1,300
Tobacco (takes a lot of hands)
18. Child labour in planting (stecken!) potatoes

(19) 220-230 planters of tobacco (a total of about 100
hectares)
20. *Friedrichsthal* income from tobacco = 147,473 marks
a year
23. Friedrichsthal leases meadows and buys hay
24. The growth of *dairy* farming.
24. Everyone sells 2-3 litres of milk, rich families—
10-20 litres
In *Hagsfeld* milk is sold, and butter (partly *ma r-
g a r i n e*) bought instead
25. Creamery in Friedrichsthal, "speculative mode of
business", its precarious dependence on the cattle-
dealers
26. Friedrichsthal—17,200 marks a year from the sale
of pigs.
27. Growth in the number of *g o a t s* in **Hagsfeld**:
disintegration of the peasant estate.
28-29. Backwardness of *B l a n k e n l o c h* with its more
natural economy.
29-30. Reason: much land.
!! {The *community* facilitates the struggle for
existence
30. Although the disintegration of the community
pays from the standpoint of production, it
is socially wasteful—maintenance of workers
(especially with *B l a n k e n l o c h's tran-*‖ N.B.
sition from agriculture to i n d u s t r y).
30. The people of Friedrichsthal carry manure from
Karlsruhe (20-30 cartloads).

31. There is no day-labourer category: most peasants
do without labourers
few "request" help
payment increases where town is near

32-33. Complete collapse of handicrafts.

35. The majority in *Hagsfeld* are factory workers (300-350), most of them *walking* the $3^1/_2$ kilometres (only 100 ride)

factory workers	Hagsfeld	350
	Blankenloch	103
	Friedrichsthal	10-12

35. Factory working day = 10 hours

36. Factory working women sometimes *take work home* !!

38. *Celebration* of the fact that the *Hagsfeld* worker has a *patch of land:* "more important sense" of property !!

Utilisation of spare time
4 a.m.—at 7 a.m. to the factory
after 7 p.m.— $1-1^1/_2$ more !!

39. The worker has better nutrition, relaxes from factory work. The women stay at home—better from the moral standpoint.

40. *Hecht* is clearly making fun of the *socialists* "capitalists", "serfdom".

40. House owners socially higher

41. Social "poetry of own house".

58-59. The growth of Karlsruhe, *m a r k e t,* etc.

62. It is a sad fact that in the sale of tobacco the well-to-do farmers sometimes cheat the poor.

63. In *B l a n k e n l o c h* and *Hagsfeld* grain is sold in **autumn** and bought in *s p r i n g.*

65. The purchase of manure and **liquid** manure.

78. The richer families (3-4 hectares) have meat 5-6 times a week
the poorer—3-4 times
a handful—only on Sundays.

79. The *Hagsfeld worker*—wife takes dinner to town (150 out of 300 get their dinner from home, 150 have theirs in eating-houses)....

79. Poor women ... carry dinner to the factory....

79-80. Cookery courses are read annually at *Blankenloch* and *Friedrichsthal* (on the initiative of her royal

!

80   !

!

highness the grand duchess) ... an undertaking equal in importance perhaps to the founding of a consumers' co-operative or a savings bank. (That's Dr. Hecht, that's him all over!)

90. The *Hagsfeld* man ... is no longer a peasant, he is a townsman.

91. Strict religious convictions—Social-Democrats are ignored, except possibly by factory men, but only the 20-30-year olds.

92-93.

!

93

!

There is no "social gulf" between the rich and the poor. The "master" peasant (with 3-4 hectares) is on thee-and-thou terms with the labouring man and woman, and calls them by their first names.— They "sir" him, but eat at the same table: "patriarchal relations".

Consequently, in "the three villages"

On the one hand, rich petty bourgeois, tobacco-planters, dairy farmers, etc. (virtuosi raising special grades of potatoes, etc.).

Example of paying nature of tobacco-growing.
Wage labour in general. (Master and labourer)
Swindling of the small by the big.

The rich sell 10-20 litres of milk	The poor 2-3 litres
" eat meat 5-6 times a week	" 3-4 and a very few on Sundays only.

On the other hand. About one-half the total population are factory workers (4,000 inhabitants—about 1,000 working, of whom 464 are factory workers). Of the *factory workers,* the greater part walk. Poor women carry dinners to the factory.

Under-consumption (margarine)
Overwork (working at home for the manufacturers; work morning and night)
Growth in the number of goats.
Sale of grain in autumn and purchase in spring.
"Fiercely industrious" (and example)

Factory workers		Number of families roughly	hectares		
350	Hagsfeld	$1,273 \div 6 = 212$	1 —	= 9	
			6 with 7 = 42 roughly		
103	Blankenloch	$1,684 \div 6 = 281$	5 with 5 = 25 roughly		
11	Friedrichsthal	$1,140 \div 6 = 190$	10 with 4 = 40 roughly		
			22	116	
464		$4,097 \div 6 = 683$	29 —	0	
		$^1/_2 = 341$			
		$^2/_5 = 273$			
		464 factory workers			

Hagsfeld
    212
   —
      9 (without side line)
    —
    203 — 350 factory workers
about 200 — 350 about

$$\frac{200}{350} = \frac{1}{460}$$

$$\frac{460 \times 200}{350} = 263 \text{ families of workers in all 3 villages} * + 29 \text{ landless} = 292$$

A total of *a b o u t* 700 families

of whom factory workers — *a b o u t* 300

I	25 —	30%
II	25 —	30%
III	50 —	40%
	100	100

For fertilisers

	hectares	*marks*	*per hectare*	
Friedrichsthal	258	28,000	108	$28,000 \div 258 = 108$
Hagsfeld	397	12,000	30	
Blankenloch	736	8,000	11	

* The words "of workers in all 3 villages" have been inserted according to the meaning.— *Ed.*

Distribution of crop area in %

Inhabit-ants	Total land ha	Cattle	Pota-toes	Tobacco	Grain	Pigs	Goats	Horses
1,140 Friedrichsthal	258	435	30%	45%	18%	497	—	40
			about 100 ha p. 19		(51.48 *) ha)			
1,684 Blankenloch	736	634	17%	$10._4$%	47%	445	8	96
			(40 ha)		about 236 ha			
1,273 Hagsfeld	397	225	42%	$0._6$%	—	220	93	35

4,097

Crop yields are much higher in Friedrichsthal (p. 29 Hecht).

To sum up:

$1/_4$ rich and well-to-do peasants | only the *Friedrichsthal people* are well-to-do — and they are about $1/_4$

$1/_4$ middle ones (those of Blankenloch — more backward economy, etc.)

$1/_2$ factory workers with patches of land (p.t.o. for rough calculation)

	Families roughly	Cost of land			Cattle in terms of horned 1 bull = 1 horse = 4 pigs = 10 goats
		ha	'000 marks	'000 marks	
Friedrichsthal	190	258	×9.5 =	2,451	599
Blankenloch	281	736	×4.9 =	3,606	842
Hagsfeld	212	397	×4.3 =	1,707	324
	683			7,764	1,765

Friedrichsthal:

       100 ha of tobacco   45% $258._0 \div 1._8 = 143^{69}$

about   50 ha of grain   18% $736._0 \div 2._5 = 294$

about   65 ha of potatoes   30% $397 \div 2 = 196$

      ($2/_3$ of tobacco)   93% $143 + 294 + 196 = 633$ families

*) 143 Morgen = $51._{48}$ ha. (Hecht, 28) $258 \times {}^{18}/_{100} = 46._{44}$ ha [68] hence **678 Morgen** = consequently **$236._6$ ha.**

"The little man" (in Friedrichsthal) obtains 30 kilogrammes of tobacco from $^1/_4$ Morgen (9 ares)—"the rich one" (with 3-3$^1/_2$ hectares)—only 25 kilogrammes. The poor one is more diligent (p. 71).

Twenty-four years ago one had 110 ares. Now he has 3$^1/_2$ hectares—made additional purchases. And all that | ! due only to being "fiercely industrious" (71). "There are | many more such examples."

Then there is also the "sober marriage policy".

The well-known peasant saying: "We work not so much for our mouth as for our pockets" (71).

Hagsfeld—the cause of progress is not only the entry into market relations, not only the free division of land, but also *education in the spirit of a higher morality, endeavour and self-help* (71).

The virtues: diligence, thrift, temperance, which now mark the Hard peasant, are not innate but acquired (72).

And Hecht extols education by state, church, and school: in the sweat of your face shall you eat bread! Why does one get 4 centners of tobacco from 9 ares, and the other, 1? Why does one raise tobacco and the other rye? Laziness. Why do neighbours (say, in the Bruchsal district) live worse, despite similar market conditions?—In our opinion the major cause of the better economic condition of our 3 villages is the more pronounced existence and development of *moral factors*. But the education of the Hard peasant is revealed not only in his greater industry, hardiness, the truly remarkable thrift and temperance (73)—but also in self-help.

Sale:	Potatoes annually	Carrots	Tobacco annually	Cereals annually	Milk	Pigs	Tobacco
Friedrichsthal					750 litres a week	17,200 marks a year	147,473 marks a year
Blankenloch	4,000 double centners	1,750 double centners	3,500 double centners	500 double centners	4,700	?(p. 26)	?
Hagsfeld					1,400	?	?

Purchase	Friedrichsthal	(marks) Blankenloch	Hagsfeld
Manure	25,000	5,000	3,000
Liquid manure	—	—	8,000
Artificial fertilisers	3,000	3,000	1,000
Concentrated feed		40,000	
Hay	10,000	20,000	10,000
Grain	23,100	12,510	
Sugar	45-50 thousand marks		
Coffee	60,000 marks		

ha		marks
100 tobacco	100 ha	147,473
? 65 potatoes	65 ha about 600 marks per ha	about 36,000
($^2/_3$ of	(p. 18:150 double centners	
tobacco	at 4 marks)	
30% and 45%)		

? 50 grain 50 ha at 26 double centners (p. 22) = 1,300 double centners

? 15 beetroot about 15 ha	p. 22=6%	= 18,000 = about 18,000
230 at 1,200 (cf. p. 18)	=$^1/_7$ of 100 =45%	

milk   750   litres × 50 = 37,500   at   15   pfennigs = about   5,625
                    (p. 64)

pigs   17,200

                                                      ======
                                                     224,298

How big is the *average gross* income of a Friedrichsthal man? 1.$_8$ ha.

224,000 marks is, of course, *not all*; taking the round
figure of 258,000 marks, this gives 1,000 marks per hectare
and 1,800 marks for 1.$_8$ hectares.

The peasant of the 18th century, with his eight to ten
hectares of land, was a peasant and a manual labourer;
the dwarf peasant of the 19th century, with his one or two
hectares of land, is a brainworker, an entrepreneur, and
a merchant (p. 69).*

---

* See present edition, Vol. 5, p. 163.—*Ed.*

Concluding words: The dwarf peasant and the factory worker have both raised themselves to the position of the middle class.... "The three villages of the Baden Hard" *now* belong to *one great, broad middle class* (94).*

Amen!

Written in June-September 1901

First published in 1938
in *Lenin Miscellany XXXI*

Printed from the original

---

* Ibid., p. 167.— *Ed.*

ANALYSIS OF MATERIAL
FROM H. AUHAGEN'S ARTICLE,
"ON LARGE- AND SMALL-SCALE PRODUCTION
IN AGRICULTURE" [70]

Hubert Auhagen, "Ueber Gross- und Kleinbetrieb in der Landwirtschaft" (*Thiels Jahrbücher,* Band 25, Jahrgang 1896. S. 1-55).

Auhagen is definitely for small farming	The village of Clauen (Hannover province) (Peine District)			
	I—4.$_{625}$ ha	{ 100	{ 100	} { *Excellent example!!* }
	II—26.$_{50}$ "	·573 }	625 drainage }	

The author says that he tried to find a village with a "possibly uniform soil" (p. 1), but does not give any soil classification for I and II.

Both farms are among *the best in the area* (p. 1).

Cultivation of land—see *separate sheet.**

In I, cows are used in ploughing and on working days (105) receive more feed. On hot summer days, they are *overworked* (p. 9), but then the owner gives them more fodder beet.

Drai- in I— *480* marks (3%=14.$_{40}$) { cf. table ** }
nage II—*3,000* " (3%=90.$_{00}$)

The *same* value of the product is taken. There are no facts.
On the *small* farms, the cattle are given better care: "The cattle fatten under the owner's eye" (p. 27).

---

* See p. 134.— *Ed.*
** See p. 130.— *Ed.*

In I and II, the same system and character of farming.

Not so livestock farming. In II, the cattle are fattened for slaughter and are not bred, and in I, *each head of cattle has been raised on the farm* (p. 28). It is very, very common for the big peasant to buy lean cattle from the small peasant and fatten them up—all over Germany (p. 28): small farming has advantages over big farming in the raising of cattle (p. 29).

N.B.

Maintenance of structures—the small peasant mostly repairs everything *himself* (p. 30).

In II *dead stock* is on a very high level (machines), but I is not backward (p. 31), for the small peasant *makes do* (!!) just as well with simpler implements.

Depreciation in I—2%, in II—6%. II has had a cart for 10-12 years; I has farmed *22 years* after his father, and *has not bought a cart*, and does not remember ***his father buying one either,*** and he had farmed for 30 years. Small implements are used on small farms to the utmost (31).

!

II spends 3,872.$_{93}$ marks on hired labour = 36.$_{53}$ per Morgen, while the small peasant economises *on all this,* because he is both ***master and labourer*** (p. 33, *too wordy*). That is the tremendous advantage of small farming!!!

Small farming—dearth of land.

The buyer of a small holding is usually very well aware that it would be better for him, financially speaking, to work for a daily wage and in addition to receive an income in the form of interest on his capital. But he rejects this higher profit for the sake of greater convenience (33)....

In the coal area of Saarbrücken "these small holders make up the best nucleus of the mine workers" (33)—as the author was told by a factory manager at Neunkirchen, and, contrary to *Social-Democratic agitation,* Auhagen believes:

!!

‼ {

    "The best thing the state could do in this area to solve the labour problem is to help workers to acquire small plots of land, by granting credits" (33).

!

    Advantage of I: "He (the small peasant) frequently has the assistance of his children about the farm almost as soon as they learn to run" (34)!

    Pp. 39-40—an example of the thriftiness of the small peasant (*cited by Kautsky*): a wife wore out one pair of shoes in 17 years of married life, etc., etc.

    Why I has *higher* crop yields

1) more thorough working of the fields—work *themselves;*

N.B.

    "The ordinary day labourer, especially on the big farms, thinks as he works: 'I wish the holiday would come round sooner'; whereas the small peasant, in doing all kinds of urgent work anyway, hopes, 'I wish I could have another couple of hours today'" (p. 42).

2) I does his work in time: he has more *labour* per hectare. **The small peasant can get up earlier and go to bed later**(43) when time is very short.

3) I is not afraid of work: beetles were collected by hand.

4) I takes in his crop faster, the grain has no time to drop.

5) I has better seed material: it is picked by hand in winter (no grain-sorter!).

6) I uses *more fertilisers, because he has more cattle (no figures)*.

    Sale I= $3,400._{80}$ — $735._{31}$ per hectare

         II= $14,097._{41}$ — $531._{98}$ per hectare

    The net income is also higher (see table of per cent on *capital**).

    Auhagen himself is aware that the *living standards* are different (p. 49) and excludes housekeeping (*see table***)

---

* See p. 131.— *Ed.*

** See pp. 130-31.— *Ed.*

—but what I should like to point out, as a phenomenon common for the whole of Germany, is the higher rent on small peasant farms as compared with the big peasant farms and landed estates (49) } Sic!

that is why *land fetches more under small farming*. Fragmentation of estates ... leads to ... *an increase in the value of the national property* (50)

Auhagen admits that the small peasants are *more* liable to have backward systems of farming (51). These are impossible among big peasants: they can hold on only by improving. But progress comes not only from the big farm, but also from the *well-to-do* owner (!).

Remarks on various parts of Germany (cursorily on the advantages of different-size farms in different areas).

"Ausgebaute" (those who settle on separate farmsteads outside the village) mostly run their farms better (54-55); there is more routine in the village.

Receipts

	I marks	II marks
I. Cash from sales:		
products of field cropping	1,596.40	7,991.15
„ „ vegetable gardening	—	90
„ „ livestock farming	1,804.40	21,171.26
Other receipts (payments for tillage and cartage)	42	200
Total receipts in cash	3,028.80*	29,452.41
II. For use in household:		
products of field cropping	182	178
„ „ vegetable gardening	30	50
„ „ livestock farming	346.15	233.50
	558.15	461.50
III. For feeding hired labourers:		
products of field cropping	—	350
„ „ vegetable gardening	—	35
„ „ livestock farming	—	377.04
	—	762.04
Total receipts in kind	558.15	1,223.54

* So in the original.—*Ed.*

Outlays

		I	II
A. Farming costs		marks	marks
Taxes		63.55	321.54
Insurance		89.95	600.13
Maintenance and depreciation of drainage (3%)		14.40	90.00
Depreciation of capital in structures ($^3/_4$%)		47.25	187.50
(α	*Maintenance of structures*	15.00	178.60 ‖ N.B
(β	Depreciation of *dead stock* (2%) (and 6%!!!)	14.42	291.66 ‖ N.B
(γ	Maintenance of *dead* stock	15.00	285.05 ‖ N.B
	Restocking of livestock	—	15,641.00*)
	Hired labour	—	3,872.93
	Artificial fertilisers	198.00	2,052.00
	Concentrated feed	141.50	1,537.50
	Cost of pairing	8.00	
	Veterinary	6.00	48.00
	Restocking of seed	2.80	60.00
	Sundries	6.00	35.00
	Total farming costs	621.87	25,200.91

B. Housekeeping costs

	I	II	
Income tax	12.00	104.00	
Church tithes	22.10	100.95	
Products for farm	558.15	461.50 ⎫	
Supplementary purchases of potatoes	—	50 ⎬ ‖ N
„ „ „ meat	18.00	124.80 ⎭	

---

*) Including 14,355 for the purchase of 55 bull-calves sold for 19,420.50. Without this   !!

$$\alpha+\beta+\gamma \qquad \text{I has 0, whereas II has 1,286 marks}$$
$$\text{I has } 44.42 \qquad \text{II has } 755.31$$

44.42	2,041.31

The total value of structures,
dead and livestock =   9,151.60   43,259

	I marks	II marks
Groceries	81.$_{90}$	216.$_{00}$
Clothes	220.$_{00}$	588.$_{00}$
Footwear	52	61
Son at school *)	—	700
Doctor and pharmacy	25	60
Tobacco	24	80
Drinks	26	70
Festivities, etc.	25	120
Fuel	59.$_{15}$	—
Sundries	35.$_{20}$	—
Total housekeeping costs	1,158.$_{50}$ **)	2,736.$_{25}$
Total outlays	1,780.$_{37}$ **)	27,955.$_{16}$

C

Total receipts	3,586.$_{95}$	30,675.$_{95}$
Total outlays	1,780.$_{37}$	27,955.$_{16}$
In hand	806.$_{58}$ **)[71]	2,720.$_{79}$
% of selling price (33,651.$_6$ and 149,559)	2.$_{39}$ % ***)	1.$_{82}$%
Adding housekeeping costs to income (p. 49), we have:	1,965.$_{08}$	5,457.$_{04}$
% of selling price	5.$_{58}$% ***)	3.$_{71}$%
Total income from cropping	1,778{?p. 26}	8,519.$_{15}$
(p. 26) from livestock farming	2,150.$_{55}$	6,613.$_{80}$ ****)

Family: I husband+wife   II   husband+wife

              2 daughters (16 and 9 yrs)   1 daughter (9 yrs)

5 persons.   1 son (7 yrs)   1 son—14 yrs*)

                             5 persons 1 nephew 17 yrs

*) Board and tuition fees.

**) Author is mistaken: 1,750.$_{37}$ and 836.$_{58}$, in view of the erroneous figure of 1,128.$_{50}$ (cf. p. 48 and p. 13), instead of 1,158.$_{50}$.

***) Author is mistaken: !! 5.$_{45}$% and !!! 8.$_{81}$%, because he takes the totals of 836.$_{58}$ instead of 806.$_{58}$, and 2,965.$_{08}$ (sic!) instead of 1,965.$_{08}$; what is more, he is **very badly** out in his %% calculations!!!

****) Additional income from bull-calves sold for 19,420.$_5$ =5,065.$_{50}$.

	I			II	
Land 4.6520 ha		marks	26.50 ha		marks
Farmland 4 ha	at 5,400	=21,600	25	at 4,000	=100,000
Meadow 0.50	at 3,800	= 1,900	1.25	at 3,600	= 4,500
Vegetable garden 0.125	at 8,000	= 1,000	0.25	at 7,200	= 1,800
4.625		24,500	26.50		106,300

(land II may be *worse*)
[reason for lower crop yields??]

Structures	6,300	25,000
→Dead stock	721.20	4,861
Live "	2,130.40	13,398
Total (selling price)	=33,651.60	149,559

	I	II	
Carriage	0	350	marks
Seed drill	0	400	"
Fertiliser spreader ..	0	150	"
Harvesting ma- chine	0	400	"
Thresher	0	700	"
Grain cleaner	0	100	"
Cattle weighing ma- chine	0	150	"
Plough	25(1)*	80 (2)* etc.	

Labour

I	II
Family—3 family workers	4 family workers?? or 3?
	(son at school)
(+help in threshing)	

Hired	—	5—year round
		6—from May 1 to Nov. 10
		4—harvest (4-5 weeks)
		3—threshing (4 weeks)

* Bracketed figures indicate number of ploughs.—*Ed.*

Consequently,
working days 3×360   1,440   (?1,080)
mine *about*=1,080   1,800   ⌠5×360
                              1,140   ⌡6×190
         ┌─────────┐   140   4× 35
         │ p. t. o.* │
         └─────────┘

[about 100:400?]? about=100:450   84   3× 28
                                      ─────
                                      4,604

	ha	ha		total labour	
Land	4.625	26.50		3	11.8
Land	100	573		100	393

Teams
   I—3 cows
   II—4 horses+3 oxen

Livestock

	I	*marks*	II
3 cows	1,260		1,200 (3)**
2 pigs	120		450
oxen	270 (1)**		6,750
horses and oxen	0		4,950 (4) (3)**
			0
young stock	260 (2)**		

(25 bull-calves
for fattening)**

Consequently,

	I	II
Cattle	3	10
Horned+young stock	3	25
Pigs	2	3
Sow+12 piglets		0

Mine, all in terms of cattle

I	II
3	10
1.5	12.5
0.5	0.75
0.5	—
5.5 total	.23.25

─────────────────

* See pp. 136-37.—*Ed.*
** Figures in round brackets indicate head of cattle: see table on p.136.—*Ed.*

Soil management
Cultivation

	Ploughing depth		Artificial fertilisers per *ha*		Crop yield in centners per ha	
	I	II	I	II	I	II
Sugar-beet ⌈ Fodder beet ⌉ │ similarly │ └ p. 6 ┘	25 cm.	*30* cm	31.$_{50}$ marks ($3^1/_2$ cent.)	40.$_{50}$ marks ($4^1/_2$ cent.)	816	740
Rye	6 cm.	*15* cm	4 cent. superphosphate + 120 lbs Chile saltpetre	6 cent. 120-300	64	56
Barley	6 cm.	*15* cm	4 cent. superphosphate	4 cent.	60	56
Potatoes	6 cm + 25 *cm*	*10* cm + 20 cm	—	—	320	320
Beans	*9* cm	*24* cm	796 cent. of stall manure	1,440	66	56
Clover	?	?	8 cent. superphosphate	4 cent.	260	210
Winter wheat	25 *cm*	20 cm	480 cent. of stall manure	{ 8 cent. of super- phosphate } ?	80	64

And so, II's cultivation and fertilisers are much better and the crop yields much worse!! {II clearly has the worse land} [No soil classification given]

$$\text{Total outlays on artificial fertilisers} = \underset{\text{I}}{198._0} - \underset{\text{II}}{2,052._0} \text{ marks}$$
$$\text{per } ^1/_4 \text{ ha} \ldots\ldots 10._{70} - 19._{36} \text{ marks}$$

Maintenance of cattle:

Pp. 8 and 20:   Feed for cattle

	I		II	
	centner	marks	centner	marks
Beans	44.$_{64}$	290.$_{16}$	250.$_0$	1,625.$_{00}$
Rye	—	—	10.$_0$	70.$_{00}$
Wheat	0.$_{40}$	3.$_{20.}$	15.$_0$	120.$_{00}$
Barley	19.$_{81}$	118.$_{86}$	67.$_0$	402.$_{00}$
Oats	—	—	239.$_0$	1,505.$_{70}$
Sugar-beet tops	408.$_0$	81.$_{60}$	2,312.$_0$	462.$_{40}$
Fodder beet	192.$_0$	96.$_{00}$	—	—
Potatoes	10.$_{20}$	20.$_{40}$	—	—
Clover (dry)	65.$_0$	195.$_{00}$	210.$_0$	630.$_0$
Total		805.$_{22}$		4,815.$_{10}$
Milk (I counted the prices)	1,320 litres	105.$_{60}$	240 litres	19.$_{20}$
Purchased feed	25 centners	141.$_{50}$	275 centners	1,537.$_{50}$
(My) total % (mine)		1,052.$_{32}$ 100	·	6,371.$_{80}$ 606

> There is no doubt that feed for cattle is
> better and more abundant in II

Milk production

I	II
3 cows *9,700* litres	3 cows *9,600* litres

From September 15, II keeps 25 bull-calves, which he fattens and sells by January 1. Then from January 1 to April 1, he keeps 30 bull-calves, fattening and selling them. Hence, the 55 bull-calves in the receipts and the outlays. It appears that Auhagen reckons the feed for 25 bull-calves a year. ⎱ N.B.

Let us compare with this the *full* data on the quantity of livestock

	I	marks		II marks
horses	—	—	4	3,600
draught oxen	—	—	3	1,350
cows	3	1,260	3	1,200
cattle and young stock	3	530	25	6,750
pigs	2	120	3	450
sow and piglets	13	200	—	—
chickens	17	20.4	40	40
pigeons	—	—	40	8
Total value of livestock	—	2,130.4		13,398
% (mine)		100	:	629
Quantitatively		100	:	423
		(5.5)		(23.25)

If all are put in terms of cattle, then

cattle		3	—	10
small cattle	at 1/2	1.5	—	12.5
small cattle	at 1/4	0.5	—	0.75
small cattle	at 1/8	1.5?? (1)*	—	—
		6.5 (5.5)*		23.25

And the keep of workers?

I. 3 workers of the *family* (p. 3) and 2 non-working members of the family.

Their keep = *1,158.50 for three workers*

II. 3 workers (!!) of the family (p. 15 "always as supervisors, *when necessary*, as workers").

Non-working members of the family 2 ⎱ 1? for the son is at school? ⎰

---

* Here Lenin gives in round brackets the difference (of one unit) in reckoning 12 piglets as cattle against his own calculation (see p. 133).—*Ed.*

Their keep=$2,736._{25}$ for 3 workers.
Hired   labourers $5+3+0._8=8._8$ annually.

Marks

Their   keep = $3,872._{93}$÷$8._8$= 440 }
$\left\{ \text{N.B.} \begin{array}{c} 440 \\ 386 \end{array} \right\}$ $1,158._{50}$÷3 =386 }

Hired labourers: **5** the year round; **6** from May 1 to November 10, i.e., $6^1/_3$ months, i.e., $6×6^1/_3$=38 months= $3^1/_6$ years: **4** for 4-5 weeks, i.e., $4×5$=20 weeks, and **3** for 4 weeks, i.e., $3×4$=12 weeks, a total of **32** weeks. $^1/_6$ of year + $\frac{32}{52}$ =$^1/_6$+$^8/_{13}$= $\frac{61}{78}$ =78.2%, i.e. less than 80%.
The small holder lives worse than the hired labourer of the big one, considering paid labour in I—**386** marks, II—**440** marks per labourer.

Results: for the s m a l l p e a s a n t
1. Soil management *w o r s e:* ploughing depth (p. 6)* smaller, *less* fertiliser. **Con:** crop yields. This means his land is better.
2. Keep of cattle *w o r s e:* statistical data p. 7.**
3. Keep of labourer *w o r s e:* p. 7*** (and p. 5****).
4. Maintenance of dead stock *w o r s e:* p. 5.*****
5. Productivity of labour *l o w e r* (cf. number of workers, p. 6****** and 5*******).
The small peasant lives worse than the hired labourer of the big peasant and gives scantier "nourishment" to land and farm.
The small peasant works harder: 3.********

Written in June-September 1901
First published in 1938
in .Lenin Miscellany XXXI   Printed from the original

* See p. 134.—Ed.
** See p. 135 –Ed.
*** See pp. 136-37.—Ed.
**** See pp. 130-31.— Ed.
***** See p. 130.—Ed.
****** See pp. 132-33.—Ed.
******* See p. 131.—Ed.
******** See p. 128.—Ed.

CRITICAL REMARKS ON K. KLAWKI'S ARTICLE,
"THE COMPETITIVE CAPACITY
OF SMALL-SCALE
PRODUCTION IN AGRICULTURE" [72]

Landwirtschaftliche Jahrbücher. Zeitschrift für wissenschaftliche Landwirtschaft. Herausgegeben von Dr. *H. Thiel.** Berlin 1899. XXVIII (28). Band (1899). (Six issues a year.) (1081 pp.+tables.)

Dr. juris *Karl Klawki.* "Ueber Konkurrenzfähigkeit des landwirtschaftlichen Kleinbetriebes" (S. 363-484).

Most extensive calculations for 12 farms in the Braunsberg district of East Prussia. (From paging through) make note of: p. 453 (and 452).

αα (p. 452). "Big farms use an average of $\frac{1}{4}$ of their gross income in their own economy, medium farms, about $\frac{1}{3}$, and small, roughly $\frac{1}{2}$. Nevertheless, the share remaining on the small farms for marketing is greater than those on big and medium farms. The reason is above all that small peasants tend to limit their household expenses to the utmost. *We c a n n o t decide outright whether or not this partially results in some underconsumption,* because the available material does not enable us to draw the correct conclusions on the overall household budget of the farmer and his family."

---

* *Agricultural Yearbooks.* Scientific agricultural magazine. Published by Dr. Thiel.— *Ed.*

Nutrition for one member of the family in marks (only from own farm?)*

	Big farms				Medium farms				Small farms			
χχ	I	II	III	IV	I	II	III	IV	I	II	III	IV
(p. 453)	—	269	—	185	240	222	252	159	136	142	163	97

(My calculation)
average=227   =218   =135

According to Klawki (373)

Small	farm	1- 10	ha
Medium	"	10-100	ha
Big	"	>100	ha

ββ ... (453). Part of the small peasants also diligently work as day labourers, and on such days receive from their employers board, in addition to their pay.... Whether there is any *under-consumption* among the small farms or not, we cannot say, but we *think it is probable* in the case of a small farm falling into Group IV. *But the fact is that the small peasants live very frugally and sell much of what they, so to speak, save out of their mouths.* (Sic!)

P. 479: If we find in the final analysis that it is the medium farm that can produce a certain quantity of products at the lowest cost, we must take into account that the small farm may assess all its labour-power at a correspondingly lower figure than that used on the large and medium farms, because it is its own. In time of agricultural crisis, and even at other times, it is. the small farms that are most stable; they are *able to sell a relatively larger quantity of products than the other categories of farms by severely curtailing domestic expenses,* which, it is true, *must lead to a certain amount of under-consumption.*** (!)

---

* For an analysis of the table, see pp. 153-54.— *Ed.*
** See present edition, Vol. 5, p. 177.—*Ed.*

Crop yield	Small farms	Medium farms	Big farms	p. 441 averages
Wheat:	6-7 cent-ners	7-8	8-9	*(per Morgen)* given by Klawki
Rye:	7	8-9	10	himself

"The case is similar with all other crops" (441).

"Only in flax, which is an extensive-farming crop, is there evidence of a growing tendency in favour of the small farms." *

Namely, medium	I	5	Stein of flax	(per Morgen?)	
farms	IV	6	"	"	
Small farms	I	6.$_5$	"	"	(4.$_{50}$ Mk of income)
	III	8	"	"	(4.$_{50}$ Mk ")
	IV	8	"	"	(4.$_{50}$ Mk ")

$\boxed{^1/_2 \text{ Stein of flax} = 18^1/_2 \text{ pounds (406).}}$

Disregarding the flax crop, which is on the whole of small importance at the present time, we have the highest yields on the big farms, and the lowest, on the small (441).

Causes: 1) Drainage is almost entirely absent on the small farms. Or the pipes are laid by the farmers *themselves*, and laid *badly*.

$\boxed{\text{On the big farms the soil is fertilised with marl}}$
2) Ploughing is not deep enough—horses are weak. (Yoking of cows is doubtful. Doing heavy work, the cows will yield little milk.)
3) Mostly insufficient feed for cattle—horned cattle.
4) Their manure production is inferior—their straw is shorter, most of it goes into feed, and less remains for litter (Unterstreuen).**

* See present edition, Vol. 5 p. 171.—*Ed.*
** Ibid., Vol. 5, p. 171, and Vol. 13, pp. 193-94.—*Ed.*

(442). Those are above all the four causes for which small farms now lag in terms of income behind the big farms. Klawki then goes on to say that, in agriculture, machines are not all that important (common arguments. *Not a single fact*)....

The list of machinery refutes *Klawki*:

	Big farms				Medium farms				Small farms			
	I	II	III	IV	I	II	III	IV	I	II	III	IV
Steam thresher	0	1	0	0	0	0	0	0	0	0	0	0
Horse-driven thresher	1	0	1	1	1	1	1	1	0	1	0	0
Grain-sorter	1	1	1	1	0	0	1	0	0	0	0	0
Winnowing machines	1	1	2	—	1	1	0	0	0			
Seed drill	1	1	0	—	0	0	0	0	0			
Manure spreader ..	1	1	0	1	0	0	0	0	0			
Horse-drawn rake	3	2	2	1	1	1	1	0	0			
Ring rollers	1	1	1	1	1	0	0	0	0			
Total=	29				11				1			

The big farmer willingly lends the small farmer his roller, his horse-drawn rake and grain-sorter, if the latter promises to supply a man to do the mowing for him in the busy season ... (443). (Characteristic "exchange of good turns"!)*

Agriculture suffers from unfavourable marketing conditions. The peasants mostly sell "locally" and merchants in small towns force down prices very considerably (373).

The large estates are better off in this respect, for they can send considerable quantities of their products to the provincial capitals right away. This usually gives them 20 to 30 pfennigs more per centner than selling in small towns.**

* Ibid., Vol. 5, p. 173.—*Ed.*
** Ibid., p. 173.—*Ed.*

But Klawki took the same prices for all (373).

The *big* landowners alone have exact book-keeping (374). Only as an exception among the peasants.

There are no technical agricultural enterprises. "Peat extraction is primarily of great importance to the small farms, because they have the necessary time and manpower for it" (439).

Flax growing has remained only among the small farmers: it requires a great expenditure of human energy. It is available in the families of the small holders, but the big farmers find hire hard and costly (440).

Improved crop
   rotation: .... Big farms Medium farms Small farms
                   I-IV   I, II and IV   II
Old   three-field
   system: .... Big farms Medium farms Small farms
               —   III   I, III and IV   (44

Livestock farming. The big farmers I process their milk into butter: "their own very profitable use of milk". The big farms II-IV send their milk to the towns and obtain a higher income than the middle farmers, who process their milk into butter at home and sell it to traders.

The *middle farmers* concentrate on the sale of well-fattened cattle.

The *small farmers* sell their cattle younger—they cannot feed them as long as the middle farmers because they are short of feed (444).

The butter produced on the medium farms (Klawki always calls them big *peasant farms*) is *s u p e r i o r* to that produced on the small farms (separators, daily churning), so that the latter are paid 5-10 pfennigs less per pound by the traders.*

---

* See present edition, Vol. 5, p. 173.—*Ed.*

Per Morgen (in marks)	Big farms	Medium farms	Small farms	
		(Average of 4 farms)		
(per Morgen of tilled farmland (444))*				
Receipts from cropping	16.$_5$	18.$_2$	22.$_7$	c. 445 [1])
Receipts from livestock farming	15.$_8$	27.$_3$	41.$_5$	
Total	32.$_3$	45.$_5$	64.$_2$	p. 447
Sale of crop products	11	12	9	
Sale of animal products	14	17	27	pp. 448-49
Total	25	29	36	
Including sale of milk and butter	7	3	7	p, 450)[2])
Consumption of crop products on home farm	6	6	14	(p. 452)
Consumption of animal products on home farm	2	10	14	
Total	8 ($^1/_4$)	16 ($^1/_3$)	28	(about $^1/_2$ of all receipts)

[1]) In general, the drop in prices leads to a displacement of crop farming by livestock farming.

The reason why small farms are superior in crop farming: the big farms spend more on the production of feed and the feeding of stock (*Klawki excludes the feeding of stock from receipts* (p. 441) *from agriculture*: this, he says, applies to livestock farming).

The small farms keep *many more* animals per Morgen, although their cattle are, of course, not as valuable (446), and their horses are worse (447). The stock on the medium farms is *not worse* than that on the big farms.

[2]) Medium farms use relatively much on the farm; for the big farms—marketing is profitable; on the small farms, butter and whole milk are used in very small quantities... not used at all on the small farms of Group IV (450).

---

* Ibid., Vol. 5, p. 170.—*Ed.*

Per Morgen
(in marks)

	Big farms	Medium farms	Small farms	
	(Average of 4 farms)			
Capital in structures	89	91	147	(p. 455)
Dead stock	13	21	37	(my calculation)
Capital in drainage	14	8	2	(")
Livestock	29	49	59	(p. 459)
Artificial fertilisers	$0._{31}$	$0._{38}$	$0._{43}$	(p. 460)
Concentrated feed *)	2	0	0	(p. 461)
Management and supervision......................	$1._7$	0	0	(p. 461)
Level of outlays: (aggregate) *Without* cost of labour-power (α)	$21._{51}$	$16._{94}$	$5._{53}$	(pp. 478-79)
with cost of labour-power (β)	$23._{31}$	$27._{03}$	$51._{67}$	
Quantity of produce valued at 100 marks is produced on expending .... (α)	65	38	8 (marks)	(p. 479)
(β)	70	60	80	

per Morgen of landwirtschaftlich benutzte Fläche [73] in marks

In giving these 2 tables, Klawki says:

Both these tables most clearly show the great importance of the farmer's and his family's own labour-power. If we find in the final analysis that it is the medium farm that can produce a certain quantity of products at the lowest cost, we must take into account that the small farm may assess all its labour at a correspondingly lower figure than that used on the large and medium farms, because it is its own. In time of agricultural crisis, and even at other times, it is the small farms that are most stable; they are able to sell a relatively larger quantity of products than the other categories of farms by severely curtailing domestic expenses, which, it is true, must lead to a certain amount of under-consumption. This, as we have seen, is already taking place on the small farms of Group IV. Unfortunately, many small farms are reduced to this by the high rates of interest on loans. But in this way, although with

---

) Our peasant farms spend nothing on Kraftfuttermittel. They are very slow to adopt progressive methods and are particularly chary of spending cash (461).

---

* See present edition, Vol. 5, p. 172.—*Ed.*

!! great effort, they are able to stay on their feet and live
from hand to mouth. Probably, it is the great diminution
in consumption that chiefly explains the increase in the
number of small-peasant farms in our locality, as indicated ‖
in the Reich statistics (cf. table on p. 372). (480.)* ‖ !

In the Königsberg Administrative Area (p. 372)

	Number of farms		Farmland under cultivation, ha		
	1882	1895	1882	1895	
Under 2 ha	55,916	78,753	26,638	33,890	And Klawki hastens to declare that this is an undesirable phenomenon. *But* there is progress even among the small farms: everything is for the best.
2-5 "	11,775	14,013	37,998	44,596	
5-20 "	16,014	18,933 **	174,054	196,498	
20-100 "	13,892	13,833	555,878	555,342	
100 and over	1,955	2,069	613,038	654,447	

The *advantage* of the big farmer—that he sells in carloads,
etc., which is much more profitable, and he is better able
to assess the value of his grain (451). *The same* goes for
cattle.

The big farmer sells his corn in centners, and his cattle
by weight.

The peasant sells his grain by measure (Scheffel),
and cattle by appearance, which makes him lose a great
deal.***

The small peasants do all the repairs of buildings (etc.)
themselves.

Medium farms III and IV and small farms lay their own
drainage pipes. (Drainage is necessary in the locality, and
there is an ever greater demand for pipes.)

P. 460: most of them (farms) began using fertilisers by
way of experiment.

---

* Ibid., pp. 177-78.—*Ed.*
** Ibid., p. 178.—*Ed.*
*** Ibid., p. 173.—*Ed.*

Labour costs.

Per 100 Morgen

	Big farms	Medium farms	Big farms				Medium farms			
			I	.II	III	IV	I	II	III	IV
Hired labour in days	887	744	1,061	970	771	613	750	895	622	488
			1,061	970	771	746[1])	972[2])	895	622	488[3])
Manual labour in days ...	887	924 [4])	(including the labour of the peasants) (p. 463)							
Value of produce per 100 working days (marks)	372	481 [5])	(p. 463)							
Total cost of manual labour per 100 Morgen	1,065	1,064	(p. 465)							
Cost of 1 working day ...	1.30	1.53	(p. 466)							
Average annual earnings of labourer	391	458								
Income per 100 marks of labour costs	305	470								

Ratio (p. 467) of kind to cash payments (p. 467):

Big farms 7 : 6
Medium farms 24 : 6

Disability and old-age insurance .... 0.29 mark per 0.13 Morgen   {None at all on small farms (p. 469)

Hired labour in days per 100 Morgen	887	744

Working days per 100 Morgen

Permanent labourers	822		638	Instleute, etc. (p. 472)
Day labourers	112		30	"free workers" (!!)

There can be no calculation for the small farms. But it is obvious that they have some surplus-labour (464).

---

[1]) The owner's two sons substitute for 2 full labour-power units.	Upper row— without correction for substitution.
[2]) 2 unmarried sisters of the owner substitute for 2 hired labouring women.	
[3]) 2 sons of the owner substitute for the old owner himself.	Lower row— with corrections.
[4]) A part of the work is said to relate to housekeeping: maids. This partially reduces the difference.	

[5]) Working much harder: the "example" set by the owner stimulates the labourers *"to greater diligence and thoroughness"*.

	Area	Stock (marks) Live	Stock (marks) Dead	Hired labour Married	Scharwerker Unmarried	Scharwerker Year round	Scharwerker Harvest-ing	Day labourers Summer	Day labourers Harvest & Potatoes	Day labourers Beetroot	Receipts	Outlays — Profit	Net profit	Per ha
Big farms L	513.71 ha	55,954	19,270.21	21	8	23	6	6		25	53,996.57	— 15,745.90	13,745.30 [1]	35.24
" " " II.	362.50 ha	35,394	20,133.13	13	2	19	—	3	12	—	— 43,459.90	— 12,094.73	10,094.73 [3]	31.28
" " " III.	430.20 ha	18,027.30	11,545.7	7	5	7	—	14	—	—	— 23,156.46	— 6,295.33	7,483.10 [4]	33.36
" " " IV.	125.00 ha	15,427	5,291	4	5	3	—	2	—	—	— 17,187.90	— 8,436.25	6,536.30	58.08
	1,431.41 ÷4 = 357.85	124,802.50 ÷4 = 31,201	56,239 ÷4 = 14,059											
Medium farms [Big peasant estate] L	74.25 ha	13,933	5,303	3	2	—	—	2—			12,586.74	— 7,147.96	5,431.86 [2]	80.44
II.	57 ha	10,600	4,990	2	4	—	—	2—3			— 9,708.71	— 5,226.98	3,726.98 [5]	67.76
III.	55.5 ha	9,170	3,458	—	3	—	—	3			— 7,433.28	+ 4,649.12	3,149.12 [6]	69.20
IV.	15.875 ha	2,923	1,545	1	—	—	—	2			— 3,181.32	+ 2,419.63	1,219.63 [7]	76.91
	202.625 ÷4 = 50.6	36,626 ÷4 = 9,156	15,296 3,824											
Small farms (Husband+wife +parents) L [8]	7.125 ha	1,192	754								1,292.66	+ 1,184.90	184.90 [8]	25.32

Box (Big farms L, stock): About 50 Morgen goes to the hired labourers

Box (Big farms II–IV, labour): Services: corvée, small jobs and casual work

Box (Medium / Small, net profit): Net profit

Box (Medium / Small, profit): Balance-profit

Box (Medium farms L): Old husband + wife + 2 adult sons + daughter

Box (Medium farms IV): Brother working as farm-hand, receives 100 marks

Husband+wife +adult son+adult daughter		ha						
	II.[20]	7.00 ha	1,109	1,403	1,673.94	+ 1,535.29	535.39?)	76.32
(2 sons+daughter) (Husband+wife) +1 adult son +2 adult daughters	III.[21]	5.00 ha	576.30	1,039	1,135.08	+ 1,039.99	159.09?)	31.40
	IV.	2.875 ha	709	916	1,093.73	+ 992.83	192.83?)	67.90
		22.900÷4 =5.5	3,148 [787]	4,570 [1,142]				

1) Klawki deducts 2,000 Mk as remuneration of the farmer's labour.
2) Addition because of lower management costs (due to a combination of farming with forestry).
3) A deduction of 1,900 Mk (1,200 and 700 respectively) for the labour of the farmer and his three adult sons, who attended agricultural schools (397) and have in earnest [—resolutely, seriously] dedicated themselves to farming.

4) Deductions: 1,500 for the labour of the farmer and his wife + 216 (2 sisters of the wife).
5) —1,500 (husband, wife +17-year-old daughter)....
6) —1,500 (wife, daughter + 2 sons)...5,916÷4=1,479
7) —1,200 (husband and wife)....

8) The farmer does 20 days of day labour. Engaged (like middle farmer IV) in peat extraction.
9) —1,000 ("assessment of labour-power" of husband+wife+parents).
10) The farmer used to be a carter, and so does all the repairs and jobs himself (430).
11) —1,000 (idem) [for 2 men + 2 women]
12) The value of the farm produce going into the personal consumption of the farmer is relatively low on this farm and on small farm IV. But it should be borne in mind that on both these farms their owners and their respective household members diligently work as day labourers, and receive board, in addition to their pay (435)*.

13) —900 (2 sons and 1 daughter—orphans?)

14) —800   [For 5 persons!!]   !!Sic!

* See present edition, Vol. 5, p. 177.—Ed.

1,000	
1,000	
900	
800	

$\left\{\begin{array}{l}\text{Hence deductions for farmer's keep:}\\ \text{Grossbetrieb: 2,000-1,900 Mk}\\ \text{Mittelbetrieb: 1,716-1,200}\\ \text{Kleinbetrieb: 1,000-800}\end{array}\right\}$*

3,700÷4
=925?

Labourer's income=850

There is no insurance of labourers on the small farms, and on the medium farms: No. I—$36._{78}$; II—$32._{31}$; III—$24._{60}$, and No. IV, insurance of employees—$7._{54}$

Big farm I. There is an *inspector*. The owner comes over from his main estate once a month (374)—(sic! 2,000 Mk for this) for a few days.** There is an experienced stewardess and a housekeeper. Outlays on salaries + office expenses= 1,350+150 marks + maintenance of inspector, etc.= 1,350. (Over and above the wages of the hired labourers and the day labourers!). Insurance of labourers=$644._{04}$.

Big farm II. *Inspector* and experienced woman pig-keeper. Owner—only direction and general supervision. (Salary— 1,100, general management—100). Insurance of labourers= $159._{76}$.

Big farm III—owned by a bishop—run by manager with a fixed annual salary. (Salary=1,800. Office expenses= 150). Insurance of labourers=$338._{25}$ marks.

Big farm IV ... would consider it more correct to call it a big-peasant estate. Insurance of labourers=$108._{10}$.***

---

* See present edition, Vol. 5, p. 175.— *Ed.*
** Ibid.— *Ed.*
*** Ibid.— *Ed.*

Crop in centners per Morgen (p. 441)

	Big farms				Medium farms				Small farms			
	I	II	III	IV	I	II	III	IV	I	II	III	IV
Wheat	8.4	7	9.8	9.3	7	8.4	7.6	6.8	5.1	7.2	6.8	—
Rye	10.83	10.5	10.6	7.6	8.4	10.1	8.6	7.9	6	8.0	7.3	8.4
Barley	11.05	9.2	9.0	8.5	7.9	7.5	8.4	4.8	4.9	7.0	7.7	—
Oats	9.08	7.3	8.6	9.0	8.3	9.3	9.0	7.3	5.0	8.7	8.3	10.0
Peas	9.49	—	7.2	7.4	—	6.7	9.0	7.5	—	7.6	—	10.8
Potatoes	84	62	50	55	57	53	69	40	38	32	50	50
Fodder beet	225	200	135	200	200	200	125	100	70	100	200	100
Flax	—	—	—	—	5 Stein	—	—	6 Stein	6½ Stein	—	8 Stein	8 Stein

	Big farm	Medium farm	Small farm			Big farm	Medium farm	Small farm
Wheat	8.7	7.3	6.4	=	=	34.7	29.8	19.1
Rye	9.9	8.7	7.7	=	=	39.5	35.0	29.7
Barley	9.4	7.1	6.5	=	=	37.7	28.6	19.6
Oats	8.5	8.7	8.0	=	=	34.0	33.9	32.0
Peas	8.0	7.7	9.2	=	=	24.1	23.2	18.4
Potatoes	63	55	42	=	=	251	219	170
Fodder beet	190	156	117	=	=	760	625	470
Flax	—	5.5	7.5*	=	=	—	11	22.5

* See present edition, Vol. 5, pp. 170-71.—Ed.

Subsistence for one member of the family*) (Quantity of
food products consumed on the farm itself)
(p. 453)

XX	Big farms				Medium farms				Small farms			
	I	II	III	IV	I	II	III	IV	I	II	III	IV
Number of persons	—	$5^{1)}$	—	$6^{3)}$	8	6	5	5	4	5	3	5
Marks per person	—	269	—	185	240	$222^{2)}$	252	$159^{2)}$	136	142	163	97
(My calculation)	Average 227				218				135			

$^{1)}$ Inspector, housekeeper, stewardess and 2 maids engaged
in housekeeping.
$^{2)}$ 2 children under 10 years = "one adult"
$^{3)}$ $1,108._{28} \div 6 = 185$. Husband + wife + 3 sons + ?

Big farm IV even has to buy butter for itself. Furthermore, we must take into account that the larger the farm,
the greater is, as a rule, the quantity of additional food
products purchased (453).*
The medium farm consumes very much, surpassing the
"average rational nutrition standard".
It is interesting how Klawki makes an (absurd) attempt
to smooth out this difference:
Let us assume, however, that the small farms are able
to secure a higher cash income only by some under-consumption. To smooth out this fact, let us take the cost of consumption per person as 170 marks a year (?? why not 218-227?),
an amount which should be regarded as being exaggerated
rather than minimised, if we take into account the fact
that the estimate includes food products coming only
from the home farm itself. If on the strength of the figures

---

*) The food of the menials and, for example, flax have
been deducted from natural consumption. The other amounts
are divided per head.

---

* See present edition, Vol. 5, p. 176.—*Ed.*

in the given table we assume that the small farm has an average size of 20-25 Morgen, and that the number of family members engaged in farming is 4, consumption would come to an average of 135 marks per person. Comparing with this figure the hypothetical consumption of 170 marks per person, we get +35 marks, and with 4 persons, 140 marks. Dividing that by 20-25 Morgen, the figure comes to 6-7 marks per Morgen. This means that for this purpose the market would have to be deprived of produce worth that much. Thus, the small farm would be receiving only 29-30 marks of net income per Morgen, and would then be equalised with the medium farm; but it would still have an edge over the big farm.*

Let us take not 170 but 218 marks—$135=83$; $4+5+3+5=17$; $17 \div 4 = 4^1/_4$; $83 \times 4._{25} = 351._{15}$: $351 \div 20 = 17._5$ marks; $351 \div 25 = 14._4$; $14._4 + 17._5 = 31._9$; $31._9 \div 2 = 15._9$

Consequently, $14^1/_2$-$17^1/_2$ marks per Morgen

> average 15.$_9$

$\{36 - 14._5 = 21._5; 36 - 17._5 = 18._5\}$ $36 - 15._9 = 20._1$

	Big farm	Medium farm	Small farm
Receipts from sales	25	29	*20.$_1$*

P. 464: The small farms have the greatest capacity for resistance.

The small farmer can assess the ... labour-power used ... at a correspondingly lower price, because that is his own labour, whereas the big peasant and the landowner depend on the general conditions of wages and must more or less reckon with the demands of the labourers. The small farmer is also more capable than the big one, and above all than the landowner, to reduce the portion going into the management of his enterprise, the entrepreneur's profit, because at critical moments he is able to restrict himself severely (sic!) in his housekeeping.

This is the small farm's advantage in a crisis.

* See present edition, Vol. 5, pp. 176-77.—Ed.

...In peasant households, the labourers are certainly better fed than by the landowners (467).*

The labourers cost more but produce more. (The exception is the big farm IV—rather, the big-peasant farm.)

					Wages for Schar-werker	
Income	of Instmann family [75]	(big farm	I)	$=799-120=679$		Mk
”	of Deputant family [75]	(big farm	I)	$=704-\ 60=644$		
”	of Instmann family,	big farm	II	$=929-120=809$		
”	of Deputant family,	big farm	II	$=658-\ 60=598$		
”	of Instmann family,	big farm	III	$=779-\ 89=690$		
”	” ”	”	” IV	$=861-\ 75=786$		

Medium farm II (Instmann family) $=737-\ 30=707$
Medium farm I   ”   ” $=$same.

If the Scharwerker are the Instmann's children, his family income		$=800\text{-}900$ marks (p. 475)
If the Scharwerker are the Deputant's children, his family income		$=600\text{-}700$ marks

(number of family members not given anywhere!)

Thus, it is not for the sake of higher wages that the Instmann is more willing to work for the peasant owner. The reason: the author says, it gives him more spare time, so he can do day labour (!?) (p. 476).

When lucky, such Instleute purchase a few Morgen of land out of their savings (from wages). For the most part they find themselves worse off financially; they are aware of this but are tempted by the greater freedom (476). Many— not the worst, by far—go to the towns.

The most important task of modern agrarian policy for the solution of the agricultural labourer problem in the East is to encourage the most efficient labourers to settle down by affording them the opportunity of acquiring a piece of land as their own property, if not in the first, then at least in the second generation (476).** !!

On p. 477, Klawki declares that the peasant finds it easier to obtain labourers. But the labourer problem is *being aggravated* even for the peasant. The peasants complain of the difficulty of obtaining labourers, especially labouring women.

* See present edition, Vol. 5, p. 174.— *Ed.*
** Ibid., p. 178.— *Ed.*

Final compar

Marks per Morgen	Large farms			
	I	II	III	IV
1) Total receipts	35.$_{05}$	33.$_{88}$	25.$_{85}$	38.$_{18}$
2) Total outlays	26.$_{24}$	25.$_{86}$	17.$_{48}$	23.$_{66}$
Net profit per Morgen	8.$_{81}$	7.$_{82}$	8.$_{34}$	14.$_{52}$
" " " ha	35.$_{24}$	31.$_{28}$	33.$_{56}$	58.$_{08}$

Average per *Morgen*   9.$_{87}$

Average: 1) $33._{18}$-$44._{18}$-$64._{24}$ Strangely enough, this calcu figures!

2) $\dfrac{23._{30}\text{-}27._{03}\text{-}51._{66}}{9._{88}\quad 17._{15}\quad 12._{58}}$

Con Klawki's calculations:

1) he takes the same prices (p. 3).* But the big farms get

2) he makes a correct reduction in the assessment of the to the medium farm and the small one (pp. 7 and *8*)*

3) he fails to take account of labour on the medium and (laying pipes themselves), etc.

4) Consumption of own farm products tends to decrease milk))* (*9*-10).* (Included also: hired labour of the labourers!! Klawki's reasoning about this pp. 1 and 2,

5) The labourers work more intensively on the *medium* on the *big* ones.

6) The *big farms* have greater outlays on disability and (artificial fertilisers, concentrated feed, drainage).

7) No account is taken at all of labour in *supervision* on

---

* References to the pages of the MS. relate to the following pages of p. 5—p. 145; pp. 7-8—pp. 148-50; p. 5—pp. 145-46; p. 2—p. 140; p. 3—p. 141; p. 7—pp. 148-50; p. 11—p. 155; p. 1—pp. 138-39; this volume: p. 3 of the MS.—p. 142 of this volume; pp. 3-4—pp.

ison: (p. 483)

Medium farms					Small farms			
I	II	III	IV		I	II	III	IV
$46._{61}$	$44._{14}$	$40._{83}$	$50._{69}$		$45._{34}$	$59._{78}$	$56._{75}$	$95._{10}$
$26._{50}$	$27._{20}$	$23._{53}$	$30._{88}$		$38._{86}$	$40._{65}$	$48._{80}$	$78._{35}$
$20._{11}$	$16._{94}$	$17._{30}$	$19._{21}$		$6._{48}$	$19._{13}$	$7._{95}$	$16._{75}$
$80._{44}$	$67._{76}$	$69._{20}$	$76._{84}$		$25._{92}$	$76._{52}$	$31._{80}$	$67._{00}$

$18._{39}$ | cf. Bulgakov I 58 | $12._{58}$ Mk

lation (which is mine) differs somewhat from Klawki's!

more (pp. 3-4, p. 5)*

value of a family's labour-power from the big farm down

small farms for repairs (p. 5)*, drainage (pp. 2 and 5)*

from the big to the small farms (pp. 1, 2, 4 bottom (no small farms: p. 3 top, p. 7, p. *11* for allotting land to pp. 5, 10).*

farms (p. *6* | note 5 |)* (and receive more: p. 11)* than

old-age insurance and on improvements in agriculture

the *medium farms.*

142-43; p. 5—p. 146; p. 1—p. 139; p. 2—p. 139; p. 4—p. 143; pp. 9-10—pp. 153-54; p. 2—pp. 139-40; p. 5—pp. 144-45; p. 10—p. 154; p. 6—p. 147; p. 11—p. 155.—*Ed.*

Klawki's data are highly inadequate: very many gaps. For instance, there are no data at all on feed. The *total* crop is not classified by requirements: sowing, feed, consumption, sales.

It is hardly possible to fill in these gaps.

Thus, big farm I. Total of $513._{71}$ ha

(consequently $2,054._{84}$ Morgen)

Farmland under cultivation = $1,540$ Morgen

(p. 375 and p. 382) $514._{84}$ Morgen

Ploughland and artificial meadow	Morgen		Morgen
Wheat	— 12	*forest*	$=449._{84}$
Winter rye	—312	unsuitable for farming	$= 2._{88}$
Spring rye	— 14		
Barley	— 22	ponds	$= 20._{88}$
Oats	—180	roads	$= 15._{04}$
			$38._{80}$
Peas	— 42		
Vetch	— 33		
Potatoes	— 42		$488._{64}+$
Beetroot	— 22	*vegetable garden*	$25._{96}$
Lupine	— 33		
Clover and timothy	—540		$514._{60}$
	1,252		
Deputants' land [76] about	50	(probably $53._{84}$)	
	1,302		$1,305._{84}$
Meadow	123		$123._{48}$
	1,425		$1,429_{32}$ $2,054._{84}$
Best pastureland (?)	$= 110._{92}$		$110._{92}$ $1,540_{24}$
	$1,535._{92}$		$1,540._{24}$ $514._{60}$
Vegetable garden	$25._{79}$		

	ha	Morgen
Roads and yards	$3._{76}$	
Ponds	$5._{22}$	
Ploughland	$326._{46}$	$=1,305._{84}$
Meadow	$30._{87}$	$= 123._{48}$
Best pastureland	$27._{73}$	$= 110._{92}$
Forest	$112._{46}$	
Vegetable garden	$6._{49}$	
Waste land and loam	$0._{72}$	
	$513._{71}$	

Since K. Klawki gives the marketed products and those consumed on the farm in cash terms *only*, it would be necessary to 1) determine the gross crop by multiplying each number of Morgen for the types of cereals by the average crop; 2) subtract the sowing; 3) multiply the difference by average prices (and these prices are not given for all the products); 4) subtract the marketed products, etc. Furthermore, since the quantity of livestock has not been reduced to a single unit, it is *quite impossible* anyway to determine in figures how well the cattle is fed.

Consequently, such calculations are *useless*.

Cf. **Brase**'s article,* especially pp. 292 and 297-98.

Written in June-September 1901

First published in 1938
in *Lenin Miscellany XXXI*

Printed from the original

---

* See pp. 160-68.— *Ed.*

160

BRASE AND OTHERS [77]

a.

ANALYSIS OF DATA FROM BRASE'S ARTICLE,
"STUDY OF THE INFLUENCE OF FARM DEBT ON FARMING"

Thiels Jahrbücher. 28. Band (1899).

Dr. Brase. "Untersuchungen über den Einfluss der Verschuldung ländlicher Besitztümer auf deren Bewirtschaftung" (S. 253-310).

A study was made of landed estates (17) and peasant farms (34) "in one district of the Liegnitz Administrative Area" (*Lower Silesia*).

The author gives a list of all these estates, but without any summing up. 17 landowners, each with 75-924 ha (9 with 200-500 ha; 1 has under 100 ha, namely 75; 1 with 127 ha; 1 with 924; 1 with 819). For each estate he gives only the number of ha (and categories of land), quantity of livestock, assessed value and debt ("according to an 1896 study").

Two of the 17 have no debt at all (204 and 333 ha); two with over 100% of the value (105 and 104%); 1—90-100%; 3—80-90%; 2—70-80%; 2—60-70%; 1—50-60%; 2—40-50%; 1—30-40%.

Among the peasants, 5 are free from debt.

$$\left\{ \begin{array}{l} \text{1 with 7 ha} \\ \text{7—10-20 ha} \\ \text{the rest—} \\ \qquad \text{20-110 ha} \end{array} \right\}$$

2 up to 10 per cent of the assessed value
5   10-20
7   20-30
3   30-40
5   40-50
3   50-60
3   60-70
1   70-80

34

The author regards as "unburdened by debt" those 1) without mortgage; 2) with mortgage but also with at least an equal amount of capital; 3) with insignificant debt (pp. 262-63).

Detailed description of the *farms* (landed estates are marked in small Latin letters: a-r)

a) 205 ha. Excellent estate: (8 horses + 14 oxen + 106 head of big horned cattle) the "pearl" of the district. (Debt=87% of value.) Very high crop yields, high culture. "The soil was only gradually brought up to this state by systematic drainage, abundant fertilisation, deep turning up and care for the ploughland by means of neat and timely cultivation, and drill and row crops" (p. 264).

All the structures are massive—"a vast amount of capital is invested here". "The livestock is highly fattened, all, without exception."

All types of machinery. The crop-rotation system is rational, the fertilisation is very heavy (manure and artificial fertilisers).

"The erection of costly structures swallows up all the rent."

b) 301 ha; debt—46.$_3$%.

The soil has been improved by many years' cultivation, cleared of stones, etc., a great quantity of lime has been added.

The structures are all good, all massive, cost 170,000 Mk.

All the livestock (10 horses + 26 oxen + 100 head of big horned cattle + 400 sheep) is fed and kept rationally.

All types of machines (no enumeration).

Fertilisers well stored. Artificial fertilisers bought.

Ploughing 17-20 cm (beetroot: 30-35 cm). Row cultivation.

c) 758 ha. (Livestock: 26 horses+54 oxen+220 head of big horned cattle+900 sheep). Debt—76.$_9$% of value. A model farm like *a* and *b*.

Land, structures and livestock are very good. Machinery. "Stall (manure) fertiliser is stored in the best way." 20,000 kg of Chile saltpetre+30,000 ammoniac superphosphate+3,000-4,000 kg of kainite are bought.

Deep ploughing; row tillage; irrigation of meadows; very high yields.

d, e, f—not model farms, but "rational".

d) (75 ha) drained systematically. Heavy use of fertiliser. Artificial fertilisers. Deep ploughing. Drill and row tillage.

e) (229 ha). Drainage started. Structures massive, part of them new. Livestock well fed. Artificial fertilisers (10,000 kg of Chile saltpetre; 25,000 of superphosphate; 50,000 kg of potassium salts and lime).

Ploughing 12-17 cm, potatoes 20-25 cm, still deeper for beetroot.

f: drained. Deep ploughing, etc. "Rather more than less is being done for the structures and their maintenance" (272).

Very good feed for livestock. 8 litres of milk a day per cow.

5,000-6,000 marks' worth of artificial fertilisers a year (15,000 kg of Chile saltpetre; 30,000-40,000 of superphosphate, 50,000 of kainite).

g (819 ha). Good structures. Stables new in part. Drainage.

Milk—3,000 litres per cow (a year).

All livestock of the best quality. Feed good.

Artificial fertilisers. Machinery. Deep ploughing.

h (693 ha). Drainage. Good fertilisers. Massive structures, some of them new.

Livestock fed well. Concentrated feed purchased.

Artificial fertilisers. Deep ploughing.

i (527 ha). Massive structures, in good condition. Livestock well fed. Machinery. Deep ploughing. Artificial fertilisers.

k (445 ha). (Debt 95.$_7$ per cent.) Farming in a "simple" way. "Ramshackle" structures, thatched roofs.

Deep ploughing 12-17 cm. Row tillage.

Owner lives very frugally.

No artificial fertilisers, no feed is purchased. The horses are overworked (despite intensive feeding).

l (347 ha). Debt 42.$_3$ per cent. (Row tillage introduced, artificial fertilisers used, concentrated feed purchased, steam machines introduced, but the result was negative.)

A return to "extensive" farming: as little as possible artificial fertilisers and feed bought.

Livestock feed simpler. Milk—5 litres a day per cow.

m (924 ha, 750 ha of forest). Mainly forestry. Way of farming is simple and cheap.

n (572 ha) {very heavily in debt}. Unfavourable conditions. 1872 drainage *run down*. No money for new one. Too much was paid for the land.

All structures massive, but house for labourers is old thatched mud hut. There are machines, some out of order, lack of feed, poor soil—in short, everything is bad.

o (281 ha). New stables. 6-8 litres of milk a day. Artificial fertilisers. Intensified feeding of livestock.

"The manure comes from the intensively fed livestock; it lies in the dung channels of the cattle shed until it is taken out into the fields, and is rationally preserved by means of kainite and superphosphate. Only rye and wheat straw is used as litter, heather and wood and other foliage no longer being used" (286-87).
Ploughing 17-20 cm. Row tillage.

p (127 ha). Bought at too high a price. Debt 57 per cent. The new owner buys more artificial fertilisers and feed, better machinery, etc.

---

q (204 ha) (Farming operations are too costly for this kind of land: "splendid estate", "everything that is best in technical but not in economic terms is being done").
The structures are massive, the stables are vaulted and adapted for the storage of manure. Feed is bought.
Machinery—rather in excess.
Intensive farming. Artificial fertilisers

	kg
120,000	kainite
35,000-40,000	Thomas slag
5,000	superphosphate
5,000	ammoniac
2,500	Chile saltpetre

r (333 ha). Massive structures.
Cow sheds are not vaulted, maintenance careful.
New living quarters for labourers.
Modest dead stock. Ploughing 12-17 cm.
Irrigation of meadows.

Peasant farms are not listed separately.
"The big and middle peasants as a rule farm better, more intensively, than the small peasants, the big vegetable gardeners (Grossgärtner) and owners of dwarf plots" (292):
deeper ploughing (cows weak)
row tillage
artificial fertilisers and feed purchased.

"If, finally, the crop yields of the peasant farms lag behind those of most landed estates, this is due above all to the peculiarity of small and medium land holdings. The peasant ploughs 5 or 8 cm shallower, in an effort to spare his young horses, which he wants to sell at a profit. In general, he knows how to take care of his livestock much better than hired farm-hands usually do. He cannot have special implements for each separate purpose, improve cultivation methods endlessly, stage long experiments in tillage and the use of fertilisers, and many other things" (292).

"The peasant tries to improve his farming methods by introducing artificial fertilisers and purchasing feed, and machinery.

"The peasant has long since realised the importance of deep ploughing and timely cultivation, the need for correct selection of valuable sorts of seeds for sowing, the keeping of stall manure, and many other similar things. Where he fails to eliminate the shortcomings which can be righted, thereby acting against his own convictions, or is forced to do so, he is, as a rule, short of capital to do this" (293).

The structures are "almost everywhere" massive and in good repair. The livestock is well fed.

This is the first group of peasant farms, *12* (south of a Kreisstadt (district town)) out of 34 (No. 1-11 and No. 18)

> No. 18 = 110 ha

The second group consists of *22* (to the north) out of 34 (of these 22: 4 with 10-20 ha; 11, with 20-50 ha; 7 with 50-95 ha). The land is *damp* sand, which suffers from stagnant moisture. Ploughing 10-13 cm.

"*A primitive wooden plough is pulled* by a small *overworked horse* or weak *half-starved* team of cows" (296).

Too much ploughed under for cereal grains... *short straw,* thin stalks, empty ears and flat grains.... They usually keep *more cattle than the scanty stocks of feed warrant. There is frequently a shortage of feed and litter....* In winter, this quantity of cattle somehow survives on straw, chaff, glume, and small quantities of roots and putrid hay Feed

N.B.

is short at all times, and is of poor quality; in some
parts, the drinking water, with a high iron-content,
is harmful for the animals. *In consequence, the
cattle are small, lean, with coarse wool, or simply
grow sickly and starve in small dark sheds.* That is why
one cannot expect them to be used correctly, or
expect great quantities of good manure.

"*Fertilisers are produced for each crop,* but *in
homeopathic doses.* It is impossible ...
to make up for this poor and inadequate fertiliser
by purchases of *kainite.* It is not fair to expect a sick
man to be efficient. *Alongside the lack of means,*
there is lack of management and experience. The
peasant never uses lime, and green fertiliser only
in separate cases ... (297). *The cultivation of the
fields is hopelessly primitive* but still burdensome;
the collected manure is scattered, $^2/_3$ or $^3/_4$ of
the seeds is sown by hand, then the field is ploughed,
and then the other $^1/_3$ or $^1/_4$ is sown on the surface
and harrowed with a home-made harrow. Rye
is sown occasionally, from time to time, because of
the lack of fertiliser. *It would, of course, be better
to change the seeds, but that and much else is not
done because of the shortage of capital.* The peasant
avoids anything *that costs money,* as a matter of
principle, if he wishes to last. He continues to
thresh his grain the old way, *with a flail, either
picking by hand or sifting all the rubbish.* Recently,
some holders who are better off bought themselves
a small horse-driven thresher. The straw is used
mostly as feed, whereas it would do better (predom-
inantly) as litter for the animals. Furthermore,
there is need to chop up hay and straw for feed, to
cover the potato and beet stores with straw, mend
the holes in the thatch, and mix some hay with the
straw to make it last as long as possible, so that
when the straw crop is poor, nothing or very little
remains for litter. It so happens that the use of
forest leaves becomes the general rule. No more
chopped straw goes into litter, but only conifer
which is collected in the forest every year. The

upshot is that the few pines growing on the denuded sand go to seed, and that, despite the vast forests, there is a shortage of timber for building, once the dilapidated structures, repaired innumerable times, threaten to collapse altogether. Even the holders with more money at their disposal are in no position to erect new structures. There is lack of stone, gravel, clay, timber, and above all, *money....* *Everything is in short supply. The unfortunate farmer* of these sad parts labours and toils with his *often numerous family* from dawn to dusk, day in, day out; his toil-hardened hands *and lean face are a sign of nothing but unceasing hard work.* He struggles for his unenviable existence, fights misfortune and care, and barely *manages to keep body and soul together; he strains his every fibre* to obtain some money, *before it is too late*, to pay off the urgent interest and *taxes*, but fears that he may be ruined anyway. He has *no means* for any radical *improvements*; but the fact is that *they alone* could help him and make his naturally poor scrap of land solidly productive and capable of giving better sustenance to its owner" (298)

— the only happy exception among these 22 holdings in the second group is the estate of the village headman at R. (No. 18: 110 ha, 43 head of big horned cattle, 4 pigs + 6 horses, a debt of $50._3$ per cent; only three of these 22 peasants have a higher debt percentage than this).

On average, the master of R. takes in 2-3 times more grain, 3-4 times more potatoes, 6-8 times more beetroot than all the other holders in R., who farm the old way, and who, because of their debts, have no opportunity or reason to farm any other way. The master of R. raises crops which his neighbours are *unable to introduce successfully into their crop rotation*, because their soil *lacks the necessary cultivation and manuring....* He (the master of R.) paid for his estate in cash, and has *c a p i t a l* at his disposal. It is capital and labour that have yielded such excellent results. No peasant could have created "an oasis in a desert" if he had no financial support, as a prerequisite to back up his efforts (300).

He has *"dry sand" which is being gradually brought into cultivation* (green fertiliser). He uses kainite, etc., "on a large scale" ...*he does row tillage, ...there is no lack of straw, new cow sheds* ...various machines.... Cattle well fattened.... Cow shed is built advantageously, and is spacious and full of light.... The cattle have clean and dry litter (299), etc.—yield a great quantity of good manure, etc., etc.

Keeps farm-hands....

(In conclusion the author argues hotly against the assumption that debts help to improve farming. On the contrary, he says, debts tend to oppress, etc. A farm needs capital; examples of rich peasants with capital, traders, a former policeman, etc., etc.).

Crop yield in kg per *h a*:

	wheat	rye	barley	oats	potatoes	fodder beets
Landowners	1,000-2,800	600-2,200	1,200-3,000	600-2,800	10-21 thous.	20-80 thous.
Peasants	400-1,800	300-1,400	250-2,000	450-1,800	$4\frac{1}{2}$-14 thous.	4-52 thous.

b.

BIBLIOGRAPHICAL NOTES AND ANNOTATIONS

Dr. Michael *Hainisch*: "Die Zukunft der Deutsch-Oesterreicher". Eine statistischvolkswirtschaftliche Studie. (Wien, 1892.) *S. 165.**

There appears to be very little statistics proper here, but there seems to be something on the debts of peasants and the ruin of peasant farms under the influence of the *money* economy: Section IV (pp. 114-53): "Plight of Peasantry, etc."

Dr. Carl von Grabmayr (Landtagsabgeordneter in Meran). *Schuldnoth und Agrarreform.* Eine agrar-politische Skizze

---

* Dr. Michael Hainisch: "The Future of the Germano-Austrians". A Statistical-Economic Study.—*Ed.*

mit besonderer Berücksichtigung Tirols. Meran 1894. (S. 211).*

$\left.\begin{array}{l}\text{General}\\\text{figures on}\\\text{the growth}\\\text{of debt}\end{array}\right\}$ *Also his. Die Agrarreform im Tiroler Landtag.* Meran 1896. (S. 157).**

Statistische Monatsschrift. Wien 1901, Neue Folge, VI. Jahrgang (der ganzen Reihe 27. Jahrgang).

(*Alfred Hölder.* k.u.k. Hof- und Universitätsbuchhandler. Wien I. Rothenthurmstrasse. 13.) ***

Also issued by his publishing house
Sociale Rundschau, herausgegeben vom k.k. arbeitsstatistischen Amte. Monthly; 2 K. a year=2 Mk. Einzelne Hefte=20 H.=30 Pf.****

Written in June-September 1901

First published in 1938
in *Lenin Miscellany XXXI*

Printed from the original

---

* Dr. Carl von Grabmayr (Landtag Deputy in Meran). *The Debt Burden and Agrarian Reform.* An Agrarian-Political Essay with Special Consideration of the Situation in Tyrol.—*Ed.*
** *Agrarian Reform in the Tyrolean Landtag.*—*Ed.*
*** *Statistical Monthly.* Vienna 1901, New Series. Sixth year of publication (27th year of publication of the whole series).
(Alfred Hölder, bookseller to the imperial and royal court, and universities. 13, Rothenthurmstrasse. Vienna.)—*Ed.*
**** *Social Survey,* published by the Imperial and Royal Labour Statistics Department. Monthly; 2 kronen a year=2 marks. Each issue=20 hellers=30 pfennigs.—*Ed.*

CRITICAL REMARKS ON A. SOUCHON'S BOOK,
PEASANT PROPERTY[78]

N. B. Souchon.
Note in *S o u c h o n*'s book:
Pages

  6. Small property (in the opinion of French social-
    ists)—without hired labour.

  12. *Social value of peasant property—defen-*
    ders of property

(N.B.) 14. *A factor of social conservation*

  16. *Safeguard against the urge for social innova-*
    tions....

  23. The small-farm regions are losing population
    more rapidly than the big-farm regions.

  24. Figures on holders

	1862	—*different* from	Bul-
day labourers with land	1882	—the same as	ga- kov's
day labourers without land	1892	—*different* from	

and a reference to the 1892 Inquiry![79]

N.B.? N.B. II.195-96

  25. The smallest holders are more inclined to move
    to the towns.

  39. *Three* main arguments in favour of large-scale
    production:

    (a) lower general costs —Con—(41) *associations*
    (b) more division of   —Con : machinery cannot
      labour and use of   always be used (43),
      machinery   disadvantages of the
                big: drop in the prices
                of corn (46)

N.

(c) more melioration,
   industries, etc.   — Con: co-operatives (47)

57. **Both the large ("model") and the small property are
   necessary (!)**

57-58. There is a decline in the number of day labourers with land—con the theory of the importance
   of small holders as hired labourers.

61. It is believed that there are 57.4% holders per
   100 plots.

67. *Holders with collateral employment (not day labourers)*

68. Peasant   farm=5-20   ha   (<5 ha can- N.B.
   not provide sustenance for a fam-
   ily: pages 68 and 69, note 2)

                                              ha

72: 1,427,655—agricultural labourers
              without land
   1,400,000—agricultural labourers ⎫
              with land   ⎪
   1,300,000—small holders with   ⎪
              collateral employment ⎬ 7 million
              (cf. 71 and 67)   ⎪
              (handicraftsmen, etc.)⎭
   1,000,000—peasants   10 million
     140,000—big farmers (>20 ha)
              with hired labour   23 million

Σ=   5,267,655   40 ⎧—minus⎫
                                        ⎨ state ⎬
                                        ⎪ lands,⎪
                                        ⎩ etc. ⎭

79. Agricultural crisis—very uncertain thing. They
   have been shouting about it for *40* years.

87. Since 1883, the number of land plots has been
   decreasing...
   —a tendency towards concentration.

88-89—*The smallest holders m o v e to the towns*
89—*"Victims of concentration—the smallest* N.B.
    holders"

92-93. The agricultural crisis should end soon.
94. The number of agricultural *machines has been
    growing very slowly, moderately.*
156-158. *Allotments Act*[80]—of small importance (not
    less or more than 1 acre, conditionally, etc.)
163. *Rentengüter*—created by the *feudal* party
164. ———————— against the socialists
                    "   exodus to the towns
                    "   shortage of labour.
167—by 1896, 605 estates with 53,316 ha were broken up
    into 5,021 Rentengüter
                1,088   2.5-5 ha
                1,023   5 -7.5 ha
169. *Facilitating the supply of labour* (N.B.)

Written in June-September 1901

First published in 1938   Printed from the original
in *Lenin Miscellany XXXI*

CRITICAL REMARKS ON F. MAURICE'S BOOK,
AGRICULTURE AND THE SOCIAL QUESTION.
AGRICULTURAL AND AGRARIAN FRANCE[81]

F. Maurice

[Only paged through. The author has the wildest ideas of the most primitive anarchism. There are some interesting factual remarks.]

Pp. Note

48. Farmers complain.... Which farmers?

small: 5 million—12 million ha   (N.B.)

big $0._{869}$ —37   "   "

85. (French) soldier's ration—1 kg of bread

300	grammes	of meat
160	"	vegetables
16	"	salt
15	"	coffee
21	"	sugar

117. 14,074,801 plots; $59._3$% farms—consequently— 8,346,000 holders (?)

119. *1882*: $84._7$% farms—$25._1$% of the area ⎫ "Extreme"
         $15._3$% (868,000)—$74._9$% ($37._1$ mil- ⎬ concentra-(!!)
                    lion ha) ⎭   tion

122. Distribution of rural population according to 1886 statistics.

122-123. Almost 720,000 absentee owners (Absenteeism).

131-132. Small cropping can feed many more people.

160.   From 1831 to 1886, the countryside gave up
         6 million persons to the towns.

165.   Rural population in *1851* and *1886*

$$\left. \begin{cases} < \text{number} & \text{of} & \text{holders} \\ = & " & " & \text{half-croppers} \\ + & " & " & \text{labourers} \end{cases} \right\} \text{N.B.}$$

167.   Permanent labourers in 1862 and 1882 (—). [The
         figures are the same as *Bulgakov's* (6)]

174.   The growth of big towns from 1831 to 1886.

194-195. The author favours social peace, "stability of
         our institutions", and is against "excessive indus-
         trialisation of agriculture"

> And he calls himself a socialist! Konfusionsrath! *

195-197. Agriculture is now *extensive* (on big farms), yields
         little produce, etc.
             It should be *small* and intensive.

197.   Maurice's slogan: *small property, small-
         scale production.*

197.   The new (future) phase of agriculture is the "*period
         of vegetable gardening*" (author's italics) or "*small
         cropping*" (!)—the only possible outcome (!).
         The tendency in modern society is towards a
         coalescence of labour and property.

198.   How is this to be achieved?
             "Very easy" (!)—

199.   there is need for a *reform*—account must be taken
         of the current ideas prevailing among the *masses*—
         with *individual property* (!!) and the
         family (!!)

200.   "Gradual" supplanting of big farms.

203.   The right of every citizen to use the national
         territory must be proclaimed

║ meaning, the nationalisation of land. ║

---

* Bungler.—*Ed.*

204. Initially state lands are to be leased to small farms
205. —large land holdings to be taxed.
       etc.
234. (234-266) (!!)—Draft law (!!) Casting of lots for
       land, etc.
278. —Descriptions of separate departments.
       {The best thing in the book.}
       Nord. Beetroot production (287. staple crop).
       Intensified fertilisation.

Prevalence of (??) small cropping			
1-10 ha:	32,000 farms	—	248,000 ha
10-50 :	10,000	”	206,000
50 and>:	690	”	53,000

N.B.
Farms:
  232 ha. Sugar refinery, etc. Model farm. Per ha: 30
      hectolitres of wheat "are not appreciably superior
      to those of the region" (p. 291) ??? (cf. Nord *24*)
N.B.
      50,000 kg of beetroot (cf. Nord *45,000*)
  140 ha. 20 milch cows. 30 hl, 50,000 beetroot.
    7 ha. 6 milch cows. 25 hl, 40,000 beetroot (sic!)
      "With all the costs covered, and the family partly
      supplied with sustenance, **the profit, rather,**
      the wages, in this case, comes to between
      15 and 1,800 francs a year" (291).
      Great development of *industry* and *mines.*

294. ‖ *An entire population is semi-*‖
      ‖ *agricultural and semi-indus-*‖
      trial, with a plot of land. **Impos-**
      sible to survive on less than 5 ha.
295. — **pays for the cultivation of his land** (*!*)
      [Sometimes with his labour!]
      —fattens livestock for traders for a remuneration.
296. Cultivation of beetroot with the aid of *machinery.*
      Child labour.
      —*working for garment merchants*
      in Lille (N.B.) N.B.
             (14-hour working day—*per family* (!)—
             $1-1^{1}/_{4}$ francs).
297. The condition of the rural labourer is *rather hard....*
      Meat *on Sundays....* Poverty....

298-299. *Growth in the number of small holders doing hired labour.*
Maurice's "moral":
"there is danger" in industrialising agriculture (beetroot),
"it is a mistake" (308) to regard agriculture as an industry, etc., etc. There is need to develop small-scale production!! etc.

309. *A i s n e.* Big cropping prevails—in contrast to *Nord.*
Worse soil, lagging agriculture.

315.

	farms	ha
<1 ha	29,000	14,000
1- 10	22,000	94,000
10- 50	7,000	169,000
50-100	991	
100-300	1,016	404,000
300 and >	69	

320. Growing production of beetroot. (Idem 316)
322. The labourers are highly dissatisfied ("not much better than serfdom"!)
...meagre pay and food....
340. Nor is the condition of the labourer better in Picardie or in Beauce

342. *Vegetable gardening* in the suburbs of Paris ... of 28,000 ha ... *1,800* ha are vegetable gardens divided into *10,000* enterprises.... From 1,000 sq. m. to 1 ha (344)....

	farms	ha
<1 ha	11,000	5,000
1- 10	2,600	
10- 50	290	
50-300	13	23,000
300-500	2	

28,000

Vegetable gardeners mostly lease land at 2,000 fr. ...

345. — — Gross receipts from 1 ha = 20,000 fr.
(working capital 25,000 fr.)
net income = 10,000 fr.

345.   Labourers per *ha*   husband and wife
                                                (entrepreneurs) — 2
         { Wages and keep =   { 3 labourers, men   — 3
              6,000 fr.   2 girls   — 2
                                     1 day labouring
                                        woman   — 1 (for
                                                              sum-
                                                              mer)

Normandy

358.   *The very small holders go in for wage labour.*
361.   —For a minority Normandy is a "rich country",
         but for the mass of peasants, it is *"harsh and
         inhospitable"*....
375.   Vegetable gardeners near Cherbourg (sale of cabbage,
         etc., to Britain). Land costs 15,000-20,000 fr.
         (1 ha).
376.   Farms from 1 to 10 ha....
         (N.B.) *Each ha needs 2-3 men labourers* (300-
         500 fr.) and Maurice is jubilant: *"small* cropping"!

Written in June-September 1901

First published in 1938   Printed from the original
in *Lenin Miscellany XXXI*

REMARKS ON
A. CHŁAPOWO-CHŁAPOWSKI'S BOOK,
AGRICULTURE IN BELGIUM
IN THE 19TH CENTURY[82]

From Chłapowo-Chłapowski.
Gainfully employed population in Belgian agriculture

	Members of families taking part in farming	Gesinde * and day labourers	Total (both sexes)
1846)	906,575	177,026	1,083,601
1880)	982,124	217,195	1,199,319
1895)	1,015,799	187,106	1,204,810
		+1,905 Hofbeamte **	

ibidem 69-71—"modern" large-scale production
       71-72. Parcel holders as labourers of big farmers.
       99-100. Idem (N.B.)
       102. Competition between small and big farms.
       137. Growth of parcel holders=labourers.
       139. Plight of rural labourers.
       Idem *145-146.*
       144. *More intensive work done by small farmers.* (N.B.).

---

* Farm-hands.— *Ed.*
** Farm employees.— *Ed.*

148. Elevation of labourers to small holders.
148. Relations between small and big farmers.
      (Support.)

Written in June-September 1901

First published in 1938
in *Lenin Miscellany XXXI*   Printed from the original

REMARKS ON THE MATERIAL
OF THE BADEN INQUIRY [83]

*Erhebungen über die Lage der Land-
wirtschaft im Grossherzogthum Baden.**
1883. Karlsruhe.

(Three big volumes, rather 4, because to the 3rd is append-
ed *Ergebnisse* der Erhebungen.**

A number of monographs on separate communities,
followed by results. Very many budgets.)

Volume 1. Note (after paging)

Sandhausen community (Heidelberg district) Vol. I,
VIII *), p. 30 [Vol. I, VIII* (community)].
Budgets. Big peasant. $9._{80}$ ha. 1 farm-hand +1 maid+
379 days of hired labour.

Small peasant. $2._{96}$ ha ($1._{62}$ ha *his own*+
$1._{34}$ *leased*)
raises tobacco and hops.

10 man-days (hired day labour).

[with tobacco and hops $1^1/_4$ working days of labour should
be reckoned per *are.* Consequently, total=370 days.

husband	—300		Total	receipts=2,032.$_{32}$
wife	— 60	370.]	Outlays	1,749.$_{91}$
day labourer	— 10			282.$_{41}$

*) The description of each community is a special issue
with its own pagination. That is why references must
include volume and community: Vol. II, XI—XIth community in Volume II.

* *A Study of the State of Agriculture in the Grand Duchy of
Baden.*—Ed.
** Results of the Study.— *Ed.*

ibidem

Day labourer=small leasehold farm.

$2._{30}$ ha $12._6$ ares of own land   16 *working days of*
     $217._2$,,   of leased land   *hired labour.*

a total of $229._8$ ares $1^3/_4$ working days per are.

Gross receipts—$1,543._{50}$ ⎰ 16—day labourer
     outlays—$1,472._{58}$ Σ=410 work- ⎱ 300—husband
         $+70._{92}$ ing days ⎰ 94—wife

Ergebnisse, pp. 56-57. The per-head consumption of meat on *big-peasant* and *middle-peasant* farms.

Everywhere (8 examples) it is *much higher* on the big farms.

Volume II. II, XI community, p. 48. 18 *ares* of tobacco require 80 working days.

[The whole Baden Inquiry is a study of 37 typical communities. In the Ergebnisse, there are the most *detailed*, incredibly detailed, budgets (70), the *main* results of which are given in the table I have borrowed.

Of interest in the Ergebnisse is Anlage VI: "Uebersichtliche Darstellung der Ergebnisse der in den Erhebungsgemeinden angestellten Ertragsberechnungen" (S. 149-65).*
This is a *tabulated* summing up of the budget (and economic) data on the separately described households. (37+33=70 budgets.)

See extract of data on these 70 budgets in notebook[84]	31 big peasants (or farmers)
	21 middle peasants
	18 small peasants (including one wine-grower).
	——
	70

In the Ergebnisse [I have **only** *paged through* the Ergebnisse, but not the material (Vols. 1-3) itself, for the essence is given in the budget table, and there is no time to make a special study of them] one is struck by the indiscriminate nature of the conclusions: the big, middle and small peasants are *not discriminated* systematically anywhere in the results either; it is always "in general", e.g., even on the

---

* Appendix VI: "Brief Review of the Results of the Assessment of Incomes in the Investigated Communities".—*Ed.*

question of consumption. A comparison is made of the *communities*, and not of the big, medium and small enterprises. (E.g., pp. 55-56.)

This table (on 1873 data) appears on p. *21* of the Ergebnisse.

		Number of agric. enterprises	%	Area ha	%
I "mixed" enterprises (of "day labourers and artisans")	0-10 Morgen (0-3.6 ha)	160,581	72.0	227,213	28.5
II small-peasant enterprises	10-20 Morgen (3.6-7.2 ha)	38,900	17.5	193,923	24.3
III middle-peasant enterprises	20-50 Morgen (7.20-18 ha)	18,346	8.3	193,936	24.3
IV big-peasant enterprises	50-100 Morgen (18-36 ha)	3,721	1.6	90,152	11.3
V large (among them big-peasant) enterprises	100-500 Morgen (36-180 ha)	1,177	0.5	65,671	8.4
VI	500 and over (180 ha and over)	21	0.01	5,542	0.6
Community land, etc.		—	—	21,060	2.6
		222,746	100	797,597 *	100

Collateral employment—handicraft industries (Görwihl, Wittenschwand, Neukirch) (p. 43)
        lumbering
        day labour
        factory work, stone quarries, etc., etc.
There is also seasonal outside earth moving and lumbering (p. 45 from Neusatz).

In Neukirch, *40* ha is considered to be a minimum area for subsistence. P. 44.

It is interesting to note concerning data $\frac{\alpha}{\alpha}$ and $\frac{\beta}{\beta}$ **(see tables in notebook):

---

* There is an error of addition in this column (should be 797,497).— *Ed.*

** $\frac{\alpha}{\alpha}$ average annual profit per ha (marks); $\frac{\beta}{\beta}$ —permissible limit of taxation of estate, together with debt, as % of its taxable capital value.— *Ed.*

With the *big* and *middle peasants*, whose holdings come to 7-10 ha in the corn areas and 4-5 ha in the commercial crop and wine-making areas ... (and to 20-30 ha when there are forests) ... the results of calculations ($\begin{smallmatrix}\alpha & \beta\\ \alpha & \beta\end{smallmatrix}$) are not bad (p. 66).... Here, there is no danger in having a 40-70 per cent, average 55 per cent, debt.

By contrast, the conditions for the *small peasant* population are taking on a less favourable shape, i.e. ... for those with *4-7 ha* under cropping, *2-4 ha* under commercial crops and wine-making ... up to 30 ha under forests.

For these small peasants, the average limit of permissible indebtedness lies ... in all respects much lower than should be established for the middle and big peasants.

...For the estates of these sizes, with an *average* family and in the *pure* corn areas, the limit of indebtedness... must not exceed 30 per cent of the assessed value of the holding if the *regular* payment of interest and of instalments is to be *fully* secured... (p. 66).

> The above-given statistics, consequently, confirm the widespread opinion that those owners of peasant holdings, who are on the borderline [*in the middle*] between the day labourers and the middle peasants [in the rural districts the farmers of this category are usually called the *"middle estate"*— Mittelstand], are frequently in a worse position than those in the groups above and below in size of holdings; for, although they are able to cope with *moderate* indebtedness, if it is kept at a certain and not very high level, they find it difficult to meet their ˙ obligations, being unable to obtain *regular* collateral employment (as day labourers, etc.), by which means to increase their income.* They can meet their obligations only when their children have grown up and are placed, so that family expenses are less of a burden on these small farms. By contrast, *day labourers* (or handicraftsmen) with *small holdings*, insofar as they have some regular collateral employment, are frequently in

---

* See present edition, Vol. 5, pp. 187-88.—*Ed.*

N.B. ‖ a much better position materially than those belonging to the "middle estate", for, as computations in numerous cases have shown, collateral employment at times yields such a high net (i.e., money) income as to enable them to repay even *large* debts*; this explains the frequently observed fact that where such conditions obtain, small holders, like day labourers and others, gradually manage to take small-peasant holdings out of debt. These computations also show that it is the rural owners, who belong to the lowest sections of the independent peasant population, that have most reasons to make *cautious* use of their credit, which is why they have to make an especially careful review of their financial possibilities when buying any real estate (pp. 66-67).

Data for *communities* also *prevail* on the question of indebtedness.

Cf. especially p. 97: "The final conclusion [on the question of indebtedness]: relatively less favourable position of the *small*-peasant population."

The study of indebtedness by groups of holdings has shown:

Almost everywhere ... it has turned out that it is the *lowest* groups of holders (day labourers with a land allotment) that have the *highest percentage* of indebtedness, and that, on the contrary, this proportion markedly declines for the *peasant population proper*, and in general tends to *drop* with the growth of the estates in size, sometimes *very rapidly* indeed, *frequently disappearing almost entirely* in the higher groups (big-peasant holdings) (p. 89).

In the final count, the studies of debt levels in the communities concerned give the following picture on the strength of these data:

Almost everywhere, there is a very considerable debt burden on the holdings of *day labourers*. Nevertheless, this part of the debt is the least dangerous (p. 97)—for this section of the rural population relies mainly on earnings not from the land, and experience shows that, given regular earnings ("to any extent"), day labourers manage to cope

---

* See present edition, Vol. 5, p. 188.—*Ed.*

with their debts (which mostly arise from the purchase of land).

The debt on holdings among *middle* and *big* peasants in the overwhelming majority of the communities studied, even in those which are considered *heavily in debt*, remains within the limits marked out by the size of estates, and such debt is *very small* in a rather large number of communities, to be found in *all* economic areas....

On the other hand, in a considerable number of the communities studied, the indebtedness of the *small-peasant population* is relatively larger and not entirely safe, considering the permissible limit of indebtedness, and in view of the fact that this higher indebtedness should *ultimately* be due largely to definite *external* conditions... (p. 97) (land, climate, land hunger, etc.), the same thing may be assumed for the country's other communities.

This indebtedness is the result mainly of *credit for land* (purchase of land and transfer of estates).

...in purchasing land, particular business-like caution must be exercised—something to which most study reports point—primarily by the *small-*   N.B. peasant population and by the day labourers, ranking next to it (p. 98).

The small peasant *sells* relatively little *for cash*, but he stands particularly in need of money, and

...because of his lack of capital, he is especially hard hit by every murrain, hailstorm, etc.*

Written in June-September 1901

First published in 1932
in *Lenin Miscellany XIX*

Printed from the original

---

* See present edition, Vol. 5, p. 188. —*Ed.*

186

REMARKS ON M. E. SEIGNOURET'S BOOK, *ESSAYS ON SOCIAL AND AGRICULTURAL ECONOMICS*[85]

M. E. Seignouret, Essais d'économie sociale et agricole, Paris 1897. (p. 232 et seq.)—in one of the essays he makes a comparison between small, big and medium wine-growing (*1869*—Gironde Agricultural Society) farms

> ### fictitious example N.B.

I. small	1 ha 60 ares—	works himself and family only
II. medium	10 ha 25 ares—	himself and family and one labourer (ploughman helper) + day labourers
III. big	51 ha 25 ares—	does not work himself. Senior servant 1, ploughmen-servants (3) and wine-growers (6-7) at settled wages

To I: it takes working days: 250 male + 200 female
{ 50 male + 50 female }
{ remain for day labourers }

Value of property	small fr.	medium fr.	big fr.
Vineyards	4,800	24,000	110,000
Other land	900	10,500	55,000
House	1,000	2,000	18,000
Implements and livestock	—	1,000	4,000
	Σ=6,700	Σ=37,500	Σ=187,000

Outlays	small	medium	big
4%	268	1,500	7,480
taxes and prestations	36	190	805
Vine-props	25	120	550
Vine	15	70	350
Manure	40 various expenses	+ 125 shoeing of cattle and re-payment *	525
		33	
Straw	16	fertiliser	400
Transportation	15		
House repairs	15	45	200
Fire insurance	4	10	30
Repair of barrels, etc.	+10 30	+130 60	150
Grape gathering (No. 1) ...	20	250	+2,000 1,170
wages		$+\frac{600}{187}+$	2,450
250 male days at $2._{25}=562$		300 male days $2._{25}=675$	more wages = 1,350 cane rush 210
200 female days at $0._{75}=150$		250 fem. days $0._{75}=187$	% −215
			various = 625
	Σ=1,210 **	Σ=4,182	Σ=18,510

(No. 1) Payment or compensation for several days of work by men or women, purchase of food, estimated at 20 fr. (p. 241).

---

* In this column, Seignouret says: "Veterinary insurance of animals or loss of their value is more considerable than with a small holder".— *Ed.*

** In the listing of outlays for the small farm, there is an omission of interest — 4 fr.— *Ed.*

Receipts small	medium	big
4 barrels of wine at 240=960	$18^1/_2$ barrels at 250=4,625 from land—732 ══════ receipts=5,357	75 barrels at 275=20,625 90 hl. of wheat = 2,250 the rest from land= 655 Σ=23,530

Balance—**250** *Balance* +*1,175 Balance +5,020*

In other words

Receipts= 960−198=462
(498=1,210−562−150)
day labour
50 male days at 2.₂₅=112.₅₀
50 fem. days at 0.₇₅= 37.₅₀

───────
612

and as *senior servant*
(labourer)
he would have had **840** francs.

Written in June-October 1901
First printed in the Fourth
Russian edition
of the *Collected Works*

Printed from the original

FROM GERMAN AGRARIAN STATISTICS[86]

((pp. 1-20))

1882

Number of farms using machinery in *1882*

	Steam ploughs	Sowers *)	Mowers	Steam threshers	Other	Σ
<2	3	4,807	48	4,211	6,509	
2-5	7	4,760	78	10,279	23,221	
5-10	6	6,493	261	16,007	51,822	74,589
10-20	18	9,487	1,232	18,856	86,632	116,225
5-20	24	15,980	1,493	34,863	138,454	190,814
20-100	92	22,975	10,681	17,960	115,172	
100 and >	710	15,320	7,334	8,377	15,011	
	836	63,842	19,634	75,690	298,367	

These are apparently the machines taken on p. 5 of these extracts* for comparison with 1895 (the number of cases of use of five agricultural machines). Here are the 1907 data on these same machines (number of *cases* of use):

1907

<2 ha	131,489;	per 100 farms of group			=	3.8")
2-5	313,641;	"	"	"	"	= 31.2
5-20	968,349;	"	"	"	"	= 90.9
20-100	469,527;	"	"	"	"	=179.1
100 and >	64,098;	"	"	"	"	= 271.9
	Σ=1,947,104					33.9

) A reduction in the number of farms using sowers in 1895 is allegedly due (p. 36) partly to the fact "dass die Landwirte jetzt an Stelle der Säemaschinen die Drillmaschinen in Gebrauch genommen haben".**

* See p. 194.— *Ed.*
** "That farmers now use seed drills instead of ordinary sowers".— *Ed.*

Note the distribution of land under *vegetables* (gärtnerisch benutzt) and under *forest*

Total farms	Their total area	Including vegetable gardens only	%	Land under vegetables ha	Farms with forest	%	Their forests ha	1907 Forests in 1907 ha
Under 2 ha 3,236,367	2,415,914	367,402	11.35	99,034	147,777	4.57	413,033	514,279
2-5 " 1,016,318	4,142,071	1,387	0.14	50,420	222,749	21.92	546,860	654,607
5-20 " 998,804	12,537,660	536	0.05	79,154	400,557	40.10	1,850,277	2,121,024
20-100 " 281,767	13,157,201	69	0.02	57,091	146,997	52.17	2,197,830	2,186,484
100 and > 25,061	11,031,896	5	0.02	43,642	13,754	54.88	2,574,276	2,203,360
5,558,317	43,284,742	369,399	6.65	329,341	931,834	16.76	7,582,276	7,679,754

These data show that there is concentration even in vegetable gardening, but its scale defies definition.

The forests are concentrated on the big farms (>20 ha—4.$_{77}$ million ha out of 7.$_{58}$, that is, over 60%).

Taking *all* the forests (and not only those connected with agriculture) we find that 953,874 farms have 13,725,930 ha of forest and 30,847,317 ha of all the land. Almost half these forests (6,733,044 ha out of 13.$_7$ million, that is, 49.$_{05}$%) is on farms with *1,000 ha and over.*

There are special data on the concentration of truck gardening (*Kunst-und-Handelsgärtnerei* = "hothouse industry", etc.?):

	Number of farms	%		garden	%		total farmland	garden	other farmland
Farms by size of truck gardens				**Their land**			**Average land per farm**		
Under 10 ares	7,780	23.$_{01}$		344	1.$_{46}$		17,313	0.$_{04}$	2.$_2$
10-50 ares	13,724	42.$_{17}$	59.71	3,230	13.$_{70}$	29.30	56,519	0.$_{24}$	4.$_1$
50 ares-1 ha	5,707	17.$_{54}$		3,677	15.$_{60}$		77,945	0.$_{64}$	13.$_6$
1 ha-2 ha	3,397	10.$_{44}$		4,208	17.$_{85}$		162,277	1.$_{24}$	47.$_7$
2 ha-5 ha	1,441	4.$_{43}$	5.94	3,987	16.$_{92}$	51.39	157,934	2.$_{76}$	109.6
5 ha and >	491	1.$_{51}$		8,124	34.$_{47}$		66,119	16.$_{54}$	134.$_7$
Total	32,540	100.$_{00}$		23,570	100.$_{00}$		538,107	0.$_{72}$	16.$_5$

B.

Cf. David, p. 152, 40%—under 20 ares

Weinbaubetriebe:
Farms with vineyards

Size of vineyard	Number of farms	%	vineyards	%	other farmland	vineyards	other
						Area per holder	
Under 10 ares	88,362	25.63	4,962	3.94	221,340	0.05	2.5
10-20 ares	81,936	23.76	11,399	9.04	258,756	0.14	3.1
20-50 ares	103,777	30.09	32,179	25.51	371,357	0.31	3.5
50 ares-1 ha	47,148	13.67	31,407	24.90	201,888	0.66	4.3
1-5 ha	22,542	6.53 } 20.52	35,399	28.07 } 61.51	158,247	1.57	7.0
5 ha and >	1,085	0.32	10,763	8.54	30,599	9.92	28.2
Total	344,850	100.00	126,109	100.00	1,242,187	0.36	3.6

$$\left. \begin{array}{l} 49\%\text{-}13\% \\ 30\%\text{-}26\% \\ 21\%\text{-}61\% \end{array} \right\} {}^{87}$$

Categories by size of *farmland* (landwirtschaftlich benutzte) area:

Under 20 ares	1,134.3	ha
20-50 "	4,476	"
50 ares-1 ha	9,867	"
1-2 ha	20,794	"
2-5 ha	41,158	"
5-20 ha	37,649	"
20-100 ha	8,746	"
100 and >	2,285	"
Σ=126,109		"

vineyards 36,271

Under 1 ha — 15,477 ha } 102,367 =
1-10 — 86,890 " } 87.17%
10-50 — 19,015 "
50 and > — 4,727 } 12.83%

Σ=126,109

In France

			%	%
Under 1	ha 136.2	thousand ha	7.56 } 42.98	
1-10	637.5		35.42	
10-40	467.9		25.98 } 57.02	
40 and >	558.9		31.04	
	1,800.5		100.00	

The (relatively) large percentage of *dependents* in the 100 and > group ($0_{.35}\%$ and $0_{.39}\%$) is due to the fact that *only* administrative personnel and supervisors have been included here among the *dependents* in agriculture (p. 49 ⋆).

Furthermore, in the 100 and > group, the A—C independents are mostly *owners of forests, industrialists* and *traders.*

P. 47 ⋆
1 = A 1 Independents
2 = A 1 Dependents
3 = A—C Dependents+D
4 = A — C Independents
5 = Other occupations

Farms by main occupation %%

	1. Agriculture independents	2. Agriculture dependents	3. Agriculture+industry+trade+local industries and other dependents	4. Veg. gardening+industry+trade+other independents	5. Other occupations	Σ %
Under 2 ha	$17._{43}$	$21._{30}$	$50._{31}$	$22._{53}$	$9._{73}$	100
2- 5	$72._{20}$	$2._{48}$	$8._{63}$	$16._{31}$	$2._{86}$	100
5- 20	$90._{79}$	$0._{21}$	$1._{11}$	$6._{96}$	$1._{14}$	100
20-100	$96._{16}$	$0._{05}$	$0._{17}$	$2._{52}$	$1._{15}$	100
100 and>	$93._{86}$	$0._{35}$	$0._{39}$	$1._{50}$	$4._{25}$	100
Total	$44._{96}$	$12._{90}$	$31._{08}$	$17._{49}$	$6._{47}$	100

2,499,130+(717,037)+1,727,703+971,934+359,550=5,558,317

Data on the percentage of *independent* rural owners with subsidiary employment clearly show the *especially* advantageous position of holders of 100 ha and >(their subsidiary employment=forestry, large-scale industry, agricultural industries, military and civil service, etc.).

Under 2 ha	26.08	% of independent
2- 5	25.54	farmers with sub-
5- 20	15.26	sidiary employment
20-100	8.82	
100 and >	23.54	(P. 48★)
	──────	
	20.10	

Independents		Dependents	
A 2—6)	31,751	A 1)	717,037
B	704,290	A 2—6)	67,605
C 1—10	130,682	B)	790,950
C 11—21	32,994	C)	12,757
C 22	72,217	C)	101,781
	───────	C)	836
	971,934	D)	36,737
			═══════
+	1,727,703		1,727,703
Other occupations	359,550		
	───────		
	3,059,187		
+			
A 1	2,499,130		
	───────		
	5,558,317		

The use of machinery vastly prevails among the large farms (79% and 94%—as against 46% among the medium, and 14%-2% among the small) (p. 36★).

The same is the case with machinery for *dairy* farming (N.B.: p. 39★) (31%-3% among the large, 3%-1% among the medium, and 1%-0.02% among the small).

A comparison with *1882*:

Steam ploughs:		>20 ha farms	Mowers:		Steam threshers:	
			total	>20 ha		
1882:	836	802	19,634	18,015	75,690	26,337
1895:	1,696	1,602	35,084	27,493	259,364	62,120
	+ 860	+ 800	+15,450	+ 9,478	+183,674	+35,783
1907:	2,995	2,873	1907:301,325	155,526	1907:488,867	86,472
	(+ 1,299)	(+1,271)				

The *percentage* increase in the number of farms using machines is naturally highest among the *lower* categories: the small magnitudes grow faster in percentages.

(p. 36* + p. 39*)

	Farms using machines in general per 100 farms	Cases of use of agric. machine per 100 farms	(see p. 2)* 1907	Cases of use of five agricultural machines per 100 farms		
				1882	P. 36*	1895
Under 2 ha	$2._{03}$	$2._{30}$	$3._8$	$0._{50}$	$1._{59}+$	$1._{09}$
2– 5	$13._{81}$	$15._{46}$	$31._2$	$3._{91}$	$11._{87}+$	$7._{96}$
5– 20	$45._{80}$	$56._{04}$	$90._9$	$20._{59}$	$43._{86}+$	$23._{27}$
20–100	$78._{79}$	$128._{46}$	$179._1$	$59._{17}$	$92._{01}+$	$32._{84}$
100 and >	$94._{16}$	$352._{34}$	$271._9$	$187._{07}$	$208._{93}+$	$21._{86}$
Total	$16._{36}$	$22._{36}$	$33._9$	$8._{68}$	$16._{59}+$	$7._{91}$
5-10 ha			$71._1$	$13._5$	$32._9$	
10-20			$122._2$	$31._2$	$60._8$	

(cf. *Deutsche Volkswirtschaft am Schlusse 19. Jahrhunderts,* S. 51)**

Concerning the comparison of the number of farms using various machines in 1882 and 1895, it should be borne in mind that small and medium farms make wide use *only* of threshers, and use very few other machines.

Steam ploughs are being used (being *introduced*) only on the big farms.

Seed drills are used by	18-57%	of big farms	5% of medium farms
Manure spreaders	3-37%	" "	$0._2$% medium
Separators	10-15%	" "	4% medium

---

* See p. 189.—*Ed.*
** *The German National Economy at the End of the 19th Century.*—*Ed.*

Then (*N.B.*) there is only a handful of cases in which farmers use their own *and hired* machinery. Hence, the concentration of machinery should be even greater.

Also note on the concentration of livestock that in 1895 the figures were taken for the *whole* of the Deutsches Reich.

N. B.

	Without land		663 agric. enterpr.			Horned cattle		
						They have 6,905		
Under	0., are		663	"	"	"	"	4
	0.,-2 ares		76,223	"	"	"	"	1,310
	2-5	"	212,331	"	"	"	"	4,986
	5-20	"	748.653	"	"	"	"	47,414
	20-50	"	815,047	"	"	"	"	176,987

On the question of "*latifundia* degeneration" (Bulgakov). Data on farms with 1,000 ha and>:
1895: *572* farms with

802,115 ha cultivated farmland
(2.$_{46}$% against 2.$_{22}$% in 1882)
1,159,674 ha total area (2.$_{68}$% against 2.$_{55}$% in 1882) including
798,435 ha farmland proper
3,655 " vegetable gardens
25 " vineyards
298,589 " forests (25.$_{75}$%)

Waste and unsuitable land—1.$_{72}$% *minimum* of all categories.

1907: 369 farms with *693,656* ha total area including
497,973 ha farmland
2,563 " vegetable gardens
0 " vineyards
145,990 " forests

In [   ] data for 1907.

Livestock kept—in general—by $97._{90}\%$; big cattle—$97._{73}\%$; sheep—$86._{01}\%$; pigs—$90._{73}\%$, etc. Number of livestock: horses: 55,591 [42,502]; horned cattle: 148,678 [120,754]; sheep: 703,813 [376,429]; pigs: 53,543 [59,304]; goats: 175 [134].*

The use of agricultural machinery: in general—*555*. Steam ploughs—81 [120]; sowers—448 [284]; manure spreaders—356; mowers—211 [328]; steam threshers—500 [337]; separators—72 [137]+140. (Σ of *cases* of use of machines=*2,800.*)

Furthermore, of these (farms with 1,000 ha and>) linked with sugar refineries   16

distilleries   228

starch factories   16

flour mills   64

breweries   6

$$\Sigma=330 \quad (33,000 \div 572)=57._{7}\%$$

211 grow beetroot (26,127 ha)
302 grow potatoes for distillation and starch-making
 21 have dairy trade in town (1,822 cows)
204 take part in dairy co-ops (18,273 cows)
        $20,400 \div 572 = 35._{6}\%$
      Of *572—544* are independent landowners by main occupation
(of 544—227 (42%) have no subsidiary employment
            317 (58%) have subsidiary employment)
  9—main occupation: independent foresters, traders and industrialists
 19—other occupations.
    Without leased land—$63._{29}\%$ of these farms
    Leased land=$12._{56}\%$ of their total area.

---

* See present edition, Vol. 5, p. 199.—*Ed.*

		Number of farms using separators			1907	
	Total farms	with manual drive	with mechanical drive	Σ	Total farms	Number of farms using separators
Prussia only _1895: number of farms using separators_						
No land	—	13	11	24	—	—
Under 0.₁ are	262	—	1	1	488	—
0.₁-2 ,,	45,554	7	3	10	69,774	10
2-5 ,,	146,672	28	12	40	206,958	27
5-20 ,,	525,466	147	76	223	560,511	128
20-50 ,,	520,236	326	56	382	515,114	378
50 ares-1 ha	410,944	555	83	638	385,867	1,515
1-2 ,,	398,979	1,415	141	1,556	362,265	7,606
2-3 ,,	233,596	1,618	189	1,807	223,325	11,828
3-4 ,,	163,126	1,747	317	2,064	166,117	14,058
4-5 ,,	126,058	1,697	433	2,130	131,472	14,991
5-10 ,,	314,634	6,137	3,111	9,248	349,352	58,347
10-20 ,,	214,095	6,492	4,565	11,057	233,808	60,777
20-50 ,,	155,539	7,574	4,575	12,149	147,724	47,349
50-100 ,,	32,575	2,279	953	3,232	28,252	8,506
100-200 ,,	8,697	876	306	1,182	8,236	2,330
200-500 ,,	8,050	798	589	1,387	7,871	2,031
500-1,000 ,,	3,110	307	445	752	2,670	899
1,000 and > ,,	533	70	132	202	340	129
Σ	3,308,126	32,086	15,998	48,084	3,400,144	230,909

Number of draught animals (horses+oxen)

	1882	1895	±	Difference
Under 2 ha	62,912	69,366	+	6,454
2-5 "	308,323	302,310	−	6,013
5-20 "	1,437,384	1,430,512	−	6,872
20-100 "	1,168,544	1,155,438	−	13,106
100 and > "	650,450	695,230	+	44,780
Total	3,627,613	3,652,856	+	25,243

Number of farms with draught animals

	1882	1895	±	Difference
Under 2 ha	325,005	306,340	−	18,665
2-5 "	733,967	725,584	−	8,383
5-20 "	894,696	925,103	+	30,407
20-100 "	279,284	275,220	−	4,064
100 and > "	24,845	24,485	−	360 *)
Total	2,257,797	2,256,732	−	

Total draught animals (horses+oxen+cows)

	1882	1895
Under 2 ha	501,212	459,337
2-5 "	1,385,769	1,412,015
5-20 "	2,086,251	2,222,431
20-100 "	1,193,319	1,213,350
100 and > "	650,607	698,129
Total	5,817,158	6,005,262

	% 1882	% 1895	±
Under 2 ha	10.61	9.46	−1.15
2-5 "	74.79	71.39	−3.40
5-20 "	96.56	92.62	−3.94
20-100 "	99.21	97.68	−1.53
100 and > "	99.42	97.70	−1.72
Total	42.79	40.60	−2.19

% of cows in total draught animals

	1882	1895	±
5-20 "	31.1	35.6	+4.5
20-100 "	2.1	4.8	+2.7
100 and > "	0.02	0.4	+0.38

*) Con: number of farms using steam ploughs

	1882	1895
20-100 ha	92	277+185
100 and > ha	710	1,325+615

	% using cows only			% using cows in general*			% using horses and oxen		
	1882	1895		1882	1895		1882	1895	
Under 2 ha	83.74	82.10	−1.64	85.21	83.95	−1.26	14.79	16.05	+1.26
2-5 "	68.29	69.42	+1.13	72.95	74.93	+1.98	27.05	25.07	−1.98
5-20 "	18.49	20.30	+1.81	29.71	34.75	+5.04	70.29	65.25	−5.04
20-100 "	0.25	0.28	+0.03	3.42	6.02	+2.60	96.58	93.98	−2.60
100 and > "	+0.00	0.03	+0.03	0.25	1.40	+1.15	99.75	98.60	−1.15
	41.61	41.82	+0.21	48.18	50.48	+2.30	51.82	49.52	−2.30

* I. e., using cows as well as horses and oxen.—*Ed.*

These data on the use of draught animals show the *greatest worsening of farming conditions*, and a *worsening of the quality of draught animals on the middle-peasant farms.*

Of the 5-20 ha farms, draught animals are incomparably worse in the 5-10 ha group

	Total farms	With draught animals	Including those using cows	only cows	% of total farms with draught animals
5-10)	605,814	548,378	50,619+30,970	+172,094	=31.3% (!!) ⎫ 20.30%
10-20)	392,990	376,725	31,373+20,671	+ 15,704	= 4.2% ⎬
%		90.5			=46.3% (!) ⎫ 34.75%
		95.8	253,683	....	=17.9% ⎬
			67,748	....	(rather 18.0%)

It is the 5-10 ha group that grew most from 1882 to 1895:

	% of farms			% of all area			% of farmland		
	1882	1895		1882	1895		1882	1895	
5-10 ha	10.50	10.90	+0.40	11.90	12.37	+0.47	12.26	13.02	+0.76
10-20 "	7.06	7.07	+0.01	16.70	16.59	−0.11	16.48	16.88	+0.40

Data for 1895 on the use of machinery: [below: for 1907]

1895 Farms using listed machines in 1894/95

	steam ploughs	broad-cast sowers	seed drills	manure spreaders	mowers	steam thresh-ers	other thresh-ers	row cultiva-tors	separators on own farm *) with manual drive	with mechan-ical drive	(My) Σ of last 2 columns
Under 2 ha	4	214	14,735	105	245	35,066	15,951	2,369	5,295	673	5,968
2-5	25	551	13,088	283	600	52,830	66,653	9,224	12,004	1,834	12,477 13,838
5-10	32	1,121	19,083	607	1,528	58,115	138,376	14,169	13,941	5,066	56,955 19,007
10-20	33	2,131	29,668	1,324	5,218	51,233	180,145	16,553	13,769	7,521	85,986 21,290
5-20	65	3,252	48,751	1,931	6,746	109,348	318,521	30,722	27,710	12,587	94,655
20-100	277	12,091	49,852	7,002	19,535	46,778	180,575	22,311	15,256	8,292	23,548
100 and >	1,325	12,565	14,366	9,328	7,958	15,342	15,169	7,911	2,539	1,797	80,137 4,336
Σ	1,696	28,673	140,792	18,649	35,084	259,364	596,869	72,537	62,804	25,183	6,696 87,987

	1895	1907
<2 ha	0.16	0.02
2-5	1.18	0.18
5-20	2.77	1.26
20-100	5.41	2.94
100 and>	10.13	7.17
Σ	1.13	0.45

		1895	1907
Σ cases of use of 5 machines=	5-10)	199,172	464,197
	10-20)	238,760	504,152
		437,932	

[See data on Prussia (separators) above, special *]

*) Note. "Farms using cultivators and separators could not be ascertained with adequate reliability; cf. the introductory text." [N.B. exaggerated for the most part; p. 39★ contains a review of reports for the states on the reasons (and nature) of mistakes in the information on separators. The review suggests that for the *most part* these data on the number of separators are *exaggerated*; these machines were frequently confused with others. Ergo, they could after all be used for a comparison with 1907 with reservations.] The text (p. 38★) says, on the other hand, that the data on these machines are for the most part **wrong**, *with the exception of Prussia* (ibidem). **Still** (p. 39★) the percentage (of the number of farms) has been calculated!

---

* See p. 198.—*Ed.*

P. 60//1898:

	Tobacco-planters	Their approx. tobacco area ha	ha (maximum)
I Under 1 are	61,040		
II 1-10 ares	27,132 } 88,000		600
III 10 ares-1 ha	49,420 } 51,000		2,700
IV >1 ha	1,579		3,300
	139,171	139,000 17,652 ha	

N.B.:

88,000 (63%) — not >3.3 thousand ha (20%)

51,000 (37%) — about 15 thousand ha (80%)

139,000

[N.B. fiscal statistics!]

In view of the extremely rough classification into groups (4 groups only!!) it is impossible to make any, even approximate, distribution between groups III and IV.

It is clear only that 88,000 planters (about 63%) have no more than c. 3,000 ha (not>3,300=20%).

Meanwhile, 51,000 planters (c. 37%) have about 15,000 ha (c. 80%).

Number of farms linked with the following industrial enterprises

1895:

	<2 ha	2-5 ha	5-10 ha	5-20 ha	10-20 ha	20-100 ha	100 ha and>	Σ
(1) Sugar refineries	154	34	(21)	52	(31)	34	76	350
(2) Distilleries	689	388	(465)	1,041	(576)	1,042	2,762	5,922
(3) Starch factories	33	29	(28)	45	(17)	58	274	439
(4) Flour mills	8,847	11,372	(11,754)	20,867	(9,113)	5,316	696	47,098
(5) Breweries	1,641	1,719	(1,905)	3,874	(1,969)	1,823	198	9,255
Total	11,364	13,542		25,879		8,273	4,006	63,064
	% 0.35	% 1.33		% 2.59		% 2.97	% 15.98	% 1.14
Total number of farms	3,236,367	1,016,318		998,804		281,767	25,061	5,558,317
Number of farms linked with the same five types of industrial enterprises in 1907	10,660	20,884		33,514		8,464	5,588	79,110

cf. Bulgakov II, 116 distorted

"And one should not imagine that they (agricultural industries) are linked mainly with the big farms" (Bulgakov II, 116). Caught out!!

!!"The bulk (of the beetroot and potatoes) was raised on the small farms" (ibidem) !!
!! *Here are the data on the farms growing beetroot:*

	farms	% of total	beetroot ha*)	%	Area under beetroot in 1907 ha	Number of farms raising potatoes for distillation and starch-making	% of total farms
Under 2 ha	10,781	0.33	3,781	1.0	9,730	565	0.01
2-5 "	21,413	2.10	12,693	3.2	18,858	947	0.09
5-20 "	47,145	4.72	48,213	12.1	77,582	3,023	0.30
20-100 "	26,643	9.45	97,782	24.7	125,961	4,293	1.52
100 and>"	7,262	28.98	233,820	59.0	281,691	5,195	20.72
Σ=	113,244	2.03	396,289	100	513,822	14,023	0.25

There are no figures for the area under potatoes. The figures on the farms totally refute Bulgakov

*) $\left[\begin{array}{l} \text{5-10 ha—18,752} \\ \text{10-20 ''—29,461} \end{array}\right]$

On the question of the role of small and large farms in dairy farming [Bulgakov II. 117 has distorted this question as well] the data are:

	Total number of farms	% of them with horned cattle	Farms with dairy trade or milk products *in towns*				Farms participating in butter co-ops and amalgamated dairies			
			Number of farms	%	Number of cows on them	Cows per farm	Number of farms	%	Number of cows	Cows per farm
<2 ha	3,236,367	28.59	8,998	0.3	25,028	2.8	10,300	0.3	18,556	1.8
2- 5	1,016,318	92.41	11,049	1.1	30,275	2.7	31,819	3.1	73,156	2.3
5- 20	998,804	97.65	15,344	1.5	70,916	4.6	53,597	5.4	211,236	3.9
20-100	281,767	98.60	5,676	2.0	58,439	10.3	43,561	15.4	418,563	9.6
100 and >	25,061	97.72	863	3.4	31,213	36.1	8,805	35.1	361,435	41.0
	5,558,317	56.52	41,930	0.8	215,871	5.1	148,082	2.7	1,082,946	7.3

	%		%		%		%		%	
Under 2 ha	58.23		21.46		11.59		6.95		1.71	
2- 5	18.28		26.35		14.03		21.49		6.76	
5- 20	17.97		36.59		32.85		36.19		19.51	
20-100	5.07		13.54		27.07 } 41.53		29.42		38.65 } 72.02%	
100 and>	0.45		2.06		14.46		5.95		33.37	
	100		100		100		100		100	

Consequently, the concentration of dairy farming is *enormous*, with *large capitalist farms* producing the *bulk* of the marketed dairy products.

Of course, the concentration of *dairy* farming does not at all have to coincide with the concentration of *cropping*. That is why classification by *area* is not enough. There is also concentration *within* each group by size of farmland:

	Dairy farms under 2 ha			Dairy farms with 2-5 ha			Dairy farms with 5-20 ha			5-10 ha		
	farms	cows	per farm	farms	cows	per farm	farms	cows	per farm	farms	cows	per farm
With 1 cow	4,024	4,024	1	1,862	1,862	1	756	756	1	551	551	1
„ 2 cows	2,924	5,848	2	4,497	8,994	2	2,687	5,374	2	1,946	3,892	2
„ 3 and >	2,050	15,156	7.4	4,690	19,419	4.3	11,901	64,786	5.4	6,103	29,213	4.9
	8,998	25,028	2.8	11,049	30,275	2.7	15,344	70,916	4.6	8,600	33,656	

Unfortunately, only *three* groups are given. Let us also note that the group of under-2-ha dairy farms include farms *without any farmland at all*. These number 471, and they have 5,344 cows (i.e., $11_{.3}$ cows per farm!); of these farms only 6 have one cow each and only 17, two; consequently, the other 448 have 5,304 cows, i.e., $11_{.8}$ **cows** per farm. Clearly, the concentration of dairy farming is *much* greater than the data for area indicate, and special *dairy farmers are emerging within dairy farming*.

More examples: among the same peasants with dairies, etc., in towns, we find the following proportions in the *under-2-ha group*:

from *2 to 5 ares*... 158 farms (38 with 1 cow, 23 with 2 cows)—1,287 cows ($8_{.1}$ *cows* per farm), minus the farms with 1-2 cows, we have 97 farms with 3 and > cows, and a total of 1,203 cows ($12_{.4}$ per farm).

[Similarly among the farms taking part in dairy co-ops, we find in the under-2-ha group 56 farms with 466 cows ($8_{.3}$ per farm) **without land**, and also 52 farms with 574 cows ($11_{.0}$ *per farm*) on *2 to 5 ares*.] In general, if we divide the under-2-ha group of farms into two subgroups: those with under 50 ares, and those with from 50 ares to 2 ha, we find that the *first* subgroup has many more cows *per farm* than the second; a clear indication that *dairy and livestock farming is* **specialising** *away from cropping.*

Farms *under 2 ha* with milk sales in *towns*:

farms:	Including			Their cows	Per farm	Total cows	Farms under 2 ha participating in dairy co-ops		
	with 1 cow	with 2 cows	hence with 3 and >				farms	cows	per farm
0-50 ares	1,944	722	372	850	9,789	11.5	11,255	869	3,514	4
50 ares-2 ha	7,054	3,302	2,552	1,200	5,367	4.5	13,773	9,431	15,042	1
	8,998	4,024	2,924	2,050	15,156	7.4	25,028	10,300	18,556	1.8

Furthermore, as regards the maximum scale of dairy farming concentration in Germany, the subdivisions of the *highest* groups are also of interest. In the category of farms selling milk in towns, we have

500-1,000 ha: 73farms with 4,888 cows. Average: 66 cows
1,000 ha and>:21   ”   ” 1,822 ”   Average: 87 cows

In the category of farms participating in dairy co-ops:

500-1,000 ha: 1,573 farms with 97,403 cows. Average: 62 cows.
1,000 and> ha: 204   ”   ” 18,273   ”   ”   89 cows.

500 and>ha: 1,777   ”   ” 115,676   ”
200-500 ha: 3,708   ”   ” 158,702   ”

200 and>ha: 5,485   ”   ” 274,378   ”   Average: about 50 cows.

Quantity of cattle
auf je *100 ha* landwirtschaftliche benutzter Fläche*:

		(*horned cattle*)	pigs
Germany	1882	$-48._{49}$	$-26._{46}$
	1895	$-52._{44}$	$-41._{71}$
Great Britain	1885	$-50._{37}$	$-18._{20}$
Denmark	1893	$-59._{81}$	$-29._{24}$
Holland	1895	$-74._{02}$	$-31._{76}$
Belgium	1880	$-69._{71}$	$-32._{59}$

See statistics for 1895, text, pp. 60*-65*

Cattle by categories:

	horned cattle			pigs		
	1882	*1895*		*1882*	*1895*	
Under 2 ha	$10._5$	$8._3$	$-2._2$	$24._7$	$25._6$	$+0._9$
2- 5 "	$16._9$	$16._4$	$-0._5$	$17._6$	$17._2$	$-0._4$
5- 20 "	$35._7$	$36._5$	$+0._8$	$31._4$	$31._1$	$-0._3$
20-100 "	$27._0$	27.3	$+0._3$	$20._6$	$19._6$	$-1._0$
100 and>"	$9._9$	$11._5$	$+1._6$	$5._7$	$6._5$	$+0._8$
	100	100		100	100	

But the tremendous decline in commercial *sheep-breeding* (from 1882 to 1895, the number of sheep fell by $8^1/_2$ million ($21._1$-$12._6$), with 7 million of this loss on the >20 ha farms!) makes the position of the large farms less favourable in respect of the total quantity of livestock:

Total cattle (value):

	1882	*1895*	
Under 2 ha	$9._3$	$9._4$	$+0._1$
2- 5 "	$13._1$	$13._5$	$+0._4$
5- 20 "	$33._3$	$34._2$	$+0._9$
20-100 "	$29._5\}44._3$	$28._8\}42._9$	$-0._7$
100 and>"	$14._8$	$14._1$	$-0._7$
	100	100	

Germany 1907 (*without
0-2 ha*) per farm=
$12._8$ ha
2,357,573 farms with
30,103,563 ha of
farmland.
Of them
1,006,277 2- 5 ha
652,798 5-10 ha

* Per 100 ha of cultivated farmland.—*Ed.*

Needless to say, the *proportion* of the big farms here has been understated, for the value of the livestock has been assumed to be the same everywhere, whereas livestock on the big farms is, of course, better, and fetches a higher price, so that the *ratio* between the groups could also be brought out incorrectly (improvement of livestock on the big farms).

But the total number of livestock did, of course, increase *less* on the big farms than on the small.

The big farms lost *most* from the great decline in commercial sheep-breeding, and the *more considerable* (as compared with the small farms) increase in their raising of *horned cattle* and *pigs only made up* some, but not all of their loss.

The following ratio for converting livestock into big cattle is given on p. 54 of the book, *Die deutsche Volkswirtschaft am Schlusse des 19. Jahrhunderts* * :

"*1 c o w = 4 p i g s = 10 s h e e p.*"

If we add that 1 cow = 10 goats, we find:

	1895	1882
1895. horses	3,367,298	3,114,420
horned cattle	17,053,642	15,454,372
sheep ($^1/_{10}$)	1,259,287	2,111,696
pigs ($^1/_4$)	3,390,660	2,107,814
goats ($^1/_{10}$)	310,525	245,253
	25,381,412	23,033,555
	− 23,033,555	
	2,347,857	

---

* *The German National Economy at the End of the 19th Century.—Ed.*

	farms
With 1 cow	6,718— 6,718 cows
" 2 "	10,338—20,676
	17,056—27,394
With 3 and > cows	24,874—188,477÷24,874=7
Total	41,930—215,871[88]

N.B.

N.B.

P. 69★ says that in America "*nicht* mitgezählt (from among the agricultural enterprises) sind dabei alle landwirtschaftlichen Betriebe unter 3 Acres (=1.$_{20}$ ha), sofern sie nicht im Censusjahr wenigstens einen Brutto-Ertrag im Wert von \$500 geliefert haben, was nur bei einigen wenigen in der Nähe von Großstädten gelegenen Gärtnereibetrieben u.d.gl. zutrifft",* which is why, allegedly, no comparison with Germany is *possible*.

---

* "At the same time no account was taken of any under-3-acre farms, which in the census year failed to yield a gross income of at least \$500, this generally being the case only with some few vegetable and similar other farms situated in the vicinity of big towns."—*Ed.*

Statistics of occupations of Germany's agricultural population in 1882 and 1895

(Gainfully employed population)

N.B. Agriculture *proper* [A 1] (thousand)

	Persons for whom agriculture is the *main* occupation:				Persons for whom agriculture is either the main occupation or a side line:		
	1882	1895			1882	1895	
A Independents (owners, leaseholders)	2,253	2,522	+269	A)	4,372	4,682	+310
C 1 (members of their families)	1,935	1,899	−36	C 1)	2,599*	2,960**	+361
I	4,188	4,421	+233 +5.6%		6,971	7,642	+671
C 3 (agricultural labourers with own or leased land) II	866	383	−483 −55.8%	C 3)	876	443	−433
A+C1+C3 =	5,054	4,804	−250		7,847	8,085	+238
B (employees)	47	77	+30 +63.8%	B)	48	78	+30
C 2 (farm-hands, men and women)	1,589	1,719	+130	C 2)	1,872	1,942	+70

C 4 (agricultural labourers without land) III	1,374	1,445	+ 71 +7.7%
	3,010	3,241	+231
Total	8,064	8,045	−19 −0.2%

I	51.9 } 62.7	54.9 } 59.7	+3.0
II	10.8	4.8	−6.0 } −3.0
III	37.3	40.3	+3.0
	100.0	100.0	

C 4)	1,441	1,518	+ 77
	3,361	3,538	+177
	11,208	11,623	+415

Same data *only* for subsidiary employment

	1882	1895	
A)	2,120	2,160	+ 40
C 1)	664	1,061	+397 +59.8%
	2,784	3,221	+437
C 3)	9	60	+51
B)	1	1	± 0
C 2)	283	223	−60
C 4)	67	73	+ 6
	351	297	−54
	3,144	3,578	+434

*) Of them 21.7% for whom agriculture is subsidiary employment
**) " " 35.8% " " " " "

In studying the changes in occupations, the following must be adopted as a basis:

1) agriculture *proper*: A1, and not A1-6 (Mr. Bulgakov, II, 133, takes precisely these A1-6, thereby obtaining a + number of gainfully employed population, i.e., adds to agriculture *truck gardening, forestry* and *fishery*, which is clearly wrong)

2) main occupation, i.e., persons for whom agriculture is the *main* occupation. Data on subsidiary employment are highly indefinite in the sense that they fail to show the importance of the subsidiary employment, etc.

Conclusions:

1. Bulgakov is quite wrong in saying that there is an *increase* in the quantity of agricultural labour. In the main occupation it has *decreased*. We *cannot* judge how far this is offset by an increase of agricultural labour in subsidiary employment.

2. Changes in the distribution of occupations (main occupation) show:

a) a growth of expropriation: the total number of land-*holders* (owners, leaseholders and labourers) has *dropped* by 250,000. The number of owners has increased by 233,000, and the number of labourers with land has *decreased* by 483,000. Consequently, it was the *poorest* section of the farmers that was expropriated.

The number of labourers used the capitalist way *increased* by 231,000 (+7.7%, i.e., a greater increase than that in the number of owners, which was 5.6%).

Consequently, agriculture developed precisely and specifically the *capitalist* way.

[Let us note that it is quite wrong to include working members of farmer families (C 1) among hired *labourers*—as statistics, and Mr. Bulgakov, II, 133 along with it, do. C 1—co-owners, and C 2-C 4—hired labourers. Therefore, when determining the *capitalist* application of labour, C 1 should be added to A.]

As for C 3, it is, of course, an intermediate category: on the one hand, they are hired labourers, and on the other, holders. And it is this intermediate category that has been *eroded* most in 13 years.

Written in June-September 1901,
with additions in 1910

First published in 1938
in *Lenin Miscellany XXXI*

Printed from the original

ANALYSIS OF DATA FROM THE BOOK,
AGRICULTURAL STATISTICS OF FRANCE.
GENERAL RESULTS
OF THE 1892 DECENNIAL INQUIRY[89]

Part I

Pp.
80. Wheat crops (Nord — most of all)
87. Oat crops (idem)
90. *Reduction* in the area under cereals 1862-1882-1892
100. *Growth* of gross output of cereals 1834-1865-1885-1895
105. Especially great *growth* in 1882-1892 (!)
106. Reason: fertilisers, etc.
108. Wheat crops from 1815 to 1895 {Hertz, p. 50}
113. Wheat production (total) from 1831 to 1891 (++
and *114* especially averages for decades
115. Growth in consumption of wheat per head (and for *industrial* purposes *N.B.*)
137. Reduction in the raising of beans, etc.
143. Increase in the raising of *potatoes* et al., and higher yields (p. 144)
158. Growth in the production of *feed* in 1862-1882-1892

	1862	1882	1892		
artificial meadows	2.8	3.1	3.2	mill.	ha
natural meadows	5.0	5.9	6.2	"	"

161. *N.B.* percentage growth of *meadows* from 1862 (N.B.)
163. Sugar plants *prevail* among the industrial crops (52.14%)
164. — Nord leading.

180. Sugar-beet: especially *Nord*
183. Growth in sugar production from 1887 to 1897.
198. Vegetable gardens mostly near big towns (N.B.).
203. Vegetable gardens decline from 1882.
206. Fallow declines.
242. Comparison with 1840 of all types of crops.
257. Nord is especially rich in livestock.
340. Consumption of *meat*.

	Wheat hl per 100 ha total farm-land	output hl	hl per ha
1. Nord	594	3,144,749	25.5
2. Pas-de-Calais	505	3,205,744	20.2
3. Somme	469	2,778,499	21.2
4. Ardennes	297	1,498,899	21.4
5. Oise	436	2,455,795	22.8
6. Aisne	482	3,412,329	23.9
7. Seine-et-Oise	409	2,167,158	23.9
8. Seine	381	103,379	26.8
9. Eure-et-Loire	455	2,579,191	21.5
10. Seine-et-Marne	453	2,570,100	22.5

24

Average for France

230 Σ= 117,499,297   16.4
in the whole of France

France. 1892:   (*Pp. 356-59*)

	% of farms	Average size of farm	Area cultivated	not culti-vated	total
Under 1 ha	39.19	0.59	2.88	1.35	2.67
1-10 "	45.90	4.29	24.07	13.83	22.80
10-40 "	12.48	20.13	30.00	21.96	28.98
40 and > "	2.43 } 14.91	162.21	43.05 } 73.05	62.86	45.55 } 74.53
Σ=100		100	100	100	100

Distribution of Cultivated Area

	Ploughland	Mead-ows	Vineyards	Vegetable gardens	Woods and forests
Under 1 ha	2.78	3.20	7.56	16.26	1.18
1-10 "	25.71	29.27	35.42	34.48	11.96
10-40 "	32.33 } 71.51	36.43	25.98 } 57.02	25.99 } 49.26	18.94
40 and>"	39.18	31.10	31.04	23.27	67.92
Σ=100		100	100	100	100

Number of farms (part 2, pp. 221-25)

	Under 1	1-10	10-40	40 and >
1862	?	2,435,401	636,309	154,167
1882	2,167,667	2,635,030	727,222	142,088
1892	2,235,405	2,617,558	711,118	138,671

Agricultural Machinery (part 2, pp. 256-59)

	Steam machines and traction engines	Ploughs *)	Horse-drawn hoes	Thresh-ers	Seeders	Mowers	Har-vesters	Tedders	Total
1862	2,849	3,206,421	25,846	100,733	10,853	9,442	8,907	5,649	3,367,851
1882	9,288	3,267,187	195,410	211,045	29,391	19,147	16,025	27,364	3,765,569
1892	12,037	3,669,212	251,798	234,380	52,375	38,753	23,432	51,451	4,321,401

Souchon (p. 94) should not be too happy about the number of machines having shown a moderate growth. If
ploughs are not included in the "machines", the growth
turns out to be rather strong (p. 195).

(p. 195)

	(part 2, p. 201)			Quantity of milk	
Growth of production	Cheese '000 kg	and Butter '000 kg	Milch cows	per cow	total mill. hl
1882	114,696	74,851	5,019,670	15	68.206
1892	136,654	132,023	5,407,126	16	77.013

*) double and multi-share

1862 — ?
1882 — 157,719
1892 — 198,506

Vineyards

Part II, p. 89: from 1882, the number of ha has declined, but the number of hl of wine per ha increased from $15._{28}$ to $16._{12}$

Beet (sugar) (part 2, p. 63)

	ha	quintals per ha
1862	136,492	324
1882	240,465	368
1892	271,258	267

Number of farms: (part 1, 363)

	>40 ha	40-100 ha	%	100 ha and >	%
1882	142,000	113,000	$1._{98}$	29,000	$0._{52}$
1892	139,000	106,000	$1._{84}$	33,000	$0._{58}$
	−3,000	−7,000		+4,000	

Increase: <1 ha

		%
1882	2,168,000	$38._{22}$
1892	2,235,000	$39._{21}$

and 5-10 ha

		%
1882	769,000	$13._{56}$
1892	788,000	$13._{82}$

by % of area under potatoes
10 and >%

Basses-Alpes	Loire
Rhône	Vosges
Puy-de-Dôme	Pyrénées-Orientales
Sarthe	Haut-Rhin (Belfort)
Haute Vienne	Seine
Saône-et-Loire	Ariège
Dordogne	Ardèche
Correze	

15

by % of vineyards 5% and >	Indre-et-Loire Gard	
Vaucluse Lot Maine-et-Loire Loire-et-Cher Tarn-et-Garonne Puy-de-Dôme Var Haute-Garonne	Lot-et-Garonne Rhône Pyrénées-Orientales Gironde Gers Aude Hérault	Over 10%

17

% of *area* under *cereals* p. *65*
area (without %!!) under industrial crops: p. 164
vegetable gardens p. *199* without %
vineyards p. *211*, % given
All (?) (not all) crops by %%: p. *238*.
potato % given p. *139*.

Area **under** vineyards in France (Bulgakov, II, 193)

	of total farmland	Total area (ha)		This is area under vineyards c.
Under 1 ha	11%	1,327,253		145,000 ha
1-10 ,,	6%	5,489,200 } 5,755,500 }	=11,244,700	675,000 ha
10-40 ,,	2.7%	14,313,417		386,000 ha
40 and > ,,	3%	22,493,393		675,000 ha
Average	4.5%	49,378,763		1,881,000 ha

according to Note 4 on p. 18
vineyards total 1,800,000 ▮

Departments with the most developed beetroot production: (p. 180)

	ha under beetroot	Area under farms 40 ha and >	Total area under all farms ha	Under potatoes ha		p. 139 % of plough-land
						%
1. Nord	47,903	167,836	511,166	$1/3$	19,714	5.3
Aisne	61,429	392,007	674,860	$>1/2$	13,286	2.6
Pas-de-Calais	37,325	250,733	629,350	$<1/2$	24,279	4.6
Somme	35,096	253,496	591,250	$<1/2$	15,374	3.1
5. Oise	24,828	296,201	529,983	$>1/2$	7,601	1.9
Seine-et-Marne	16,278	339,419	547,800	$>1/2$	10,001	2.4
Seine-et-Oise	9,992	287,377	501,302	$>1/2$	16,802	4.4
8. Ardennes	5,212	271,518	485,290	$>1/2$	17,149	6.0
$\Sigma=$	238,063	2,258,587	4,471,001	$>1/2$	124,206	

Of total ha
271,258

$>1/2$ with average for France
45.55%

(of 1,474,144)

average
for
France
5.72%

(products on
them—64 mill.
quintals out
of 72)

1892 = 271,000 ha

1882 = 240,000 "

1862 = 136,000 "

1840 = 58,000 "

Written in 1901

First printed in the
Fourth Russian edition
of the *Collected Works*

Printed from the original

SUMMARISED DATA ON FARMS IN GERMANY, FRANCE, BELGIUM, BRITAIN, U.S.A. AND DENMARK FROM THE CENSUSES OF THE 1880s AND 1890s[90]

	Farm area	Number of farms 1882	%	Number of farms 1895	%	Area under farms 1882	%	Area under farms 1895	%
Germany	Under 2 ha	3,061,831	58.03	3,236,367	58.23	1,825,938	5.73	1,808,444	5.56
	2- 5	981,407	18.60	1,016,318	18.28	3,190,203	10.01	3,285,984	10.11
	5- 20	926,605	17.56	998,804	17.97	9,158,398	28.74	9,721,875	29.90
	20-100	281,510	5.34	281,767	5.07	9,908,170	31.09	9,869,837	30.35
	>100 ha	24,991	0.47	25,061	0.45	7,786,263	24.43	7,831,801	24.08
	Total:	5,276,344	100	5,558,317	100	31,868,972	100	32,517,941	100
		1882		**1892**		**1882**		**1892**	
France	Under 1 ha	2,167,667	38.22	2,235,405	39.21	1,083,833	2.19	1,327,253	2.68
	1- 5	1,865,878	32.90	1,829,259	32.08	5,597,634	11.29	5,489,200	11.12
	5-10	769,152	13.56	788,299	13.82	5,768,640	11.63	5,755,500	11.65
	10-40	727,222	12.81	711,118	12.47	14,845,650	29.93	14,313,417	28.99
	>40 ha	142,088	2.51	138,671	2.42	22,296,105	44.96	22,493,393	45.56
	Total:	5,672,007	100	5,702,752	100	49,591,862	100	49,378,763	100
		1880		**1895**					
Belgium	Under 2 ha	709,566	78.0	634,353					
	2- 5	109,871	12.1						
	5-20	74,373	8.2						
	20-50	12,186	1.3						
	50 ha and >	3,403	0.4	3,584					
	Total:	909,399	100	829,625					

Britain

	1895	%	1895	%
1-5 acres	117,968	22.7	366,792	1.13
5- 20	149,818	28.8	1,667,647	5.12
20- 50	85,663	16.5	2,864,976	8.79
50- 100	66,625	12.8	4,885,203	15.00
100- 300	81,245	15.6	13,875,914	42.59
300- 500	13,568	2.6	5,113,945	15.70
500-1,000	4,616	0.9	3,001,184	9.21
1,000 and >	603	0.1	801,852	2.46
	520,106	100	32,577,513	100

America

	1880	1895	1880	1895
Under 10 acres	139,241	150,194		
10- 20	254,749	265,550		
20- 50	781,574	902,777		
50- 100	1,032,810	1,121,485		
100- 500	1,695,983	2,008,694		
500-1,000	75,972	84,395		
>1,000	28,578	31,546		
	4,008,907	4,564,641	536,081,835	623,218,619

Denmark

	1885	1895	Tönde Hartkorn * 1885	Tönde Hartkorn- korn aver- age 10 ha 1895
Under 2.5 ha	117,816	125,602	6,226	6,349
2.5-10	67,773	66,591	34,506	34,102
10-40	43,740	44,557	96,685	98,107
40-120	27,938	27,301	172,282	169,195
Over 120 ha	1,953	2,031	55,153	56,822
	259,220	266,082	364,852	364,575

623 (G. Bang) ZN, XIX, 2

Written in June-September 1901
First printed in the Fourth Russian edition
of the *Collected Works*

Printed from the original

* Hartkorn—unit of area for the purposes of land-tax assessment by crop. Tönde—ton.—*Ed.*

FROM THE DUTCH

From the Dutch Agricultural Inquiry of 1890. {Thiels Grohmann's}

Insurance of dead and livestock of labourers

Of them

Number of typical communities		Total number of insured	Owners	Lease-holders	Both simultaneously
30	Labourers	4,551	1,693	2,055	803
44	Small peasants and peasants	4,319	1,700	1,363	1,256
44	Big peasants	2,671	972	1,013	686
30	Labourers	4,551	1,693	2,055	803
45	Small peasants and peasants	4,149	1,553	1,331	1,265
45	Big peasants	2,670	1,022	955	693

---

* Thiel's *Agricultural Yearbooks*, Vol. 22 (1893).— *Ed.*

AGRICULTURAL INQUIRY OF 1890 [91]

Landwirtschaftliche Jahrbücher. B. 22 (1893).*
Article

and peasants by categories and percentages

Of the total number of insured
those insured by items and percentages

Dwellings	%	Household effects	%	Livestock	%	Crops	%
2,020	44.4	1,524	33.5	730	16	720	15.8
3,084	71.4	2,263	52.4	1,712	39.7	1,787	41.4
2,059	77	1,827	68.4	1,472	55.1	1,631	61.0

Head of insured livestock by categories
and percentages

Milch cows	%	Young stock	%	Sheep	%	Fattened pigs	%	He- and she-goats	%
4,062	89.3	1,416	31.1	4,041	88.8	6,028	132.5	3,089	68
17,470	421.0	11,129	268.3	11,441	275.8	12,414	299.2	802	19.3
28,166	1,050.5	22,513	843.2	21,667	811.5	13,562	507.9	349	13

Continued:

				Horses			
Draught oxen	%	Geldings and mares	%			Young horses	%
85	1.9	103	2.3			3	0.0
253	6.0	3,545	85.5			346	8.4
84	3.1	7,159	268.2			1,504	56.3

From the *Dutch* Agricultural Inquiry of 1890

Communities	Categories of farmers	Their land ha	Their total land ha	Their (Farmers') number	Number of those using fertilisers other than manure		Number of those with farm-hands (dinstboden)					Number of those who have labourers										
					Artificial fertilisers	Compost	1	2	3	4	5 and >	y. 1	t. 1	v. 2	t. 2	v. 3	t. 3	v. 4	t. 4	v. >4	t. >4	t.*
Laren	Labourers	1–2	?	359	4	2	27	7	3	—	—	7	40	1	4	1	1	—	—	—	—	1
	Carters	2–10	?	181	1	—	51	18	4	1	—	2	30	1	2	—	1	—	—	—	—	—
	Small peasants	10–20	?	108	—	—	35	29	8	1	1	1	24	—	1	1	2	—	—	—	—	2
	Big "	30–40	?	29	—	—	8	8	4	3	5	—	5	—	1	—	—	—	—	—	—	—
	Total			677	5	2	121	62	19	15	5	10	99	2	8	2	4	—	—	—	—	3
Geldermalsen	Farmers	50 and >	396	6			7	3	—	—	—	1	1	3	—	—	—	—	—	—	—	—
	"	25–50	333	9			10	—	—	—	—	3	3	2	—	—	—	—	—	—	—	—
	"	10–25	272	17			16	4	—	—	—	4	3	—	4	—	—	—	—	—	—	—
	"	1–10	225	78			16	—	—	—	—	5	11	—	3	1	1	—	—	—	—	—
? (voor–Vracht)	Labourers	1 and <	16	24			—	—	—	—	—	1	1	—	1	—	—	—	—	—	—	—
	Carters	1–10	87	15			—	—	—	—	—	—	3	—	—	4	9	—	—	—	—	—
	Total			149			49	7	—	—	—	14	22	5	8	5	10	—	—	—	—	—
Wamel	Big peasants		530	13			17	1	—	—	—	3	3	6	5	—	8	—	—	—	—	—
	Small peasants		406	39			25	—	—	—	—	14	6	4	5	—	5	—	—	—	—	—
	Tobacco-planters		84	38			—	—	—	—	—	4	13	—	—	—	—	—	—	—	—	—
	Labourers		26	65			1	—	—	—	—	—	—	—	—	—	—	—	—	—	—	—
	Total		1,046	155			43	1	—	—	—	21	19	10	10	—	13	—	—	—	—	—
Leeuwen	Big peasants		334	12			12	6	—	—	—	1	1	—	1	—	6	—	—	—	—	—
	Small peasants		360	40			27	—	—	—	—	9	14	1	19	1	2	—	—	—	—	—
	Tobacco-planters		191	90			13	—	—	—	—	—	43	3	4	—	—	—	—	—	—	—
	Labourers		28	37			—	—	—	—	—	—	—	—	—	—	—	—	—	—	—	—
	Total		913	179			52	6	—	—	—	10	58	4	24	1	8	—	—	—	—	—

Voorst	Big peasants	20-70	64	24	1	35	46	13	—	2	16	28	3	13	1	1	—
	Small peasants	10-20	42	4	2	33	5	—	—	2	2	16	—	2	—	—	—
	Carters	5-10	33	4	—	14	—	—	—	—	—	7	—	—	—	—	—
	Labourers	2-6	35	6	—	5	—	—	—	—	—	4	—	—	—	1	—
	Total		174	38	3	87	51	13	—	2	18	55	3	15	1	1	—
Raalte	Labourers	1-2	591	—		2	—	—	—	—	—	—	—	—	—	—	—
	Carters	2-10	18	—	—	12	—	—	—	—	—	—	—	—	—	—	—
	Small peasants	10-20	195	—	2	58	17	1	—	2	—	—	2	—	—	1	—
	Big "	20-60	191	—	10	50	71	11	10	2	2	2	2	—	1	1	1
	Total		995	—	12	122	88	12	10	4	—	2	—	2	1	1	1
Dalfsen	Big peasants		129	2	2	72	17	—	—	2	2	—	2	—	3	—	—
	Peasants		257	2	—	56	1	—	—	1	3	—	1	—	1	—	—
	Small peasants		176	—	1	6	—	—	—	—	1	—	2	—	—	—	—
	Labourers		379	1	—	5	—	—	—	—	3	—	3	—	—	—	—
	Total		941	3	3	139	18	—	—	3	11	1	—	4	—	—	—

This column sometimes gives an amount in excess of the total because I summed up the number of farms keeping 1 (2 and so on) *men* and *women* farm-hands, whereas there are some farms which keep both. Unfortunately, the *total number of farms* using hired labour *is not given.*

This means that what can be summed up is only *either* the number of cases of labour hire *or* the number of hired labourers (by multiplying by 1, by 2, by 3, etc.). (Farming by "labourers" (1-2 ha) appears to be typical for all the communities.)

*) v.=vast (ferme, bleibend)—permanent, t.=tijdelijk (temporel, passager)—temporary, v.=vrouwelijk (weiblich)—female.

The Inquiry is called *Uitkomsten van het Onderzoek naar den Toestand van den Landbouw in Nederland*,* and was carried out by an agrarian commission appointed by royal decree on September 18, 1886. Four big volumes (The Hague, 1890).

Descriptions by communities are on the lines of the Baden and other inquiries (but almost without budgets). Of special interest are the tables on many communities showing the distribution of farms among *labourers*, "carters", small peasants, and big peasants—(in Community No. 1 Laren, labourers usually have 1-2 ha; "carters", 2-10 ha; small peasants, 10-20 ha and big peasants, 30-40 ha; p. 7, Vol. I). Here are some of the heads in the table: 1) Getal =number of farms by size; 2) "state and location of land established with the participation of a definite number of farmers" (the location of the land ... on the farms is advantageous, middling, bad);—"gebruikte Mest" (use of fertilisers: manure, artificial fertilisers—by number of farms).—Number of horses and livestock of all categories.—Number of farms making butter and cheese (Zuivelboeren = peasants engaged in dairy farming). Number of farms using "old" (alt) and "new" methods of "dairy farming". Number of farms keeping "farm-hands" and "labourers" under three heads: 1 each, 2 each, "3 and more each".

N.B.
In the summing up in Vol. IV, there are summaries for some few data relating to the communities, *but there is no a single summary for all the communities together* (a total of 95 communities were studied).

There are different classifications by groups: 1) labourers, small peasants, big peasants; 2) land area 1-5 ha, etc. 60-70 ha, 70 ha and over, etc.; 3) *horses* (Community No. 92: small peasants—with one horse; peasants, with horses; big peasants, with 3 or more horses); 4) vegetable gardeners, tobacco-planters, etc., are singled out.

Written not earlier than April 1902-
not later than April 1903
First published in 1938
in *Lenin Miscellany XXXII*

Printed from the original

* *Results of a Study of the State of Agriculture in the Netherlands.—Ed.*

REMARKS ON E. STUMPFE'S WORKS[92]

A

AN ANALYSIS OF DATA FROM STUMPFE'S ARTICLE, "ON THE COMPETITIVENESS OF SMALL AND MEDIUM LAND HOLDINGS AS COMPARED WITH LARGE LAND HOLDINGS"

Stumpfe."Über die Konkurrenzfähigkeit des kleinen und mittleren Grundbesitzes gegenüber dem Grossgrundbesitze."

> *Thiels Landwirtschaftliche Jahrbücher*, 1896, Band 25.

Stumpfe comes straight to the point by saying that if large units in agriculture were superior to the small, as they are in industry, the law on the settlement of Eastern Prussia would have been a mistake, and *the Social-Democrats would have been right* (p. 58).

According to the 1882 data, medium farms (10-100 ha!!)=12.$_4$% of the farms and 47.$_6$% of the land—hence the "great economic importance of the *peasantry*" (p. 58).

9 farms [Big and medium—kept books. Small farms—"strongest mistrust" p. 59].

Group   I. Glogau district—sandy soil, rye and potatoes.
      "   II. Neumarkt and Breslau districts—good soil, beet crops, very intensive.
      "   III. Liegnitz district—lower intensiveness, weaker root crops.

	Group I	How much land *ha*?	Land classification Class ha	Crop area ha	Crop yield per *Morgen* Centners rye potato	Livestock horses horned cattle
Group I	Big farm {1892-93}	1,033	V— 52 VI—203 VII—198 VIII— 23	476 (1,903 Morgen)	7.5 79	23+170
	Medium farm	21.25	? almost the same land Note *No. 1**￼	19	5 50 oats: 7.5	2+ 9 (+6 pigs)
	Small farm	11.25	V—0.25 VI—3 VII—3.50 VIII—3	10	5.25 ?	1+ 5 (+4 pigs)
Group II	Big farm (1892-93)	471.5	I—212.5 II—120.5 III— 59.0	361³/₄	10.7 beet 146 wheat 12.75	30+180 (111 sheep **)
	Medium farm	51.5	III—25 IV—13 V— 4 VI— 0.75	47.5	8.9 beet 137 wheat 11.3	6+29 (14 pigs)
	Small farm	8.5	II—1 III—4 IV—3.5	7.25	?	0+ 5 (6 pigs)
Group III	Big farm (1893-94)	445	?	?	?	29+173 ⎰324 sheep ⎱ 47 pigs
	Medium farm	40.75	III—11.5 IV—22.25 V— 3.5	37.25	?	7+29 19 pigs
	Small farm	8.0	III—3.60 IV—1.75 V—2.60	7.75	?	?

* See p. 236.— *Ed.*
** A figure denoting the increase of sheep in 1892-93.— *Ed.*

Receipts (marks)		Sundries	Farm economy	*Amount* (Total receipts)
Sales grain	livestock and milk			
38,136 ⌣ +453*	27,289	62,111 distillation	5,500 ("on manor account")	133,489
1,257	758	—	—	2,015
618	491	—	—	1,109
64,476 milk livestock 19,370 sheep 6,455	21,357 beet + potatoes + fruits in general	46,144 1,457 4,767	from lease 2,866 5,852 (=stocks in hand)	*172,714*
5,574 ⌣ +198*	4,050 beet potatoes	767 40	rape and clover 437	*11,066*
1,010	1,095	—	—	*2,105*
34,334 other cereals +seed 12,005	18,201 potatoes receipts from sheepyard	1,145 2,865	from lease 117	68,667
3,584 live- stock milk poultry	potatoes 1,910 780 76 ⌣ +530*	504	clover 153 pigs *1,007*	8,544
632 livestock milk pigs	176 beet 290 120	105 155=cucumbers and cabbage		1,478

(ctd on next page)

* Stumpfe lists these receipts (453, 198 and 530 marks) under the head of "Insgemein" ("General Receipts").—*Ed.*

[ctd]

Outlays

a) taxes b) fire and hail insurance	a) salaries and wages of farm-hands b) day wages	Sundries	purchases a) livestock b) feed c) artificial fertilisers	a) building repairs b) transportation, carriage, mail c) others	total
a) 953 + b) 2,120	7,093 + 19,221	4,939 (farm requirements) 36,593 (distillation)	a) 12,506 + b) 11,175 + c) 11,796	1,617 / 1,162 / 2,223	111,398
34 / 40	a + b { 347	50 (sundries)	90 / — / —	64 (blacksmith, saddle-maker, cartwright)	625
a+b=33	a + b { 90	42 + 30	63 / — / —	29 (blacksmith, etc.)	287
a) {1,374 / 734 b) {1,084	a) 9,933 b) 24,725 c) 4,089 food for farm-hands	sundries: 2,355 purchase of grain=5,423 steam plough= 2,530	a) 14,557 b) 24,552 c) 10,052 sheepyard expenses= 4,962	a) 692 b) 1,111 c) 2,914 6,168=pay to artisans 1,595 heating 1,500 firewood and timber	**120,350**
a + b { 379	a + b { 1,560	purchase of seed 239	a) 554 b) 890 c) 634	general expenses 969 275 black- smith, etc.	**5,500**
a) 30 b) 26		sundries; 65	a) 100 b) 225 c) 26	blacksmith, etc. 31	**503**
a) 1,288 b) 2,238	a) 5,336 b) 13,228 farm-hands and food	2,836 firewood and coal 432 sundries: 661 sheepyard expenses 113	a) 2,070 b) 5,320 c) 775 seeds: 177	a) 375 b) 117 c) 618 2,714 artisans	38,298
a) 159 b) 152	a + b { 1,137 / 218 food for farm-hands	262 artisans old-age insur- ance=34	a) 549 b) 900 c) 305	a) — b) — c) 770 seed 147	4,633
a) 34 b) 22	— general 68		a) 90 b) 110 c) 40	46 blacksmith, etc.	410

Profit (less remuneration to owner)	Net income marks	Same *per ha*		
— 22,091 1,500	20,591	36.72	Big farm	
— 1,390 350 (!!)	1,040	50.12	Medium farm	Group I
— 822 300 (!!)	522	52.20	Small farm	
— 52,364 1,500	50,864	118.40	Big farm	
— 5,566 450	5,116	99.32	Medium farm	Group II
— 1,602 450	1,152	135.56	Small farm	
— 30,369 900	29,469	76.04	Big farm	
— 3,911 450	3,461	84.92	Medium farm	Group III
— 1,068 350	718	89.72	Small farm	

Notes to Tables*

No. 1. "It was impossible to establish the land assessment there (medium farm of Group I), but the ploughland was almost of the same quality as on the landowner's estate (big farm I), possibly slightly more uniform" (p. 63).

About Group I, the author (who was employed on the estate for two years and has a knowledge of the countryside (p. 66)), says:

While, on the strength of the big outlays under the head of feed and artificial fertilisers, and also the large expenditure on wages, and taking account of the sandy soil, the landowner's estate should be characterised as highly intensive and undoubtedly quite up to the modern standard, the very opposite has to be said of the two peasant farms.

"In almost every respect they are still being run on the old lines, and their production should be classified as extensive, in terms of capital and labour. No feed or fertilisers are purchased; on the contrary, considerable quantities of straw and also rye and potatoes, especially, are sold. In consequence, there is insufficient compensation of nutritive substances.... The result is worse crops and a shortage of livestock.

"The stubbornness with which local peasants stick to their old habits is very hard to understand, especially in view of the good example they daily have before them, which could, after all, stimulate them to competition. However, in the recent period, it appears, there, too, a turn for the better is beginning" (p. 61).

Remuneration for the owner's labour is reckoned at 7,500 for the big farm (the usual salary of a manager!!)÷5 (the owner has 5 estates!!)=1,500. For the medium farm—350 ("the usual pay for the country" (p. 64) for managing such a farm!). For the small farm—300 ("a unit!!! half the size of the preceding one" p. 66).

No size of family is given.

Concerning Group II, Stumpfe remarks that the farms are not quite comparable, because the *land is better* on the big farm (the whole farm is a pearl among the Silesian estates (p. 74), according to a professor from Halle!!),

Sic!

!??

* See pp. 232-35.— *Ed.*

and it is *much better* situated; only 1 mile from Breslau (the small farms are much farther away). Still!! small farming is particularly profitable!!!

About the medium farm of Group II: "But the especially great advantage of peasant farming is that it is entirely in the owner's hands, and that work in one's own interest and for one's personal profit will nearly always be of higher value, and more economical and profitable than work in the interest of others" (p. 69).

For the small farm, remuneration is 450 marks=(1) for the owner—350+(2) 100 marks to his wife's parents, who substitute for *hired labour* (pp. 72-73). [I must say that the substitution is cheap!]

The medium farm is said to be on the modern level as well, and is in general quite faultless, not worse than the big farm.

(No detailed data on machinery!!)

The village has an amalgamated dairy, and there is joint use of machinery, joint purchase of fertilisers, etc.

About Group III we learn only that the big farm is excellently run (p. 74) [The entire description of Group III is **highly** superficial (pp. 74-77).]

Stumpfe's conclusion: the smaller the holding, the larger the rent (p. 77).

...There is not the slightest doubt that on peasant farms where the owner takes due care of the progress of operations or takes part in them himself, the work is performed qualitatively and quantitatively very differently from the way it is done on the landowners' estates, with the exception, perhaps, of the quantitative side in case of piecework (p. 78).

...which is why, despite the partially insignificant gross income, the net profit of the small farms was still higher... (p. 78).

Group I. Receipts in marks from (p. 78)

	cropping		livestock farming		general		total	
	total	$1/_4$ per ha	total	$1/_4$ per ha	total	$1/_4$ per ha	total	$1/_4$ per ha
Big farm	63,652	28.37	27,289	12.16	773	0.34	91,715	40.89
Medium "	1,257	15.14	758	9.13	—	—	2,015	24.27
Small "	618	15.46	491	12.27	—	—	1,109	27.72

etc., etc., the same thing all over again.

!! The peasant is also able to slash his expenses in the household budget (p. 80), etc.

!!{ The same: *p. 83* ("living within their means")

He argues that there is a tendency on the part of sugar and distillation enterprises to branch out from agriculture, etc., and that *c o - o p e r a t i v e s* place the advantages also *within reach* of the small farms (p. 85), etc. (cf. *D a v i d* —echoes this).

The *machine* does not play the same part in agriculture (*cf. D a v i d !*).

!! "It is at any rate beyond doubt that the steam plough does not at all reduce production costs" (p. 87) (*cf. Bensing and Fischer*)

The small farmer *d o e s   t h e   r e p a i r s   h i m - s e l f* (!!) (p. 92) and his implements last longer (p. 92)—"This is undoubtedly also connected with the higher earnings of artisans on the big farms (not because the big ones pay more, but because) there are all sorts of discards of tools and wood ends, which would be in use on a small farm *for a long time yet* (!!). In general, this effort to make use even of the smallest objects, this possibility of pressing down

!! to a minimum expenses on the farm's small current requirements is an important characteristic advantage of the small farm..." (p. 92).

The Social-Democrats have also issued their threats in the countryside—there will be strikes as well, and all this is a much greater danger to the big farms (94).

The big farmer's expenses on labour are higher, because he has to feed whole families of labourers, whereas the small farmer for the most part takes on unmarried men, and although the labourer's food is considerably better on the peasant farms and is, consequently, costlier than on the land-owners' estates, we have here, on the other hand, the resultant much higher productivity of labour by young, strong and well-fed labourers, and this fact is of great importance, especially since much

N.B. account has to be taken also of the incentive and educational element in the owner's preliminary and joint work (p. 95).

"All the organisation of the work on the big and small farms, in Silesia at least, is such that *there is decidedly no reason to doubt* the lower cost of labour on the peasant farms" (p. 96). | **N.B.**

—again there is mention of the stimulating influence of the labour of the owner and *his children* (p. 96). The peasants provide better food for the farm-hands.

Disability and old-age insurance is another burden on the big farm: } !

Group II

	total	490	marks	big	farm	$0._{30}$	marks	
		34	"	medium	"	$0._{16}$	"	
		0	"	small	"	0	"	

per **Morgen**

(p. 101) The Social-Democrat gentlemen have blundered badly over agriculture....

p. 102. Sering on settlement ("putting labour at the disposal" of the landowning gentlemen!!),— and "Landed estates are unable to compete with the immense capital which is contained in the *hands* and *feet* of these men [the settlers]" (Sering, quoted p. 102). } !

p. 106: the big farms are mostly superior in *commercial* terms, but the **co-operatives** will help the peasant.

p. 108: the *peasants* usually sell their corn and livestock *less* profitably [but that is said to be balanced out by other things].

"It is not the German Junker that is the enemy of the peasant; the two have, apart from inessential issues which are mostly of internal importance, the same interests and the same adversaries. This is a conviction which has lately been strongly making its way" (p. *113*). | **N.B.**

> There you have Stumpfe!

Written between June 1901 and March 1903

First published in 1938 in *Lenin Miscellany XXXII*

Printed from the original

B

REMARKS ON E. STUMPFE'S BOOK, SMALL HOLDINGS AND GRAIN PRICES

Dr. Emil *Stumpfe* (*Der kleine Grundbesitz und die Getreidepreise.* Leipzig 1897, Band III, Heft 2 der *Staats- und Sozialwissenschaftliche Beiträge* von *Miaskowski**) gives a rather interesting summary of quite extensive budgetary data on small farms (**181** under-10-ha farms) in various parts of Germany, but *only* on their sale and purchase of *farm* products.

Stumpfe argues with David (*Neue Zeit* No. 36, 1894/5), who took the data of the Hessen Inquiry and reckoned the sales and purchases. (Kühn simply reckoned the sales per hectare.) Stumpfe deducts 33-40% as the cost of fabrication from the purchase price, on the plea that you cannot take the price of the purchased product but only the price of the *raw material* which has gone into the making of the product!! This approach (an absurd one) spoils the whole work terribly. (Although this recalculation is done *only when* it gives a different result!)

N.B.:
reckoning
the *sum*
of all types of
pluses
and
minuses

However, I shall go over the cases of this recalculation, which the author always indicates: *No. 19* (Baden, 2-3 ha), the minus becomes a plus, *No. 31* (Baden 2-3 ha), same thing, No. 50, the minus remains, *No. 112,* Württemberg 2-3 ha

---

* Miaskowski's *Contribution to State and Social Science.*

No. 40	still plus	No. 143 still	plus
No. 41	same	No. 151	,,
No. 48	,,	No. 152	,,
No. 49	,,	Nos. 154-161	,,
No. 51	,,	No. 169	,,
No. 60	,,	No. 170	,,
No. 75	,,	No. 171	,,
No. 79	,,	No. 172	,,
No. 94	,,	No. 173	,,
No. 98	,,	No. 174	,,
No. 100	,,	No. 175	,,
No. 111	,,	Nos. 179-181	,,

This means that only in three cases has Stumpfe's absurd approach distorted the state of affairs, by turning an overall minus (excess of purchases over sales) into a plus.

In the vast majority of cases, the result is still an *overall minus*. (Stumpfe calculates three types of plus and minus, separately for cereals (I), livestock products (III) and the rest (II).)

That is why I find that I can take Stumpfe's table with its conclusions on the *pluses and minuses* (sales and purchases, as a sum total), making note of *t h r e e* corrections.

Stumpfe makes a separate comparison of *sales* and *purchases* in I, II and III:

I cereals and pulses	giving tables for
	(1) I
II all other cropping products	(2) I+II
III livestock products	(3) I+II+III

Stumpfe then gives separate results for the states, separating *s o u t h e r n   G e r m a n y* (Baden 60*), Hessen 44, Württemberg 12+Bavaria) from *n o r t h e r n* Germany (Saxony 6+28, Silesia 24, Hannover 7). I take only the results for **southern** and **northern** Germany.

(On 52 of these Stumpfe collected **himself**!!: 24 in Silesia +28 in the Kingdom of Saxony.)

---

*) The number of under-10-ha farms. Stumpfe takes only the under-10-ha farms, putting the over-10-ha farms in a special annexe.

Farms	Southern and northern Germany	Number of farms	Mouths over 14 years	Mouths under 14 years
Under 2 ha	Southern	20	56	50
	Northern	7	19	12
	Σ	27	75	62
$1^1/_2$-2 ha	Southern	5	19	10
	Northern	7	19	12
	Σ	12	38	22
2-3 ha	Southern	21	66	47
	Northern	9	23	19
	Σ	30	89	66
3-4	Southern	10	40	17
	Northern	12	32	24
	Σ	22	72	41
4-6	Southern	26	103	55
	Northern	(25)	(74)	(49)
	Σ	51	177	104
6-8	Southern	23	102	31
	Northern	2	7	4
	Σ	25	109	35
8-10 ha	Southern	19	88	39
	Northern	7	25	18
	Σ	26	113	57

In general, Stumpfe's book is a grossly *biased defence* of taxes.

In his opening pages, Stumpfe analyses the question of the effect corn prices have on those of other farm products, insisting (correctly) on the tremendous and all-decisive importance of *corn* prices.

On how many farms sales greater (+) or purchases greater (−)		Total farmland	Per ha		Adults+ children (2 children= 1 adult)
+	**−**		adults	children	
6	14	$24._{54}$	$2._{28}$	2	$3._{30}$
7	—	$13._{06}$	$1._{45}$	$0._{9}$	$1._{9}$
13	14				
3	2	$8._{73}$	$2._{2}$	$1._{1}$	$2._{7}$
7	—	$13._{06}$	$1._{45}$	$0._{9}$	$1._{9}$
10	2				
16*)	5	$52._{83}$	$1._{25}$	$0._{89}$	$1._{69}$
9	—	$24._{42}$	$0._{94}$	$0._{77}$	$1._{32}$
25*)	5				
9	1	$37._{20}$	$1._{07}$	$0._{45}$	$1._{29}$
12	—	$42._{93}$	$0._{74}$	$0._{55}$	$1._{01}$
21	1				
26	—	$131._{69}$	$0._{78}$	$0._{41}$	$0._{98}$
25		$120._{75}$	$0._{61}$	$0._{40}$	$0._{81}$
51	—				
22	1	$156._{99}$	$0._{65}$	$0._{20}$	$0._{75}$
2	—	$14._{50}$	$0._{48}$	$0._{27}$	$0._{61}$
24	1				
19	—	$168._{88}$	$0._{52}$	$0._{23}$	$0._{63}$
7	≡	$60._{75}$	$0._{41}$	$0._{28}$	$0._{55}$
26	—				

---

*) Stumpfe has 19 and 2, and Σ of 28 and 2.

The area under cereals in Germany in 1878-52.$_{59}$% of total farmland

1883-53.$_{46}$%
1893-54.$_{37}$%

> The extension of the area under other cereals (and of livestock farming correspondingly) is rapidly leading to their respective overproduction, which ·tends again to even out prices (cf. Marx on Smith. But Stumpfe does not quote Marx and does not apply the theory of rent to the question)

Stumpfe's italics

> "Thus, there is good ground for the thesis that there can be no prolonged disproportions in the rent yielded by the several crops per area unit, and that a levelling off must follow sooner or later" (p. 15).

Stumpfe also analyses the prices of livestock products, arguing along the same lines.

Stumpfe polemises with Reichschancellor Hohenlohe, who said on March 29, 1895, that only the over-12-ha farms wanted higher prices, that is, only 4 million out of the 19 million agricultural population, reckoning 3.5 persons per farm. Stumpfe makes roughly the following estimation of the agricultural population (1882 data) (p. 40)

			millions of agricultural population
Parcel farms under	2 ha		$0._6 \times 3._5 = 2._1$ million
Small "	2 to	5 ha	$0._{99} \times 4._5 = 4._4$ "
Medium "	5 to	20 ha	$0._{96} \times 7 = 6._7$ "
Big-peasant	20 to	100 ha	$0._{29} \times 13 = 3._7$ "
Big "	over	100 ha	$0._{025} \times 90 = 2._2$ "

19.$_1$ million

Stumpfe believes that there is no·more than 0.6 million agricultural population on the *3* millions of under-2-ha farms. "The owners of under-1-ha parcel farms... are mostly craftsmen, small industrialists, factory workers, etc., consequently, anything but peasants or independent farm owners" (p. 39).

Sic! Stumpfe says something quite different on another occasion!

3.5 persons per farm with less than 2 ha, for "after all, grown up children mostly go into employment right away" (p. 40).

Here are the statistics of family size, according to Stumpfe's data:

The number per farm was (p. 82)

Groups	Number of farms	Adults	Children	Total
ha: 0- $1\frac{1}{2}$	15	2.5	2	4.5
$1\frac{1}{2}$- 2	12	3.16	2.6	5.76
2- 3	30	3	2.2	5.2
3- 4	22	3.27	1.86	5.1
4- 6	49	3.6	2.1	5.7
6- 8	25	4.3	1.4	5.7
8-10	26	4.34	2.2	6.5
10-20	37	6	2	8
20 and over	12	8.75	2.1	10.85

And Stumpfe concluded: the "average" for the 5 to 20 ha group will be precisely about 7, for the 20 to 100 ha, about 13, if it is about 11 for the 20 to 30 ha group.

(A funny character! he's forgotten all about *hired* labour!!)

(Stumpfe's distribution of agricultural population is of some interest for the picture of *hired labour*.)

He says that all peasants—including the labourers on the big farms!!—all want higher corn prices. } !

Stumpfe himself suspects that the data he has collected (for Silesia, etc., see above*) will appear unlikely (p. 50),

* See p. 241.—*Ed.*

and so he defends himself in advance: why is it that, according to his data, the conditions in *northern* Germany are much better, when *southern* Germany is regarded as being more civilised?

And Stumpfe attacks *southern* Germany "...incredible fragmentation of holdings" (p. 48)—10-12-20 parcels per hectare!—hence "the intensified supply of farms with labour everywhere" (p. 49)—in general the population in the south is much more static (p. 49)—see, he says, the *Bavarian* Inquiry of *1895*, the new one!—a prevalence of three-field farming (Bavaria; inquiry)—"great backwardness of the whole economy" (p. 51), very frequently the system of compulsory crop rotation still *in evidence*, furthermore "fragmentation and stripping of farmlands prevent or hamper any kind of melioration" (p. 52), frequently make almost impossible the introduction and use of

ha-ha!! these new remarkably improved agricultural implements (p. 52), for example, out of 24 *Bavarian* communities only 4 use the seed drill. "The advantages of farming with the use of the seed drill are

ha-ha! so well-known and incontestable" (p. 52) etc., and other machines are rare too, old ploughs are "often of the most primitive form" (p. 52), rollers

! are unknown, etc.... This backwardness in machine and technical equipment....

ha-ha! The very same Stumpfe who, on another occasion, deprecates the importance of machinery—when he defends the small farms!

—not a single centrifuge (p. 53) in the places described by the *South-German* inquiries. "This technical backwardness is crowned" with reports from Christazhofen and Ingerkingen of threshing by horses (on horseback)—"such is the antediluvian method of husking grain"—Stumpfe exclaims.

...Fertilising methods leave very much to be desired (53), etc.

—meanwhile, quotations from *The Condition of the Peasants, in favour* of small farms in the north (pp. 54-55). I must say these quotations look very much like Bulgakov's!*Make a comparison!*

In Silesia, peasants have seed drills, manure spreaders, etc., etc. (p. 55), the crop rotation system prevails, rollers (pp. 56-57).

"One need only list these very important (sic!) implements to discover the extremely different state of farming in southern and northern Germany" (p. 57). Then "there is the usual under-estimation" (p. 58)—in the north, the *good example*" (p. 59) set by the landowners (sic!), the "teachers" of the peasants (!), a model, "pioneers in farming" (p. 59)! As for the South, it more or less completely lacks big farms (p. 60).

!!

Oh,
Herr
Stumpfe!!

Written not earlier
than April 1902-
not later than April 1903

First published in 1938
in *Lenin Miscellany XXXII*

Printed from the original

REMARKS ON G. FISCHER'S WORK,
THE SOCIAL IMPORTANCE
OF MACHINERY IN AGRICULTURE[93]

Gustav Fischer. Die sociale Bedeutung der Maschinen in der Landwirtschaft. Leipzig 1902. (Schmollers *Forschungen,* XX. Band, 5. Heft.)

> The introduction quotes the writings of Social-Democrats on small farming. Among them *Sering, The Agrarian Question and Socialism* (con Kautsky), Schmoller's *Jahrbuch für Gesetzgebung, Verwaltung und Volkswirtschaft.** Band 23, 4. Heft.

Sering has already said that agriculture is unlike industry, especially in the matter of machinery.

Chapter I. "The Cost of Machine Labour and the Limits of Its Profitability".

"It was on the big farms that conditions first existed for the use of agricultural machinery" (p. 4)—initially even the manufacturers were concerned only with machinery for the big farms. Now they supply machines for the small ones as well.

The author wants to discover the limits for these new machines according to the new data.

| Here is the result of his calculations (pp. 24-25) | Kautsky on p. 94 of his *Agrarian Question* says, that, according to Kraft, the limits of full use are α) *1,000* ha; and β) *70* ha (p. 5) |

---

* *Yearbook for Legislation, Administration and National Economy.—Ed.*

Type of machine	Limit of economic usefulness ha	Cost of machine labour under full use *) $marks$ $per\ ha$	manual labour $marks$ $per\ ha$	*) This is full use ha	AA see below *
(α) Steam plough (20 h.p.)	192	34	$51._{20}$	500	
Steam plough (12 h.p.)	121	$33._8$	$42._7$	250	
Broadcast sower	—	$0._{88}$	$0._{44}$	>360	ha
Seed drill ($3._{766}$ m)	$21._6$	$2._{56}$	$6._{04}$	360	17
(β) Seed drill ($1._{88}$ m)	$13._6$	$3._{48}$	$6._{04}$	160	$8._8$
Manure spreader	—	$1._{12}$	$0._{55}$	>280	
Cultivator ($3._{766}$ m)	4	$2._{13}$	16	180	$3._7$
Cultivator ($2._0$ m)	$1._2$	$2._{06}$	16	75	$1._1$
One-row cultivator	$0._{27}$	$4._2$	16	$22._5$	$0._{23}$
Hay mower	$13._4$ (or $6._7$)	$3._5$	5	58	$3._4$
Reaper with self-throwing	$9._5$	$6._9$	11	76	$7._1$
(β) Reaper-binder	—	$11._{25}$	$11>$	76	$24._3$
Reaper with manual rake	$8._1$	$7._0$	11	68	$5._1$
Tedder	$2._9$ (or $1._5$)	$6._3$	$12._5$	35	$0._{95}$
Horse-drawn rake with seat	$13._8$ (or $6._9$)	1	$1._6$	90	$8._0(4)$
ditto without seat	$9._{45}$ (or $4._{73}$)	$1._2$	$1._6$	$67._5$	$3._9(1._9)$

The author calculates his limits of usefulness as follows: he takes performance per day (5 ha per steam plough), determines the price of manual (resp. with the use of a team) labour in that time, and calculates the *minimum number of days* of machine work required for the price to be *t h e s a m e*. This minimum (in terms of ha) is his limit.

(Hence, that is the *minimum* limit where the machine is still *not* cheaper than manual labour.)

The author frequently quotes Bensing (countering his statements, for instance, with that of Rimpau, to the effect that a horse-drawn plough works as well as the steam plough, provided it ploughs to the same depth: p. 8). ‖ !

Potato planters are still not feasible (the potatoes vary in size, and weigh 8 centners to $^1/_4$ ha, while

---

* See p. 250.— *Ed.*

	seed-grain comes to less than 1 centner). But one recent invention is a hole potato-planter which makes regular holes, helps to furrow and hoe, although the potato is inserted by hand (p. 11).
N.B.	Saves labour, and the *income increase* is reckoned at 5% (p. 12).

There has been no success so far in making *reasonably* good potato and beet lifters.

Chapter II. "The Possibilities of Using Machinery on Small Farms"   (p. 27)

	Cereals		Sugar-beet	Meadow hay
Reduction of costs *per hectare*	17.$_{52}$ marks:	52 cent-ners (crop)	30.$_{78}$	8.$_{30}$
As compared with manual labour *per centner*	0.$_{34}$ marks per centner		0.$_{05}$ (640 cent-ners)	(:80) 0.$_{10}$ (cent-ners)

Consequently, the cost reduction is *not large*. This, he says, is against *Bensing*, for he *fails to debit to the machine costs the cost of the teams* (p. 28)—"not quite right".

Considering that the cost of the teams does not apply to some machines set into motion by draught animals (for the cattle is there anyway, and is not fully used), we find the limits of economic usefulness still further reduced (p. 28) (see, AA in table *).

> "It goes without saying that farmers whose hold-ing hardly, if at all, allows them to use machinery because of its size, are at a disadvantage, as com-pared with those who attain the highest possible use of machinery or are close to it, in view of the fact that the per-hectare cost of using machinery does

---

* See p. 249.— *Ed.*

not fall in proportion to the time of use, but at first
drops sharply and then slower and slower" (p. 29).
For instance, a mower costs 5.94 Mk per ha for 8 days

" " 5.24 " per ha for 20 days

"...70 pfennigs per hectare is, of course, not much" ‖ ha-ha!
(p. 30).

Moreover, the "really" *lower* % of machine depreciation
should be allowed the small farmer: he takes more care.
See, he says, Auhagen,* Stumpfe,** *Herkner* (!) *(The
Labour Problem*, Berlin, 1897, p. 226).

The *small* farmer can make *co-operative* use of machinery:
hire of machinery (thresher very often, p. 31) (it is also
most convenient with regard to the steam plough, p. 32)
(although the *small* one cannot use the steam plough even
on hire: p. 33, his fields are not long enough).

The hiring out of machinery ... is very com- ‖ N.B.
mon (p. 33). "The big landowner lets ... ‖ cf.
his small neighbours ... use his seed drill on ‖ Klawki!!
hire".... ‖ N.B.

The *co-operatives* are developed to a greater
extent than the statistics show. In 1890, Bavaria had 282
machine (thresher) co-operatives. But very many farms
pool machines privately.

Chapter III. "*The Importance of Machinery for the Labour
Problem*".

Machines are frequently introduced, even when they
are *more expensive* (seeders, etc.) because of the *labour
shortage*. Can the machines help when there is a shortage
of labour?

Most say: yes (p. 37). *Von der Holtz is sceptical* (they tend
to increase winter unemployment, etc.).

Here is the author's calculation of the labour saving
through machinery: (p. 39)

---

* See p. 130.— *Ed.*
** See p. 238.— *Ed.*

	ha worked per day	this requires		for equal performance by manual labour		saving in labour through machinery	
		men	youngsters or women	man-days	youngster- or woman-days	man-days	youngster- or woman-days
Broadcast sower	9	1	—	2	—	1	—
Seed drill $3._{77}$ m	9	4	—	2	—	—2	—
Seed drill $1._{88}$ m	4	3	—	1	—	—2	—
Manure spreader	10	1	1	$2._2$	—	$1._2$	—1
Cultivator $3._7$ m	9	3	—	—	120	—3	120
Cultivator c. $2._{00}$ m	$3._{75}$	1	1	—	50	—1	49
Hay mower	$3._2$	1	—	8	—	7	—
Reaper with self-throwing	$3._8$	1	1	8	—	7	—1
Reaper-binder	$3._8$	1	1	8	8	7	7
Reaper with manual rake	$3._4$	2	—	7	—	5	—
Beet lifter	$1._7$	2	9	—	13	—2	4
Tedder	7	1	—	—	14	—1	14
Horse-drawn rake with seat	6	1	—	—	$4._8$	—1	$4._8$
ditto without seat	$4._5$	1	—	—	$3._6$	—1	$3._6$

"With the exception of the seed drill, which is used in the spring and autumn seasons, and the manure spreader, which requires a roughly similar application of labour, all the machines, therefore, show a saving of labour, as compared with manual operations" (p. 38).

especially the cultivator (very important)
and the reaper—which is why it is used with the binder, even if it is more expensive (there are few hands during the harvesting!). The same goes for the steam plough.

"All the above-mentioned machines have the advantage of making the farmer more independent of the demand for labour. He can oppose the excessive wage demands, at whose mercy he would otherwise have been placed without being able to offer any resistance, and, what is much more important, he can perform operations for which he would otherwise not have found any labour at all" (p. 40).

The manure spreader works better, more evenly, than the unskilled labourer.

The seed drill *helps to save* seed stock.

"The milk separator is also one of those machines which yield a qualitative performance coefficient unattainable under manual labour" (p. 41). In 1900, Germany had 2,841 dairy co-operatives.

The 1895 statistics show furthermore that it was the peasant farms that led in the absolute number of participants in them, whereas the large farms, at any rate, are still very far ahead in proportion to their total.

"Participation in dairy co-operatives or amalgamated dairies"

(p. 41)

	farms	percentage of each group
under 2 ha	10,300	0.3
2 to 5 ha	31,819	3.1
5 to 20 ha	53,597	5.4
20 to 100 ha	43,561	15.4
100 ha and over	8,805	35.1

"However, the relatively insignificant participation of the small farms in dairy co-operatives is partly due to the fact that they are mostly situated on the immediate outskirts of towns and sell more of their milk than large farms to urban buyers, without processing it" (p. 41). **!?**

The thresher leads to a substitution of *free labourers* for indentured day labourers who do the threshing (p. 42) (cf. Max Weber). Payment in kind is supplanted by payment *in cash*—"as a result of which even the smaller holder becomes more depend-

N.B. ent on ready cash than ever before.... Such are
     the socially unfavourable consequences of the
     introduction of the thresher" (p. 42).

Agricultural machines demand more intelligent workers
(as compared to the industrial??)....

Chapter IV. "*Electricity in Agriculture*".

The author finds the expectations of Kautsky and Pringsheim exaggerated, gives two examples of *actual* use of
electricity (on royal estates in 1895-96), contests one calculation, obtaining a higher cost of production instead of the
lower one (inferred by the author of a report on the royal
estates) and says that "electrification of farming is not yet
able to yield any considerable reduction of costs, although
it does provide all sorts of conveniences and comforts for
the performance of operations" (p. 51).

Is it cheaper for the big farms? Not much, for the motors
in agriculture are all too small.

The substitution of electric motors for field machines
(Pringsheim) is a realm of speculation.

Finale:

"The production of electric power will remain cheapest
at the big central stations, with which the small farmer
can just as easily obtain a connection as the big one. The
advantages secured by the latter from a somewhat better use
of motors and any possible small rebate that he may be
given will be insignificant. That is why any shift of social
relations to the detriment of small farming should not be
expected" (p. 54).

Chapter V. "*Machinery in North-American Agriculture*"

The limit of the economic usefulness of machines is (must
be) even lower, because wages are higher.

There is the most rapid growth of *m e d i u m* farms
(George *K. Holmes* on the progress of American agriculture
in *Yearbook of the United States Department of Agriculture*,
1899).

320 acres=128 ha is taken to be a medium farm,
because the whole of farming is more extensive: p. 58.

There is nowhere any swallowing up of the small by the big (p. 62), machines cannot give the big farms the edge they do in industry (p. 63).

The farms will be increasingly smaller with the growth of intensivor ess.

The small farms have the same machines as the big ones.

Example: 300-320 acres   1 plough   1 disc   1 seed
                             with seat   harrow   drill
and 6,500 acres   22   "   32   "   10   "

etc. (Fischer sees no advantages from diversified machinery!)

"Thus, large-scale farming there does not obtain any advantages from the use of machinery" (p. 59)? |?

The small holder is more careful, more painstaking, he saves the $100 which the big farmer pays to his labourers as a bonus for the best cultivated lots, etc. (p. 59). |!!

The large wheat farms, with very extensive farming, are to be found only in North Dakota.

Greater use? (156 acres per binder in one case, and 65 acres, on a small farm), but that is "only little" (p. 61). |?!

Final conclusions (pp. 64-66)

...the machines are used mostly because of the labour shortage; more and more are being introduced on the small farms

% increase from 1882 to 1895 (p. 65)

	Steam ploughs	Seed drills	Reapers	Steam threshers	Other threshers
under 2 ha	33	211	410	733	145
2- 5 ha	257	187	669	414	187
5- 20 ha	171	226	352	214	130
20-100 ha	201	169	83	160	57
over 100 ha	87	76	9	83	1

ha-ha! | "This comparison shows that the percentage increase in the number of farms using machinery among the small farms ... is considerably greater than among the big ones...."

...These figures best of all prove (!?) that machinery in agriculture is not at all a domain of the big farms (p. 66), for there is a rapid growth in the understanding of its importance and the possi-

Sic! | bility of its use even on the parcel farms.

Written in 1902

First printed in the
Fourth Russian edition
of the *Collected Works*

Printed from the original

NOTE ON P. TUROT'S BOOK, *AGRICULTURAL INQUIRY* 1866-1870 [94]

Paul *Turot, Enquête agricole de 1866-1870, resumée par...* Paris 1877.

The Inquiry consisted of 33 volumes, which were not on sale. The first 4 volumes gave a general summary of which a résumé was made by Mr. Turot. Although his work has been "crowned" with a gold medal, it is on the lowest possible level. It is not a summary of the Inquiry data, but a summary of the "data on the decisions" of the central commission in charge of the Inquiry. And its decisions are such, for instance, as that machinery should be imported duty-free, that inventors must be rewarded (pp. 84-87: no data at all on the use of machinery!!),—that labour cards should not be introduced (pp. 81-84), etc. The rest of the chapters can be judged from the content of this "Chapter III. Wages. Piece Work" (content—nil).

No wonder its pages remain uncut (at the British Museum).

Written not earlier than April 1902-
not later than April 1903

First printed in the
Fourth Russian edition
of the *Collected Works*

Printed from the original

258

REMARKS ON H. BAUDRILLART'S BOOK,
THE AGRICULTURAL POPULATION
OF FRANCE.
PART III.
THE POPULATION OF THE SOUTH[95]

Baudrillart (Henri), *Les populations agricoles de la France.*
3-me série. *Les populations du Midi.* Paris 1893.

Only some small notes can be made while looking through this book, which is written in the same style and spirit as the earlier volumes.

Les bouches-du-Rhône. The city of Marseilles. Very superficial description of agriculture. Note is made of the common practice of *share-cropping* (métayer, *méger*). Among others: lé comte de Tourdonnet, *Étude sur le métayage en France** (without any indication of time or place).

For example. "...The peasant farmers, who share the status of small holder and rural labourer, are fairly well off"—for instance, outlays are 510 francs (husband+ wife), receipts=850 francs. "Consequently, a household is able (!!!) to live in a comfortable (!!) manner, having 500 francs and making savings" (!!). That's Baudrillart all over!

Pp. 267-69 on "the solidarity" of agriculture (at Hérault) and industry (cloth manufacture)—for instance, the factory at Villeneuvette (100 men+300 women). The same line of employers since 1792 (Maistre), the workers are at the factory all their lives, "Christian" spirit in the master's

* Count de Tourdonnet, *An Essay on Share-cropping in France.*— *Ed.*

attitude to his workers. The owner of the factory "runs" it through "a small commune, with the aid of the municipal council which has sprung from its midst [of the factory management]", etc. Such is Baudrillart! Volume Three especially appears to be incredibly dry, monotonous, matter-of-fact and *absolutely empty*. It is quite impossible and unnecessary to read the meanderings of this "titled old man", and only "critics" of the Bulgakov stripe can take such a writer seriously.

Written not earlier than 1901-
not later than January 1903

First published in 1938   Printed from the original
in *Lenin Miscellany XXXII*

REMARKS ON E. COULET'S BOOK

Élie Coulet, Le mouvement syndical et coopératif dans l'agriculture française. La fédération agricole (thèse pour le doctorat). Montpellier 1898.*

[Contains a bibliography; there are indications of rural labourers being expelled by the syndicates; not a Socialist but *appears* to be a "Katheder", judging from a bird's-eye view. Rouanet's source. There seems to be some pretty interesting data there.]

Written before February 10 (23), 1903

First published in 1938   Printed from the original
in *Lenin Miscellany XXXII*

---

* *The Syndicalist and Co-operative Movement in French Agriculture.* The Agricultural Federation. (Doctoral thesis.)—*Ed.*

REMARKS ON G. ROUANET'S ARTICLE, "ON THE DANGER AND THE FUTURE OF AGRICULTURAL SYNDICATES"

*Revue socialiste**)   (Vol.   29)   *February*   1899
(pp. 219-37)

(Revue économique. "Du danger et de l'avenir des syndicats agricoles" par *M. Gustave Rouanet.*)

quotes Rocquigny, p. 42 in *Les syndicats agricoles*[96]

G. Rouanet's article was written on *Élie Coulet*'s book.[97] G. Rouanet slights the "syndicates" as the handiwork of the "agrarian party"—they consist *mainly* of large and middle landowners; their efforts in favour of the *labourers are ridiculously insignificant*; their aim: a landowners' trust, an association for marketing farm produce; their political programme: the interests of the big landowners, who are leading all this movement, carrying the small farmers and labourers with them, and whose goal is to establish complete domination of the state by the big landowners' party.

Like all trusts, the syndicates are working assiduously in favour of socialism.

Out of *1,391* syndicates with 438,596 members (1897) were established:

N.B.‖   "societies against accidents at work: *one*; orphanages—*one*; employment agencies and offices: *thirteen*; courts of arbitration, reconciliation chambers: *three*; societies for aid to manual labour: *two*;
N.B.‖   aid in kind (gifts of things to children)—*one*; aid

---

*) Manager: M. Rodolphe Simon. (78 Passage Choiseul, Paris) 1 franc an issue. Free: contents since 1885.

in supply of implements (service for the hire of tools and farming implements): *two*" (p. 225) and Rouanet ridicules Deschanel.[98]

Rouanet repeatedly quotes Rocquigny, mentioning by the way that his démocratie rurale = 300,000 large land-owners!! (p. 231).

Written before February 10 (23), 1903

First published in 1938 in *Lenin Miscellany XXXII*

Printed from the original

ANALYSIS OF DATA FROM NOSSIG'S BOOK[99]

Nossig (*Revision des Sozialismus.* Band II. *Die moderne Agrarfrage**) gives the following interesting data on restoring soil fertility.

Grandeau (manager of the Station agronomique de l'Est) believes that there are 25 million ha of farmland in *France*

	taken from the land annually: metric tons	given same *thousands*	
Nitrogen	613,000	285 ⎤	fertilisers produced
Phosphoric acid	298,000	147 ⎪	by 49 million head
Potash	827,000	549 ⎬	of cattle (according
	—	+ ⎦	to Tisserand)

⎧ That is the total ⎫
⎨ cattle, but not all ⎬
⎩ should be reckoned in
   terms of fertiliser! ⎭

i.e., *the deficit averages about 50 per cent!* (p. 101)

And the artificial fertilisers do not, by a long shot, make up for all that is taken from the soil.

In Britain, an average of $1._9$ million centners of phosphoric acid is taken from the soil, while *guano* and *bone fertiliser* cover only *one-half* (p. 109).

Thus, only the private owners, and not the land, have benefited from intensive agriculture with the use of artificial fertilisers (p. 109).

It is now being recognised that mineral and artificial fertilisers alone are not enough.

60,000 kg of fertilisers per ha is required.

---

* *Revision of Socialism*, Vol. II, *The Contemporary Agrarian Question.—Ed.*

In the past, they wanted to substitute them
(p. 111)   by 125 kg of phosphoric acid
+60 kg of nitrogen
+60 kg of potash

It is now recognised that mineral fertilisers alone tend
to dry up the soil, and that an addition of manure is also
necessary.

Grandeau believes that out of 60,000 kg there must be at
least

20,000 kg of natural fertiliser.

Grandeau: *Annalles de la Station agronomique de l'Est.*
Déherain: *Les plantes de grande culture**
especially pp. 27-29 (also 188-93).

} The result arrived at by Nossig (who makes use of the
} *latest* agronomical data, and cites Grandeau, Déherain,
} Wollny, Hellriegel, Dünckelberg, Cohn, and many others)
} is that even intensive farming frequently comes to *plun-
dering the soil.*

It increases yields temporarily, but fails to bring about
a long-term and stable increase in soil fertility.

(Human fertilisers must also be returned to the land
((pp. 102, 108, 112).

Written before February 10 (23), 1903

First published in 1932   Printed from the original
in *Lenin Miscellany XIX*

---

* Grandeau, *Annals of the East Agronomic Station*; Déherain,
Major Crop Plants.—Ed.

CRITICAL REMARKS ON E. DAVID'S BOOK, *SOCIALISM AND AGRICULTURE*[100]

A

David.

20 Marxism has "simply" "applied" the laws of industry to agriculture.

23 A reference to *"The Peasant Barbarians".* *

28 "Success" (of agitation among peasants for Marxist programme)=zero.

> typical narrow-mindedness of the opportunist: he starts out with the International resolutions, instead of a theoretical analysis.

{ The *Communist Manifesto* is ignored. Utopian socialism as well and Sismondi, etc. }

33 Engels's Prefatory Note to the *Peasant War* left out

33 In Vol. I Marx gives very little attention to agriculture.

36 Improvement of the peasants' condition in the third quarter of the 19th century

(clay floors, etc., have disappeared south and west.)

"The peasantry" on "the upgrade" (and not the peasant bourgeoisie??)

43 Engels in 1894[101]—"das Heitere"—} he Rettungsvorschläge —"unheilbarer } got Widerspruch". (Absturz ersparen)** it!

---

* See pp. 111-15.—*Ed.*
** What Lenin meant was the following statement by David: "The funny thing (das Heitere) is that Engels, while pointing to the peasant's absolutely hopeless condition (absoluten Rettungslosigkeit des Bauern), puts forward a proposal for his salvation (Rettungsvorschläge)", a proposal "to spare the peasant this downfall (Absturz ersparen)" ...These proposals are in "irreconcilable contradiction (unheilbarer Widerspruch)" with Engels's views on the

49   A "*heavy blow*" at the Marxist doctrine:
             1895 census, the *advance* of the middle
             peasantry.

49   Note. *Definition* of the **small farm** =
             without *permanent* employment of outside
             labour and without collateral employment
             below: dwarf farms
             above: medium farms (the owner also works)
                      big farms (owner's *supervision*)

51   1895 census: **supplanting of large-scale by
             small-scale production(!)**

52   Kautsky's *Agrarian Question*—"*desperate
             attempt*"

             ┌───┐
             │ 52: the question of landed property—   │
             │ in Vol. II   │
             └───┘

53   *Hertz* annihilated Kautsky. Bernstein.

56   *Small-scale* production is superior in the
             intensive branches: the transition to inten-
             sive farming calls for *small-scale* production
             ((=without hired labour ! ! ? ? cf. 49)).

57   Science *must* stand *above* parties—
             Sering, Conrad—for the *small farm*

59   The   peasant   *prepares   socialism
             after   his   own   fashion*: **co-ope-
             ratives** ("während die marxistischen Theore-
             tiker" etc.) (die Wege ... dem Sozialismus)*
             —*Producers*' co-operatives: "a compromise
             between the principles of association and
             individualism"
             —"not socialist forms as yet"
             —far from it. But even less—"transition
             to capitalism" (K. Kautsky).

60   ‖—"mighty burgeonings of the process of
             ‖socialisation" (=co-operatives)

future of the small peasants.— *Ed.*
    * In full, David's sentence runs as follows: "While the Marxist
theorists (Während die marxistischen Theoretiker) were trying to
make socialism plausible and palatable for the peasant in their own
manner, the peasant himself worked energetically to pave the way
for   socialism   after   his   own   fashion   (die   Wege...   dem
Sozialismus)."— *Ed.*

61   *...Chapter I. "Essential* Distinction"....

66   *Concentration...* absolutely lacking.... (1895
census!!)

70   *...industry—mechanical process, agriculture—organic process* (=**essence!**)
Wrong. {ferment, etc.}
(1) no continuity;
(2) change of operations;
(3) territorial change. (Change in place
     of work);
(4) pace of work determined by nature;
(5) roomy working premises;
(6) production of manure—(no analogy!);
(7) there can be only a slow increase in the
     quantity of produce.

77   "nutrition (sic!), reproduction, care, protection" of vegetable and animal organisms:
small farm not inferior, but often superior

77   empty talk on the "*conservatism of nature*"
(!!)
—in connection with this the "*law of
diminishing returns*" (!)
("misunderstood, but basically the right
idea").

Simple co-operation

82   "Neighbourly help" to the peasant (ha-ha!).
It is (not need as such but) the example of the
neighbours that impels the small peasant
to *tireless effort.!!!*

84   Marx, "incidentally"??? "***absolutely fails
to see***" (nonsense) that capitalism causes
supervision owing to the labourer's resistance. (And gives quotations from Marx!)

86   **Hubert Auhagen** (N.B.)—"instructive
study"
cultivation of fields better on the small
farm.

88	The big farm gets a worse job done and *pays more for it*!
89	Against agricultural training ...*the peasant learns from childhood!!!*
90	Of course, *there is a lot of backwardness*, but then *most* of the big farms are not model ones either!!
	(An example of dodging!)
92	"Critical moments." Marx is not right: there's a shortage of labour there. (He got it!!)
92	The peasant has>manpower per area, the greatest intensity, etc., feverish work ⎱ ("advantages")
94	*Simple co-operation does not allow large-scale production to attain the same results as the peasant community with the same labour reserve* (Nonsense!!)
95	A "normal" family (6-4 persons) is mostly sufficient... —ha-ha! "Help" ("Ausbitten").
97-99	*Saving* of means of production on the big farm. *Not a single fact!*
101	*In general* the big farm *obtains*>from the land....
107	*Rentengutsbildung** in *Prussia* ... *are to be welcomed in principle* ... (Sic!!) ... (Sic!!)
	(Sering .... is quite right ...)... a greater quantity of labour for the remaining estate owners...
109 and *110*	*The small one builds cheaper* (David's italics)—"Advantage" (*Auhagen*)
	—"personal participation rules out high cost and jerry-building"
	(very nice, indeed!)
113	*Stumpfe*: "the smaller the farm, the higher the rent"....
114	Saving of implements (on big farms) is>

---

* See Note 18.—*Ed.*

than made up by the *"painstaking care"* ("repairs done personally"!!) (lovely!)

Stumpfe: ("...no rakes for 6 years....")
Auhagen

117
The commercial advantages of the big farm? The small farmer sells to *consumers* (Sic!)

117-118
Conclusion: the *advantages* (of co-operation and savings on implements, etc.) are> than balanced out by the *disadvantages* (ha-ha!)

Simple co-operation does not give the big farms any advantage at all....

Chapter III. *Division of Labour*

Cropping and livestock farming resist radical (!!) specialisation.

> That is why David ignores *greater*, not "radical" specialisation in large-scale farming

141
On the *big farms*, livestock is neglected. The opposite on the *peasant farm*... (Denmark).

146
(145 and a welter of reasoning of every kind:)

the peasant's "personal stake".

149
There is nothing more absurd than to imagine that the peasant is stupid: *diverse labour*, etc.

152
On the whole, it is the small farm that *prospers* in gardening. (Very characteristic! "figures"!!) (*Precisely!!*) (lovely!)

[only 6% over 2 ha]

155
Agriculture rules out the Nacheinander being transformed into "Nebeneinander" (wrong!)

159   On the big farm there are no differentiated
           tools (wrong)

170   Marx on machinery in agriculture (Vol. I)...
           "applies without hesitation"....

173   Does not deny the advantages of combining
           agricultural   production   with   industries,
           but this is not of general importance (!!!)

178   Thresher. (Cheaper and better. Bensing
           (p. 175).) More often on the big farms.
           (The small ones frequently have nothing
           to thresh!!! Funny character.)
           "Technically" there is nothing to prevent
           the small ones as well (!!!)

181   Steam plough *has not yet supplanted a single*
           small farm | that's audacious! |

183   *Deep   ploughing* ... not   only   with
           the use of the steam plough | pathetic dodge! |

185   The steam plough is not a universal plough
           | very novel! |

191   K. Kautsky's "fantastic notions" about the
           steam plough (where?? charlatan).

192-193   *Hand and Machine Labor**—The machine
           is *cheaper.*

201   Electricity is also within reach of the
           small (dodges!)

207   There has been no sort of revolution from
           the electric plough (his wit is on the petty
           dullard level)

209   A reference to *Fischer* (that the machine is
           not a threat to the small holder)....

221   "On the small-peasant farm, the *cow* is
           the *ideal*, i.e., the cheapest and most
           rationally used draught animal" (N.B.
           N.B.)

---

* See pp. 282-86.— *Ed.*

some muscular activity out in the fresh
air is beneficial....
...better feeding [Manilovism![102]]
cheap and again:

Auhagen (**without** **any** **mention** of
shallower ploughing!)

239   Seed drill *"quite accessible"*
[Growth of small figures!] (Swindler.)

246   ...Reaping machines... can be introduced....

250-253   *Conclusions* on *machinery*. A series of
swindles. ***Big*** ***farm*** ***not*** ***mechanical!***
Advantage not great (*one* example from
Fischer, and nothing about the others!!)
Does not give any increase in products.
[*A lie: con Bensing*]

257-258   What *absolutely* tends to *paralyse*
the effect of the agricultural machine in supplanting hand labour ... intensiveness tends
to create much more hand labour than
that supplanted by the agricultural machines.

> A funny character: he has failed to
> think through the $\frac{c}{v}$!!

262   **only** (??) the transition to extensive farming
brings about a redundancy of agricultural
labour.

265   Decline of rent in Britain=*depreciation of
the nation's land*.

267   Agricultural machines do not result in
automatic operations?

> Reaper?

271   The agricultural machine is *not* at all
to blame for *female* and *child* labour (?)

281   The "machinomaniacs" notwithstanding,
there has been no reduction in hard mechanical labour

> Reactionary. Why? Slaves are cheap

| 284-285 | Child labour: the small-peasant farm offers the **most** *favourable* condition. |

(Scoundrel)

| $\begin{cases} 282 \\ 288 \end{cases}$ | physical *labour* will *remain* such (and not pleasure) —"*many millions* will have to take up mechanical labour as an occupation" $\Big\}$ an opportunist's ideal of the future! |
| 292 | Labour protection and child protection—at the expense of the big farm.... |

> "Saving on high wages"—that's forgotten!!! Cf. Bulgakov

| 301 | Lengthening of the working day by the machine v.s.* **nirgends** boxed[very bold] .... |

299	the labourers' movement in East Prussia.... "isolation" of the countryside
323	Condition of labourers in East Prussia. Not the small farms, but the *big* ones manage to survive only by making use of the labourer's need....
325	The agricultural labourer cannot understand *how the big farm can be more paying than the small one.* Sic!
327	***Producers'*** *co-operatives* in the country? Ideal?

> He has *confused* them with associations in the commodity economy. Cf. 328: corn tariffs would have been demanded. | Bungler!

| 328 | *Rising to the small peasantry*!! ("'Heaven forbid!' the orthodox Marxist will say.") |

---

* The words beginning with v.s. are not clear. David says: "Nowhere (nirgends) was anything heard about the use of agricultural machines lengthening the working day".—*Ed.*

342-343   "Intensive (deep... p. 344) mechanical cultivation of the soil" (to conserve the heat).... Small farm???

352   Deep ploughing... not *always, must be* "*reasonably applied*"

352-355   The bigger the farm, the harder it is to have efficient supervision—but the small peasant—*heart and mind*!!

357   Melioration.   Small farm???

360   The small holder *likewise* participates in melioration.   Downright lie!

362   By no means is melioration confined to the big farm....
figures *without % to group*!!
"Whence it is sufficiently clear...."

389   Artificial fertilisers.
The small farmer has> practical knowledge
ha-ha!
————takes more care
————"nothing in the way...."

415-417   The smaller the farm, the more feasible is harmony (in the sense of fertiliser) and the *raising* of fertility....   (?

417   Combination of parcel agriculture and industrial work—"*h a r m o n i o u s   l i f e*"... change of occupations, etc. ("Narodniks")

420   Abolition of antithesis between town and country... "only" it will take **centuries** (Merci!)

424   *The   small   farmer   has>livestock*   **per**   ha—*hence*   **manure**....

Simple!

427   ..."solid holding": extolled by David... "gives an interest"....

428   —"Idealist or ass!" | characteristic... hm!

429   "Illusion" about the supplanting of proprietary farming by leasehold farming.

Chapter VIII

439   Introduction of >diverse plants in Europe, especially in the 19th century—*small farm*?

440-441   Selection and cultivation of improved varieties.————Small farm?

455   Grain cleaning. "The modern grain cleaner, etc".
            "   "   *Small farm*?

456   "   "   Painstaking work *on those long winter evenings*!!! "The small farm has a *decided* advantage."

459   *Crop rotation* is one of the most effective ways of combating weeds.... **Small farm?**

463   ...the interested eye... ————

465   Fighting harmful insects and animals—care of plants, etc.

466   *The big farm cannot obtain the advantages which the small holder, cultivating the land himself, has by reason of his very status in all these operations* (killing of insects, protection of plants, etc.). (David's italics.) It is true that today, because of the ignorance of their owners, many small farms present a still sadder sight than the big ones. However, ignorance is in no sense the specific, *organic* flaw of the small farm" (David's italics).
The whole of David is there!

479   Livestock breeding. Cf. the weight of horned cattle.

480   *Growth of average weight—on the small farm*??

481

"It is the **regions** with the small- and middle-peasant farms that are at the head of livestock breeding organisations"

(!is that all!)

486

The small farms breed the livestock and the big ones utilise it $\boxed{\text{cf. V. V.}}$ [103]

490

Supply animals ... with clean straw in sufficient quantities.— — — — —
Small farm?

494-495

Stumpfe: peasants are the best livestock breeders.

504

Around 1850-80 (p. 503)
thatched roofs disappeared in the southern part of Germany, better stables, etc., etc., were built.

N.B.
(cf. p. 36)

509

Repair work....
The peasant does not pay, he does the repairs himself.... That saves the peasant many a thaler.

well,
of
course!

511

It is not true that "the cottage industry" is "a normal supplement" (Marx) "not true in any case".

this is interesting!
Con
Narodniks!

512
(and 518)

"The *lowest* (!) (which then is the "highest" ???) area limit for the *small farm* is a plot which provides *sufficient!!* work and normal sustenance to the members of the independent farming peasant family."

sufficient! that's extremely rare

Care must be taken not to confuse these with the *dwarf holdings*—which are *below* these limits ... otherwise the question will be merely confounded (!!)
It's a home truth that people who have not enough land ... need another occupation....

513	Reduction of minimum size of area... under the influence of intensification. **Hecht** 513-516, *special note 516*
	(Optimist)
518	The rural handicraftsmen belong to the army of *industrial workers* *"The independent farming peasant belongs to another economic category"* (true!! But *which* category, my dear David?)
528	Kautsky's "totally groundless assertion" that the sugar industry is a classical example of the agricultural big industry and %... *of the total* } charlatan! "This requires no further comment"— precisely!
528-529	"...All the advantages that the big farm has because of better or cheaper power and tools are more than made up by painstaking effort on the small farm" (("Gist."))
529	Not *"dependence"* (of the peasant on the sugar refinery), but "organisation"—!
531	Figures on industrial enterprises: *the fool has copied them without understanding them.*
532	"The vast majority of enterprises processing farm produce are connected with *small* farms" │ Downright distortion! │
533-534	There is no industrialisation—*on the contrary* (!!),—with Kautsky it's only "St. Hegel", "the good old dialectical process".
539	Co-operation—*a transforming force; producers'* co-operatives—*a new economic principle of co-operation.*
540	*The making of milk products is developing most vigorously——*
541-542	Denmark ... "sound" division of labour... (*546* cf. trusts)

550-551

In Denmark in 1898   *179,740 cow houses*
30 and>cows   7,544$=4\%$
10-29   "   49,371$=27._{82}\%$
<10   "   122,589$=68._{97}\%$incl.*1-3*head
                                       70,218$=39._{85}\%$c.

(???)   179,504 100$._{79}$ (??)
                            hence:
                                       c.
  7,500 (30 and>) $\times30=225,000$ ⎫
 49,400 (10-29) $\times11=536,000$ ⎪
 52,400   (4-9) $\times 5=250,000$ ⎬
 70,200   (1-3) $\times1._5=100,000$ ⎪
 —————   —————————   ⎭
179,500   1,111,000

Out of 1,111,000 milch cows—about 900,000
are in co-operative dairies.
i.e. *33% have about 75% !!!*   ‖

555   *Jibes over the sale of milk wors-*
       ening nutrition—What a bore!
556   Note: *Bang—the peasant eats better*
       than the worker.
560   The small farmer has more staying power ‖
       in face of the crisis: *"the small ones can* ‖
       more easily stint themselves to the extreme" ‖
561   Dairy co-operatives—"far from being a
       socialist phenomenon" are *however* "even
       less" "purely capitalistic".
569   (Trusts)—with corn, milk, etc.   ⎤
       David compares them with trade   N.B.
       unions!! ("no objections can be pro-
       duced")
573   France—highly developed co-operatives.
576   *Danish peasant+English worker* (direct
       marketing) ((oh, what a bore!
581   The two sections of the co-operative ⎞
       world—peasants and workers—are   ⎟ !
       winning ground from the *capitalist* ⎠
       entrepreneurs
586   British consumer societies have abandoned
       the idea of *collectivising peasantry* in agri-
       culture

588   against "theoretical optimists"!! (personal interests, etc.!)

592   Credit co-operatives—death to the *usurer* (con *Marxism!!*)

> The "creative power" of the co-operative idea has led the Marxist doctrine on the "necessary ruin" of the peasant ad absurdum.

598   Full implementation of consumers' co-operatives will rid the peasant of *capitalist middlemen.*

> The root of David's mistake lies in the fact that he confounds release from middlemen and traders with release from *capital.*

601   "*A pooling of the interests of the farmers and the industrial workers*" (David's italics).

604   —Associations of peasants and consumers' societies of workers—*a cell of the organisation system* ((*à la* trusts, of course))

611   "Law" of diminishing returns—the *distinction between mechanical and organic production culminates in it!!* of tremendous importance

614   Turgot (cf. "art can do no more").

615   (1) only from a definite level of intensiveness does the income (per outlay) decline (2) the law says *nothing* about transition from one scientific-technical stage to another. (*At one stage only.*)

617   J. S. Mill—"basically right"....

619   *Marx* disdains *the great truth which lies at the root of the soil fertility law*....

620   —— His excursus into the history of economy is *false*

621   Marx contradicts himself in *Capital* III, 2,277— This David is an ass

626   Rent ... from the land...!!!

635   *Division of labour... has no part* to play... in agriculture

that's audacious! a specimen of his garbling!

637   ...there is no arbitrary decupling (of labour)...

643   In Germany (some big farms) have *doubled* their crops in 100 years (France 10.,-15 $_8$ hectolitres)

644   Productivity has not *doubled* ("definitely not") (more outlays, fertilisers, etc.)

Higher productivity—productivity of *labour*, Mr. David? probably>than double! What has that got to do with the growth of outlays on C??* Marvellous economist!

644   there is no doubt at all... the natural expenditure of *living* human labour has increased

that's bold

reference: costs of production!!!—
ha-ha!

644   Productivity has increased but on a more modest scale than in industry
1) *nature is conservative*

645   2) limited effect of labour-saving inventions. "With the growth of intensiveness, machine labour gives way *percentage-wise* (!) to manual labour" ($\frac{c}{v}$?)

654   "In *organic* production, machinism and the growing mass of products are in antagonism to each other" (!!)
"the higher the intensiveness, the less machine labour there is."

655   *M. Hecht*—"typical" (his data) (!)

---

* C—constant capital.— *Ed.*

656   Bang in *Neue Zeit:* greater income with smaller size (*r i s e* in the category of independent farmers).

659   (Fischer:) the big farmer pays the labourers a reward for good work. "The small holder saves on this."

660   In agriculture, there is a tendency towards a reduction in *hired labour* and an **increase** in the farmer's *own labour.*

667   The law of diminishing returns leads to an extension of the area under crop throughout the world (overseas competition)

670   Growth in the *weight* of livestock.

674   The small farmers have more cattle.

683   The Social-Democrats stand for the all-round boosting, etc., of *peasant farming.*

687   Marxism is inapplicable (to agriculture).

699   *T r a n s f o r m a t i o n   o f   b i g   f a r m s   i n t o   s m a l l - p e a s a n t   f a r m s.*

700   Against agricultural associations of rural labourers (cf. producers' associations!!)

701   *P r o d u c e r s'   c o - o p e r a t i v e s* are a *compromise* **between** **the** **individualist** **and** **the** **associative** **economic** **prin-** **ciples.**

701   The small peasant's work "contains more ideas"....

701   A fusion of society's supreme property right and the individual's usufruct...

703   A fusion of the small peasants and the rural labourers....

Written in March-April 1903

First published in 1932
in *Lenin Miscellany XIX*

Printed from the original

B

From *David:*

p. 109: "The small holder builds at lower cost than the big one." He works himself. "This advantage" (sic!) also applies to the maintenance of buildings.

p. 115 (from Auhagen): the small farmer bought no cart for 22 years (the big one wears out his in 10-12 years and sells it to the blacksmith)....

p. 152: "On the whole, it is the small farm that *prospers* (!) in gardening as in agriculture".

‖N.B. cf. statistics

221: "On the small-peasant farm, the *cow* is the ideal, i.e., the cheapest and most rationally used draught animal" (!!)

pp. 528-529-532. Sleight-of-hand *à la* Bulgakov, namely, that the small farm is more often combined with beet sugar and potato production.

550-551. Denmark ((and the cover))

424: The small farm has *twice* as much cattle per *ha* than the big one. (Cf. Drechsler[104].)

Written in March-April 1903

First published in 1938
in *Lenin Miscellany XXXI*

Printed from the original

EXTRACTS FROM THE BOOK,
HAND AND MACHINE LABOR

Hand and Machine Labor (Thirteenth Annual Report of the Commissioner of Labor, 1898, Vols. I and II, Wash., 1899.[105])

[A very interesting and original work, invaluable on the question of hand and machine production. Quantity of working time, the number of operations and the number of different workers in hand and machine labor, and also labor costs are compared by article produced or work accomplished ("unit"—altogether 672 units). In each unit the same data are given separately for each operation. Unfortunately, the data are excessively fragmented, and there is no attempt to summarise, or to give any general numerical, even if only approximate, conclusions.

cf. p. *93*: the general conclusion on agriculture:
"The aggregates presented by these 27 units necessarily vary very much with the crop produced, and the gains made by the supplanting of primitive methods by modern ones are quite different in different instances. With the exception noted in unit 22 there is a gain in each case, and in some instances, as in units 3 and 26, it is very large, though of course not comparable with those found in the manufacturing industries. An average deduced from the 27 units here reported shows that one man with the improved machinery in use to-day can cultivate and harvest nearly twice as large a crop as was possible under the primitive method."
(These 27 units—production of apple trees, wheat, cotton, barley, berries, tobacco, potatoes, etc. In Volume One, each unit is divided into operations.)

In general, the number of operations is much greater in machine production (division of labour! e.g., boots and shoes: 45-102 operations in hand production, and 84-173 in machine production), but in agriculture it may sometimes (perhaps more often be *vice versa*). Reason: the combination of several operations in machine production. E.g., unit 27, wheat, 20 bushels (1 acre).

Hand method 8 operations
machine   "—5   "

$$hand: \quad \left\{ \begin{array}{l} \text{motive power} \\ \text{ox and hand} \end{array} \right.$$

Ia—breaking ground
Ib—sowing seed
Ic—pulverising topsoil and cover-
                        ing seed

machine:

N.B. ‖ I—breaking ground, sowing and covering seed, and pulverising topsoil (gangplow, seeder, and harrow —motive power: steam).

See examples on separate sheet.* $\left\{ \begin{array}{l} \text{1597 pp.} \\ \text{in the two} \\ \text{volumes} \end{array} \right\}$

Information on separate operations is an excellent illustration of the *division of labour*. A pity that no effort is made to summarise for some of the "units".

Another thing that should be done is to sum up *the number of operations* (and % of operations) with motive power *other than hands*.

There are no summaries on *average ages* of workers (and sex) under hand and machine labour.

No summaries on *wages* under hand and machine labour.

All this can (and should) be calculated by number of *units* and number of *operations*. Otherwise, there remains nothing but examples, illustrations.

---

* See pp. 284-86.— *Ed.*

From *Hand and*

Some examples from "Summary of

Unit number	Name	Description		Quantity
		Hand	Machine	
2	Apple trees	Apple trees 32 months from grafts		10,000 (1 acre)
14	Onions	Onions	Onions	250 (1 acre) bush.
27	Wheat	Wheat	Wheat	20 (1 acre) (bush.)
69	Boots	Men's cheap grade, etc.		100 pairs
91	Bread	1—pound loaves bread		1,000
176	Wheels	Carriage wheels, etc.		1 set (4)
212	Trousers	Cottonade trousers, etc.		12 dozen pairs
241	Cottonades	apparently a grade of fabric		500 yards

Text (Vol. I) contains *only* explanatory notes for each unit *separately*, so that *nothing* is *summarised*.

(A very important thing for a *detailed* study of the division of labour in *separate* units, the role of machines in *separate* operations, the importance of workers' skills, and the English names of these skills. But all this is rough and raw, a handbook, and no more.)

It is very important to point out that for an *adequately exact* comparison of the level of technology in the various systems of production there must be precisely a *break-down by operations*. That is the only scientific method. It would give such a great deal in application to agriculture!

The same Report, as on the previous page—Vols. VI and VII deal with the *cost of production*. Two great volumes give the most detailed figures on each of the *hundreds* of enterprises studied for production costs, materials, wages, etc., and then the cost of living with budgets, level of labour productivity, etc. Unfortunately all of this is absolutely raw stuff, and almost useless without processing (except possibly for occasional references). Strangely enough, the authors of these works make no attempt at all to summarise or draw any general conclusions, however few!

Machine Labor

production by hand and machine methods":

Year of production		Different operations performed		Different workmen employed		Time worked hand machine		Labor cost ($)		Unit number
hand	machine	hand	machine	hand	machine	hours minutes	hours minutes	hand	machine	
$18\frac{69}{71}$	$189\frac{3}{5}$	17	20	37	125	$1{,}240._4$	$870._{24}$	$193._5$	$111._6$	2
1850	1895	9	10	28	675	$433._{55}$	$223._{23}$	$30._8$	$22._3$	14
$18\frac{29}{30}$	$189\frac{5}{6}$	8	5	4	10	$64._{15}$	$2._{58}$	$3._7$	$0._7$	27
1859	1895	83	122	2	113	$1{,}436._{40}$	$154._5$	$408._5$	$35._4$	69
1897	1897	11	16	1	12	28	$8._{56}$	$5._6$	$1._5$	91
1860	1895	13	30	2	27	37	$4._{23}$	$9._3$	$0._7$	176
1870	1895	6	13	1	16	1,440	$148._{30}$	72	$24._4$	212
1893	1895	19	43	3	252	$7{,}534._1$	$84._{14}$	$135._6$	$6._8$	241

This is from Vol. I—General table, introduction and analysis.

In Vol. II, there is nothing but tables for each *operation* in each unit. Here is a sampling of the table headings in Vol. II: 1) operation number; 2) work done (description of each operation); 3) machine, implement or tool used (in each operation separately); 4) motive power (hand, foot, horse, ox, steam, electricity, etc.); 5) persons necessary on one machine; 6) employees at work on the unit—number and sex (of the workers);—occupation (skill or shop);—age (of workers);—time worked;—pay of labour (rate per— —)—labour cost (rate by time worked or by pieces in case of piece rates).

e.g. No. *241*. Hand labour: *3* housewives (only female) worked at odd hours, *50 years*; no machines.

Machine production: mostly steam frames and machines. Working 11 hours a day. Ages from 10 years (sic!) to 50 years. Both *male* and *female*.

Or No. 27 (wheat). Hand labour: hand, oxen, 4 *labourers*, 21-30 years. Plow, sickles, flails, shovels.

Machine production: gangplow, seeder, combined *reaper* and *thresher*. Steam and horse. *10* employees (all specialists: engineer, fireman, water hauler, separator man, header tender, sack sewers, sack filler, teamsters).

Let's try to take the results for 27 units (agriculture):

			$\Sigma = 27$ acres of diverse crops	

Years	Number of different operations	Number of different workers	Time worked *hrs mins*	Labour cost $
1829-1872	hand 304	366	9,758	1,037.$_5$
1893-1896	machine 292	1,439	5,107	597.$_8$

Determining the number of different workers with the exception of No. 14 (onions), hand—28, machine—675, we get:

hand—338
machine—764
subtracting also apple trees (No. 2), hand—37, machine—125, and No. 19 (strawberries), hand—32, machine—156, we get:

hand—269
machine—583, still more than double!

Of the 27 units only in one case (No. 22, tobacco) is the time worked and labour cost higher for machine labour (199 and 353 hours: $5.$_9$ and 30.$_2$). The author observes: "Unit 22 is unique in that the total time at the later date was nearly twice that at the earlier, a fact for which no other explanation appears than that previously offered" (p. 93); page 91: "The methods used at the two periods differ so largely that no comparison can be made."

Written in the autumn of 1904

First printed in the
Fourth Russian edition
of the *Collected Works*

Printed from the original

ANALYSIS OF L. HUSCHKE'S DATA [106]
(ON SMALL-SCALE AGRICULTURE)

Huschke (on small-scale agriculture)

Wheat and rye as feed %	% going on feed *		
	oats		barley
5.84 Small farm	69.0		35.0
	77.7	(p. 52)	20.5
9.09 Medium farm I	72.39		12.22
	68.31	(p. 75)	13.90
29.56 Medium farm II	54.01		52.59
	75.91	(p 93)	46.52
3.55 Big farm	82.72		11.81
	74.70	(p. 112)	24.08
(p. 165)	$\Sigma=574.72\div8=71.84\%$		$\Sigma=216.26\div8=27.08\%$

* Top figures in each column are for 1887-1891, lower figures, for 1893-1897.— *Ed*.

Hence, data on feed:
(average amount for decade)

	Head of cattle	Cereals double centners	Feed area ha	Outlays on feed marks	ha under oats
Small farm	11	47.5	5.5	90	2
		4.3	0.50	8	
Medium farm I	29	131	15.5	1,290	7.6
		4.5	0.53	44	
Medium farm II	25	203.5	12.0	404	6.9
		8.1	0.48	16	
Big farm	67	184	42.1	3,226	8.9
		2.7	0.63	48	

	$\Sigma=132$	565.5	75.1		
		4	0.57		

below=average per head of cattle*

For a precise calculation of the area under feed on each farm, the quantities of four cereals (wheat, rye, barley and oats) fed to the livestock should be given in terms of *hectares*, (1) the grain sown should be subtracted from the total crop; (2) the net crop obtained should be divided by the number of *hectares* under each cereal; (3) the number of double centners fed to the livestock should be divided by the quotient thus obtained.

- This is too cumbersome a calculation for the four cereals, the four farms, and the two five-year periods.

On the other hand, the error could *not* be too great if we take *all* the oats as being *feed*, for the oats *not* going into feed are balanced out by the barley going into feed.

---

* This sentence was subsequently pencilled in over the table heading; it refers to the lower figures in columns 2, 3 and 4.—*Ed.*

Hence, let us assume that the *whole* area under oats is area under feed: (i.e., oats+mixture+all the fodder grasses+wheat).

	Total area under feed
Small farm	$7._5$
	$0._{68}$
Medium farm I	$23._1$
	$0._{79}$
Medium farm II	$18._9$
	$0._{76}$
Big farm	$51._0$
	$0._{76}$
	$\Sigma = 100._{50}$
	$0._{75}$

These data show such (relatively) stable averages that they can apparently be relied upon: $0._{75}$ ha per head of cattle. But for a comparison with the statistical data for the whole of Germany, it should be taken into account that Huschke's calculation of cattle is *different* from mine.

The difference is not due to any difference in rates, but to *Huschke*'s very detailed classification of cattle. He makes a distinction between foals, young cattle, calves, suckling-pigs (p. 53, Note 1), whereas I am *unable* to take account of these minute distinctions from the data of the general agricultural census of June 12, 1907.

N.B. This means that for a comparison, Huschke's data should be converted into the terms of the June 12, 1907 data, i.e., *all* horses, and *all* cattle = 1.0; *all* pigs = $^1/_4$; *all* sheep = $^1/_{10}$.

We then have:

						ha under feed
	Small farm............	$13._{45}$	}	head of	}	$7._5$
average for	Medium farm I	$31._{85}$	}	cattle	}	$23._1$
10 (8) years	Medium farm II	$36._{81}$		"		$18._9$
	Big farm	$88._8$		"		$51._0$
		$170._{91}$				$100._{50}$
						$0._{58}$

and for the whole of Germany (1907)—13,648,628 ha of feed (meadows+fodder plants+oats+mixed cereals) for 29,380,405 head of cattle, i.e., 0.$_{46}$ per head.

This looks very much like being true, because Huschke's farmers are (very) *g o o d*.

From ‖*Huschke's*‖ data follow these conclusions

1) the big farm spends much more on *artificial fertiliser* (p. *144*)
2) ,, ,, ,, has a much deeper ploughing (*p. 152, Note 2*)
3) ,, ,, ,, is better *equipped with dead stock*
4) ,, ,, ,, ensures the greatest crop increase in time
5) ,, ,, ,, feeds livestock better
6) ,, ,, ,, spends more on insurance (p. 139)
7) ,, ,, ,, obtains a better price for its products (p. *146*) (p. *155*).

{ cf. }
{ p. 144 }

To 1) *per h a.*

		1887-91	*1893-97*	(p. 139)
Small farm		17.$_{18}$	16.$_{91}$—	in marks
Medium farm		40.$_{48}$	32.$_{60}$—	per ha seed,
		22.$_{80}$	20.$_{74}$—	feed,
‖Big farm		41.$_{34}$	48.$_{95}$+	fertiliser

To 3) A list of stock, p. *107* et al., p. 47.

Outlays on maintenance of dead stock, buildings and drainage in marks per *ha*.

	1887-91	*1893-97*		
Small farm	14.$_{10}$	7.$_{43}$	−6.$_{67}$	
Medium farm	13.$_{38}$	15.$_{95}$	+2.$_{57}$	Why
	10.$_{70}$	9.$_{91}$	−0.$_{79}$	so?
Big farm	9.$_{64}$	11.$_{95}$	+2.$_{31}$	

To *4*) Yields of four cereals (rye, wheat, oats and barley) in *double centners* per *ha*.

			1887-91	1893-97	
NB:	(p. 51)	small farm	$20._{46}$	$20._{66}$	$+0._{20}$
the land on	(p. 73)	medium farm	$17._{90}$	$17._{13}$	$-0._{77}$
the big farm	(p. 92)		$19._{09}$	$21._{06}$	$+1._{97}$
is worse	(p. 111)	big farm	$17._{46}$	$19._{77}$	$+2._{31}$
(p. 125)					

Livestock feed (double centners)

Head in terms of big cattle [1])	Price of cattle			wheat	rye	barley	oats	Σ
$+$ $10._{75}$	2,765 (p. 47)		1887-91	$2._{19}$	$1._{68}$	$14._{24}$	$30._{74}$	$48._{85}$
$11._{3}$	3,019 Small farm		1893-97	$1._{44}$	$0._{40}$	$8._{81}$	$35._{56}$	$46._{21}$
				—	—	—	$+$	—
$+$ $26._{8}$	9,474 (p. 74)			$12._{78}$	$1._{34}$	$21._{16}$	$77._{04}$	$112._{32}$
$30._{6}$	11,091 Medium farm I			$14._{26}$	$6._{38}$	$29._{75}$	$99._{87}$	$150._{26}$
				$+$	$+$	$+$	$+$	$+$
$+$ $23._{5}$	10,574 (p. 87)			$12._{71}$	$2._{39}$	$59._{24}$	$94._{33}$	$168._{67}$
$25._{9}$	10,971 Medium farm II			$25._{71}$	$33._{74}$	$57._{38}$	$122._{09}$	$238._{92}$
				$+$	$+$	—	$+$	$+$
$-$ $67._{1}$	23,442 (p. 112)			$18._{61}$	$0._{63}$	$15._{90}$	$128._{83}$	$163._{97}$
$66._{0}$	23,300 Big farm			$15._{40}$	$1._{15}$	$41._{25}$	$146._{60}$	$204._{40}$
				—	$+$	$+$	$+$	$+$

[1]) Huschke gives $9._{4}$ and 10 (p. 53), but this does not follow from the rates he himself gives (p. 53).

$$? = \text{Perennial fodder plants?}$$

Use of Land (ha)

	Wheat, rye, oats+barley	Potatoes	1 — (Peas, beans, vetch) leguminous plants	2 — Fodder-beet	Fodder vetch, maize, red clover+alfalfa	3 — Sugar-beet	Σ (total)	Meadows	Σ of all land	Total area under fodder (1+2+3)
Small farm	6.6	1	0.4	1	4	—	13.00	0.5	13.64	5.50
Medium farm I	33.5	4	5	2	12[1] +1.5[2]	3 Fallow	61	—	(50.16) 61.12	15.50
Medium farm II	20.5	2.5	4	2.5 (Rape)	9	2.5 2.5	43.5	0.99	45.06	12.49
Big farm	45.0	6.0	8.0 +2.0	6.0 Rape 4.0 Beet-root	2.0 +25 (?[3]) { Mixture, maize, etc. }	3.0	101	5.08	108.42	(?)42.08

[1] Perennial fodder plants....
[2] Mixture for fattening....
[3] Others (p. 110) ? 101—76=25

Value of Livestock

α) 1st five-year period / β) 2nd five-year period	Head in terms of big cattle	marks	Price of average head of big cattle	
I (Small farm) (p. 47)	α) $53._{85} \div 5 = 10._{75}$	2,765.$_{00}$		$52._3 \times 10 =$
	β) $56._{60} \div 5 = 11._{32}$	3,019.$_{00}$		$523 \div 2 = 261._5$
	$110._{45} \div 10 = 11._{04}$	5,784 $\div 2 = 2,892._0$	261.$_5$	$5,784 \div 110._{45} =$ $52._3 \times 5 = 261._5$
II (Medium farm) (p. 69)	α) $134._2 \div 5 = 26._8$	9,474.$_0$		
	β) $153._2 \div 5 = 30._6$	11,091.$_0$		
	$287._4 \div 10 = 28._{74}$	20,565 $\div 2 = 10,282._{50}$	357.$_5$	$20,565 \div 287._4 =$ $71._5 \times 5 = 357._5$
III (Medium farm) (p. 87)	α) $70._6 \div 3 = 23._5$	10,574.$_{66}$		
	β) $129._7 \div 5 = 25._9$	10,971.$_{00}$		
	$200._3 \div 8 = 25._{04}$	21,545.$_{66}$		$21,545._{66} \div 200._3 =$ $107._5 \times 5 = 537._5$
		$\div 2 = 10,772._{83}$	430.$_0$	$107._5 \times 8 =$ $860 \div 2 = 430$
IV (Big farm) (p. 107)	α) $335._5 \div 5 = 67._1$	23,442.$_0$		
	β) $333._{25} \div 5 = 66._6$	23,300.$_0$		
	$668._{75} \div 10 = 66._8$	46,742 $\div 2 = 23,371._{00}$	349.$_5$	$46,742 \div 668._{75} =$ $69._9 \times 5 = 349._5$

This is wrong. 2,892 should be divided by 11.04, etc. But the *ratios* do not change.

P. *123*:

I—13.$_{64}$ ha   11 ⎤
II—61.$_{10}$ 29 ⎥ head of big cattle
III—45.$_{06}$ 25 ⎥
IV—108.$_{41}$ 67 ⎦

Written not earlier than September 1910-not later than 1913
First published in 1938 in *Lenin Miscellany XXXI*

Printed from the original

III

MATERIAL FOR A STUDY
OF THE CAPITALIST ECONOMY
OF EUROPE AND THE UNITED STATES

1910-1916

GERMAN AGRARIAN STATISTICS (1907)[107]

44 pages. 40 vertical×33 (horizontal) squares *

Statistik des Deutschen Reichs.	German statistical publications: *Puttkammer* und *Mühlbrecht.* Französische Strasse, 28. Berlin. (*Free* catalogue.)

Vol. 212. Census of Occupations and Enterprises of June 12, 1907.

Agricultural   Production   Statistics.

First three subvolumes: *1 a; 1 b; 2 a*

From the "preliminary remarks" to tables 4 and 5 ("Part *1 b*"). These figures were first collected in 1907. "The ground for classifying under these 11 heads according to number of personnel was the data under letter C 1-3 of the master card; consequently, account was also taken of family members helping out (C 2 b) and casual labour (C 3 c)" (p. 455). "...The number of farms classified under heads 14-64" (establishments by number of labourers: 1, 2, etc., to 200) "is as a rule smaller than the total number of farms in the first column" (the number of *all* agricultural enterprises), "because it contains, in addition, figures for farms only with the greatest number of labourers and farms without personnel" (455).

---

* Size of square-lined sheet used in MS.— *Ed.*

On the whole, the *main* substance of the *three* volumes (*1 a, 1 b* and *2 a*) is set down in this notebook.

> secondary items left out: forest estates, columns of particular and detailed data, poultry in the cattle population column, etc., etc.

To show that it is not right to classify labour in agriculture by sex and age, I give the data (*Statistisches Jahrbuch*, 1910) for the *whole of industry* according to the Census of June 12, 1907. Total personnel = *14,348,016*, including *women* — *3,510,464* (= 24.4 %). Apparently, *only* the help and labourers have been classified by age. Their total: *7,474,140* men + *1,862,531* women, together = 9,336,671; including those of 16 years and over — 6,923,586 men + 1,663,070 women; 14-16 — 527,182 men + 190,454 women, together = 717,636; *under 14*: 23,372 men + 9,007 women [together = 32,379 = 0.3% out of 9,336,671].

$$
\left\{
\begin{array}{ll}
\text{14-16 years} \quad \dots\dots & 717,636 \\
\text{under 14 years} \quad .. & 32,379
\end{array}
\right.
$$

$$750,015 = 8.0\%$$

Then family members helping out (141,295 men + 790,602 women) are classified as follows: 16 years and over — 126,738 men + 767,127 women; under *16* years: 14,557 men + 23,475 women.

Statistik des Deutschen Reichs. Band *202. Berufs- und Betriebszählung vom 12. Juni 1907. Berufsstatistik** (according to the June 12, 1907 Census), } The exact title of Vol. 202:

Vol. **202** (1909). (Price 6 Mk)   Section I Introduction

     "   211 (*in preparation*) Summaries.

---

* *Statistics of the German Reich.* Vol. 202. Census of Occupations and Enterprises of June 12, 1907. Occupations Statistics.

1895 statistics: *Statistics of the German Reich*, new series, Vol. **112** (Berlin 1898): "Agriculture in the German Reich according to the Agricultural Census of June 14, 1895".

Part *2 a*. Table 10. Wine-growing Farms
(by size of area under *vineyards*)

	Number of wine-growing farms	These farms have			Owners not farmers by principal occupation
		total area ha	area under vineyards *ha*	other farmland	
Under 2 ares	2,239	4,287	23	3,726	1,228
2-5	25,240	61,016	836	52,440	11,665
5-10	56,183	149,617	3,922	135,135	23,127
10-20	79,031	270,713	10,998	235,714	25,900
20-50	99,805	409,727	30,806	334,396	23,054
50-1 ha	44,373	227,764	29,328	171,583	7,156
1-2	16,167	124,645	20,973	85,140	2,578
2-3	2,747	35,262	6,315	19,777	541
3-4	868	25,104	2,927	10,620	189
4-5	437	10,433	1,860	5,218	114
5 and over	768	44,098	7,119	13,581	201
Total	327,858	1,362,666	115,107	1,067,330	95,753

1) top   =Total
2)   =main enterprises
3) bottom=ancillary enterprises.

I have left out many details in this table on *owned* and *leased* land.

Part *1 a*.   Table 1

	Agricultural enterprises in general		Of the total area			The farms	
	enterprises	area ha	land owned	land leased	other land	land only under vegetable gardens	land only under potatoes
Under 0.5 ha	2,084,060 / 89,166 / 1,994,894	619,066 / 142,995 / 476,071	369,752	157,132	92,182	623,711	360,944
0.5-2 ha	1,294,449 / 369,224 / 925,225	1,872,936 / 725,021 / 1,147,915	1,333,022	426,380	113,534	13,263	21,831
2-5	1,006,277 / 718,905 / 287,372	4,306,421 / 3,153,829 / 1,152,592	3,501,620	713,415	91,386	1,200	249
5-20	1,065,539 / 980,970 / 84,569	13,768,521 / 12,702,834 / 1,065,687	12,401,022	1,239,747	127,752	289	74
20-100	262,191 / 254,661 / 7,530	12,623,011 / 12,097,243 / 525,768	11,622,873	946,723	53,415	27	2
100 and >	23,566 / 23,110 / 456	9,916,531 / 9,696,179 / 220,352	7,873,850	2,028,962	13,719	3	—
incl. 200 ha and >	12,887 / 12,737 / 150	7,674,873 / 7,555,522 / 119,351	6,063,052	1,607,373	4,448	—	—
Σ	5,736,082 / 2,436,036 / 3,300,046	43,106,486 / 38,518,101 / 4,588,385	37,102,139	5,512,359	491,988	638,495	383,100
5-10 ha	652,798 / 589,266 / 63,532	5,997,626 / 5,376,631 / 620,995	5,266,586	671,655	59,385	233	54
10-20 ha	412,741 / 391,704 / 21,037	7,770,895 / 7,326,203 / 444,692	7,134,436	568,092	68,367	56	20

* The column below has been transferred here from p. 17 of the l total number of enterprises, the second, the main enterprises, and the bott

1) total
2) main enterprises
3) ancillary enterprises *

Table 2

have   Of the total area

land under forest estates	waste and unsuitable land	ploughland ha	land under vegetable gardens and orchards without decorative gardens	vineyards ha	Of the total area, farmland in general
38,762	22,788	246,961	76,431	6,256	359,553 / 24,400 / 335,153
118,994	61,782	976,345	71,296	29,046	1,371,758 / 462,317 / 909,441
237,117	117,939	2,350,006	73,454	39,346	3,304,878 / 2,446,400 / 858,478
445,922	218,712	7,728,039	138,511	34,185	10,421,564 / 9,710,848 / 710,716
141,258	80,009	7,220,699	79,810	5,878	9,322,103 / 9,064,769 / 257,334
13,630	8,775	5,910,304	42,214	657	7,055,018 / 6,953,946 / 101,072
8,411	5,231	4,683,308	31,867	236	5,555,793 / 5,495,247 / 60,546
995,683	510,005	24,432,354	481,716	115,368	31,834,874 / 28,662,680 / 3,172,194
					under 2 ha 1,731,311 / 2-20 13,726,442 / over 20 ha 16,377,121
240,369	117,892	3,379,657	69,450	23,379	4,607,090 / 4,182,257 / 424,833
205,553	100,820	4,348,382	69,061	10,806	5,814,474 / 5,528,591 / 285,883

(p. 311 of this volume), as Lenin wanted it. The top figure of three shows
the ancillary enterprises.—*Ed.*

1) top　　= *male*
2) lower = *female*
3) bottom=together

> In this table, and from here on, all the totals (male+female) are *mine*

Part *1b*. Table 4: Personnel on agric

	Number working on June 12. 1907		Maximum working from June 13, 1906 to June 12, 1907		Of the ... persons		
						personnel	
	total	of them permanent labour	total	of them casual labour	enterprises	12.6. 1907	maximum
Under 0.5 ha	522,343 1,491,964 2,014,307	325,043 528,973 854,016	964,858 1,648,732 2,613,590	516,509 231,555 748,064	1,060,700	147,753 912,947	381,957 991,575
0.5-2 ha	801,850 1,536,895 2,338,745	492,153 802,695 1,294,848	1,240,243 1,812,754 3,052,997	563,252 397,971 961,223	492,565	60,418 432,147	242,890 524,494
2-5 ha	1,330,625 1,583,252 2,913,877	1,012,783 1,066,337 2,079,120	1,709,508 1,941,006 3,650,514	519,004 498,023 1,017,027	93,154	23,101 70,053	69,240 109,349
5-20 ha	2,324,888 2,270,970 4,595,858	1,882,107 1,618,714 3,500,848	3,045,451 3,024,803 6,070,254	992,858 1,047,081 2,039,939	14,227	8,391 5,836	23,602 20,285
20-100 ha	1,139,898 929,535 2,069,433	919,070 634,009 1,553,079	1,565,150 1,310,234 2,875,384	613,760 593,277 1,207,037	755	589 166	2,353 1,382
100 ha and over	728,224 509,105 1,237,329	542,097 291,815 833,912	844,301 625,384 1,469,685	301,164 330,517 631,681	62	62 —	694 611
incl. 200 ha and over	560,063 380,727 940,790	416,934 218,221 635,155	636,171 458,853 1,095,024	218,795 239,469 458,264	30	30 —	453 494
Total	6,847,828 8,321,721 15,169,549	5,173,253 4,942,570 10,115,823	9,369,511 10,362,913 19,732,424	3,506,547 3,098,424 6,604,971	1,661,463	240,314 1,421,149 1,661,463	720,736 1,647,696 2,368,432
5-10 ha	1,239,883 1,251,454 2,491,337	1,001,675 892,956 1,894,631	1,593,788 1,616,384 3,210,172	483,185 502,028 985,213	11,822	6,563 5,259 11,822	17,668 15,890
10-20 ha	1,085,005 1,019,516 2,104,521	880,432 725,785 1,606,217	1,451,663 1,408,419 2,860,082	509,673 545,053 1,054,726	2,405	1,828 577	5,934 4,395

tural enterprises by number and sex

employed in agricultural enterprises, including managers:

	2			3			4-5	
	personnel			personnel			personnel	
enter-prises	12. 6. 1907	maxi-mum	enter-prises	12. 6. 1907	maxi-mum	enter-prises	12. 6. 1907	maxi-mum
324,880	250,567 399,193	318,171 434,458	66,372	79,406 119,710	95,129 130,939	19,644	34,269 48,554 82,823	39,695 53,319 93,014
426,043	319,863 532,223	446,119 618,457	182,016	224,209 321,839	277,889 367,778	81,584	151,820 194,193 346,013	176,531 220,032 396,563
330,535	296,159 364,911	414,281 474,573	312,821	431,143 507,320	539,652 611,119	222,679	449,854 498,361 948,215	529,782 577,755 1,107,537
121,400	126,194 116,606	212,595 208,956	252,719	385,231 372,926	542,336 537,519	475,524	1,058,301 1,032,429	1,361,568 1,344,729
2,354	2,943 1,765	7,977 6,302	8,605	15,911 9,904	33,406 24,169	57,167	150,793 111,409 262,202	247,806 193,646 441,452
32	55 9	392 375	49	95 52	522 462	158	500 233 733	1,378 999 2,377
15	24 6	237 252	14	32 10	181 209	27	88 36	362 331
1,205,244	995,781 1,414,707 2,410,488	1,399,535 1,743,121 3,142,656	822,582	1,135,995 1,331,751 2,467,746	1,488,934 1,671,986 3,160,920	856,756	1,845,537 1,885,179 3,730,716	2,356,760 2,390,480 4,747,240
102,110	104,613 99,607 204,220	166,855 165,933	194,618	290,540 293,314 583,854	389,482 397,234	274,771	590,891 599,881 1,190,772	728,042 738,760 1,466,802
19,290	21,581 16,999	45,740 42,023	58,101	94,691 79,612	152,854 140,285	200,753	467,410 432,548 899,958	633,526 605,969 1,239,495

[ctd on next page]

[ctd]   Of the ... persons employed in agricul

	6-10			11-20			21-30		
	enterprises	personnel		enterprises	personnel		enterprises	personnel	
		12.6.1907	maximum		12.6.1907	maximum		12.6.1907	maximum
Under 0.5 ha	2,239	6,007 9,095 15,102	7,203 10,338 17,541	183	1,325 1,212	1,793 1,487	33	483 356	567 454
0.5-2 ha	11,710	33,370 45,959 79,329	38,251 51,753 90,004	972	6,147 7,096	7,263 8,093	144	2,115 1,372	2,788 1,918
2-5 ha	32,692	102,339 116,750 219,089	115,989 132,611 248,600	2,450	15,942 17,842	18,246 20,252	344	4,692 3,530	5,719 4,126
5-20 ha	185,008	629,332 629,739 1,259,071	766,674 778,448 1,545,122	11,760	76,534 80,289	87,732 93,320	1,363	16,593 16,632	18,976 19,151
20-100 ha	150,553	609,305 494,583 1,103,888	827,983 690,869 1,518,852	36,727	259,354 229,139	322,736 289,113	4,026	50,242 47,615	60,187 58,008
100 ha and over	992	5,551 2,610 8,161	10,345 6,736 17,081	3,569	35,656 20,330	49,619 33,356	3,966	61,029 39,705	76,503 54,314
Incl. 200 ha and over	118	608 337 945	2,001 1,662 3,663	377	4,379 1,753	6,923 3,933	1,058	18,704 8,823	23,959 14,126
Total	383,194	1,385,904 1,298,736 2,684,640	1,766,445 1,670,755 3,437,200	55,661	394,958 355,908 750,866	487,389 445,621 933.010	9,876	135,154 109,210 244,364	164,740 137,971 302,711
5-10 ha	62,941	206,045 214,834 420,879	242,528 252,678 495,206	3,741	24,802 26,293 51,095	27,973 29,895	511	6,356 6,152 12,508	7,329 6,962
10-20 ha	122,067	423,287 414,905 838,192	524,146 525,770 1,049,916	8,019	51,732 53,996	59,759 63,425	852	10,237 10,480	11,647 12,189

ral enterprises. including managers:

31-50			51-100			101-200			over 200		
enterprises	personnel		enterprises	personnel		enterprises	personnel		enterprises	personnel	
	12. 6. 1907	maximum		12. 6. 1907	maximum		12. 6. 1907	maximum		12.6. 1907	maximum
1	590 202	976 579	16	852 229	1,322 371	11	912 436	962 556	1	179 30	179 30
50	1,484 811	1,810 1,042	25	1,099 581	1,300 667	10	862 446	1,109 569	3	463 228	516 175
1	2,758 1,381	3,229 1,790	50	2,303 1,271	2,543 1,482	18	1,548 829	1,760 930	4	786 1,004	980 945
2	10,027 8,180	11,701 9,886	174	7,244 4,289	8,867 5,294	47	3,942 2,479	4,684 3,097	15	3,099 1,565	3,273 1,650
57	23,278 19,968	28,875 25,538	320	13,236 7,763	16,475 11,525	95	8,687 4,440	10,719 6,241	27	5,560 2,783	5,936 2,946
56	141,141 95,068	164,612 118,881	6,230	255,654 177,056	289,423 212,650	2,115	160,220 119,793	176,208 136,154	406	68,261 54,249	74,315 60,858
79	87,952 48,939	103,628 64,070	5,431	229,374 152,908	258,941 183,845	2,043	154,674 116,005	169,638 131,735	388	64,198 51,910	69,826 58,191
97	179,278 125,610 304,888	211,203 157,716 368,919	6,815	280,388 191,189 471,577	319,930 231,989 551,919	2,296	176,171 128,423 304,594	195,442 147,547 342,989	456	78,348 59,859 138,207	85,199 66,604 151,803*)
4	3,441 2,760 6,201	4,087 3,366	76	3,282 1,722 5,004	3,772 2,102	16	1,460 728 2,188	1,740 930	9	1,890 904 2,794	2,041 999
8	6,586 5,420	7,614 6,520	98	3,962 2,567	5,095 3,192	31	2,482 1,751	2,944 2,167	6	1,209 661	1,232 651

*) Σ maximum (>6 labourérs)=6,088,551. Σ (maximum)=
,507,799.

vertical =male
order   =female
          =total

Ibid. Table 5. Personnel in agricultural enterprises

	Managers				Family	
		of them				β working permanently
	α total	owners	lease-holders	others (managers, supervisors, etc.)	m./f.	of them under 14 years
Under 0.$_5$ ha	279,464	135,084	98,928	45,452	31,353	2,364
	135,017	92,817	33,816	8,384	369,641	2,841
	414,481	227,901	132,744	53,836	400,994	5,205
0.$_5$-2 ha	363,273	304,138	45,309	13,826	98,286	7,904
	123,044	110,100	10,901	2,043	643,391	8,311
	486,317	414,238	56,210	15,869	741,677	16,215
2-5 ha	681,216	635,969	38,392	6,855	272,863	16,468
	73,917	70,880	2,611	426	920,203	16,647
	755,133	706,849	41,003	7,281	1,193,066	33,115
5-20 ha	936,185	906,121	25,478	4,586	626,299	26,790
	57,062	55,692	1,028	342	1,247,274	25,239
	993,247	961,813	26,506	4,928	1,873,573	52,029
20-100 ha	242,975	228,370	11,360	3,245	185,277	5,258
	13,585	12,974	451	160	275,514	4,749
	256,560	241,344	11,811	3,405	460,791	10,007
100 ha and over	22,980	12,978	5,107	4,895	4,191	104
	775	552	167	56	6,193	139
	23,755	13,530	5,274	4,951	10,384	243
incl. 200 ha and over	12,702	6,287	2,957	3,458	1,548	76
	436	301	108	27	2,138	107
	13,138	6,588	3,065	3,485	3,686	183
Total	2,526,093	2,222,660	224,574	78,859	1,218,269	58,888
	403,400	343,015	48,974	11,411	3,462,216	57,926
	2,929,493	2,565,675	273,548	90,270	4,680,485	116,814
	220,716	(total farms 225,697)			415,295	
5-10 ha	562,393	544,423	15,448	2,522	333,626	15,548
	35,692	34,868	618	206	741,594	14,927
	598,085	579,291	16,066	2,728	1,075,220	30,475
10-20 ha	373,792	361,698	10,030	2,064	292,673	11,242
	21,370	20,824	410	136	505,680	10,312
	395,162	382,522	10,440	2,200	798,353	21,554

by status in production and by sex.

members			Outside labour				
γ working temporarily only		controllers, book-keepers, etc. (α) m./f. δ	permanent labour		those in (α), (β) and (γ) under 14 years	casual labour	
m./f.	of them under 14 years		male and female farm-hands (β) ε	day labourers, labourers and Instleute (γ) ζ		m./f. η	of them under 14 years
123,306	19,191	1,003	4,297	8,926	177	73,994	681
888,204	17,871	469	19,617	4,229	259	74,787	620
1,011,510	37,062	1,472	23,914	13,155	436	148,781	1,301
184,838	38,533	1,646	12,094	16,854	717	124,859	1,564
612,088	34,070	486	27,245	8,529	647	122,112	1,192
796,926	72,603	2,132	39,339	25,383	1,364	246,971	2,756
177,721	49,761	2,131	32,958	23,615	3,028	140,121	2,766
376,646	42,233	555	59,365	12,297	2,251	140,269	1,947
554,367	91,994	2,686	92,323	35,912	5,279	280,390	4,713
170,486	66,132	4,965	254,249	60,409	16,750	272,295	9,984
358,981	56,446	1,614	281,870	30,921	7,002	293,248	5,498
529,467	122,578	6,579	536,119	91,330	23,752	565,543	15,482
32,320	12,431	10,146	359,451	121,221	13,702	188,508	12,038
82,948	10,508	3,577	278,809	62,524	4,141	212,578	8,230
115,268	22,939	13,723	638,260	183,745	17,843	401,086	20,268
1,040	117	44,341	147,731	322,854	4,301	185,087	18,118
3,052	105	6,229	68,265	210,353	3,689	214,238	18,123
4,092	222	50,570	215,996	533,207	7,990	399,325	36,241
442	20	35,494	106,702	260,488	3,223	142,687	12,907
1,163	33	4,222	48,452	162,973	2,929	161,343	13,181
1,605	53	39,716	155,154	423,461	6,152	304,030	26,088
689,711	186,165	64,232	810,780	553,879	38,675	984,864	45,151
2,321,919	161,233	12,930	735,171	328,853	17,989	1,057,232	35,610
3,011,630	347,398	77,162	1,545,951	882,732	56,664	2,042,096	80,761
101,259		6,754	497,655	91,394		288,171	
108,928	39,776	2,264	77,028	26,364	6,171	129,280	3,769
221,400	34,115	641	101,642	13,387	3,187	137,098	2,266
330,328	73,891	2,905	178,670	39,751	9,358	266,378	6,035
61,558	26,356	2,701	177,221	34,045	10,579	143,015	6,215
137,581	22,331	973	180,228	17,534	3,815	156,150	3,232
199,139	48,687	3,674	357,449	51,579	14,394	299,165	9,447

[ctd on next page]

[ctd]	Only in this column are totals (m.+f.) from the original. In other columns, the totals are mine	Ergo, there are more hired than family workers in the 20-50 ha group as well	
		(My calculation) Total labour	
	total number of persons	$(\alpha+\beta+\gamma)$ family	$(\delta+\varepsilon+\zeta+\eta)$ hired
Under 0.5 ha	522,343 1,491,964 2,014,307	1,392,862 1,826,985	99,102 187,322
0.5-2 ha	801,850 1,536,895 2,338,745	1,378,523 2,024,920	158,372 313,825
2-5 ha	1,330,625 1,583,252 2,913,877	1,370,766 2,502,566	212,486 411,311
5-20 ha	2,324,888 2,270,970 4,595,858	3,396,287	1,199,571
20-100 ha	1,139,898 929,535 2,069,433	372,047 832,619	557,488 1,236,814
100 ha and over	728,224 509,105 1,237,329	10,020 38,231	499,085 1,199,098
incl. 200 ha and over	560,063 380,727 940,790	18,429	922,361
Total	6,847,828 8,321,721 15,169,549	6,187,535 10,621,608	2,134,186 4,547,941
	1,621,244	737,270	883,974
5-10 ha	1,239,883 1,251,454 2,491,337	998,686 2,003,633	252,768 487,704
10-20 ha	1,085,005 1,019,516 2,104,521	664,631 1,392,654	354,885 711,867

(My calculation) Number of workers under 14 years			% of minors in total			Number of workers per enterprise		
total	family	hired	total	fami-ly	hired	total	fami-ly	hired
44,004	42,267	1,737	2.2	2.3	0.9	1.0	0.9	0.1
92,938	88,818	4,120	3.9	4.4	1.3	1.8	1.6	0.2
85,101	125,109	9,992	4.6	4.9	2.4	2.9	2.5	0.4
213,841	174,607	39,234	4.7	5.1	3.3	4.3	3.2	1.1
71,057	32,946	38,111	3.4	3.9	3.1	7.9	3.2	4.7
44,696	465	44,231	3.6	1.2	3.7	52.5	1.6	50.9
32,476	236	32,240	3.5	1.2	3.5	73.0	1.4	71.6
601,637	464,212	137,425	3.9	4.4	3.0	2.6	1.8	0.8
							3.3	
119,759	104,366	15,393	4.8	5.2	3.1	3.8	3.1	0.7
94,082	70,241	23,841	4.5	5.0	3.3	5.1	3.4	1.7

Part *2 a*. Table 6. Cattle population

	Number of agricultural enterprises				
	$\underline{\alpha}$ no poultry or other livestock α	$\underline{\beta}$ poultry, but no other livestock β	other livestock, but no poultry γ	both poultry and other livestock δ	total (β-δ)
Under 0.5 ha	714,035	185,382	498,870	685,773	1,370,025
0.5-2 ha	93,210	44,308	217,790	939,141	1,201,239
2-5 ha	17,812	7,884	69,634	910,947	988,465
5-20 ha	7,075	2,089	28,304	1,028,071	1,058,464
20-100 ha	1,569	207	3,346	257,069	260,622
100 ha and over	331	28	1,228	21,979	23,235
Incl. 200 ha and over	140	16	820	11,911	12,747
Total	834,032	239,898	819,172	3,842,980	4,902,050
			4,662,152		
20-50 ha					
5-10 ha	4,824	1,574	21,179	625,221	647,974
10-20 ha	2,251	515	7,125	402,850	410,490

goats		(My calculation)		
		$(\underline{\alpha}+\underline{\beta})$ no live-stock	$(\Sigma - \underline{\varkappa})$ no cattle	$(\Sigma - \underline{\varkappa}+\underline{\lambda})$ no horses
1,312,416		899,417	1,919,153	2,076,177
1,384,810		137,518	623,897	1,242,718
	<2 ha	1,036,935	2,543,050	3,318,895
419,208		25,696	51,399	812,050
429,656		9,164	12,107	376,989
99,506		1,776	2,140	8,902
8,314		359	384	547
4,440		156	165	246
3,653,910		1,073,930	2,609,080	4,517,383
255,190		6,398	8,758	308,389
174,466		2,766	3,349	68,600

Ibid. Table 7. Agricultural enterprises

	Enterprises using the following types of machines in the last year:	steam ploughs				broadcast sowers		
			own				own	
		farms	farms	number of steam ploughs owned	farms	farms	number of sowers owned	
Under 0.₅	18,466	5	1	1	2,696	68	68	
0.₅-2	114,986	13	3	4	11,442	468	471	
2-5	325,665	23	5	7	15,780	4,219	4,225	
5-20	772,536	81	25	26	87,921	63,067	63,183	
20-100	243,365	319	21	23	73,481	67,958	69,919	
100 and >	22,957	2,554	360	381	15,594	15,527	28,255	
200 and>	12,652	2,112	321	341	9,429	9,412	20,347	
Σ	1,497,975	2,995	415	442	206,914	151,307	166,121	
5-10 ha	419,170	31	15	15	33,272	19,220	19,246	
10-20 ha	353,366	50	10	11	54,649	43,847	43,937	

My symbols:

A = farms using machines in general
B = " owning machines "
C = number of own machines of a given type

with use of agricultural machinery

reapers			seed drills and planters			inter-row cultivators		
	own			own				
farms	farms	number of reapers owned	farms	farms	number of machines	A	B	C
231	178	189	998	21	23	31	13	13
1,132	569	598	3,899	224	226	270	200	202
6,812	4,422	4,459	4,983	1,573	1,581	1,140	1,052	1,060
137,624	125,640	130,561	33,123	24,319	24,370	4,146	3,726	3,773
136,104	131,292	158,375	30,795	28,125	28,438	6,011	5,597	5,794
19,422	19,297	47,381	9,327	9,274	13,493	2,814	2,793	4,978
10,943	10,887	32,270	5,761	5,741	9,479	1,716	1,706	3,537
301,325	281,398	341,563	83,125	63,541	68,131	14,412	13,381	15,820
36,261	30,816	31,128	10,443	6,273	6,280	1,395	1,214	1,227
101,363	94,824	99,433	22,680	18,046	18,090	2,751	2,512	2,546

[ctd on next page]

[ctd]

	steam threshers			(other threshers)			potato planters		
	A	B	C	A	B	C	A	B	C
Under 0.5	10,468	116	125	5,431	444	444	4	3	3
0.5-2	60,750	680	702	39,321	10,370	10,405	71	32	32
2-5	127,739	1,455	1,500	163,287	116,187	116,297	55	29	29
5-20	203,438	3,360	3,441	539,285	502,826	503,717	312	204	204
20-100	69,005	4,311	4,380	190,618	185,895	187,317	866	679	681
100 and >	17,467	9,906	10,436	9,061	8,656	9,746	1,352	1,342	1,624
200 and >	10,721	7,702	8,202	3.649	3,488	4,212	1,010	1,005	1,271
Σ	488,867	19,828	20,584	947,003	824,378	827,926	2,660	2,289	2,573
5-10 ha	118,840	1,687	1,733	275,793	249,979	250,490	116	84	84
10-20 ha	84,598	1,673	1,708	263,492	252,847	253,227	196	120	120

potato lifters			grain crushers			separators		
A	B	C	A	B	C	A	B	C
5	2	2	34	33	33	757	670	684
29	4	4	446	437	437	11,720	10,463	10,550
93	61	63	2,476	2,410	2,414	56,955	53,210	53,328
4,196	3,672	3,691	12,943	12,735	12,750	180,641	175,221	175,467
5,442	5,040	5,193	9,686	9,591	9,627	80,137	78,293	78,556
1,239	1,227	1,839	3,747	3,735	4,009	6,696	6,570	6,897
647	640	1,103	2,615	2,612	2,840	3,512	3,438	3,686
11,004	10,006	10,792	29,332	28,941	29,270	336,906	324,427	325,482
713	571	573	4,916	4,808	4,816	85,986	82,807	82,903
3,483	3,101	3,118	8,027	7,927	7,934	94,655	92,414	92,564

Σ—A alone adds up to 2,424,543 for all columns and C—1,808,704

[Only the first five categories
Ibid. Table 8. Connection between agricul

	Number of agricultural		
	sugar refineries	distilleries	starch factories
Under 0.5	8	582	9
0.5-2	12	4,199	7
2-5	23	11,459	10
5-20	67	13,859	29
20-100	118	2,750	60
100 and >	231	3,910	319
200 and >	170	3,056	281
Σ	459	36,759	434
5-10 ha	33	8,800	19
10-20 ha	34	5,059	10

were counted in 1895]
tural enterprises and side-line industries

enterprises connected with:			
flour mills	breweries	saw mills	brick works
1,265	191	360	248
3,893	494	889	616
8,383	1,009	1,908	1,285
16,747	2,812	4,895	3,178
4,193	1,343	1,504	1,952
943	185	498	1,449
656	85	386	1,072
35,424	6,034	10,054	8,728
9,467	1,281	2,511	1,621
7,280	1,531	2,384	1,557

Ibid. Table 9. Owners and other supervisory person

	Owners and other supervisory personnel at agricultu				
					A. 1. Agricul
	independent			108	
		of them			
	total	without side line	with side line	management and supervisory personnel	male and female farmhands
Under 0.5 ha	85,213	66,111	19,102	14,175	1,502
0.5-2 ha	364,755	253,337	111,418	4,591	778
2-5 ha	717,699	495,439	222,260	406	127
5-20 ha	980,145	809,107	171,038	255	30
20-100 ha	253,877	230,363	23,514	216	4
100 ha and over	22,731	18,259	4,472	140	—
200 ha and over	12,568	9,541	3,027	64	—
Total	2,424,420	1,872,616	551,804	19,783	2,441
5-10 ha	588,958	468,744	120,214	142	25
10-20 ha	391,187	340,363	50,824	113	5

Total A (A.1+A.2-6)=under 0.5 ha=494,761 ⎫
　　　　　　　　　　 0.5-2 ” =568,575 ⎬ =1,063,336

nel at agricultural enterprises by main occupation:

ral enterprises were distributed by *main occupation* as follows:

ture (day labourers, labourers)	A. 2-6 Vegetable gardening, livestock farming, fisheries, etc.		B. Industry			
			independent		ancillary personnel	
	independent	ancillary personnel	total	of them engaged in handicrafts	total	of them apprentices, assistants and workers
351,347	11,940	30,584	253,194	17,663	752,278	703,935
155,330	13,007	30,114	203,677	10,042	305,102	291,039
16,636	5,564	12,688	108,968	2,206	65,004	61,212
1,078	2,040	4,979	37,575	201	5,477	4,613
7	411	197	3,512	4	128	43
—	41	7	230	—	7	—
—	18	1	82	—	1	—
524,398	33,003	78,569	607,156	30,116	1,127,996	1,060,842
1,053	1,458	2,628	28,811	174	4,950	4,276
25	582	2,351	8,764	27	527	337

[ctd on next page]

[ctd]

	Owners and other supervisory personnel at agricul by *main occupa*						
	C. 1-11 Trade and Insurance		C. 12-26 Transport and Communications		C. 27 Hotels and Inns		
	Independent	Ancillary personnel	Independent	Ancillary personnel	Independent	Ancillary personnel	
Under 0.₅ ha	70,786	14,878	11,993	104,011	27,837	863	
From 0.₅ ha to under 2 ha	40,908	3,089	10,046	32,454	23,104	210	
2-5	17,703	540	7,544	8,286	17,454	54	
5-20	7,215	92	3,646	1,106	12,728	12	
20-100	720	8	243	20	818	—	
100 and >	36	—	3	—	10	—	
200 ha and over	13	—	1	—	2	—	
Total	137,368	18,607	33,475	145,877	81,951	1,139	
5-10 ha	5,386	75	2,768	985	9,281	10	
10-20 ha	1,829	17	878	121	3,447	2	

tural enterprises were distributed
tion as follows:

D	E	F	G	H	K		of them hired labour (Σ of the columns marked in red pencil)
Household services and casual hired labour	Private and public employment, the professions	No occupation, and no occupation reported	Domestic servants living in	Members of households without trade at all or only with side line	Managers of public enterprises	Total	This letter is mine / My figures
17,351	101,442	227,116	323	5,746	1,481	2,084,060	1,273,137 +14,175
3,780	29,086	70,333	32	2,108	1,945	1,294,449	530,889 +4,591
501	11,297	13,823	9	242	1,732	1,006,277	
52	3,916	3,307	6	30	1,850	1,065,539	
2	756	407	1	3	861	262,191	
—	61	57	—	—	243	23,566	
—	24	13	—	—	100	12,887	
21,686	146,558	315,043	371	8,129	8,112	5,736,082	
44	2,636	2,515	6	26	1,041	652,798	
8	1,280	792	0	4	809	412,741	

Part *1b*: Table 3. Ploughland

	Number of farms with plough-land	Their total area in ha	Of the total area		
			Total	of this	
				spring wheat	winter wheat
				cereals accord	
Under 0.₅ ha	1,352,763	368,098	246,961	1,299	1,912
0.₅-2 ha	1,232,970	1,588,736	976,345 / [49.₁] 5.₀	8,115 / [0.₄] 2.₆	21,819 / [0.₉] 1.₈
2-5 ha	985,613	3,948,861	2,350,006 / [54.₆] 9.₆	17,468 / [0.₄] 4.₉	99,763 / [2.₃] 7.₅
5-20 ha	1,050,696	13,124,460	7,728,039 / [56.₁] 31.₆	72,891 / [0.₅] 20.₃	430,479 / [3.₁] 32.₅
20-100 ha	259,475	11,942,678	7,220,699 / [57.₂] 29.₆	106,714 / [0.₉] 29.₈	426,074 / [3.₄] 32.₂
100 ha* and over	23,262	9,368,409	5,910,304 / [59.₆] 24.₂	151,878 / [1.₅] 42.₄	343,725 / [3.₅] 26.₀
200 ha and over	12,769	7,379,305	4,683,308	114,751	262,029
Total	4,904,779	40,341,242	24,432,354 / [56.₇] 100.₀	358,365 / [0.₈] 100.₀	1,323,772 / [3.₁] 100.₀
			<2 ha) 1,223,306 / 2-20) 10,078,045 / >20) 13,131,003	9,414 / 90,359 / 258,592	23,731 / 530,242 / 769,799
5-10 ha	641,983	5,634,959	3,379,657	26,818	178,520
10-20 ha	408,713	7,489,501	4,348,382	46,073	251,959

Bottom %% (Zahn, 1910, p. 574[109]): ☐ =% of total area of figure is % of all area under a *given* cereal, etc. [see p. 30

---

* See p. 327.—*Ed.*

and its cultivation

ploughland makes up

under { all these 7 = total area under cereals (after Zahn) }

spelt (ing to Zahn)	rye	barley	oats	mixed cereals	sugar-beet
1,615	32,386	8,511	10,667	1,444	1,257
14,235	260,602	56,479	105,499	15,809	8,473
[0.6] 6.9	[11.8] 4.8	[2.6] 4.0	[4.7] 2.7	[0.7] 1.9	[0.4] 1.9
53,576	648,844	157,406	371,046	51,873	18,858
[1.2] 23.1	[15.1] 10.6	[3.7] 9.7	[8.6] 8.8	[1.2] 5.8	[0.4] 3.7
117,920	2,106,517	542,951	1,473,212	204,784	77,582
[0.9] 50.5	[15.3] 34.5	[4.0] 33.5	[10.7] 35.0	[1.5] 22.7	[0.6] 15.1
42,730	1,795,482	476,069	1,384,181	273,528	125,961
[0.3] 18.9	[14.2] 29.4	[3.8] 29.4	[10.9] 32.9	[2.2] 30.3	[1.0] 24.5
1,460	1,262,945	379,896	865,713	354,560	281,691
[0.0] 0.6	[12.8] 20.7	[3.8] 23.4	[8.7] 20.6	[3.6] 39.3	[2.8] 54.8
282	1,018,704	298,069	651,013	288,599	221,857
231,536	6,106,776	1,621,312	4,210,318	901,998	513,822
[0.5] 100.0	[14.2] 100.0	[3.7] 100.0	[9.8] 100.0	[2.1] 100.0	[1.2] 100.0
15,850	292,988	64,990	116,166	17,253	9,730
171,496	2,755,361	700,357	1,844,258	256,657	96,440
44,190	3,058,427	855,965	2,249,894	628,088	407,652
63,433	916,289	239,689	624,989	81,684	31,327
54,487	1,190,228	303,262	848,223	123,100	46,255

[ctd on next page]

agricultural enterprises (= 43,106,486), and the second of this notebook *].

[ctd]

(This table is taken in *full*.)

	Of the total area ploughland makes up				field pasture	fallow (bare)
	of this sown to					
	potatoes	fodder plants	vege-tables in fields	other field crops		
Under 0.5 ha	166,327	8,139	7,787	3,733	745	1,139
0.5-2 ha	333,605 — 20.1 / 15.8	80,516 — 3.6 / 3.4	20,877 — 1.1 / 10.8	29,127 — 1.3 / 3.1	11,836 — 0.5 / 1.2	9,353 — 0.4 / 1.0
2-5 ha	447,484 — 10.4 / 14.1	262,426 — 6.1 / 10.1	42,916 — 1.0 / 16.2	94,397 — 2.2 / 8.9	42,207 — 1.0 / 3.9	41,742 — 1.0 / 4.2
5-20 ha	948,993 — 6.9 / 29.9	841,726 — 6.1 / 32.6	100,569 — 0.7 / 37.9	308,102 — 2.2 / 29.0	221,618 — 1.6 / 20.4	280,695 — 2.0 / 28.4
20-100 ha	609,723 — 4.8 / 19.2	720,375 — 5.7 / 27.9	62,546 — 0.4 / 23.5	310,916 — 2.5 / 29.2	492,910 — 3.9 / 45.5	393,490 — 3.1 / 39.5
100 ha and over	667,698 — 6.7 / 21.0	671,500 — 6.8 / 26.0	30,841 — 0.3 / 11.6	316,388 — 3.2 / 29.8	315,073 — 3.2 / 29.0	266,936 — 2.7 / 26.9
200 ha and over	562,501	528,225	22,351	254,403	246,139	214,385
Total	3,173,830 — 7.4 / 100.0	2,584,682 — 6.0 / 100.0	265,536 — 0.6 / 100.0	1,062,663 — 2.5 / 100.0	1,084,389 — 2.5 / 100.0	993,355 — 2.3 / 100.0
<2 ha)	499,932	88,655	28,664	32,860	12,581	10,492
2-20)	1,396,477	1,104,152	143,485	402,499	263,825	322,437
>20)	1,277,421	1,391,875	93,387	627,304	807,983	660,426
5-10 ha	470,609	381,869	49,776	134,387	79,264	102,003
10-20 ha	478,384	459,857	50,793	173,715	142,354	179,692

%% according to Zahn

	Cereals		Total area under cereals		Vegetable gardens		Meadows		Fat pastures		Vineyards	
<2 ha	13.7	4.3	21.7	3.7	5.9	30.7	12.6	5.2	0.5	1.5	1.4	30.6
2-5	19.0	10.2	32.5	9.5	1.7	15.2	18.6	13.5	1.0	4.9	0.9	34.1
5-20	19.8	34.0	36.0	33.5	1.0	28.8	16.8	38.9	1.5	24.1	0.3	29.6
20-100	18.8	29.6	35.7	30.5	0.6	16.6	12.7	26.8	3.3	49.2	0.1	5.1
100 and >	17.8	21.9	33.9	22.8	0.4	8.7	9.4	15.6	1.7	20.3	0.0	0.6
Σ	18.6	100.0	34.2	100.0	1.1	100.0	13.8	100.0	2.0	100.0	0.3	100.0

	Total farmland		Area under forest husbandry		Small pastures		Waste and unsuitable land		Other land		Total area	
<2 ha	69.5	5.4	20.6	6.7	2.2	5.2	2.4	4.0	5.3	12.4	100.0	5.8
2-5	76.8	10.4	15.2	8.5	2.2	9.1	3.1	9.1	2.7	11.0	100.0	10.0
5-20	75.7	32.7	15.4	27.6	2.6	33.5	4.4	40.9	1.9	25.4	100.0	31.9
20-100	73.9	29.3	17.3	28.5	2.8	33.7	4.4	37.4	1.6	19.5	100.0	29.3
100 and >	71.1	22.2	22.2	28.7	2.0	18.5	1.3	8.6	3.4	31.7	100.0	23.0
Σ	73.9	100.0	17.8	100.0	2.5	100.0	3.4	100.0	2.4	100.0	100.0	100.0

Ibid. Table 2. *Number and area of farms*

	Agricultural enterprises in general		Of the total area		
	number of enterprises	area	land owned	land leased	other land *)
Under 0.5 ha	357,945	85,395	16,332	20,068	48,995
0.5-2 ha	182,806	182,068	77,613	60,207	44,248
2-5 ha	34,998	113,967	73,209	35,407	5,351
5-20 ha	3,751	27,679	19,590	7,434	655
20-100 ha	—	—	—	—	—
100 ha and over	—	—	—	—	—
200 ha and over	—	—	—	—	—
Total	579,500	409,109	186,744	123,116	99,249
<2 ha 2-20 ha >20 ha					
5-10 ha	3,687	26,769	18,945	7,183	641
10-20 ha	64	910	645	251	14

*) Other land=Dienstland, Deputant land, etc.

> I have made heavy cuts in this table, leaving out details for owned and leased land, etc.

of agricultural labourers and day labourers

	Of the total area			Farms holding land exclusively	
plough-land	under vegetable gardens and orchards (without decorative gardens)	under vineyards	farmland in general	under vegetable gardens	under potatoes
64,735	11,404	580	79,383	43,904	113,345
132,140	8,210	1,627	167,420	1,034	13,388
72,877	2,222	504	101,679	45	38
16,123	409	43	24,018	—	—
—	—	—	—	—	—
—	—	—	—	—	—
—	—	—	—	—	—
285,875	22,245	2,754	372,500	44,983	126,771
15,665	398	43	23,235	—	—
458	11	—	783	—	—

per farm		Quantity of all livestock in terms of big cattle
farmland ha	all livestock in terms of big cattle	
$0._{17}$	$0._4$	826,963
$1._1$	$1._5$	1,922,168
$3._2$	$4._2$	4,243,647
		10,960,779
$35._5$	$29._2$	7,662,750
$299._3$	$159._6$	3,764,098
$5._5$	$5._1$	29,380,405
		2,749,131
		15,204,426
		11,426,848
$7._0$	$7._8$	5,141,657
$14._1$	$14._1$	5,819,122

Per permanent labourer		bottom: *of them* permanent labourers / Number of *all* labourers
Farmland ha	All livestock in terms of big cattle	
0.$_4$	0.$_9$	2,014,307 / 854,016
1.$_6$	1.$_5$	2,338,745 / 1,294,848
1.$_6$	2.$_3$	2,913,877 / 2,079,120
		4,595,858 / 3,500,848
6.$_0$	4.$_9$	2,069,433 / 1,553,079
8.$_4$	4.$_5$	1,237,329 / 833,912
		940,790 / 635,155
3.$_1$	2.$_9$	15,169,549 / 10,115,823
<2 ha:		4,353,052 / 2,148,864
2-20:		7,509,735 / 5,579,968
>20:		3,306,762 / 2,386,991
2.$_4$	2.$_7$	2,491,337 / 1,894,631
3.$_6$	3.$_6$	2,104,521 / 1,606,217

Statistics of the German
For comparison, I take the 1895 data

1895	number of agricultural enterprises	no livestock	livestock in general	total number of such enterprises
			Farms with agricultural	
				in particular
<2 ha	3,237,030	831,771	2,405,259	965,517
2-5	1,016,318	26,658	989,660	960,110
5-20	998,804	9,090	989,714	985,911
5-10 ⎱	605,814	6,542	599,272	596,429
10-20 ⎰	392,990	2,548	390,442	389,482
20-100	281,767	1,837	279,930	279,274
100 and >	25,061	380	24,681	24,638
1895:	5,558,980	869,736	4,689,244	3,215,450
1907:	5,736,082	1,073,930	4,662,152	3,127,002
	+177,102	+204,194	−27,092	−88,448
1895 ½-1 ha	676,215	91,406	584,809	521,172
1-2 ha	707,235	51,708	655,527	243,588*)
1882:	5,276,344	834,441	4,441,903	3,255,887

% of farms

	no livestock		livestock in general	
	1895	1882	1895	1882
<2 ha	25.70	26.30	74.30	73.70
2-5	2.62	2.36	97.38	97.64
5-20	0.91	0.56	99.09	99.44
20-100	0.65	0.26	99.35	99.74
100 and >	1.52	0.38	98.48	99.62
Total	15.65	15.81	84.35	84.19

*) These figures erroneously transposed:
    243,588 refers to 50 ares-1 ha
    521,172 refers to 1 ha-2 ha.

Reich, Vol. 112
on the number of farms with livestock:

or dairy production *keeping* for their farm

big cattle			in general		
specifically			sheep	pigs	goats
horses and horned cattle	horses but no horned cattle	horned cattle but no horses			
28,954	40,080	896,483	141,466	1,731,919	1,330,953
152,440	20,968	786,702	80,057	799,803	192,272
584,561	10,601	390,749	184,648	887,424	160,808
278,748	7,536	310,145	87,985	527,741	98,071
305,813	3,065	80,604	96,663	359,683	62,737
267,190	1,473	10,611	122,498	266,073	34,306
24,357	149	132	15,072	22,222	2,609
1,057,502	73,271	2,084,677	543,741	3,707,441	1,720,948
1,153,258	65,441	1,908,303	390,821	3,899,820	1,783,375
+95,756	−7,830	−176,374	−152,920	+192,379	+62,427
+87,926					
5,067	12,213	226,308	34,911	428,775	357,522
21,752	18,829	480,591	41,101	483,609	246,734
996,244	42,180	2,217,463	749,217	2,950,588	1,505,357

with

big cattle in general		horses and horned cattle		horses but no horned cattle		horned cattle but no horses	
1895	1882	1895	1882	1895	1882	1895	1882
29.83	35.84	0.89	0.91	1.24	0.64	27.70	34.29
94.47	95.18	15.00	14.83	2.06	1.47	77.41	78.88
98.71	99.17	58.53	57.31	1.06	0.78	39.12	41.08
99.12	99.68	94.83	94.87	0.52	0.28	3.77	4.53
98.31	99.55	97.19	99.07	0.59	0.13	0.53	0.35
57.84	61.71	19.02	18.88	1.32	0.80	37.50	42.03

	1895			
	Number of farms		Number of those owning horned cattle	
	without big cattle:	without horses:	1895	1907
Under 2 ha	2,271,513	3,167,996	925,437	802,120 −
2-5 ha	56,208	842,910	939,142	934,193 −
5-20 ha	12,893	403,642	975,310	1,043,516 +
5-10 ha	9,385	319,530	588,893	636,748 +
10-20 ha	3,508	84,112	386,417	406,768 +
20-100 ha	2.493	13,104	277,801	258,683 −
100 and over	423	555	24,489	23,049 −
1895	2,343,530	4,428,207	3,142,179	3,061,561 −
1907	2,609.080	4,517,383	3,061,561	
	+265,550	+89,176	−80,618	
			3,213,707	
			(1882)	

cf. Schmelzle[110]			Number of those owning		
N.B. Number of horned cattle per owning farm				livestock in general (Nutzvieh)	
				1895	1907
			Under 0.5 ha	1,164,923	1,184,643 +
1895	1907	+%	0.5-2 ha	1,240,336	1,156,931 −
1.53	1.64	7.2	<2 ha	2,405,259	2,341,574 −
2.98	3.38	10.3	2-5	989,660	980,581 −
5.05	5.89	16.6	5-10	599,272	646,400 +
8.42	10.14	20.4	10-20	390,442	409,975 +
16.74	20.51	22.5	2-20 ha	1,979,374	2,036,956 +
79.92	100.97	26.3	20-100	279,930	260,415 −
			100 and >	24,681	23,207 −
			20 and >	304,611	283,622 −
			Total	4,689,244	4,662,152 −
			1882:	4,441,903	

[Cows not counted separately in 1895]

Growth of livestock

	horses			horned cattle			
	1895	1907		1895	1907		
<0.5 ha	14,528	9,598	−	237,606	196,262	−	
0.5 to 2 ha	74,356	61,769	−	1,177,633	1,119,370	−	
50 ares-1 ha	21,866			305,904			(1895 =100)
1-2 ha	52,490			871,729			1907:
<2 ha	88,884	71,367	−	1,415,239	1,315,632	−	
2-5	225,998	241,636	+	2,802,900	3,154,323	+	112.5
5-20	1,147,454	1,323,490	+	6,227,233	7,873,092	+	126
5-10	441,345	528,088	+	2,974,531	3,748,898	+	126.0
10-20	706,109	795,402	+	3,252,702	4,124,194	+	126.8
20-100	1,254,223	1,202,174	−	4,650,993	5,305,871	+	114.1
100 and >	650,739	652,436	+	1,957,277	2,327,291	+	118.8
Σ=	3,367,298	3,491,103	+	17,053,642	19,976,209	+	
1882	3,114,420			15,454,372			
cows:				12,689,526			
1882							
bulls:				2,764,846			

population

sheep			pigs			
1895	*1907*		1895	*1907*		
223,453	179,402	—	1,473,823	1,975,177	+	
344,234	236,359	—	1,992,166	2,407,972	+	
142,297			873,416			(1895 =100)
201,937			1,118,750			
567,687	415,761	—	3,465,989	4,383,149	+	126.4
489,275	359,943	—	2,338,588	3,107,038	+	132.8
1,871,295	1,448,545	—	4,210,934	6,334,146	+	150.0
682,591	537,561	—	2,106,453	3,158,595	+	
1,188,704	910,984	—	2,104,481	3,175,551	+	
3,498,936	2,326,268	—	2,658,560	3,655,146	+	132.9
6,165,677	4,371,103	—	888,571	1,386,272	+	167.2
12,592,870	8,921,620	—	13,562,642	18,865,751	+	
21,116,957			8,431,266			

[ctd on next page]

[ctd]

In terms of big cattle

sheep $= \frac{1}{10}$; pig $= \frac{1}{4}$; goat $= \frac{1}{12}$

	goats		see p. 43*			
	1895	*1907*	1895	1907		
<0.5 ha	1,260,176	1,312,416	747,951	826,963	+ 79,012	
0.5-2 ha	1,225,174	1,384,810	1,886,552	1,922,168	+ 35,616	
50 ares-1 ha	754,841					1895
1-2 ha	470,333					=100
<2 ha	2,485,350	2,697,226	2,634,503	2,749,131	+ 114,628	
2-5 ha	295,194	419,208	3,687,071	4,243,647	+ 556,576	
5-20 ha	252,096	429,656	8,635,557	10,960,779		126.9
5-10 ha	148,328	255,190	4,023,109	5,141,657	+1,118,548	
10-20 ha	103,768	174,466	4,612,448	5,819,122	+1,206,674	
20-100 ha	64,374	99,506	6,925,115	7,662,750	+ 737,635	
100 and >	8,237	8,314	3,447,412	3,764,098	+ 316,686	
Total	3,105,251	3,653,910	25,329,658	29,380,405	+4... ...	
1882	2,452,527					

* See p. 368.—*Ed.*

	Agricultural enterprises			Total area			Cultivated farmland		
	1895	1907	+/−	1895	1907	+/−	1895	1907	+/−
Under 0.5 ha	1,852,917	2,084,060	+	522,712	619,066	+	327,930	359,553	+
0.5-2 ha	1,385,450	1,294,449	−	1,893,202	1,872,936	−	1,460,514	1,371,758	−
<2 ha	3,236,367	3,378,509	+	2,415,914	2,492,002	+	1,808,444	1,731,311	−
2-5	1,016,318	1,006,277	−	4,142,071	4,306,421	+	3,285,984	3,304,878	+
5-10	605,814	652,798	+	5,355,138	5,997,626	+	4,233,656	4,607,090	+
10-20	392,990	412,741	+	7,182,522	7,770,895	+	5,488,219	5,814,474	+
2-20	2,015,122	2,071,816	+	16,679,731	18,074,942	+	13,007,859	13,726,442	+
20-100	281,767	262,191	−	13,157,201	12,623,011	−	9,869,837	9,322,103	−
100 and >	25,061	23,566	−	11,031,896	9,916,531	−	7,831,801	7,055,018	−
20 and >	306,828	285,757	−	24,189,097	22,539,542	−	17,701,638	16,377,121	−
Total	5,558,317	5,736,082	+	43,284,742	43,106,486	−	32,517,941	31,834,874	−

{ Zahn, *Annalen* 1910 p. 588 }	Horses			Horned cattle			Sheep			Pigs		
	1907	1895	1882	1907	1895	1882	1907	1895	1882	1907	1895	1882
<2 ha	$2._1$	$2._6$	$1._8$	$6._6$	$8._3$	$10._4$	$4._7$	$4._5$	$3._6$	$23._2$	$25._6$	$24._7$
2-5 ha	$6._9$	$6._7$	$6._5$	$15._8$	$16._4$	$16._9$	$4._0$	$3._9$	$3._5$	$16._5$	$17._2$	$17._6$
5-20 "	$37._9$	$34._1$	$34._2$	$39._4$	$36._5$	$35._7$	$16._2$	$14._8$	$12._7$	$33._6$	$31._0$	$31._4$
20-100 "	$34._4$	$37._3$	$38._6$	$26._6$	$27._3$	$27._0$	$26._1$	$27._8$	$26._0$	$19._4$	$19._6$	$20._6$
>100 "	$18._7$	$19._3$	$18._9$	$11._6$	$11._5$	$10._0$	$49._0$	$49._0$	$54._2$	$7._3$	$6._6$	$5._7$
Σ	100	100	100	100	100	100	100	100	100	100	100	100

Per 100 ha of farmland

	1907	1895	1882	1907	1895	1882	1907	1895	1882	1907	1895	1882
<2 ha	$4._1$	$4._9$	$3._1$	$76._0$	$78._3$	$88._4$	$24._0$	$31._4$	$41._2$	$253._2$	$191._7$	$114._1$
2-5 ha	$7._3$	$6._9$	$6._4$	$95._4$	$85._3$	$81._8$	$10._9$	$14._9$	$22._8$	$94._0$	$71._2$	$46._6$
5-20 "	$12._7$	$11._8$	$11._6$	$75._5$	$64._1$	$60._2$	$13._9$	$19._3$	$29._4$	$60._8$	$43._3$	$28._9$
20-100 "	$12._9$	$12._7$	$12._1$	$56._9$	$47._1$	$42._1$	$25._0$	$35._5$	$55._5$	$39._2$	$26._9$	$17._5$
100 ha and>	$9._2$	$8._3$	$7._5$	$33._0$	$25._0$	$19._8$	$62._0$	$78._7$	$147._1$	$19._6$	$11._3$	$6._2$
Σ	$11._0$	$10._4$	$9._8$	$62._7$	$52._4$	$48._5$	$28._0$	$38._7$	$66._3$	$59._3$	$41._7$	$26._5$

Goats

1907	1895	1882
73.8	80.0	80.6
11.5	9.5	9.2
11.8	8.1	7.9
2.7	2.1	2.1
0.2	0.2	0.2
100	100	100
155.8	137.4	108.2
12.7	9.0	7.1
4.1	2.6	2.1
1.1	0.7	0.5
0.1	0.1	0.1
11.5	9.5	7.7

Zahn, p. 593

Forced sales per 10,000 agricultural enterprises (Bavaria) (*1903-1907*)

<2 ha	41.6
2-5	39.7
5-10	35.0
10-20	32.9
20-50	46.3
50-100	102.4
100 and >	193.2
	39.4

Odd fact:

reduction in the number of *cows* since 1882!! Possibly not comparable data

1882:

	cows	pigs
<2 ares	2,405	11,908
2-5 ares	8,164	41,524
5-20 ares	64,527	258,184
20 ares-1 ha	565,230	1,027,664
1-2	937,158	744,402
		2,083,682
2-5	2,385,617	1,487,852
5-10	2,133,423	1,307,490
10-20	2,267,912	1,339,383
		4,134,725
20-50	2,528,533	1,383,768
50-100	728,778	348,797
		1,732,565
100-200	313,957	136,012
200-500	455,384	204,181
500-1,000	249,831	116,865
1,000 and >	48,607	23,236
		480,294
$\Sigma = 12,689,526$		8,431,266

	1	2	3	4
	Population by *main* occupation of those gainfully employed			
See p. 45 *	gainfully employed	household servants living in	members of family without main occupation	total number of persons in this category (1-3)
A 1 Σ [total] m [men] w [women]	2,295,210 1,997,419 297,791	118,677 3,861 114,816	4,723,729 1,902,489 2,821,240	7,137,616 3,903,769 3,233,847
A 2 {	137,710 112,367 25,343	15,731 206 15,525	282,476 112,442 170,034	435,917 225,015 210,902
A 3 {	17,416 14,960 2,456	5,529 102 5,427	21,475 7,197 14,278	44,420 22,259 22,161
B 1 {	44,368 30,845 13,523	3,272 30 3,242	19,671 6,306 13,365	67,311 37,181 30,130
B 2 {	28,722 26,468 2,254	428 — 428	67,834 25,490 42,344	96,984 51,958 45,026
B 3 {	3,476 3,257 219	390 2 388	2,937 820 2,117	6,803 4,079 2,724

* See p. 370.—*Ed.*
** Columns 7 and 8 are here reversed, as in the original. See Lenin's

5	6	8**	7**	9
of the gainfully employed (1)		in general engaged in side line, as an occupation, specified in preceding column	of the gainfully employed (1) with side line (as an occupation) notably in agriculture	total number of persons engaged in respective occupation (1+8)
without side line	with side lines (auxiliary employment) in general			
1,779,464	515,746	1,334,235	48,749	3,629,445
1,508,547	488,872	1,221,485	42,686	3,218,904
270,917	26,874	112,750	6,063	410,541
107,089	30,621	613,701	7,590	751,411
84,176	28,191	570,865	6,520	683,232
22,913	2,430	42,836	1,070	68,179
15,130	2,286	326,049	676	343,465
12,899	2,061	303,203	568	318,163
2,231	225	22,846	108	25,302
42,547	1,821	1,001	924	45,369
29,213	1,632	769	830	31,614
13,334	189	232	94	13,755
20,074	8,648	1,064	7,927	29,786
17,871	8,597	997	7,893	27,465
2,203	51	67	34	2,321
3,109	367	229	169	3,705
2,894	363	221	167	3,478
215	4	8	2	227

remarks on p. 370.— *Ed.*

[ctd on next page]

[ctd]

	1	2	3	4
	Population by *main* occupation of those gainfully employed			
	gainfully employed	household servants living in	members of family without main occupation	total number of persons in this category (1-3)
C 1 {	3,883,034 1,051,057 2,831,977	123 — 123	94,889 37,772 57,117	3,978,046 1,088,829 2,889,217
C 2 {	1,332,717 707,538 625,179	82 — 82	24,428 9,697 14,731	1,357,227 717,235 639,992
C 3 {	259,390 213,717 45,673	776 — 776	572,324 216,958 355,366	832,490 430,675 401,815
C 4 {	236,534 219,220 17,314	1,248 — 1,248	690,610 276,140 414,470	928,392 495,360 433,032
C 5 {	1,343,225 646,236 696,989	1,231 — 1,231	691,009 265,412 425,597	2,035,465 911,648 1,123,817
Total I A {	9,581,802 5,023,084 4,558,718	147,487 4,201 143,286	7,191,382 2,860,723 4,330,659	16,920,671 7,888,008 9,032,663

5	6	8	7	9
of the gainfully employed (1)		in general engaged in *side line*, as an *occupation*, specified in preceding column	of the gainfully employed (1) with side line (as an occupation) notably in agriculture	total number of persons engaged in respective occupation (1+8)
without side line	with side lines (auxiliary employment) in general			
3,741,662	141,372	2,951,361	1,239	6,834,395
980,807	70,250	589,229	762	1,640,286
2,760,855	71,122	2,362,132	477	5,194,109
1,319,072	13,645	79,539	617	1,412,256
697,078	10,460	21,914	599	729,452
621,994	3,185	57,625	18	682,804
19,108	240,282	63,962	238,219	323,352
13,104	200,613	55,512	198,884	269,229
6,004	39,669	8,450	39,335	54,123
4,670	231,864	6,040	231,719	242,574
4,001	215,219	5,267	215,096	224,487
669	16,645	773	16,623	18,087
1,317,664	25,561	116,403	936	1,459,628
632,159	14,077	52,448	504	698,684
685,505	11,484	63,955	432	760,944
8,369,589	1,212,213	5,493,584	538,765	15,075,386
3,982,749	1,040,335	2,821,910	474,509	7,844,994
4,386,840	171,878	2,671,674	64,256	7,230,392

There seems to be a mistake here.*

Distribution (in thousands) adopted
in *The Agrarian Question*, p. 244[111]

	1882	1895	1907
a)	2,253	2,522 +	2,450 −
c 1)	1,935	1,899 −	3,883 +
I (a+c 1)	4,188	4,421 +	6,333 +
II c 3)	866	383 −	259 −
I+II	5,054	4,804 −	6,592 +
b)	47	77	76
c 2)	1,589	1,719	1,333
c 4 and c 5)	1,374	1,445	1,580
III (b+c 2+c 4+c 5)	3,010	3,241 +	2,989 −
Total............................	8,064	8,045 −	9,581 +

Also collateral employment

	1882	1895	1907
a)	2,120	2,160	2,274
c 1)	664	1,061	2,951
c 2)	9	60	80
b)			2
c 3)			64
c 4-5)			122
	351	297	188
Total............................	3,144	3,578	5,493

---

* This is a later remark; it applies to the two places of the table
Lenin subsequently corrected.— *Ed.*

Distribution of ploughland (p. 15*)

	(see p. 15*) cereals (5 first)	α oats and mixed cereals	β sugar beet and potatoes	γ fodder plants	α+β+γ	vegetables, etc.	others	Σ	field pastures and fallow	Σ
Under 2 ha	406,973	133,419	509,662	88,655	731,736	28,664	32,860	1,200,233	23,073	1,223,306
2-20 "	4,247,815	2,100,915	1,492,917	1,104,152	4,697,884	143,485	402,499	9,491,783	586,262	10,078,045
20 and>	4,986,973	2,877,982	1,685,073	1,391,875	5,954,930	93,387	627,304	11,662,594	1,468,409	13,131,003
Σ	9,641,761	5,112,316	3,687,652	2,584,682	11,384,550	265,536	1,062,663	22,354,610	2,077,744	24,432,354
	meadows ha	fat pastures	vegetable gardens and orchards (without decorative gardens)	vineyards	farmland in general	lesser pastures and grazing areas				Head of livestock in terms of big cattle
Under 2 ha	312,372	12,604	147,727	35,302	1,731,311	55,674	Under 2 ha			2,749,131
2-20 "	3,114,864	248,037	211,965	73,531	13,726,442	452,162	2-20 "			15,204,426
20 and > "	2,524,394	593,165	122,024	6,535	16,377,121	553,456	20 and > "			11,426,848
Σ =	5,951,630	853,806	481,716	115,368	31,834,874	1,061,292				29,380,405

The conclusion is that (20 and>) have *more* cereal for fodder than (2-20). And (2-20) have less than half as much again of meadows (than 20 and >) and almost 1.5 times as much livestock.

2,524,000 ha of meadows for 11,427,000 head of livestock (in terms of big cattle)=0.220 **
3,115,000 "   "   15,204,000 "   "   )=0.204 **

* See pp. 324-25.—Ed.
** The figures 0.220 and 0.204 show ha of meadows per head of livestock in the 20 ha and over group and the 2-20 ha group of farms.—Ed.

Farms in terms of hired labour	(Total labour per farm)	Number of farms	Total labour
Almost without hired labour	(1-3)	3,689,289	6,539,697
Small minority of hired labour	(4-5)	856,756	3,730,716
Majority of hired labour	(6 and >)	466,095	4,899,136
(p. 41)* Total		5,012,140	15,169,549
Proletarian and small peasant	(Under 5 ha)	4,384,786	7,266,929
Middle peasant	(5-10 ha)	652,798	2,491,337
Big peasant and capitalist	(>10 ha)	698,498	5,411,283
Total		5,736,082	15,169,549

) Estimated from % of labour given on p. 41 for the

All the details from *Wolff, Les Engrais,*** Paris, 1887.

Note sources estimating the quantity of manure: *Garola,* S. 11409), pages 121-124. *Stoeckhardt's* method: multiplied by $1._3$ (horses), $2._3$ (cows), $1._2$ (sheep), $2._5$ (pigs).

idem in Kraft's *Agricultural Dictionary* 8°. S. 10575

J. Fritsch, Les Engrais (Paris 1909?; Bibliothèque 1/2 dry matter (Trockensubstanz) of feed+litter [Einstreu] the quantity of litter and feed, weighed in a dry state]. should be multiplied by $1._3$ kg for horse; $1._5$ for draught ox; means that the methods of Heuzè and Stoeckhardt are similar.]

* See p. 366.—*Ed.*
** Fertilisers.—*Ed.*

Approximate *) figure		Per farm			Approximate *) number of agric. machines	Agric. machines per farm
Farmland ha	Total livestock in terms of big cattle	labour	land	live-stock		
5,706,798	7,263,322	1.77	1.5	1.9	167,699	0.05
7,050,002	7,515,336	4.3	8.2	8.7	547,084	0.6
19,078,074	14,601,747	10.5	40.1	31.3	1,093,924	2.3
31,834,874	29,380,405	3.0	6.3	5.8	1,808,707	0.36
5,036,189	6,992,778				210,179	
4,607,090	5,141,657				398,495	
22,191,595	17,245,970				1,200,033	
31,834,874	29,380,405				1,808,707	

three categories by group.

Bibliothèque Nationale 8°. S. 9558, page 100 et seq.

Engrais (Paris 1903.—At the Bibliothèque Nationale, 8°.
fodder (weight of the dry feed substance)+litter (litter straw)

Nationale: 8°. S. 13195), p. 98 [according to *Wolff*:
also in dry state. $\Sigma \times 4$. According to other writers, double
According to M. *Heuzè*, Σ of litter and feed (in dry state)
2.3 for cows; 2.5 for pigs; 1.2 for sheep. (Average 1.8). [This

Female and child labo

(vertical   1) men
order: 2) women
         3) total).

(α)=temporary workers as % of *total* labour.

| | Permanent labour (workers) | | | | | | | | | |
| | family | | | | hired | | | | total | | |
		%	of them under 14 yrs	%		%	of them under 14 yrs	%		%	of them under 14 yrs
Under 0.5 ha	504,658 815,475		5,205	0.6	24,315 38,541		436	1.1	325,043 528,973 854,016		5,641
0.5-2 ha	766,435 1,227,994		16,215	1.3	36,260 66,854		1,364	2.3	492,153 802,695 1,294,848		17,579
2-5 ha	994,120 1,948,199		33,115	1.7	72,217 130,921		5,279	4.0	1,012,783 1,066,337 2,079,120		38,394
5-10 ha	777,286 1,673,305		30,475	1.8	115,670 221,326		9,358	4.2	1,001,675 892,956 1,894,631		39,833
10-20 ha	527,050 1,193,515		21,554	1.8	198,735 412,702		14,394	3.5	880,432 725,785 1,606,217		35,948
20-100 ha	289,099 717,351		10,007	1.4	344,910 835,728		17,843	2.1	919,070 634,009 1,553,079		27,850
100 ha and>	6,968 34,139		243	0.7	284,847 799,773		7,990	0.9	542,097 291,815 833,912		8,233
incl. 200 ha and>											
Total	3,865,616 7,609,978		116,814	1.5	1,076,954 2,505,845		56,664	2.3	5,173,253 4,942,570 10,115,823		173,478
Under 2 ha											
2-20											
20 and>											

agriculture

Temporary labour (workers)

family				hired				total			
	(α) %	of them			(α) %	of them			(α) %	of them	
		under 14 yrs	%			under 14 yrs	%			under 14 yrs	%
888,204 1,011,510	55	37,062	3.6	74,787 148,781	79	1,301	0.8	962,991 1,160,291	58	38,363	3.3
612,088 796,926	39	72,603	9.1	122,112 246,971	78	2,756	1.1	734,200 1,043,897	45	75,359	7.2
376,646 554,367	22	91,994	16.5	140,269 280,390	68	4,713	1.7	516,915 834,757	29	96,707	11.5
221,400 330,328	11	73,891	22.4	137,098 266,378	54	6,035	2.3	358,498 596,706	24	79,926	13.4
137,581 199,139	14	48,687	24.4	156,150 299,165	42	9,447	3.1	293,731 498,304	23	58,134	11.6
82,948 115,268	14	22,939	19.9	212,578 401,086	32	20,268	5.0	295,526 516,354	25	43,207	8.3
3,052 4,092	11	222	5.4	214,238 399,325	33	36,241	9.0	217,290 403,417	32	36,463	9.0
2,321,919 3,011,630	29	347,398	11.2	1,057,232 2,042,096	45	80,761	3.9	3,379,151 5,053,726	33	428,159	8.4

[ctd on next page]

[ctd]

	family		of them under 14 yrs	%	hired	%	of them under 14 yrs	%	total	%	of them under 14 yrs	
Under 0.5 ha	1,392,862 1,826,985		42,267	2.3	99,102 187,322		1,737	0.9	1,491,964 2,014,307		44,004	2
0.5-2 ha	1,378,523 2,024,920		88,818	4.4	158,372 313,825		4,120	1.3	1,536,895 2,338,745		92,938	3
2-5 ha	1,370,766 2,502,566		125,109	4.9	212,486 411,311		9,992	2.4	1,583,252 2,913,877		135,101	4
5-10 ha	998,686 2,003,633		104,366	5.2	252,768 487,704		15,393	3.1	1,251,454 2,491,337		119,759	4
10-20 ha	664,631 1,392,654		70,241	5.0	354,885 711,867		23,841	3.3	1,019,516 2,104,521		94,082	4
20-100 ha	372,047 832,619		32,946	3.9	557,488 1,236,814		38,111	3.1	929,535 2,069,433		71,057	3
100 ha and>	10,020 38,231		465	1.2	499,085 1,199,098		44,231	3.7	509,105 1,237,329		44,696	3
incl. 200 ha and>												
Total	6,187,535 10,621,608		464,212	4.4	2,134,186 4,547,941		137,425	3.0	8,321,721 15,169,549		601,637	
Under 2 ha	2,771,385 3,851,905				257,474 501,147				4,353,052			
2-20	3,034,083 5,898,853				820,139 1,610,882				7,509,735			
20 and >	382,067 870,850				1,056,573 2,435,912				3,306,762			

α=family workers; β=supervisors, managers, etc.; γ=permanent male and female farm-hands; δ=permanent day labourers and labourers; ε=temporary labour.

Zahn 1
Annalen, 1910
p. 595

Prussia

	α	β	γ	δ	ε	Σ=100% absolute figure
< 2 ha	88.5	0.1	1.5	0.8	9.1	2,594,470
2- 5 "	84.5	0.1	3.2	1.2	11.0	1,497,799
5- 20 "	72.1	0.1	10.9	2.1	14.8	2,518,338
20-100 "	38.9	0.6	29.5	9.9	21.1	1,374,647
100 and>	2.9	3.9	17.5	44.4	31.3	1,035,270
Σ	65.9	0.6	10.5	7.6	15.4	9,020,524

Bavaria

	α	β	γ	δ	ε	Σ=100% absolute figure
< 2 ha	89.3	0.1	1.9	1.0	7.7	382,369
2- 5 "	89.6	0.1	3.6	1.0	5.7	461,674
5- 20 "	79.2	0.1	13.2	1.3	6.2	934,697
20-100 "	50.8	0.3	35.8	3.9	9.2	301,141
100 and>	5.0	4.6	22.1	41.5	26.8	21,771
Σ	78.5	0.1	12.4	2.0	7.0	2,101,652

Saxony

	α	β	γ	δ	ε	Σ=100% absolute figure
Under 2 ha	84.9	0.3	1.4	2.1	11.3	94,372
2- 5 "	81.7	0.2	4.4	2.0	11.7	68,985
5- 20 "	69.0	0.3	19.9	2.0	8.8	166,231
20-100 "	34.4	1.6	42.4	8.3	13.3	86,601
100 and over	3.4	6.1	18.2	39.8	32.5	34,972
Total	62.6	1.0	17.8	6.2	12.4	451,161

Württemberg

	α	β	γ	δ	ε	Σ=100% absolute figure
Under 2 ha	90.9	0.1	1.2	0.8	7.0	220,355
2- 5 "	90.8	0.1	2.7	0.8	5.6	238,979
5- 20 "	77.6	0.1	12.7	1.8	7.8	236,082
20-100 "	46.8	0.8	32.5	5.1	14.8	51,785
100 and over	5.5	4.7	23.3	29.7	36.8	4,821
Total	83.1	0.1	7.6	1.6	7.6	752,022

All Germany (Σ=15,169,549 persons)

	α	β	γ	δ	ε
Under 2 ha	88.5	0.1	1.4	0.9	9.1
2- 5 "	85.9	0.1	3.2	1.2	9.6
5- 20 "	73.9	0.1	11.7	2.0	12.3
20-100 "	40.2	0.7	30.8	8.9	19.4
100 and over	3.1	4.1	17.4	43.1	32.3
Total	70.0	0.5	10.2	5.8	13.5

> Zahn (1910, p. 567) calls the 2-5 small-peasant farms
> the 5-20 middle-peasant farms
> the 20-100 big-peasant farms {ha-ha!

Owners of agricultural enterprises who are independent by main occupation

(Zahn 1910, p. 567)

	1907 absolute	%	1895 absolute	%	State on June 12, 1907 as a percentage of the 1906-1907 maximum**)		
					men	women	total
Under 2 ha	449,968	13.3	564,077	17.4	60.1	87.5	76.8
2-5	717,699	71.3	733,813	72.2	77.8	81.6	79.8
5-20	980,145	92.0	906,786	90.8	76.3	75.1	75.7
20-100	253,877	96.8	270,931	96.2	72.8	70.9	72.0
100 and over	22,731	96.5	23,523	93.9	86.3	81.4	84.2
Total	2,424,420	42.3	2,499,130*)	45.0	73.1	80.3	76.9

) cf. p. 38 of this notebook below.
**) Zahn, 1910; p. 568: comparison of the total number of workers on June 12, 1907 with the *maximum*.

* See p. 361.—*Ed.*

Owners of agricultural enterprises who were not independent farmers by main occupation

Volume *211.* p. 89 ("Die berufliche und soziale Gliederung")[112]		in industry	employed in communications	in trade and innkeeping	hired labour, casual work	Total
Total	1907	1,127,996	145,877	19,746	21,686	
	1895	790,950	101,781	13,593	36,737	
Under 0.5 ha	1907	752,278	104,011	15,741	17,351	
	1895	514,840	67,632	10,493	29,078	
0.5-2 ha	1907	305,102	32,454	3,299	3,780	
	1895	227,928	27,250	2,513	6,910	
2-5 ha	1907	65,004	8,286	594	501	
	1895	44,479	6,146	472	685	
5 ha and over	1907	5,612	1,126	112	54	
	1895	3,703	753	115	64	

In view of the very confusing nature of German occupations statistics, it is important to make the following clear and simple comparison for C *1* (members of families), according to Zahn (p. *486*), where those in the given occupation are the "gainfully employed, including members of their families without any occupation and their domestic servants".

	in the occupation 1882	1907	increase	millions
Independents (A including A 1,C 1)	20,586,372	20,881,542	295,170	+0.3
Employees	829,865	3,067,649	2,237,784	2
Workers (Class A 1,C 1)	18,398,378	28,396,761	9,998,383	10
Total	39,814,615	52,345,952	12,531,337	

Data on live

	Straw	Oats, fodder grasses and hay			
	α 7 cereals *) ha	β oats	γ fodder grasses	δ meadows	$\beta+\gamma+\delta$
Under 0.5 ha	57,834 7	10,667	8,139 1	29,370 3	48,176 5
0.5-2 ha	482,558 25	105,499	80,516 4	283,002 14	469,017 24
2-5	1,399,976 33	371,046	262,426 5	800,045 19	1,433,517 34
5-10	2,131,422 41	624,989	381,869 7	1,056,821 20	2,063,679 40
10-20	2,817,332 45	848,223	459,857 8[1]	1,257,998 22[2]	2,566,078 44
20-100	4,504,778 59	1,384,181	720,375 9[3]	1,595,781 21[4]	3,700,337 48
100 and>	3,360,177 89	865,713	671,500 18	928,613 25	2,465,826 65
Total	14,754,077 50	4,210,318	2,584,682 9	5,951,630 20	12,746,630 43
Under 2 ha					
2-20 ha					
20 ha and over					

) All the first 7, including oats and mixed cereals.

[1] 7.9; [2] $21.6 \Sigma = 29.5$

[3] 9.4; [4] $20.8 \Sigma = 30.2$

* See pp. 324-25.—*Ed.*

stock feed   [bottom=*per 100* head of total livestock in terms of big cattle]

| Pastures | | | | Mixed cereals +sugar- beet+pota- toes | Total area under feed $\beta+\gamma+\delta$ +mixed cereals |
ϵ field pastures	ζ fat pastures	η small pastures	$\epsilon+\zeta+\eta$		
745	535	13,833	15,113 2	169,028	49,620 6
11,836	12,069	41,841	65,746 3	357,887	484,826 25
42,207	42,027	96,771	181,005 4	518,215	1,485,390 35
79,264	77,783	140,225	297,272 6	583,620	2,145,363 41
142,354	128,227	215,166	485,747 8	647,739	2,689,178 46
492,910	419,935	357,443	1,270,288 16	1,009,212	3,973,865 52
315,073	173,230	196,013	684,316 18	1,303,949	2,820,386 75
1,084,389	853,806	1,061,292	2,999,487 10	4,589,650	13,648,628 46
					534,446
					6,319,931
					6,794,251

In the tables columns 3 and 4 are designated as they are here, but in the text Column 3 is called: landwirtschaftlich benutzte Fläche

1895:	Agricultural enterprises	Total area	Total farmland (with vegetable gardens and vineyards)	ploughland, meadow, pasture and other cultivated farmland (without vegetable gardens and vineyards)
$^1/_2$-1 ha	676,215	617,416	462,711	430,351
1-2 ha	707,235	1,275,786	997,803	947,796
5-10 ha	605,814	5,355,138	4,233,656	4,168,205
10-20 ha	392,990	7,182,522	5,488,219	5,436,867
Σ	5,558,317	43,284,742	32,517,941	32,062,491

Number of farms with leased land per 100		Leased land per 100 ha	
1895	1882	1895	1882
51.66	49.94	24.79	27.71
49.55	44.79	15.93	14.61
35.91	31.41	8.17	7.25
22.62	19.08	7.30	7.09
37.56	36.77	19.18	22.39
46.91	44.02	12.38	12.88

1895

	Farms with				Of total land	
	own land only	leased land only	more	less	own land ha	leased land ha
			than half land leased			
Under 2 ha	1,009,126	831,107	377,190	463,510	1,575,672	598,851
2-5	443,268	47,185	95,745	360,663	3,364,418	659,894
5-10	323,420	12,194	36,686	197,422	4,726,447	550,978
10-20	261,101	7,513	14,256	90,597	6,626,528	473,903
5-20	584,521	19,707	50,942	288,019	11,352,975	1,024,881
20-100	208,674	9,969	8,202	45,558	12,102,060	960,200
100 and>	15,401	4,991	1,229	3,193	8,875,255	2,116,215
Σ	2,260,990	912,959	533,308	1,160,943	37,270,380	5,360,041

As for other land, it is given in 1895 under 4 heads (Deputant, Dienst, common and share-cropping) which it is not worth while citing

	%	%	%	%	%	%
Under 2	31.18	25.68	11.65	14.32	65.22	24.79
2-5	43.62	4.64	9.42	35.49	81.23	15.93
5-20	58.52	1.97	5.10	28.84	90.55	8.17
20-100	74.06	3.54	2.91	16.17	91.98	7.30
100 and>	61.45	19.92	4.90	12.74	80.45	19.18
Σ	40.68	16.43	9.59	20.89	86.11	12.38

1895	A 1 Agriculture		A 2-6 Vegetable gardening, fisheries, etc.		B Industry		C 1-10 Trade		C 11-21 Transport and communications		C 22 Inn-keeping, etc.	
	independent	dependent	independent	dependent	independent	dependent	independent	dependent	independent	dependent	independent	dependent
<2 ha	564,077	689,523	24,163	52,329	534,323	742,768	105,018	12,234	23,539	94,882	41,971	772
2-5	733,813	25,212	4,578	10,602	121,263	44,479	17,315	419	6,432	6,146	16,308	53
5-20	906,786	2,066	2,286	4,476	44,204	3,588	7,519	99	2,818	729	12,715	11
20-100	270,931	148	592	194	4,320	111	787	5	197	24	1,209	—
100 and>	23,523	88	132	4	180	4	43	—	8	—	14	—
	2,499,130	717,037	31,751	67,605	704,290	790,950	130,682	12,757	32,994	101,781	72,217	836
5-10	538,417	1,822	1,567	2,386	33,123	3,252	5,541	75	2,132	655	8,872	6
10-20	368,369	244	719	2,090	11,081	336	1,978	24	686	74	3,843	5

1895	Casual hired labour d	Other types of occupation	N	Independent farmers	Independents in industry, trade, etc.	Hired labourers	Others and unidentified	Details about A 1 agriculture — independent: without subsidiary employment	independent: with subsidiary employment	dependent: managers, super-visors	dependent: male and female farm-hands	dependent: day labourers, labourers
<2 ha	35,988	314,780	3,236,367	588,240	704,851	1,628,496	314,780	416,983	147,094	18,888	57,039	613,596
2-5	685	29,013	1,016,318	738,391	161,318	87,596	29,013	546,361	187,452	437	481	24,294
5-20	64	11,443	998,804	909,072	67,256	11,033	11,443	768,440	138,346	205	54	1,807
20-100	—	3,249	281,767	271,523	6,513	482	3,249	247,037	23,894	142	—	6
100and>	—	1,065	25,061	23,655	245	96	1,065	17,986	5,537	88	—	—
	36,737	359,550	5,558,317	2,530,881	940,183	1,727,703	359,550	1,996,807	502,323	19,760	57,574	639,703
5-10	52	7,914						444,417	94,000	110	45	1,667
10-20	12	3,529						324,023	44,346	95	9	140

Checked with *Statistics of the German Reich*, Vol. 112 (incorrect figures in ☐) For a comparison I take the main data for 1882 and 1895 from *Handwörterbuch* (1909, 3. A), I, pp. 245-246.

		<2 ha	2-5	5-20	20-100	100 and>	Σ
Number of farms	1882: %	3,061,831 / 58.03%	981,407 / 18.60%	926,605 / 17.56%	281,510 / 5.34%	24,991 / 0.47%	5,276,344 / 100%
"	1895	3,235,169 / 58.22	1,016,239 / 18.29	989,701 / 17.97	281,734 / 5.07	25,057 / 0.45	
According to Statistics of the German Reich	1895	3,236,367 / 58.23	1,016,318 / 18.28	998,804 / 17.97	281,767 / 5.07	25,061 / 0.45	5,558,317 / 100%
	1907:	58.9	17.5	18.6	4.6	0.4	100
Their	1882: %	1,825,938 / 5.73	3,190,203 / 10.01	9,158,398 / 28.74	9,908,170 / 31.09	7,286,263 / 24.43%	31,868,972 / 100%
	1895	1,807,870	3,285,720	9,720,935	9,868,367	7,829,007	
cultivated farmland	1895	1,808,444 / 5.4	3,285,984 / 10.4	9,721,875 / 32.1%	9,869,837 / 29.3%	7,831,801 / 22.2%	32,517,941 / 100%
	1907	5.56	10.11	29.90	30.35	24.08%	100%

					Total area
1882	2,159,358	3,832,902	11,492,017	12,415,463	10,278,941	40,178,681
	5.37	9.54	28.60	30.90	25.59	100%
1895	2,415,914	4,142,071	12,537,660	13,157,201	11,031,896	43,284,742
	5.58	9.57	28.96	30.40	25.49	100%
1907	5.8	10.0	31.9	29.3	23.0	100%

N.B. The 1895 statistics have no classification of ploughland (Ackerbau) by cereals, and the ploughland is not even differentiated from the cultivated farmland.

1882:		Their	
Number of farms	total area ha		farmland
5-10	554,174	4,780,980	3,906,947
10-20	372,431	6,711,037	5,251,451

(ibidem 249)

Cultivated area by groups of main crops (ha and %)

	cereals and pulses	root crops	fodder grasses	commercial crops	field pasture and fallow
Deutsches Reich 1893: [from Handwörterbuch der Staatswissenschaften*]	15,992,120	4,237,661	2,519,375	261,090	2,760,347
	60.9%	16.2%	9.6	1.0	10.5%

* Socio-Political Manual.—Ed.

Essay at compiling tables with

	Number of farms	Workers (12.6.1907)			Of them *temporary* workers		
		total	family	hired	total	family	hired
Under 0.5 ha	2,084,060	2,014,307	1,826,985	187,322	1,160,291	1,011,510	148,781
0.5-2 ha	1,294,449	2,338,745	2,024,920	313,825	1,043,897	796,926	246,971
2-5 ha	1,006,277	2,913,877	2,502,566	411,311	834,757	554,367	280,390
5-10 ha	652,798	2,491,337	2,003,633	487,704	596,706	330,328	266,378
10-20 ha	412,741	2,104,521	1,392,654	711,867	498,304	199,139	299,165
20-100 ha	262,191	2,069,433	832,619	1,236,814	516,354	115,268	401,086
100 ha and >	23,566	1,237,329	38,231	1,199,098	403,417	4,092	399,325
Total	5,736,082	15,169,549	10,621,608	4,547,941	5,053,726	3,011,630	2,042,096
Groups		Average per farm (of those *classified* by number of workers)					
<0.5		1.3	1.2	0.1			
0.5-2		1.9	1.7	0.2			
2-5		2.9	2.5	-0.4			
5-10		3.8	3.1	0.7			
10-20		5.1	3.4	1.7			
20-100		7.9	3.2	4.7			
100 and >		52.5	1.6	50.9			
Σ		3.0	2.1	0.9			
Under 2 ha	3,378,509	4,353,052 1,324,193	3,851,905	501,147			395,752
2-20	2,071,816	7,509,735 3,655,513	5,898,853	1,610,882			845,933
20 and >	285,757	3,306,762 1,868,122	870,850	2,435,912			800,411

in pencil=incl. men **

---

  * At the top of the table in the MS., there is a pencilled note:
  ** This remark of Lenin's, pencilled in the MS., applies to the bottom.— *Ed.*

bottom—number of men *

more rational classifications:

Farms by total number of workers employed

Maximum of workers	of them temporary	1-3 workers			4-5 workers		
		Number of farms	Number of workers	ditto maximum	Number of farms	Number of workers	ditto maximum
2,613,590	748,065	1,451,952	1,909,576 / 477,726	2,352,229	19,644	82,823 / 34,269	93,014
3,052,997	961,223	1,100,624	1,890,699 / 604,490	2,477,627	81,584	346,013 / 151,820	396,563
3,650,514	1,017,027	736,510	1,692,687 / 750,403	2,218,214	222,679	948,215 / 449,854	1,107,537
3,210,172	985,213	308,550	799,896 / 401,716	1,153,062	274,771	1,190,772 / 590,891	1,466,802
2,860,082	1,054,726	79,796	215,288 / 118,100	392,231	200,753	899,958 / 467,410	1,239,495
2,875,384	1,207,037	11,714	31,278 / 19,443	75,589	57,167	262,202 / 150,793	441,452
1,469,685	631,681	143	273 / 212	3,056	158	733 / 500	2,377
19,732,424	6,604,971	3,689,289	6,539,697 / 2,372,090	8,672,008	856,756	3,730,716 / 1,845,537	4,747,240
			%			%	
			$94._8$			$4._1$	
			$80._9$			$14._8$	
			$58._1$			$32._5$	
			$32._1$			$47._8$	
			$10._2$			$42._8$	
			$1._5$			$12._6$	
			$0._0$			$0._1$	
5,666,587		2,552,576	3,800,275	4,829,856	101,228	428,836	489,577
9,720,768		1,124,856	2,707,871	3,763,507	698,203	3,038,945	3,813,834
4,345,069		11,857	31,551	78,645	57,325	262,935	443,829

[ctd on next page]

"Σ farms=5.012,140" and "Σ (maximum)=19,507,799".— Ed.
lower figures in Column 2, in the first three lines at the

[ctd]
Farms by total number of workers employed

(absolute figures: p. 7)*
% of women in *total* number of workers

Groups	6 workers and more			Total farms by number of workers			% of women in total number of workers		
	number of farms	number of workers	ditto maximum	number of farms	number of workers	ditto maximum	total	family	hired
Under 0.5 ha	2,504	21,908 / 10,348	26,817	1,474,100	2,014,307	2,472,060	74.1	76.2	53.2
0.5-2 ha	12,924	102,033 / 45,540	117,254	1,195,132	2,338,745	2,991,444	65.7	68.1	50.3
2-5 ha	35,669	272,975 / 130,368	310,602	994,858	2,913,877	3,636,353	54.4	54.7	51.6
5-10 ha	67,458	500,669 / 247,276	586,402	650,779	2,491,337	3,206,266	50.2	49.8	51.9
10-20 ha	131,391	989,275 / 499,495	1,226,351	411,940	2,104,521	2,858,077	48.4	45.3	49.8
20-100 ha	192,915	1,775,953 / 969,662	2,357,151	261,796	2,069,433	2,874,192	44.8	44.7	45.1
100 ha and >	23,234	1,236,323 / 727,512	1,463,974	23,535	1,237,329	1,469,407	41.0	26.2	41.6
Total	466,095	4,899,136 / 2,630,201	6,088,551	5,012,140	15,169,549 / 6,847,828	19,507,799	54.8	58.2	46.9

Groups	% of workers to Σ of classified workers	Average number of workers per farm				
< 0.5	1.1	8.7				
0.5-2	4.3	7.0				
2-5	9.4	7.7				
5-10	20.1	7.4				
10-20	47.0	7.5				
20-100	85.9	9.2				
100 and >	99.9	53.2				
Σ		10.5				
Under 2 ha	15,428	123,941	144,071	2,669,232	4,353,052	5,463,504
2-20	234,518	1,762,919	2,123,355	2,057,577	7,509,735	9,700,696
20 and >	216,149	3,012,276	3,821,125	285,331	3,306,762	4,343,599

* See p. 308.— *Ed.*

	(p, 2)* Subsidiary farms	Total farms	B A 1 and B A 2-6	B and C	pp. 13-14** marked in red pencil	E, F, H and K
				including farmers by main occupation		
			Independent farmers	Independent industrialists, craftsmen, traders, etc.	Hired labourers	Employees, others and unidentified
Under 0.5 ha	1,994,894	2,084,060	97,153	363,810	1,287,312	335,785
0.5-2	925,225	1,294,449	377,762	277,735	535,480	103,472
2-5	287,372	1,006,277	723,263	151,669	104,251	27,094
5-10	63,532	652,798	590,416	46,246	9,918	6,218
10-20	21,037	412,741	391,769	14,918	3,169	2,885
20-100	7,530	262,191	254,288	5,293	583	2,027
100 and >	456	23,566	22,772	279	154	361
Total	3,300,046	5,736,082	2,457,423	859,950	1,940,867	477,842
Under 2 ha	2,920,119	3,378,509	474,915		1,822,792	
2-20	371,941	2,071,816	1,705,448		117,338	
20 and >	7,986	285,757	277,060		737	

[ctd on next page]

---

* See p. 300.— *Ed.*
** See pp. 320-23.— *Ed.*

[ctd]

Use of agricultural machines: (below: per 100 farms)

	(% of farms) Number of farms using machines in general	Total of A — Number of cases of use of all types of machines	Number of machines owned — All except hand threshers and centrifuges	(others) Hand threshers	Milk separators	Total	(p. 21)* Total live-stock in terms of big cattle	Number of cases of farms linked with industries (p. 12)**
Under 0.5 ha	18,466 0.9%	20,660	457	444	684	1,585 0.1	826,963	2,663
0.5-2	114,986 8.8%	129,163	2,676	10,405	10,550	23,631 1.1	1,922,168	10,110
2-5	325,665 32.3%	379,343	15,338	116,297	53,328	184,963 18.3%	4,243,647	24,077
5-10	419,170 64.2%	567,766	65,102	250,490	82,903	398,495 61.4	5,141,657	23,732
10-20	353,366 85.6%	635,934	176,900	253,227	92,564	522,691 126.6	5,819,122	17,855
20-100	243,365 92.8%	602,464	282,430	187,317	78,556	548,303 209.1	7,662,750	11,920
100 and >	22,957 97.4%	89,273	112,396	9,746	6,897	129,039 547.5	3,764,098	7,535
Total	1,497,975 26.1%	2,424,603 ? 543	655,299	827,926	325,482	1,808,707 31.5	29,380,405	97,872
Under 2 ha	133,452					25,216	2,749,131	12,773
2-20	1,098,201					1,106,148	15,204,426	65,664
20 and>	266,322					677,342	11,426,848	19,455

* See p. 338.—*Ed.*
** See pp. 318-19.—*Ed.*

Austrian Statistics, Vol. LXXXIII, Part 1, *Austria.* Agricultural Census of June 3, 1902
For all this and details see black notebook[113]

| Total for Reich | | A. Purely family farms | | | Number of economically active persons | | | | | |
Groups by size of productive area	Total number of farms	1. Only owner participating	2. Members of family participating	total	a) owners	b) family members	c) employees	d) supervisory personnel	e) servants	f) day labourers
As a result:	2,856,349	547,107	1,677,830	9,070,682	3,424,016	4,389,405	12,294	57,657	942,766	244,544
-0.5	343,860	150,944	181,323	676,498	378,485	285,573				
0.5-1 "	369,464	115,117	227,109	846,265	427,081	401,905				
1-2 "	561,897	126,203	379,991	1,477,786	662,367	775,754				
2-5 "	792,415	114,833	545,274	2,454,298	954,844	1,384,305				
5-10 "	383,331	29,719	227,476	1,412,013	476,644					
10-20 "	242,293	8,565	91,456	1,044,972	325,083					
20-50 "	127,828	1,441	23,602	706,665	171,126					
50-100 "	17,372	182	1,299	126,291	17,791					
over 100 "	17,889	103	300	325,894	10,595					

Concerning the table on page 22.*
It is Table 1 taken from Vol. *202.*
I have two mistakes in the table: inadvertent transposition of columns *7* and *8.* That's one.

Then, the figures in Column 8 have been shifted.** Both mistakes have been *noted.*

The table refers to *Occupations Group* I (type of occupation A 1)=agriculture, breeding of animals used in agriculture, dairy farming, milk collector, agricultural wine-making, fruit-growing, vegetable gardening, tobacco-growing, etc. (p. 5) (types of occupation A 1)

"The subgroups of occupations under A, etc. (p. 4) include: a) independents, also managing employees and other managers of enterprises; b) non-managing employees, in general scientifically, technically and commercially trained administrative and supervisory personnel, and also book-keepers and office workers; c) other assistants, apprentices, factory wage workers and day labourers, including family members employed in industry and servants" (p. 4).

"The subgroup of occupations I A (type of occupations A 1) includes:

A 1) owners and co-owners; A 2) leaseholders, hereditary leaseholders; A 3) managing employees, other managers of production; B 1) employees on farms, also trainees and apprentices; B 2) supervisory personnel; B 3) book-keepers and office workers; C 1) family members working on the farm of the head of household; C 2) agricultural farm-hands, male and female; C 3) agricultural labourers, day labourers, cultivating their own or leased land; C 4) agricultural labourers, day labourers, not cultivating their own or leased land, but other land; C 5) agricultural labourers, day labourers, not cultivating any land" (p. 5).

I leave out the subgroups of occupations I B = vegetable gardening and livestock farming (types of occupations A 2, A 3); II A: forestry and hunting (type of occupations A 4) and II B: fisheries (types of occupations A 5, A 6), which together with I A constitute the *group A of*

---

* See pp. 342-45.—*Ed.*
** In the MS., the figures in Column 8 (groups 1-5) were displaced. In this volume they are given as indicated by Lenin (see p. 343).—*Ed.*

occupations. In this section totals are given for A, B, C, but *without subdivision* into A 1-3, B 1-3, C 1-5.

Written September 1910-
later than June 1913

First published in 1938
in *Lenin Miscellany XXXI*

Printed from the original

PLAN FOR PROCESSING THE DATA
OF THE GERMAN AGRICULTURAL CENSUS
OF JUNE 12, 1907[114]

*Capitalism in German agriculture.
The economics of German agriculture
according to the data of the 1907
Census.*

The capitalist system of agriculture in Germany according to the June 12, 1907 Census

The following main groups of questions (or themes) in processing the June 12, 1907 (agricultural) Census.

pp. 1-8 [115]

1. 0.　　*Introduction.*　　General statement of the question: "areas". My analysis of the Σ data.

(I. 8-20)
§ I. (pp. 8-20)

2. 1. *Main Groups.*
Proletarian,—peasant,—capitalist.
Co-relation of the three groups.

"*3 main groups
of farms
in Germany*"

§ II. Proletarian
farms.
(20-30)

Importance of this grouping. Proof of its being correct.

§ III. (30-40)

§ IV. (40-50)

I+II

§ V   (50-59)

§ VI (60-73)

§ VII (73-87)

3. *Hired Labour.*

4. 2. Female and child labour. The
odious privilege of small-scale production.

5. 3. Labour vs. farmland and quantity
of livestock. (Waste in small-scale
production)

6. 4. Machines (cf. with *Hungarian* statistics [116])

*

7. 5. *Livestock* { Increase in quantity of livestock. Decrease in number of livestock *owners.* } Hence, growth of expropriation

Comparison with *Danish* data
(cf. Dutch and **Swiss**)

group-
ing { N.B.
American
and
Russian
statistics }

6 bis

9. 6. Main *occupation* of owners
(cf. 1895) [117] (Farms as side lines.)

10. 7. Family, *family*-capitalist and
capitalist farms *by number of
workers.*

8. Industries:

8. 9. Use of land. [*Quantity of livestock
vs. fodder area.* Cf. Drechsler [118]
and *Hungarian* statistics.]

10. Rural population by status in
production (data not comparable).

11. Wine-growing farms (nothing interesting).

* This line was red-pencilled in the MS. to denote that up to there
the plan for the processing of German agricultural census data was
used by Lenin in his article, "The Capitalist System of Modern
Agriculture" (Article I).—*Ed.*

{ **American**
and
Russian
statistics }

11. 12. *Comparison   with   1895.*
Growth   of   *medium*   (peasant)
farms.   Transition   to   *livestock
farming.*
1) American statistics, on grouping,
2) Danish ⎫   on concentration of
3) Swiss   ⎭   livestock,
4) Hungarian on implements,
5) Russian on co-operatives.

---

*The following themes remain for
a second article*:

8. Livestock farming. Increase in quantity along with a decrease in the
number of owners=expropriation.
Cf. Danish and Swiss data.

9. Livestock feed. Cf. fodder area (cf.
Drechsler).

10. Main   and   auxiliary   occupation.
Non-farmers   and   semi-farmers.
Cf. 1895.

11. Family, family-capitalist and capitalist farms. Three main groups.

12. Cf. 1895. N.B.: American statistics
on 2 groups.

Tables: (in 1st article[119])

1) p. 19—**3** main groups (and hired labour)
2) p. 31—number of workers (family and hired) per farm in the seven groups
3) p. 38—% of temporary workers in the seven groups
4) p. 42—% of women in the seven groups
5) p. 45—% of children in the seven groups—
6) p. 52—average size of farm and area per worker in the seven groups
7) p. 62—machinery (%, number of machines owned and %) in the *seven* groups
8) p. 69—hired labour and machines (*3* groups)
9) p. 79—ploughs on farm—8 groups
10) p. 86—% of cases of use of machinery in 1882, 1895, 1907 in the seven groups

Written September 1910-
later than June 1913

First published in 1938
in *Lenin Miscellany XXXI*

Printed from the original

DANISH STATISTICS[120]

Danmarks Statistik.

I had the last 5 (⊔) (1888-1909)

Livestock: *1838*: Statistical Tables Earliest Series, Part Five.—*1861*: ibid. Third Series, Vol. 3.—*1866*: ibid., Third Series, Vol. 10.—*1871*: ibid., Third Series, Vol. 24.—*1876*: Fourth Series, C No. 1.—*1881*: Fourth Series. C No. *3*.— |1888| : Fourth Series, C No. 6.— |1893| : Fourth Series, C No. 8.— |1898| : Fifth Series, C No. 2 (and *Statistical Bulletins*, Fourth Series, Vol. 5, Part 4)— |1903| : *Statistical Bulletins*, Fourth Series, Vol. 16, Part 6.— |1909| : *Statistical Tables*, Fifth Series, C No. 5.

Quantity of livestock in Denmark:

	Horned cattle (head)	Total livestock in terms of big cattle[1]:	Population	Number of farms with horned cattle	Carts	Other vehicles	Two-horse teams	1898. p. 13★ Unification of livestock [horse=3; horned cattle=1; sheep=$\frac{1}{6}$; pig=$\frac{1}{4}$]	1898. p. 25★ Population in rural areas (roughly)	Total farms	Their total horned cattle (head)
1838:	854,726	1,565,538						2,162,707			
1861:	1,118,774	1,856,041						2,464,768			
1871:	1,238,898	2,008,606	1,811,000					2,606,293			
1881:	1,470,078	2,278,135	1,999,000	176,452				2,902,718			
1888:	1,459,527	2,338,042	2,140,000	177,186	265,775	123,305	136,534	2,983,022	1,411,547		
1893:	1,696,190			179,800				3,343,148	1,423,613		
1898:	1,744,797			180,641	292,703	159,330	143,875	3,563,975	1,444,700	278,673	1,744,797
1903:	1,840,466			179,225	327,003	206,076	166,531	3,815,000			
1909:	2,253,982			183,643						274,248	2,218,350

1838–
1888:+70.76%+49.34%

[1] 1 head of horned cattle=1; 1 horse=$1\frac{1}{2}$; 1 donkey=$\frac{1}{2}$; 1 sheep and 1 goat=$\frac{1}{10}$; 1 pig=$\frac{1}{4}$. Totals *without goats and donkeys* (1888, p. xvi).

(In 1903 — no data on quantity

Number of farms with...

	1	2	3	4-5	6-9
1909:	9,167	16,785	19,092	31,273	32,710
1903:					
1898:	18,376	27,394	22,522	27,561	26,022
1893:	20,596	27,714	21,908	26,877	25,494
1888:	29,394	32,115	19,982	22,889	23,013

Danish 1909
Pages:

	(p. 48 ★)			
	farms	%	Land %	Horned cattle %
<3.3 ha	101,124	42.2	2.6	4.9
3.3-9.9 ha	50,732	21.2	9.1	12.3
9.9-29.7 ha	55,703	23.3	31.2	35.2
>29.7 ha	31,916	13.3	57.1	47.6
Σ=239,475	100.0	100.0	100.0

of horned cattle by groups.)

head of *horned cattle*:

10-14	15-29	30-49	50-99	100-199	200 and >	Total
22,498	37,384	11,360	2,440	640	294	183,643
20,375	30,460	5,650	1,498	588	195	180,641
19,802	29,865	5,335	1,447	594	168	
19,855	24,383	3,638	1,233	555	129	177,186

statistics
48 *; 162

(p. 162) Number of farms with horned cattle	%	Head of horned cattle
38,696	38%	105,923
49,558	98%	267,817
55,188	99%	767,355
31,781	99%	1,039,740
175,223	73%	2,180,835
+4,738		+37,515
179,961		2,218,350

α) Under 3.$_3$ ha = roughly proletarians and semi-proletarians

β)   3.$_3$-9.$_9$ ha=small peasants
γ)   9.$_9$-27.$_7$ ha=big peasants, peasant bourgeoisie
δ)   >29.$_7$ ha=capitalist agriculture

	Farms	Land	Horned cattle
	%	%	%
α+β))	63.$_4$	11.$_7$	17.$_2$
δ))	13.$_3$	57.$_1$	47.$_6$
γ+δ))	36.$_6$	88.$_3$	82.$_8$%

Number of farms by head
of horned cattle

	1881	1888
1-3 head	79,320	81,491
4-14 "	67,122	65,757
15-49 "	28,089	28,021
50 and over	1,921	1,917
Total	176,452	177,186

(Page 42[*])
Number of farms by head of horned cattle

	1898	%	1909	%	+ or − 1898-1909
1-3 head	68,292	37.$_8$	45,044	24.$_5$	−34.$_0$%
4-14	73,958	40.$_9$	86,481	47.$_1$	+16.$_9$%
15-49	36,110	20.$_0$	48,744	26.$_6$	+35.$_0$%
50 and >	2,281	1.$_3$	3,374	1.$_8$	+46.$_3$%
Σ=	180,641	100.$_0$	183,643	100.$_0$	+ 1.$_7$%

Number of *horned cattle* compared:

(p. 18 ★)

	per '000 population	per' 000 ha
Denmark	837 (682) [1]	578 (38) [2]
Germany	330 (343)	382 (29)
Russia	270 (292)	68 (5)

> In Germany, 10-20 ha farms
> have 33% of the hired labour
> *N.B.*

1898

	Number of farms %
Without land	4.82
< 1 Tönde Hartkorn *	52.49
1-4 " "	16.34
4 and > " "	10.69
	84.34
Unidentified area	16.46
	$\Sigma = 100.80$

[1] Bracketed figures are for 1883-1888
[2] idem. *per sq. km.*

> 100 ha = 1 sq. km.

* Under 1 Tönde Hartkorn means "areas with a crop yield of under 1 ton".—*Ed.*

Number of farms
by quantity of
horned cattle

1885			*1888*	*1881*		
_147,584	50 and more head		1,917	1,921	−	4
2,671	15-49	"	28,021	28,089	−	68
144,913	+ 4-14	"	65,757	67,122	−1,365	
87,621	1-3	"	81,491	79,320	+2,171	
232,534				176,452		

Written in December 1910-1913

First published in 1938
in *Lenin Miscellany XXXI*

Printed from the original

AUSTRIAN AGRICULTURAL STATISTICS[121]

EXTRACTS

N.B. *Oesterreichische Statistik,* Band *83* (Vol. LXXXIII), Heft 1, (1902).

The name of this volume: Results of the Farm Census of June 3, 1902 (etc.). Vienna, *1909.*
Austrian Agricultural Statistics.
Austrian Statistical Handbook
         Vol. 27 — 1908 etc. (back)
         Vol. 28 *) — 1909 (last one)
Results of the Farm Census of June 3, 1902 (Vol. 27, p. 138).

		%
Number of enterprises in general 2,856,349		100
" " purely agricultural 2,133,506		$74._7$
" " agricultural and forestry 713,382		$25._0$
" " purely forestry 9,461		$0._3$

Average size of enterprise in ha:
               total area = $10._5$ ha
               productive area = $9._9$ ha

---

*) Vol. 29 — 1910 (Vienna, 1911, 6 kronen).
Nothing about agricultural statistics. Only references to previous years.
   There are data on industry.

Agricultural and forestry enter

By type of

Number of enterprises with indication

	in general*)	under 2 ha	2-100 ha	over 100 ha
Machinery in general	947,111	139,548	796,811	10,752
Straw-cutters	804,427	109,218	685,418	9,791
Cleaners and graders	372,501	33,273	332,186	7,042
Threshers	328,708	10,089	310,316	8,303
Seeders	75,331	3,580	66,208	5,543
Crushers	45,117	9,073	33,682	2,362
Rakes and tedders	14,326	76	9,859	4,391
Mowers	13,151	68	10,182	2,901
Separators	8,674	248	7,543	883
Rootcrop lifters	6,175	205	4,720	1,250
Maize cultivators	4,608	277	3,863	468
Manure spreaders	2,438	25	979	1,434
Hay and straw presses	1,668	255	1,147	266
Steam ploughs	383	—	45	338
Narrow gauge lines	122	—	16	106

*) Percentage of farms using machinery .... $33._2$ $10._9$ $51._{10}$ $60._1$

---

* Figures from *Austrian Statistics*, Vol. LXXXIII, Part 1, p. XXXIV and (p. 385) is a selective summary from a number of tables.— *Ed.*

prises using agricultural machinery:

machinery:

of use of machines: with cultivated area*

2-5 ha	5-10	10-20	20-50	50-100
288,931	220,588	174,876	100,520	11,896
248,163	190,237	149,706	87,038	10,274
87,271	92,355	95,292	52,322	4,946
43,142	76,744	109,982	72,595	7,853
6,592	11,993	25,450	19,840	2,333
9,216	7,417	8,403	7,475	1,171
155	417	2,134	5,511	1,642
261	575	2,530	5,616	1,200
562	799	2,488	3,246	448
608	904	1,498	1,356	354
490	698	1,321	1,113	241
54	97	183	406	239
250	248	276	284	89
1	—	4	19	21
—	3	1	5	7

pp. 27-29. The first part of the table (p. 384) is given in full, the second

13—738

Classification of agricultural and forestry enterprises by size of *productive* area (distinct from total area, farmland, ploughland and meadow, etc.)

(Vol. 27, p. 141)

Under 0.5	ha	343,860	
0.5- 1	"	369,464	
1- 2	"	561,897	
2- 5	"	792,415	
5- 10	"	383,331	
10- 20	"	242,293	
20- 50	"	127,828	
50-100	"	17,372	
>100	"	17,889	

My total

Σ   2,856,349

*

100- 200	8,099
200- 500	6,050
500-1,000	2,100
> 1,000	1,640

No general grouping by area, only data on enterprises (by produc

	Number of enter-prises	Plough-land	Meadow	Vegetable gardens	Area Vineyards
Total	2,856,349	10,624,851	3,072,230	371,240	242,062
with 100 ha and over	17,889	1,640,937	391,047	32,617	7,372
under 100 ha	2,838,460	8,983,914	2,681,183	338,623	234,690

---

* These detailed figures by groups of area over 100 ha are taken 149).— *Ed.*

** The data in the following table are taken from the same source,

*** The data are from the same source, 27th year of publication

(Vol. 27, p. 143)

	Enterprises by farmland	%	by productive area **	%
Under 2 ha	1,322,565	46.5	1,275,221	44.6
2- 5 ha	810,225	28.5	792,415	27.7
5- 20 "	613,290	21.6	625,624	21.9
20-100 "	89,342	3.1	145,200	5.1
Over 100 ha	11,466	0.3	17,889	0.7
	2,846,888	100.0	2,856,349	100.0

with 100 ha and over and enterprises with <100 ha
tive area) ***

in *ha*:

Pastures	Mountain pastures	Forest	Lakes, swamps, ponds and unsuitable land	Total
2,655,371	1,399,724	9,777,933	1,857,373	30,000,784
652,273	900,899	5,477,565	750,866	9,853,576
2,003,098	498,825	4,300,368	1,106,507	20,147,208

from *Austrian Statistical Handbook*, 28th year of publication, 1909 (p.

27th year of publication, 1908, pp 141 and 142.—*Ed.*
1908, pp. 146-47.—*Ed.*

(*Vol.* 28,

Enterprises by personnel

	Purely family enterprises	
	owner only	family members
Under 0.5 ha	150,944	181,323
0.5-1 ″	115,117	227,109
1-2 ″	126,203	379,991
2-5 ″	114,833	545,274
5-10 ″	29,719	227,476
10-20 ″	8,565	91,456
20-50 ″	1,441	23,602
50-100 ″	182	1,299
over 100 ″	103	300
	——	——
Total	547,107	1,677,830

p. 152)

and productive area:

Enterprises with non-family personnel				
without employees or supervisory personnel				
servants only	day labourers only	servants and day labourers	outside labour only	with employees and supervisory personnel
	with casual outside labour			
7,569	1,093	79	1,000	1,852
10,326	2,688	173	12,960	1,091
25,146	5,441	503	22,945	1,668
72,380	13,675	1,952	41,286	3,015
81,182	12,027	3,302	26,546	3,079
107,401	8,193	6,955	15,960	3,763
79,277	3,469	9,887	4,702	5,450
9,189	579	2,060	332	3,731
3,844	207	828	79	12,528
——	——	——	——	——
396,314	47,372	25,739	125,810	36,177

[ctd on next page]

[ctd]

	Personnel								
	male					female			
	All persons	over	%	under	%	over	%	under	%
		16 years old							
Under 0.5 ha	676,498	295,781 ⎫		28,917 ⎫		321,197 ⎫		30,603 ⎫	
0.5-1 ha	846,265	366,460 ⎬ 43.1		44,368 ⎬ 5.7		389.709 ⎬ 45.4		45,728 ⎬ 5.8	
1-2 ha	1,477,786	632,150 ⎭		96,609 ⎭		651,033 ⎭		97,994 ⎭	
2-5 ha	2,454,298	1,045,423	42.6	191,088	7.8	1,032,920	42.1	184,867	7.5
5-10 ha	1,412,013	612,615 ⎫		114,465 ⎫		578,558 ⎫		106,375 ⎫	
10-20 ha	1,044,972	466,357 ⎭ 43.9		70,279 ⎭ 7.5		444,227 ⎭ 41.6		64,109 ⎭ 7.0	
20-50 ha	706,665	329,369 ⎫		44,257 ⎫		296,132 ⎫		36,907 ⎫	
50-100 ha	126,291	66,803 ⎭ 47.6		6,311 ⎭ 6.1		48,233 ⎭ 41.3		4,944 ⎭ 5.0	
over 100 ha	325,894	228,949	70.3	7,500	2.3	83,220	25.6	6,225	1.9
Total	9,070,682	4,043,907	44.6	603,794	6.6	3,845,229	42.5	577,752	6.3

Number of gainfully employed persons

owners	family members	employees	super- visors	servants	day labourers
378,485	285,573	86	1,895	8,935	1,524
427,081	401,905	18	1,103	12,440	3,718
662,367	775,754	24	1,686	29,984	7,971
954,844	1,384,305	40	3,051	91,136	20,922
476,644	789,325	67	3,114	120,151	22,712
325,083	474,248	116	3,884	214,674	26,967
171,126	237,972	320	5,716	259,787	31,744
17,791	27,642	533	4,146	60,306	15,873
10,595	12,681	11,090	33,062	145,353	113,113
3,424,016	4,389,405	12,294	57,657	942,766	244,544

[ctd on next page]

[ctd]

	Purely family farms	Farms with non-family personnel	Total farms*
Under 0.5 ha	332,267	11,593	343,860
0.5-1 ,,	342,226	27,238	369,464
1-2 ,,	506,194	55,703	561,897
2-5 ,,	660,107	132,308	792,415
5-10 ,,	257,195	126,136	383,331
10-20 ,,	100,021	142,272	242,293
20-50 ,,	25,043	102,785	127,828
50-100 ,,	1,481	15,891	17,372
>100 ,,	403	17,486	17,889
	2,224,937	631,412	2,856,349
Under 5 ha		226,842	2,067,636
5-10 ,,		126,136	383,331
10 and >,,		278,434	405,382
		631,412	2,856,349

* The three boxed figures are combined from Table 6 of *Austrian*
** Source of this and the following tables: *Austrian Statistics*. Vol.

Number of farms connected with **			(My total) Farms providing hired labour	Number of farms connected with handicraft industries
agricultural wage labour	industrial	wage labour without further specification		
103,949	47,585	25,072	176,606	27,266
131,738	36,152	27,587	195,477	27,271
190,504	44,314	39,090	273,908	39,782
186,271	38,381	37,082	261,734	47,611
} 58,173	11,437	14,036	83,646	23,833
670,635	177,869	142,867	991,371	165,763
(α+β) total with hired labour and craftsmen			(α)	(β)
1,049,655			907,725	141,930
} 107,479			} 83,646	} 23,833
1,157,134			991,371	165,763

[ctd on next page]

Statistical Handbook, 28th year of publication, 1909 (p. 152).— Ed.
LXXXIII, Part 1, p. 41.— Ed.

[ctd]

	Number of farms connected with				
	other agricultural enterprises	industrial enterprises	Total men	Total women	%
Under 0.5 ha	⎫		324,698	351,800	52.0
0.5-1 "	13,187	127,088	410,828	435,437	51.5
1-2 "	⎭		728,759	749,027	50.7
2-5 "	8,659	72,385	1,236,511	1,217,787	49.6
5-10 "	5,540	35,551	727,080	684,933	48.5
10-20 "	4,922	21,689	536,636	508,336	48.6
20-50 "	4,130	12,595	373,626	333,039	47.1
50-100 "	1,354	2,702	73,114	53,177	42.1
over 100 "	3,396	4,726	236,449	89,445	27.4
	41,188	276,736	4,647,701	4,422,981	48.7

Under 5 ha	221,319
5-10 "	41,091
10 ha and over	55,514
	317,924

Total children (under 16 yrs)	%	Total family workers	Total hired labourers	Total workers	
59,520	8.8	664,058	12,440	676,498	
90,096	10.6	828,986	17,279	846,265	
194,603	13.2	1,438,121	39,665	1,477,786	
375,955	15.3	2,339,149	115,149	2,454,298	
220,840	15.6	1,265,969	146,044	1,412,013	
134,388	12.8	799,331	245,641	1,044,972	
81,164	11.3	409,098	297,567	706,665	
11,255	9.0	45,433	80,858	126,291	
13,725	4.2	23,276	302,618	325,894	
1,181,546	13.0	7,813,421	1,257,261	9,070,682	
					Number of farms using machinery
		5,270,314	184,533	5,454,847	428,479
		1,265,969	146,044	1,412,013	220,588
		1,277,138	926,684	2,203,822	298,044
		7,813,421	1,257,261	9,070,682	947,111

Vol. 28, p. 150
Maintenance of livestock in
connection with size of productive area

	Horses	Horned cattle	Goats	Sheep	Pigs	Number of farms with livestock in general*
a) Number of farms with this livestock						
Under 2 ha	78.750	720,490	244,373	71,004	486,891	
2-5 "	230,079	714,530	62,709	73,713	462,421	761,527
5-20 "	307,765	595,890	66,541	97,087	473,947	
20-50 "	79,769	121,655	20,797	32,657	110,988	122,844
50-100 "	10,410	14,692	3,265	6,679	12,816	14,934
over 100 "	10,771	12,110	2,156	4,178	7,695	12,620
Total:	717,544	2,179,367	399,841	285,318	1,554,758	2,544,792
b) Quantity of livestock						
Under 2 ha	110,101	1,232,007	446,808	503,187	813,836	
2-5 "	379,087	1,975,503	148,818	599,797	981,935	
5-20 "	626,149	3,343,032	145,683	890,110	1,680,992	
20-50 "	215,739	1,493,417	50,397	379,272	674,273	
50-100 "	39,286	301,599	15,339	127,702	108,629	
over 100 "	170,569	679,699	19,711	302,278	105,430	
Total:	1,540,931	9,025,257	826,756	2,802,346	4,365,095	
Number of farms with this livestock						
Under 0.5 ha	5,790	86,197	93,321	14,501	98,340	215,941
0.5-1 "	13,973	199,278	80,781	19,627	135,465	298,474
1-2 "	58,978	435,015	70,271	36,876	253,086	507,990
5-10 "	176,081	362,559	34,941	55,561	275,007	373,892
10-20 "	131,684	233,331	31,600	41,526	198,940	236,570
Quantity of livestock						
Under 0.5 ha	7,535	121,406	157,412	103,588	151,416	
0.5-1 "	18,515	297,048	149,762	130,128	217,274	
1-2 "	84,051	813,553	139,634	269,471	445,146	
5-10 "	336,128	1,616,774	80,243	503,797	808,701	
10-20 "	290,021	1,726,258	65,440	386,313	872,291	

Written not earlier than
1910-not later than 1912

First published in 1938
in *Lenin Miscellany XXXI*

Printed from the original

* Source: *Austrian Statistics,* Vol. LXXXIII, Part 1, p. 21.—*Ed.*

REMARKS ON SCHMELZLE'S ARTICLE,
"DISTRIBUTION OF RURAL LAND HOLDINGS, ITS INFLUENCE ON THE PRODUCTIVITY AND DEVELOPMENT OF AGRICULTURE" [122]

Dr. *Schmelzle.* "Die ländliche Grundbesitzverteilung; ihr Einfluss auf die Leistungsfähigkeit der Landwirtschaft und ihre Entwicklung" (*Annalen des Deutschen Reichs,* 46. Jahrgang, 1913, No. 6, S. 401-33).

The author talks platitudes; refuses to differentiate between various, small, medium and large farms, but he does give many interesting indications of and references to the latest writings.

(Stumpfe)   Marks

		Cost of buildings per *ha*	
		on the big farms	360
(p. 407)	"	medium "	420
	"	small "	472

Quante[1] [123]: Cost of buildings per *ha* for Marks

The implication is "higher cost of repairs, insurance and depreciation".	under-5-ha farms	1,430
	5-20 ha	896
	20-100 "	732
	100-500 "	413
	500 and over "	419

Dr. Vogeley[2] [124] reckons the averages

	for this per *ha*	Marks
	on middle-peasant farms	64.$_{48}$
	" big " "	57.$_{63}$

"Untersuchungen betreffend die Rentabilität der schweizerischen Landwirtschaft." Bericht des Bauernsekretariats. Bern 1911.*

			The earnings of an entrepreneur and his family per male working day 1901-09
Capital in implements			
per *ha* under 5 ha	395	francs	$2._{01}$ francs
5-10 "	309	"	$2._{27}$ "
10-15 "	253	"	$2._{31}$ "
15-30 "	231	"	$2._{26}$ "
over 30 "	156	"	$4._{15}$ "
		cultivated farmland ha	of which ploughland
Per person working on the farms			
$^2)$ $_{125}$ over 15 ha		$4._{67}$	$2._{87}$ ha
10-15 "		$3._{63}$	$1._{88}$ "
under 10 "		$2._{59}$	$1._{32}$ "

Literature:

   Werner und *Albrecht. Der Betrieb der deutschen Landwirtschaft am Schlusse des 19. Jahrhunderts.* Berlin 1902.**
   M. Sering. Die Bodenbesitzverteilung und die Sicherung des Kleinbesitzes. Schriften des Vereins für Sozialpolitik. Band 68. (1893).***
   Fr. Brinkmann: Die Grundlagen der englischen Landwirtschaft. Hannover 1909.****
   Keup-Mührer: Die volkswirtschaftliche Bedeutung von Gross- und Kleinbetrieb in der Landwirtschaft. Berlin 1913. [Price 11 frs 25]*****
$^2)$ *Arbeiten der Deutschen Landwirtschafts-Gesellschaft. Heft 118; 133; 123; 218; 130.*******

   * *A Study of the Profitability of Swiss Agriculture,* Report of the Peasant Secretariat.— *Ed.*
   ** *German Agricultural Production at the Close of the 19th Century.*— *Ed.*
   *** *Distribution of Land Holdings and the Security of Small Holdings. Transactions of the Social Policy Association.*— *Ed.*
   **** *The Principles of British Agriculture.*— *Ed.*
   ***** *The National Economic Importance of Large- and Small-scale Production in Agriculture.*— *Ed.*
   ****** *Transactions of the German Agricultural Society.*— *Ed.*

[1])   *Thiels Landwirtschaftliche Jahrbücher.* 1905. S. 955.*
E. Laur. Grundlagen und Methoden der Bewertung etc.
in der Landwirtschaft. Berlin 1911.**
(Sammelwerk): *Neuere Erfahrungen auf dem Gebiet*
*des landwirtschaflichen Betriebswesens.**** Berlin 1910.
Petersilie: "Schichtung und Aufbau der Landwirtschaft
in Preussen." Zeitschrift des Königlichen Preussischen
Statistischen Landesamts. 1913.****
H. Losch: *Die Veränderungen im wirtschaftlichen etc.*
Aufbau der Bevölkerung Würtembergs. (Würtembergische
Jahrbücher für Statistik. 1911.) *****
M. Hecht: *Die Badische Landwirtschaft.* Karlsruhe
1903.******

Germany 1907 (Dr. Arthur Schulz where?) (P. 410)

Calculated total number of permanently employed persons	Per permanently employed person				
	horses	horned cattle	pigs	sheep	poultry
2- 5 ha 2,346,000	0.$_{10}$	1.$_{34}$	1.$_{19}$	0.$_{15}$	6.$_{25}$
5- 20 " 3,891,000	0.$_{34}$	2.$_{02}$	1.$_{62}$	0.$_{37}$	7.$_{09}$
20-100 " 1,804,000	0.$_{67}$	2.$_{94}$	2.$_{02}$	1.$_{28}$	7.$_{85}$
over 100 " 1,068,000	0.$_{61}$	2.$_{18}$	1.$_{29}$	4.$_{10}$	3.$_{35}$

On the whole, says the author, small-scale production
is weaker (p. 414). There are special crops, vegetable gardening, but their part is weak.

(P. 415.) Area under *cereals* per 100 ha of cultivated
farmland in 1907

	Germany	Bavaria
< 2 ha	31.$_2$	29.$_4$
2- 5 "	42.$_4$	38.$_8$
5- 20 "	47.$_5$	41.$_8$
20-100 "	48.$_3$	43.$_5$
100 and over	47.$_6$	34.$_9$

---

* Thiel's *Agricultural Yearbooks.—Ed.*
** *Principles and Methods of Assessment, etc., in Agricul-*
ture.—Ed.
*** (Collection); *The Latest Experiments in Agricultural*
Production.—Ed.
**** "Stratification and Structure of Agriculture in Prussia."
Journal of the Royal Prussian Statistical Board.—*Ed.*
***** *Changes in the Economic, etc. Structure of the Population*
in Württemberg (Württemberg Statistical Yearbooks).—Ed.
****** *Baden Agriculture.—Ed.*

Crop statistics (1901-10)

<table>
<tr><th colspan="2"></th><th colspan="2">(double centners)</th></tr>
<tr><th colspan="2"></th><th>wheat</th><th>rye</th></tr>
<tr><td rowspan="5">The result is said to be not in favour of small-scale production</td><td>Germany ....</td><td>19.6</td><td>16.3</td></tr>
<tr><td>Belgium ....</td><td>23.6</td><td>21.7</td></tr>
<tr><td>Denmark ....</td><td>27.8</td><td>17.3</td></tr>
<tr><td>France ....</td><td>13.6</td><td>10.6</td></tr>
<tr><td>Great Britain ....</td><td>21.4</td><td>17.6</td></tr>
</table>

Livestock farming: in Bavaria (1907) per 100 ha of cultivated farmland

head of horned cattle (p. 419)

<table>
<tr><td rowspan="5">The big farms are said to have better livestock in general: (p. 419) Cf. Part 218. Transactions of the German Agricultural Society</td><td>under 2 ha</td><td>137.6</td></tr>
<tr><td>2- 5 "</td><td>125.1</td></tr>
<tr><td>5- 20 "</td><td>109.8</td></tr>
<tr><td>20-100 "</td><td>98.7</td></tr>
<tr><td>100 and over</td><td>62.7</td></tr>
</table>

p. 420: (From Part 81 of *The Contribution to the Statistics of the Kingdom of Bavaria*, p. 146*)

N.B.	Bavaria: Per farm with the following species of livestock						Head of horned cattle per 100 ha of cultivated farmland		
	horned cattle			pigs					
	1907	1882	increase from 1882 to 1907% %	1907	1882	increase % %	1907	1882	increase % %
Under 2 ha	1.9	1.7	11.8	1.9	1.6	18.8	137.6	131.9	4.3
2- 5 "	3.7	3.2	15.6	2.7	2.1	28.6	125.1	107.3	16.6
5- 20 "	8.7	7.3	19.2	4.6	3.4	35.3	109.8	92.3	19.0
20-100 "	21.4	17.3	23.7	10.2	7.1	43.7	98.7	80.7	22.3
100 and over "	82.7	54.1	52.9	48.7	21.1	130.8	62.7	50.3	24.7

Cost-price per kilogramme of milk on farms with

5-10 ha of area	16.$_{34}$ centimes
10-20 " " "	14.$_{97}$ "
20-30 " " "	14.$_{43}$ "
over 30 " " "	12.$_{60}$ "

Schmelzle in *Weekly of the Agricultural Society in Bavaria*. 1912, No. 47 et seq.

{ *A Study of the Profitability of Swiss Agriculture*. l. c. (p. 422) }

	Gross income per ha without forest (1901-09)	Net profit as % of production capital (1901-09)	Growth of gross income per *ha* of cultivated area in 1906-09 as compared with 1901-05	
			Gross income in general	Gross income from livestock farming
			%	%
	%			
Small-peasant farms .... under 5 ha	169.$_{70}$	2.$_{35}$	+3.$_7$	14.$_6$
Small middle-peasant farms 5-10	148.$_{20}$	2.$_{91}$	17.$_7$	21.$_2$
Middle-peasant farms 10-15	128.$_{55}$	3.$_{34}$	16.$_2$	21.$_8$
Big middle-peasant farms 15-30	122.$_{00}$	3.$_{42}$	20.$_5$	22.$_0$
Big-peasant farms .... over 30	100.$_{00}$	4.$_{48}$	16.$_9$	15.$_7$

Both wings of the Social-Democrats are said to be wrong: the Radicals in that they tend to forget the difference between agriculture and industry, and the revisionists in that they allege the superiority of small-scale production to be the cause (of the development towards small-scale production) (p. 433). The author is a *middle-of-the-roader* (!!), a fool. He says small and middle (5-20 ha) peasant farms are growing stronger, area statistics for 1907, etc., etc.

Written not earlier than July
1913

First published in 1938
in *Lenin Miscellany XXXI*   Printed from the original

REMARKS ON E. LAUR'S BOOK, *STATISTICAL NOTES ON THE DEVELOPMENT OF SWISS AGRICULTURE OVER THE LAST 25 YEARS*[126]

Statistische Notizen über die Entwicklung der schweizerischen Landwirtschaft in den letzten 25 Jahren. (E. Laur.) Brugg 1907.

Participation of Swiss agriculture in supplying the country with corn (estimated).

In the early 1880s = 1,850,000 quintals * = 38.$_5$% of demand

Now . . . . . . = 850,000 " ' = 14.$_3$%

Reduction in area under corn.

%

Cantons	Zurich	(1885)→15,490	ha—(1896) 13,590—12.$_3$
	Berne	(1885)—48,170	" —(1905) 43,340—10.$_0$
	Waadt	(1886)—38,510	" — (1905)28,330—27.$_2$

Maintenance of livestock	1886	1906	±%
Number of livestock owners	289,274	274,706	− 5.$_{04}$
Livestock owners with farms	258,639	239,111	− 7.$_{55}$
Owners of horses	56,499	72,925	+29.$_{07}$
Owners of big horned cattle	219,193	212,950	− 2.$_{85}$
Owners of small cattle	232,104	206,291	−11.$_{55}$
Horses	98,622	135,091	+36.$_{98}$
Horned cattle	1,212,538	1,497,904	+23.$_{54}$
Pigs	394,917	548,355	+38.$_{86}$
Sheep	341,804	209,243	−38.$_{78}$
Goats	416,323	359,913	−13.$_{55}$

* Double metric centners (100 kg).—*Ed.*

Value of livestock

	1886	1906	±%
Horses	51,245(000 fr.)	94,523	+ 84.45
Horned cattle	360,853	527,797	+ 46.26
Pigs	20,997	42,655	+103.15
etc.			
Total	448,579	680,722	+ 51.75

Milk production

	1886	1906	±%
Milch cows	663,102	785,577	+ 18.47
Milk goats	291,426	251,970	− 13.55
Milk from cows	14,678,000 hl*	20,818,000 hl	+ 14.84
	(2,210 l)	(2,650 l)	
" " goats	874,000 hl	756,000	− 13.55
	(300 l)	(300 l)	
Total milk output	15,552,000 hl	21,574,000 hl	+ 38.72
Consumption of milk by population	7,217,000 hl	10,391,000	+ 44.00
	(250 l)	(300 l)	
Consumption of milk for breeding and fattening of calves	2,437,000	3,124,000	+ 27.80
Consumption of milk for breeding goats	87,000	75,000	− 13.80
Consumption of milk for breeding pigs	117,000	160,000	+ 36.75
Consumption of milk for condensation and baby food	369,000	886,000	+140.11
Consumption of milk for making chocolate	15,000	100,000	+566.67
Consumption of milk for technical processing on Alpine farms	5,311,000	6,838,000	+ 28.75
Milk consumed on farms and in households	5,450,000	6,563,000	+ 20.42
Milk marketed	10,102,000	15,095,000	+ 49.43
of this, milk and milk products for export	3,500,000	4,502,000	+ 28.63
of this, milk and milk products at home	6,602,000	10,593,000	+ 60.45
Value of milk output	215,500,000 francs	333,210,000 francs	+ 54.62
Value of milk output less milk going into breeding and fattening of livestock	175,597.000	286,180,000	+ 62.05

* hl—hectolitres; l—litres.— *Ed.*

	1886	1906	±%
Total value of Swiss meat production	126,612,000 francs	214,810,000	$+70._{72}$
Total value of Swiss meat consumption	172,080,000	285,171,000	$+65._{71}$
Cost of one kg of meat	$1._{514}$	$1._{625}$	$+ 7._{33}$
Per-head consumption of meat	$39._{353}$ kg	$50._{103}$ kg	$+27._{31}$
Consumption of meat (quintals)	1,136,000	1,755,000	$+54._{48}$
of this, nationally produced	829,000	1,333,000	$+60._{79}$
of this, imported	307,000	422,000	$+37._{45}$

Value of total output (estimated)

	'000 fr. in mid-1880s	%	'000 fr. now	%	±%
Cereals	39,000	$7._{16}$	21,300	$2._{92}$	$-45._{38}$
Potatoes	24,471	$4._{50}$	27,000	$3._{70}$	$+10._{33}$
Hemp and flax	1,894	$0._{35}$	1,900	$0._{26}$	$+ 0._{32}$
Tobacco	1,000	$0._{17}$	1,000	$0._{14}$	—
Various crops	250	$0._{04}$	400	$0._{05}$	$+60._{00}$
Hay for horses not used on farms	3,600	$0._{66}$	4,500	$0._{62}$	$+25._{00}$
Wine-growing	49,240	$9._{05}$	45,000	$6._{16}$	$- 8._{61}$
Fruit-growing	49,500	$9._{09}$	60,000	$8._{21}$	$+21._{21}$
Vegetable-gardening	25,926	$4._{76}$	26,400	$3._{61}$	$+ 1._{83}$
Horned cattle breeding	6,485	$1._{19}$	5,600	$0._{77}$	$-13._{64}$
Fattening of horned cattle (including export)	96,250	$17._{68}$	156,300	$21._{40}$	$+62._{39}$
Horse breeding	288	$0._{05}$	350	$0._{05}$	$+21._{52}$
Pig breeding	38,221	$7._{02}$	61,480	$8._{43}$	$+60._{85}$
Sheep breeding	3,800	$0._{70}$	2,590	$0._{35}$	$-31._{84}$
Goat breeding	12,250	$2._{25}$	13,260	$1._{81}$	$+ 8._{24}$
Poultry farming	13,256	$2._{43}$	14,000	$1._{01}$	$+ 5._{61}$
Bee-keeping	2,286	$0._{41}$	3,000	$0._{41}$	$+31._{23}$
Milk products	176,597	$32._{49}$	286,180	$39._{20}$	$+62._{05}$
Total	544,314	$100._{00}$	730,260	$100._{00}$	$+34._{16}$

Import of agricultural raw materials and machinery	mid-1880s quintals	now quintals	±%
Fertilisers and waste	181,720	913,340	+ 402.60
Feedstuffs	516,000	1,456,390	+ 182.25
{ Bran, oil-cakes (idem ground)	27,410	366,310	+1,236.41
Maize	287,370	634,620	+ 120.83
Flour	86,230	171,850	+ 99.30
Straw and straw for litter	110,000	567,410	+ 415.82
Seed	24,130	11,450	− 52.55
Agricultural machinery and implements	1,340	40,340	+2,910.45

	1885-1888	1905	
Import of competitive farm items	198,381,000 francs	351,681	+77.27
Export of competitive farm items	78,399,000 francs	81,512	+3.97

Agricultural population	1888	1900	%
Relating to agriculture	1,092,827	1,047,795	−4.12
Male	568,024	555,047	−2.28
Female	524,803	492,748	−6.10
Technical and managing personnel, men	—	464	
„ „ „ „ women	—	14	
Man servants	61,320	57,849	−5.66
Maid servants	9,927	6,779	−31.71
Day labourers men	35,258	37,234	+5.60
„ „ women	8,921	8,348	−6.42
	115,426	110,210	

Written in 1913

First published in 1938
in *Lenin Miscellany XXXI*

Printed from the original

REMARKS ON E. JORDI'S BOOK,
THE ELECTRIC MOTOR IN AGRICULTURE[127]

*Ernst   Jordi,   Der   Elektromotor   in   der
Landwirtschaft.* Bern 1910

The author is a practitioner from an agricultural school
at Rütti, Berne. This school itself uses an electric motor
for farming operations. The author has collected data on
electric motors in Swiss agriculture. Result: highly recom-
mends that peasant co-operatives use electric motors.

"At present, no other mechanical engine can match the
electric motor's simple and reliable operation, insignificant
wear and tear, great adaptability, instant readiness for
use, minimal requirements in supervision and maintenance,
and the consequent low overhead costs.... Production-wise,
it will pay big farms to have their own motor in most cases.
Medium and small farms are advised to purchase and run
an electric motor co-operatively..." p. 79

1 volt×1 ampere   =   1 watt
h.p. { kilowatt   =   1,000   watts
{   1 h.p.   =   736   watts

Cost of
electricity:
"effective h.p.—hour with
the use of" (p. 78)

a. electric motor
(4 h.p.)—*26* centimes
b. manpower—300   cen-
times
c. one-horse   drive—100
centimes
d. water (very cheap)—a
few centimes
e. internal-combustion engine (4 h.p.)—60 cen-
times

Consequently, the elec-
tric motor is cheaper than
anything (except water).

The author reckons Switzerland's water-power (according to official statistics) at *722,600* h.p. Roughly $^3/_4$ of a million h.p. (in a 24-hour day). Rather, up to 1 million = the work of 14-24 million men (p. 13)

Written in September-October
1914

First printed in the
Fourth Russian edition
of the *Collected Works*

Printed from the original

CAPITALISM AND AGRICULTURE
IN THE UNITED STATES OF AMERICA[128]

OUTLINE OF INTRODUCTION

AMERICAN AGRICULTURAL CENSUSES

The importance of America as a leading country of capitalism. A model. Ahead of the others. Most freedom, etc.

Agricultural evolution. The significance, importance and complexity of the question.

American agricultural statistics. Decennial censuses. Similar material.

Himmer as a *collection* of bourgeois views. *In this respect* his short article is worth volumes.

The gist of his attitude: "*family-labour*" farms (or farmers) or *capitalist* farms. Main propositions. "Decline of Capitalism"?

VARIANTS OF PLAN

I

3 main divisions and *2 subdivisions*.
3 *sections* and 2 *subsections* (9 divisions)

Cf. p. 4 of the extracts from the *1900* edition: in 1900 there were 5 divisions,* which is more *reasonable*.

Population density.
Per cent of urban population.
Population increase.

---

* See p. 427.—*Ed.*

Settlement (homesteads).
Growing number of farms.
Increase in improved area.
Intensiveness of agriculture.
       { capital
       { fertilisers.
Hired labour.
Crops (agricultural).
Yields.
Average farm acreage and its changes
       { by divisions
       { in time.
Percentage distribution of total value of farms and value
of agricultural implements + machines.
Sale-purchase of feedstuffs and livestock products.
Negroes in the South and their flight to the cities. Immigrants and their urge to move to the cities.
Hired labour in agriculture.

Expenditures for wages.

Occupation statistics.
Owners versus tenants
   in general
   in the South.
Mortgaged farms. Increase.
Number of farms owning horses and changes.
Number of farms (by groups) and changes.
Acreage of improved land (idem) and changes.
Dairy *cattle* (and its concentration)....
Plantations in the South.
Overall picture of industry and agriculture in their class
structure and development.
Three methods of grouping. N.B.
              (1900)....
Latifundia and decrease in their acreage.

II

The main thing: three *sections* and
A) 2 divisions of the North (New England+Middle
Atlantic)....

> *Add*: the prices of **industrial** products

B) The South—"decline of capitalism"
C) Summaries of acreage groups.
D) Comparison of three types of groupings.
settlement.
latifundia.
Owners versus tenants.
Overall picture of agriculture and industry

III

1. *Introduction.* The importance of the question. Material. "Himmer."
2. **General** essay 3(+2) *main* sections (*general* characteristic) resp. 3-5 §§

(homestead) West	Transition from homestead to
(industrial) North	settled areas
(slave-holding) South	(1 division)
	(1 division)

3. Average farm acreage (1850-1910)

4. Acreage groups.
5. *Ibid.* Percentage distribution of total value and value of machinery.
6. Groups by income.
7.   "   "   principal source of income ("specialities").
8. Comparison of the 3 groupings.
9. Expropriation of the small farmers.
  { summaries for the United States by groupings } mortgaged
  { owners and tenants } farms.
  { ownership of horses }
10. Hired labour in agriculture.
11. Considerable decrease in the acreage of the latifundia.
12. Overall picture.

Further (after 13 §§) roughly:
14. Expropriation of small farmers

(α) flight from the countryside
(β) owners
(γ) ownership of horses
(δ) farm debt.

15. Overall picture *N.B.*+

$$\left(\!\left(\begin{array}{l} +cf. \quad America \quad and \quad Russia, \quad if \quad all \quad the \quad land \\ goes \ to \ the \ peasants. \end{array}\right)\!\right)$$

15. A comparative picture of evolution in industry and agriculture.

16. *Summary and conclusions.*

> add to § 3, the North
> % of *large enterprises*

---

add: % of high-income farms

under 3 acres	$5._2$	N.B.
3 to 10	$0._6$	
10 to 20	$0._4$	
20 to 50	$0._3$	
50 to 100	$0._6$	

+ prices of livestock
Add: Latifundia, % of land

1900	1910
$23._6$	$19._7$

+ value of land:

$7._1\%$ $7._6\%$

+ increase in livestock
meadow + land: p. 6.

VARIANTS OF TITLE

Roughly

═══════

Capitalism and Agriculture in the United States of America.
(New Data on the Laws Governing the
Development of Capitalism in Agriculture.)
New Data on the Laws Governing the Development of Capitalism in Agriculture.
Part One. Capitalism and Agriculture in the United States of America.

EXTRACTS FROM DIFFERENT VARIANTS

I

I.
From corvée to capitalist rent.
Marx.
III. Size of capital investment in land.

II

"Summary and Conclusions":
A) ⎧ Similar material.
    ⎩ Range of nuances.
B) "*Seven theses.*"

16. *Summary and
    conclusions.*

| *p. 20:* *+ quotations* |

III

Size of country and diversity.
Range of nuances, strands in evolution:
3. ‖ α) Intensification due to *vast* industry.
4. ‖ β) Extensive farming (livestock breeding—hundreds
        of dessiatines)
2.   γ) Settlement
1.   δ) Transition from feudalism to capitalism (slave-
        holding)
     ε) comparative size of farms (?)
1. | Machinery
2. | Hired labour
3. | Displacement of small-scale by large-scale farming
4. | Minimisation of the displacement by acreage group-
     ing.
5. | Growth of capitalism as farms become smaller
     (intensification).

6. ⌐ Expropriation of small farmers

    { owners and tenants   }
      ownership of livestock }
      debts.   }

7. ⌐ Uniformity with industry (§ 15).

IV

10. Defects of conventional methods of economic inquiry.
11. Small and big farms by value of product.
11. More exact comparisons of small and large enterprises.
12. Different types of enterprises in agriculture.
13. How is the displacement of small-scale by large-scale
     production in agriculture minimised?

V

4. *Average size of farms.*
     "Decline   of   capitalism"   in   the   South.
     U.S.A. the South, the North
      +   −   =
       two divisions of the North, the West, the South
                 −   ±
5. *"Disintegration   of   capitalism"   in   the*
     North. New England + Middle Atlantic.
6. *Capitalist character.*
6. *Groups   by   farm   acreage.* **Overall   result.**
7. Idem. *The South.*
8. *The North.* New England + Middle Atlantic.
9. *The West.*
10. *The   capitalist   character   of   agricul-
      ture.*
11. *Groups by value* (total value and value of machinery).
12. Groups by income.
13. Groups by speciality.
14. Comparison of the three groupings.
15. *Expropriation.*
16. *Overall picture.*

VI

10. Shortcomings in the grouping of farms by acreage
11. Grouping by income

12. Grouping by (principal source of income) speciality
13. Comparison of the three groupings.

{ cf. America and Russia, if all the land went
to the peasants } N.B.

VII

California
per acre

	1910	1900
L a b o u r	4.$_{38}$	2.$_{16}$
Fertilisers	0.$_{19}$	0.$_{08}$

Understatement of the ruin of small-scale production (when grouping is by acreage):

{ the minority of prospering farms are lumped together with the mass of backward farms and those on the way to ruin.

N.B.

Add:

among the high-income farms ($2,500 and over), there is a higher % of very small and small farms

under 3 acres — 5.$_2$
3 to 10   0.$_6$
10 to 20   0.$_4$
20 to 50   [0.$_3$]
50 to 100 0.$_6$

VARIANTS OF CONTENTS

I

Contents:

1. General Characteristic of the Three Sections. The Homestead West.
2. The Industrial North.
3. The Former Slave-owning South.
4. Average Size of Farms.
   "Disintegration of Capitalism in the South."
5. The Capitalist Nature of Agriculture.
6. Areas of the Most Intensive Agriculture
7 Machinery and Hired Labour

End

————— means: "rewrite heading" of §

II

REMARKS ON AMERICAN
AGRICULTURAL STATISTICS

The most interesting thing American agricultural statistics provide—in novelty and importance for economic science—is the comparison of *three* groupings: 1) by acreage (conventional); 2) by principal source of income; 3) by gross income—by value of products not fed to livestock (probably, gross cash income).

The second and third groupings are a novelty, which is highly valuable and instructive.

There is no need to say much about the second one. Its importance lies in showing the economic types of farm with a *bias* for some aspect of *commercial* agriculture. This grouping gives an excellent idea of the *impossibility of comparing* various types of farm (by acreage), and so of the *limits* within which the acreage grouping can be applied (resp. the conclusions to be drawn from this kind of grouping).

To 1) Farms of these types cannot be compared by acreage: *Hay & grain* as the principal sources of income. Average size of farm—$159._3$ acres (see pp. 7-8 of my extracts*). Average expenditure for labour—$76 per farm ($0._{47}$ per acre).

Flowers & plants. Average size = $6._9$ acres. Average expenditure for labour = $675 per farm, $97._{42}$ per acre, that is, $9,742 \div 47 = 207$ times greater.

Of course, the number of farms with *flowers* as the principal source of income is insignificant ($0._1\%$), and that with *hay & grain*, very large ($23._0\%$), but a calculation of

* See pp. 432-34.—*Ed.*

the average would give a false impression. The number of cereal farms (hay & grain) is 200 (214) times greater $(1,319,856 \div 6,159 = 214)$, but their average expenditure for labour per acre is 1/207 of the figure for the flower farms.

The same applies, with due alterations, to vegetables $(2._7\%$ of all farms; expenditure for labour $= \$1._{62}$ per acre, with an average of $\$0._{43})$; fruits $(1._4\%$ of all farms. labour—$\$2._{46}$ per acre), etc.

The cereal farms are large *in acreage* $(159._3$ acres on an average) but have low income (in terms of *gross* income)— an average of $\$665$ of gross income per farm. On the flower farms—$6._9$ acres—$\$2,991$ of gross income per farm Fruits—$74._8$ acres, $\$915$ of gross income per farm, etc.

Or take dairy produce. The farms are *smaller* than average: $121._9$ acres versus $146._6$—and smaller than the cereal farms $(159._3$ acres) but their gross income is *higher*: $\$787$ (versus an average of $\$656$, and $\$760$ for the hay & grain farms) Expenditure for labour per farm $= \$105$ (versus an average of $\$64$, and $\$76$ for hay & grain) and $\$0._{86}$ per acre, i.e. double the average $(\$0._{43}$ per acre). They have livestock valued at $\$5._{58}$ per acre (versus an average of $\$3._{66})$; implements & machinery, $\$1._{66}$ per acre (versus an average of $\$0._{90})$.

And that is not unique for the United States, but is the *rule* for all capitalist countries. What is the implication in the case of a *switch* from cropping to dairy farming?

For example (α) 10 grain farms switch to dairy farming.
(β) 10 farms $\times$ 160 $= 1,600$ acres
$\div 120$ (average dairy produce farm)
$= 13$ farms

The scale of production is reduced. The smaller farm wins out!
Expenditure for labour $10 \times 76 = \$ 760$ (α)
(β) $13 \times 105 = \$1,365$ (β) *Almost twice*$> !!$

This means that the switch to dairy farming—as well as to vegetables, fruits, etc.—leads to a reduction in the average farm acreage, to an increase in its *capitalist* expenditures (= intensification of its capitalist character), and to an increase in production

(gross income: $\alpha = 760 \times 10 = \$ 7,600$
$\beta = 787 \times 13 = \$10,231)$

To 2) What are the limits for applying the grouping by acreage? *Ordinary*, grain, farms are *in the majority*. In America, hay & grain = 23%; livestock (extensive N.B. [mixed with intensive]) =27.$_3$%; miscellaneous = 18.$_5$%. $\Sigma=68._8\%$. Consequently, general laws *may become apparent* even in general averages, but only in the gross totals, wherever there is known to be *no switch* from old farms to new (but where does that happen?), from farms with a similar investment of capital per hectare (per acre).

The great defect of American statistics is the failure to give *combined* tables. It would be extremely important to make a comparison of data on farms by acreage *within the limits* of one type of farm. That is not done.

Now for the third, new type of grouping—by gross income.

A comparison of it with the first, conventional grouping (by acreage) is highly instructive.

The quantity of livestock (value) per acre. By acreage: there is a *regular reduction*, without a single exception: from $\$4\ 5\ 6._{76}$ per acre (<3-acre farms) to $\$2._{15}$ per acre (1,000 acres and over), i.e., some 200 odd times greater! This is a ridiculous comparison, because *heterogeneous* magnitudes are involved.

By gross income: there is an *increase* (with 2 not very big exceptions: when income is at 0 and at $\$2,500$ *and>* to a maximum) *parallel* to the *increase* in acreage (also with two exceptions: at 0 and at the minimum).

Expenditure for labour per acre.

By acreage. There is a *reduction* (with one exception) from $\$40._{30}$ (<3 acres) to $\$0._{25}$ (>1,000 acres). 150-fold!!

By gross income. There is a regular *increase* from $\$0._{06}$ to $\$0._{72}$.

Expenditure for *fertilisers*. There is a *reduction* by acreage from $\$2._{36}$ per acre to $\$0._{02}$.

By gross income: there is an *increase* (with one exception)

from $0_{.01}$ to $0_{.08}$ ($0_{.06}$),

implements & machinery per acre.

There is a *reduction* by acreage

from $27_{.57}$ to $0_{.29}$.

There is an *increase* by gross income (with one exception)

from $0_{.38}$ to $1_{.21}$ ($0_{.72}$).

Average quantity of improved land.
‖ An *increase* by acreage from $1_{.7}$ to $520_{.0}$.
‖ An *increase* by gross income (with one exception) from $18_{.2}$ to $322_{.3}$.

The grouping by *income* combines the big and the small *acreage* farms, where they are similar in the level of capitalism. The predominant importance of such a "*factor*" as *land* remains and stands out in the grouping, but it is seen to be (co)subordinate to *capital*.

The grouping by income: the differences between the groups in expenditure for labour ($4—$786) per farm, are *tremendous*, but are relatively small per acre ($0_{.06}$—$0_{.72}$).

The grouping by acreage: the differences between the groups in expenditure for labour per farm ($16—$1,059) are *less* significant, but are tremendous per acre ($40_{.30}$—$0_{.25}$).

By acreage: income (gross per farm) by groups: $592—$1,913 ($5, 334), i.e. the differences are *very small*.

Depending on whether you take gross income or acreage as the yardstick, the ratios between small and large farms (in America) turn out to be *diametrically* opposed (by the main indicators and by the most important one for the capitalist economy, namely, expenditures for labour).

⎵It⎵ should be noted that America's agricultural statistics shows up its one *main* distinction from continental Europe.

In America, the % of parcel (proletarian?) farms is *insignificant*: 11.$_8$% of farms under 20 acres (= 8 ha).

In Europe, it is *great* (in Germany, more than one-half are under *2 ha*).

In America, agricultural capitalism is more *clear-cut*, the division of labour is more *crystallised*; there are *fewer* bonds with the Middle Ages, with the soil-bound labourer; ground-rent is not so burdensome; there is less intermixing of commercial agriculture and subsistence farming.

AMERICAN AGRICULTURAL STATISTICS *

(pp. 1-12 of extracts)

Pages
(of extracts)

1 number of farms in *acreage* groups, combined with grouping *by income.*

2 idem in %% for both groupings, combined with *each other.*

3 size of farms in divisions compared.

4 nil.

5 number of farms *by acreage* combined with the *principal source of income.*

6 grouping by *principal source of income*—% of total.

7 and 8 averages for farms by *principal source of income.*

9-10 averages (and % of total) for farms *by acreage and by income* [[without combination]]
11 and 12—nil.

The most interesting aspect of American statistics is the combination (even if not consistent) of the *three* groupings: by acreage, by income and by principal source of income.

A comparison of the groupings *by acreage* and by *income* (pp. 10 and 9 of the extracts) clearly shows the superiority of the *latter.*

---

* *Twelfth Census,* 1900. *Census Reports.* Volume V. *Agriculture.* Washington, 1902.

Acre
(absolute

The United States

Income:	Number of farms 5,739,657	Under 3 41,882	3-10 226,564	10-20 407,012	20-50 1,257,785
$ 0	53,406	1,346	5,166	8,780	12,999
1-50	167,569	6,234	38,277	33,279	45,361
50-100	305,590	7,971	55,049	64,087	89,424
100-250	1,247,731	13,813	86,470	182,573	454,904
250-500	1,602,854	4,598	28,025	89,116	471,157
500-1,000	1,378,944	2,822	8,883	21,295	154,017
1,000-2,500	829,443	2,944	3,351	6,412	25,691
2,500 and over	154,120	2,154	1,343	1,470	4,232
$ 0-100	526,565	15,551	98,492	106,146	147,784
-1,000 and >	983,563	5,098	4,694	7,882	29,923

Rough % of low-income farms (0-100)	c: $9._1$	37	43	25	12
Rough % of high-income farms (1,000 and >)	$17._2$	13	2	$1._9$	2

age
figures)

50-100	100-175	175-260	260-500	500-1,000	1,000 and over
1,366,167	1,422,328	490,104	377,992	102,547	47,276
6,159	12,958	1,451	2,149	1,110	1,288
19,470	18,827	2,333	2,290	902	596
44,547	33,168	4,922	4,197	1,428	797
271,547	176,287	33,087	21,061	5,497	2,492
495,051	358,443	87,172	53,121	12,108	4,063
420,014	492,362	152,544	97,349	22,398	7,260
101,790	310,420	182,868	149,668	34,210	12,089
7,589	19,863	25,727	48,157	24,894	18,691

| 70,176 | 64,953 | 8,706 | 8,636 | 3,440 | 2,681 |
| 109,379 | 330,283 | 208,595 | 197,825 | 59,104 | 30,780 |

5	4	$1._8$	$2._2$	3	5
8	24	43	52	57	66

Comparison of the two main groupings (by acreage and income) is given in such tables:

Per cent of the number of farms of specified values of products not fed to livestock;

	Per cent of all farms	0	1-50	50-100	100-250	250-500	500-1,000	1,000-2,500	2,500 and over
All farms	100	100	100	100	100	100	100	100	100
Under 3	0.7	2.5	3.7	2.6	1.1	0.3	0.2	0.4	1.4
3 and under 10	4.0	9.7	22.8	18.0	6.9	1.7	0.6	0.4	0.9
10-20	7.1	16.5	19.9	21.0	14.6	5.6	1.5	0.8	1.0
20-50	21.9	24.3	27.1	29.3	36.5	29.4	11.2	3.1	2.7
50-100	23.8	11.5	11.6	14.6	21.8	30.9	30.5	12.3	4.9
100-175	24.8	24.3	11.2	10.8	14.1	22.4	35.7	37.4	12.9
175-260	8.5	2.7	1.4	1.6	2.7	5.4	11.1	22.0	16.7
260-500	6.6	4.0	1.4	1.4	1.7	3.3	7.1	18.0	31.2
500-1,000	1.8	2.1	0.5	0.5	0.4	0.8	1.6	4.1	16.2
1,000 and over	0.8	2.4	0.4	0.2	0.2	0.2	0.5	1.5	12.1

increase — maximum — decrease

Per cent of the number of farms of specified acreage:

Groups of farms	Per cent of all farms	Under 3	3-10	10-20	20-50	50-100	100-175	175-260	260-500	500-1,000	1,000 and over
0	0.9	3.2	2.3	2.2	1.0	0.5	0.9	0.3	0.6	1.1	2.7
1-50	2.9	14.9	16.9	8.2	3.6	1.4	1.3	0.5	0.6	0.9	1.3
50-100	5.3	19.0	24.3	15.7	7.1	3.3	2.4	1.0	1.1	1.4	1.7
100-250	21.8	33.0	38.1	44.8	36.2	19.9	12.4	6.8	5.6	5.4	5.3
250-500	27.9	11.0	12.4	21.9	37.5	36.2	25.2	17.8	14.0	11.8	8.6
500-1,000	24.0	6.7	3.9	5.2	12.3	30.7	34.6	31.1	25.8	21.8	15.3
1,000-2,500	14.5	7.0	1.5	1.6	2.0	7.4	21.8	37.3	39.6	33.3	25.6
2,500 and over	2.7	5.2	0.6	0.4	0.3	0.6	1.4	5.2	12.7	24.3	39.5
Σ=	100.0	100.0								100.0	100.0
Under 500	58.8	6.7	3.9	5.2	12.3	30.7	34.6	31.1	25.8	21.8	15.3
500-1,000	24.0	6.7	3.9	5.2	12.3	30.7	34.6	31.1	25.8	21.8	15.3
1,000 and>	17.2	12.2	2.1	2.0	2.3	8.0	23.2	42.5	52.3	57.6	65.1

(diagonal annotations within the table: "decrease" ←, "minimum", "increase" →)

Value of products not fed to livestock

The text on page LXI gives valuable indications about *typical* farms by divisions

Divisions	Acreage	Gross income (from products not fed to livestock) $	Deriving its principal income from
North Atlantic	50-100	500-1,000	livestock or dairy produce
North Central	100-175	500-1,000	livestock or hay & grain
Western	100-175	500-1,000	" " " "
South Atlantic	20-50	250-500	cotton
South Central	20-50	250-500	"

In 19 00 there were *5 divisions*:
1) North Atlantic = New England + Middle Atlantic 1910
2) South Atlantic = idem   1910
3) North Central = West + East North Central   ”
4) South Central = East + West South Central   ”
5) Western = Mountain + Pacific   ”

V. I. LENIN

Absolute figures

Farms classified

Principal source of income	Total number of farms	Under 3	3 and under 10	10 and under 20	20-50
The United States	5,739,657	41,882	226,564	407,012	1,257,785
Hay and grain	1,319,856	1,725	26,085	59,038	190,197
Vegetables	155,898	4,533	23,780	23,922	41,713
Fruits	82,176	1,979	10,796	13,814	22,604
Livestock	1,564,714	13,969	56,196	81,680	257,861
Dairy produce	357,578	5,181	15,089	20,502	59,066
Tobacco	106,272	397	5,827	12,317	26,957
Cotton	1,071,545	997	25,025	112,792	426,689
Rice	5,717	123	996	614	1,185
Sugar	7,344	50	345	629	2,094
Flowers & plants	6,159	3,764	1,387	492	355
Nursery products	2,029	121	262	307	429
Taro	441	171	141	47	31
Coffee	512	47	200	94	68
Miscellaneous	1,059,416	8,825	60,435	80,764	228,536
Total of underlined—highly capitalistic crops	724,126	16,366	58,823	72,738	154,502

(p. 18, table 3):

by acreage

50-100	100-175	175-260	260-500	500-1,000	1,000 and over
1,366,167	1,422,328	490,104	377,992	102,547	47,276
294,822	415,737	152,060	137,339	33,035	9,818
30,375	22,296	5,069	3,086	813	311
15,813	10,858	3,061	2,131	781	339
384,874	423,741	156,623	125,546	38,163	26,061
90,814	104,932	35,183	20,517	4,514	1,780
25,957	21,037	7,721	4,836	1,063	160
238,398	164,221	52,726	35,697	11,090	3,910
814	810	396	385	206	188
1,787	1,029	391	380	233	406
112	43	4	2	—	—
387	302	96	86	32	7
31	8	2	4	2	4
30	25	16	13	7	12
281,953	257,289	76,756	47,970	12,608	4,280
166,120	161,340	51,939	31,440	7,651	3,207

An extract from

for a general characteristic of grouping

%

The United States:	Hay & grain	Vege-tables	Fruits	Live-stock	Dairy-produce	Tobacco	Cotton
Number of farms	23.0	2.7	1.4	27.3	6.2	1.9	18.7
Number of acres in farms	25.0	1.2	0.7	42.2	5.2	1.1	10.7
Total value of farm property	31.1	2.7	2.1	36.6	8.3	1.0	5.4
Value of farms & improvements	35.2	2.8	2.4	34.3	7.3	1.0	5.3
Value of buildings	24.8	3.5	2.4	33.7	12.0.	1.5	4.8
Value of implements & machinery	28.7	2.8	1.9	30.9	9.4	1.1	6.3
Value of livestock	21.7	1.2	0.7	51.3	7.9	0.8	6.1
Value of products	26.6	2.8	2.0	32.8	7.5	1.7	12.2
Amount expended for labour	27.4	4.5	4.1	27.8	10.3	1.5	7.4
Amount expended for fertilisers	14.6	10.9	3.4	14.0	7.5	5.2	22.5

Summary in 4 groups:
1) ☐ = crops with a great excess in % of expenditure for *capitalist* farms.
2) Cotton = special crops with *little* development of capitalism. omy forms; vestiges of slavery and its reproduction on a
3) Livestock—a minimum of capitalism.
4) Hay & grain = "medium" + miscellaneous.

---

*) These, the most capitalist, crops are characterised by a age (3.4% of land with 6.3% of the farms) and a use of ferti the land). And it is these crops that grew fastest over cereals increased=+3.5%, and under rice, +78.3%; tobacco, **) < = less than 0.1%.

---

* This figure has been corrected to 45.0 in the Fourth Russian edition

Table 18 (p. 248)

by principal source of income
of total

Rice	Sugar	Flowers and plants	Nursery products	Miscellaneous	Σ		By speciality of *farms*	
					Highly capitalistic □	The same without dairy produce *)	medium (hay & grain+miscellaneous)	slightly capitalistic (livestock+ cotton)
$0._1$	$0._1$	$0._1$	$<**)$	$18._5$	$12._5$	$6._3$	$41._5$	$46._0$
$0._1$	$0._3$	$<$	$<$	$13._5$	$8._6$	$3._4$	$38._5$	$52._9$
$0._1$	$0._7$	$0._3$	$0._1$	$11._6$	$15._3$	$7._0$	$42._7$	$42._0$
$0._1$	$0._7$	$0._2$	$0._1$	$10._6$	$14._6$	$7._3$	$45._8$	$39._6$
$0._1$	$0._4$	$0._6$	$0._1$	$16._1$	$20._6$	$8._6$	$40._9$	$38._5$
$0._2$	$4._4$	$0._2$	$0._1$	$14._0$	$20._1$	$10._7$	$42._7$	$37._2$
$0._1$	$0._2$	$<$	$<$	$10._0$	$10._9$	$3._0$	$31._7$	$57._4$
$0._2$	$1._0$	$0._5$	$0._3$	$12._4$	$16._0$	$8._5$	$39._0$	$35._0$*
$\boxed{0._5}$	$4._0$	$1._1$	$0._6$	$10._8$	$26._6$	$16._3$	$38._2$	$35._2$
$0._1$	$3._8$	$0._6$	$0._2$	$17._2$	$31._7$	$24._2$	$31._8$	$36._5$

labour over the % of land. In other words, these are strictly

Special economic relations (labour of Negroes, natural econ-
capitalist basis).

size of farm which is only about a little over *half* the aver-
lisers which is *7 times* the average ($24._2$% versus $3._4$% of
the 10 years (1899-1909): in that period the total area under
$+17._5$%; sugar, $+62._6$%; vegetables, $+25._5$%, flowers, $+96._1$%.

of Lenin's *Collected Works* (see present edition, Vol. 22, p. 80).— *Ed.*

Average value of

	Land per		Implements & machinery per		All livestock per	
	farm	acre	farm	acre	farm	acre
The United States	2,285	15.59	133	0.90	536	3.66
Hay & grain	3,493	21.93	166	1.04	506	3.17
Vegetables	2,325	35.69	138	2.12	244	3.74
Fruits	3,878	51.82	175	2.34	251	3.35
Livestock	2,871	12.66	151	0.66	1,009	4.45
Dairy produce	2,669	22.05	201	1.66	676	5.58
Tobacco	1,214	13.47	77	0.85	235	2.61
Cotton	653	7.82	45	0.53	176	2.11
Rice	2,205	11.59	212	1.11	317	1.67
Sugar	12,829	35.30	4,582	12.61	957	2.63
Flowers	4,550	656.90	222	32.04	63	9.07
Nursery products	6,841	83.73	266	3.26	228	2.79
Taro	968	22.56	15	0.35	107	2.50
Coffee	3,083	22.48	63	0.46	160	1.16
Miscellaneous	1,317	12.33	101	0.94	291	2.73

The United States

Value of all farm property per				
$				
farm	acre	%	Number of farms	
3,574	24.$_{39}$	100	5,739,657	All farms
4,834	30.$_{34}$	23.$_0$	1,319,856	Hay & grain
3,508	53.$_{85}$	2.$_7$	155,898	Vegetables
5,354	71.$_{54}$	1.$_4$	82,176	Fruits
4,797	21.$_{14}$	27.$_3$	1,564,714	Livestock
4,736	39.$_{12}$	6.$_2$	357,578	Dairy
2,028	22.$_{51}$	1.$_9$	106,272	Tobacco
1,033	12.$_{36}$	18.$_7$	1,071,545	Cotton
3,120	16.$_{40}$	0.$_1$	5,717	Rice
20,483	56.$_{36}$	0.$_1$	7,344	Sugar
8,518	1,229.$_{72}$	0.$_1$	6,159	Flowers
9,436	115.$_{49}$	less than	2,029	Nursery
1,276	29.$_{73}$	$^1/_{10}$	441	Taro
3,775	27.$_{53}$	per cent	512	Coffee
2,250	21.$_{07}$	18.$_5$	1,059,416	Miscellaneous

$$\Sigma = 100._0$$

Vegetables	2.$_7$	Cereals	23.$_0$
Fruits	1.$_4$	Livestock	27.$_3$
Milk	6.$_2$	Miscellaneous	18.$_5$
$\Sigma = 10._3\%$			68.$_8$

$$+$$

Cotton 18.$_7$

87.$_5$%

$+$ special
12.$_5$% crops

100.$_0$

Farms classified by principal source of income.*

The United States:	Average expenditures for labour on farms in 1899 $		(all land) Number of acres in farms	(1899) Value of products not fed to livestock $	$ Average expenditures for fertilisers in 1899	Average acres improved land	Average non-improved land in farm
	per farm	per acre	Average per farm	Average per farm	per acre	per farm	
All farms	64	0.43	146.6	656	0.07	72.3	+ 74
Hay & grain	76	0.47	159.3	760	0.04	111.1	+ 48
Vegetables	106	1.62	65.1	665	0.59	33.8	+ 31
Fruits	184	2.46	74.8	915	0.30	41.6	+ 33
Livestock	65	0.29	226.9	788	0.02	86.1	+140
Dairy produce	105	0.86	121.9	787	0.09	63.2	+ 58
Tobacco	51	0.57	90.1	615	0.30	53.0	+ 37
Cotton	25	0.30	83.6	430	0.14	42.5	+ 41
Rice	299	1.57	190.3	1,335	0.07	80.9	+110
Sugar	1,985	5.46	363.4	5,317	0.77	140.5	+223
Flowers & plants	675	97.42	6.9	2,991	7.41	5.6	+ 1
Nursery products	1,136	13.91	81.7	4,971	0.84	67.7	+ 14
Taro	51	1.18	42.9	425	0.13	6.8	+ 36
Coffee	360	2.62	137.1	568	0.08	27.6	+110
Miscellaneous	37	0.35	106.8	440	0.08	46.5	+ 60

*) Page CXXVII.

The United States*:	Low-income farms under $100	Non-capitalist farms Income <$500	Medium farms $500-1,000	Capitalist farms *) High-income farms $1,000 and>
Number of farms	9.1	58.8	24.0	17.2
Number of acres in farms	5.1	33.3	23.6	43.1
Total value of farm property	2.5	23.7	26.1	50.2
Value of farm & improvements	2.3	22.0	25.8	52.2
Value of buildings	2.6	28.8	28.4	42.8
Value of implements & machinery	2.0	25.3	28.0	46.7
Value of livestock	3.2	24.8	24.2	51.0
Value of products	0.7	22.1	25.6	52.3
Amount expended for labour	0.9	11.8	19.6	69.1
Amount expended for fertilisers	1.3	29.1	26.1	44.8

*) Farms with an income of >$1,000 must be regarded as *capitalist*, because their expenditure for *labour* is high: $158-$786 per farm.

Farms with an income of under $500 must be regarded as *non-capitalist*, because their expenditure for *labour* is insignificant: under $18 per farm.

* The table was compiled by Lenin on the basis of the data in the table on pp. 436-37.— *Ed*.

% (Table

Classification by value of products

$

The United States	Total	0
Number of farms		0.9
Number of acres in farms		1.8
Total value of farm property		0.7
Value of farm & improvements		0.6
Value of buildings		0.3
Value of implements & machinery		0.4
Value of livestock		1.4
Value of products		—
Amount expended for labour		0.3
Amount expended for fertilisers		0.2
Average expenditures for labour $ { per farm (p. CXXVIII, table, CXXII) $ { per acre		24 0.08
Average number of acres per farm	146.6	283.2
Average expenditures for fertilisers $ { per farm in 1899 $ { per acre		2 0.01
Value of all livestock $ { per farm $ { per acre	536 3.66	840 2.97
Value of implements & machinery $ { per farm $ { per acre	133 0.90	54 0.19
Average number of improved land per farm (acres)	72.3	33.4

18, p. 248)
of 1899 not fed to livestock

1-50	50-100	100-250	250-500	500-1,000	1,000-2,500	2,500 and >
2.9	5.3	21.8	27.9	24.0	14.5	2.7
1.2	2.1	10.1	18.1	23.6	23.2	19.9
0.6	1.2	6.6	14.6	26.1	33.3	16.9
0.6	1.1	6.0	13.7	25.8	34.9	17.3
0.7	1.6	8.6	17.6	28.4	31.5	11.3
0.5	1.1	6.9	16.4	28.0	30.9	15.8
0.6	1.2	6.8	14.8	24.2	29.3	21.7
0.1	0.6	5.9	15.5	25.6	32.0	20.3
0.2	0.4	2.5	7.9	19.6	35.9	33.2
0.2	0.9	7.9	19.9	26.1	27.0	17.8
4 0.06	4 0.08	7 0.11	18 0.19	52 0.36	158 0.67	786 0.72
62.3	58.6	67.9	94.9	143.8	235.0	1,087.8
1 0.01	2 0.03	3 0.05	7 0.07	10 0.07	18 0.08	63 0.06
111 1.78	118 2.01	167 2.46	284 3.00	539 3.75	1,088 4.63	4,331 3.98
24 0.38	28 0.48	42 0.62	78 0.82	154 1.07	283 1.21	781 0.72
18.2	20.0	29.2	48.2	84.0	150.5	322.3

Classification by

The United States:	under 3	3 and under 10	10 and under 20	20 and under 50	50 and under 100	100 and under 175
Number of farms	$0._7$	$4._0$	$7._1$	$21._9$	$23._8$	$24._8$
Number of acres in farms	—	$0._2$	$0._7$	$4._9$	$11._7$	$22._9$
Total value of farm property	$0._4$	$1._2$	$2._1$	$7._9$	$16._6$	$27._9$
Value of farm & improvements	$0._2$	$0._9$	$1._8$	$7._2$	$16._0$	$28._1$
Value of buildings	$0._8$	$2._7$	$3._6$	$10._7$	$20._4$	$28._9$
Value of implements & machinery	$0._3$	$1._2$	$2._2$	$9._0$	$19._0$	$28._9$
Value of livestock	$1._2$	$0._8$	$1._5$	$7._0$	$14._4$	$25._6$
Value of products	$0._7$	$1._2$	$2._5$	$10._8$	$18._3$	$27._3$
Amount expended for labour	$0._9$	$1._1$	$1._8$	$6._2$	$12._3$	$23._5$
Amount expended for fertilisers	$0._4$	$1._5$	$3._4$	$14._9$	$21._7$	$25._7$

			under 3	3 and under 10	10 and under 20	20 and under 50	50 and under 100	100 and under 175
Expenditures for labour	per	farm	77	18	16	18	33	60
	per	acre	$40._{30}$	$2._{95}$	$1._{12}$	$0._{55}$	$0._{46}$	$0._{45}$
Average number of acres	per	farm	$1._9$	$6._2$	$14._0$	$33._0$	$72._2$	$135._5$
Value of products not fed to livestock, average per farm			592	203	236	324	503	721
Expenditures for fertilisers	per	farm	4	4	5	7	9	10
	per	acre	$2._{36}$	$0._{60}$	$0._{33}$	$0._{20}$	$0._{12}$	$0._{07}$
Value of all livestock	per	farm	867	101	116	172	325	554
	per	acre	$456._{76}$	$16._{32}$	$8._{30}$	$5._{21}$	$4._{51}$	$4._{09}$
Value of implements & machinery	per	farm	53	42	41	54	106	155
	per	acre	$27._{57}$	$6._{71}$	$2._{95}$	$1._{65}$	$1._{47}$	$1._{14}$
Improved land	per	farm	$1._7$	$5._6$	$12._6$	$26._2$	$49._3$	$83._2$

Rough estimate:

In 1910, $45._9\%$ of the farms used hired labour. From 1900 to 1910, the number of hired labourers increased by (*roughly*) 27-48%.

Assuming that in 1900, *40%* of the farms used hired labour.

Take 40% of the medium, $24._8 \times 40\% = 9._{92}$. About *10%*.

Take $2._5$ times less from the small farms: $40 \div {}^5/_2 = \frac{80}{5} = 16$; $57._5 \times 16 = 9._2 = 9\%$.

Take 3 times more from the big farms: $40 \times 3 = 120\%$; $17._7 \times 120 = 21._{24}\%$. $9\% - 10\% - 21\%$.

area in acres — Amalgamation (by acreage)

175 and under 260	260 and under 500	500 and under 1,000	1,000 and over	Total	Under 20	All under 100 acres	100-175	175 and>	
$8._5$	$6._6$	$1._8$	$0._8$		$11._8$	$57._5$	$24._8$	$17._7$	Number of farms
$12._3$	$15._4$	$8._1$	$23._8$		$0._9$	$17._5$	$22._9$	$59._6$	Land
$15._1$	$15._3$	$5._9$	$7._6$		$3._7$	$28._2$	$27._9$	$43._9$	Value of land
$15._9$	$16._4$	$6._1$	$7._4$		$2._9$	$26._1$	$28._1$	$45._8$	
$13._9$	$12._0$	$4._0$	$3._0$		$7._1$	$38._2$	$28._9$	$32._9$	
$13._6$	$13._1$	$5._1$	$7._6$		$3._7$	$31._7$	$28._9$	$39._4$	Implements & machinery
$13._3$	$15._2$	$7._0$	$14._0$		$3._5$	$24._9$	$25._6$	$49._5$	Value of products
$13._7$	$13._6$	$5._2$	$6._7$		$4._4$	$33._5$	$27._3$	$39._2$	
$14._6$	$17._1$	$8._8$	$13._7$		$3._8$	$22._3$	$23._5$	$54._2$	Expenditures for labour and fertilisers
$12._5$	$10._0$	$4._2$	$5._7$		$5._3$	$41._9$	$25._7$	$32._4$	

175 and under 260	260 and under 500	500 and under 1,000	1,000 and over	Total
109 $0._{52}$	166 $0._{48}$	312 $0._{47}$	1,059 $0._{25}$	
$210._8$	$343._1$	$661._9$	$4,237._3$	$146._6$
1,054	1,354	1,913	5,334	656
14 $0._{07}$	15 $0._{04}$	22 $0._{03}$	66 $0._{02}$	10 $0._{07}$
834 $3._{96}$	1,239 $3._{61}$	2,094 $3._{16}$	9,101 $2._{15}$	536 $3._{66}$
211 $1._{00}$	263 $0._{77}$	377 $0._{57}$	1,222 $0._{29}$	133 $0._{90}$
$129._0$	$191._4$	$287._5$	$520._0$	$72._3$

Approximate:

$$((1900 : \| 22._3 \| 23._5 \| 54._2 \text{ [% of expenditure for labour]}$$
$$\times 40$$
$$9._0 + 9._4 + 21._6 = 40\%$$

About: $11 + 12._3 + 17._7 = 40$

Comparison of the
1900

(Politico-economic) significance of respective figures.	Per cent of total total of three figures in horizontal rows=100		By income [see p. 9]*		
			farms		
			Non-capita-list <$500 of income	Medium (500-1,000)	Capitalist (1,000 and>)
Common and basic figures:		Number of farms	58.8	24.0	17.2
		Acreage	33.3	23.6	43.1
Scale of produc-tion:	Scale of production	Value of product	22.1	25.6	52.3
Level of farming; machinery; care of the land	Constant capital:	Value of im-plements and machinery	25.3	28.0	46.7
		Expen-ditures for fertilisers	29.1	26.1	44.8
Capitalist charac-ter of enter-prise	Variable capital:	Expendi-tures for hired labour	11.3	19.6	69.1

% of farms

1910   % of all land

implements
and
machinery

* See p. 435.—Ed.

three groupings :

2 By acreage [see p 10]*			1 By principal source of income [see p. 6]**				
farms			farms				Commercial crops
Small (under 100 acres)	Medium (100-175)	Large (175 and >)	Slightly capitalist (livestock and cotton)	Medium (hay and grain—miscellaneous)	Highly capitalist (spec.→ crops)		
57.5	24.8	17.7	46.0	41.5	12.5	1	Index of extensive-
17.5	22.9	59.6	52.9	38.5	8.6	2	ness of enterprise
33.5	27.3	39.2	35.0***	39.0	16.0	6	
31.7	28.9	39.4	37.2	42.7	20.1	3	Index of intensiveness of enterprise
41.9	25.7	32.4	36.5	31.8	31.7	4	
22.3	23.5	54.2	35.2	38.2	26.6	5	
58.0	23.8	18.2					
17.9	23.4	58.7					
29.9	28.9	41.2					
57.5	—12.5	=45.0					
33.5	—16.0	=17.5					
31.7	—20.1	=11.6					
41.9	—31.7	=10.2					

*** In the Fourth Russian edition of Lenin's *Collected Works* (see present edition Vol. 22, p 80) the figure has been corrected to 45.0.— Ed.

Thirteenth Census of the United States, taken in the

(p. 30, table 2)

Three main sections of the United States	All farmland		Total population:					Urban population		
	mill. acres	%	(mill.) 1910	%	(mill.) 1900	%	1900-1910 % of pop. increase	(mill.) 1910	1900	1900-1910 % of increase
The North	587.8	30.9	55.8	60.6	47.4	62.3	17.7	32.7	25.2	29.8
The South	562.1	29.5	29.4	32.0	24.5	32.3	19.8	6.6	4.7	41.4
The West	753.4	39.6	6.8	7.4	4.1	5.4	66.8	3.3	1.7	89.6
The U.S.A.	1,903.3	100.0	92.0	100.0	76.0	100.0	21.0	42.6	31.6	34.8

(p. 34, table 3)

	Improved land in farms (mill. acres)			% of improved land	% of land in farms to total acreage		% of improved land in farms	% of improved land to total acreage
	1910	1900	% of increase		1910	1900	1910	1910
The North	290	261	10.9	60.6	70.4	65.1	70.1	49.3
The South	150	126	19.5	31.5	63.1	64.4	42.5	26.8
The West	38	27	39.8	7.9	14.7	12.4	34.2	5.0
The U.S.A	478	414	15.4	100.0	46.2	44.1	54.4	25.1

year 1910. Volume V. Agriculture. Washington 1913

Rural population (mill.) 1910	1900	1900-1910 % of increase	% of urban population (1910)	Number of farms ('000) 1910	1900	% of increase	All land in farms (mill. acres) 1910	1900	% of increase
23.1	22.2	3.9	58.6	2,891	2,874	0.6	414	383	8.0
22.7	19.9	14.8	22.5	3,097	2,620	18.2	354	362	—2.1
3.5	2.3	49.7	48.8	373	243	53.7	111	94	18.2
49.3	44.4	11.2	46.3	6,361	5,737	10.9	879	839	4.8

(p. 37, t. 4)   (p. 42, t. 7)

Average acreage per farm, all land: 1910	1900	% of increase	improved land: 1910	1900	% of increase	Value of all farm property ($ mill.) 1910	1900	% of increase	Value of land and buildings ($ mill.) 1910	1900	% of increase
143.0	133.2	7.4	100.3	90.9	10.3	27,481	14,455	90.1	23,650	12,041	96.4
114.4	138.2	—17.2	48.6	48.1	1.0	8,972	4,270	110.1	7,353	3,279	124.3
296.9	386.1	—23.1	101.7	111.8	—9.0	4,538	1,715	164.7	3,798	1,295	193.4
138.1	146.2	—5.5	75.2	72.2	4.2	40,991	20,440	100.5	34,801	16,615	109.5

	Value of land ($ mill.)			Value of buildings ($ mill.)			Value of implements and machinery ($ mill.)			Value of livestock ($ mill.)		
	1910	1900	%+	1910	1900	%+	1910	1900	%+	1910	1900	%+
The North	19,129	9.369	104.2	4,521	2,672	69.2	856	517	65.6	2,975	1,897	56.8
The South	5,926	2,562	131.3	1,427	717	99.0	293	180	62.9	1,325	811	63.5
The West	3,420	1,127	203.5	377	167	125.0	116	53	119.0	625	367	70.1
The U.S.A.	28,475	13,058	118.1	6,325	3,556	77.8	1,265	750	68.7	4,925	3,075	60.1

Value ($ mill.)

	p. 538, t. 8 of all crops (α)	p. 476 t.3 of dairy products (1)	p. 494 t. 21 of wool	page 507 t. 33 of poultry	p. 517 t. 41 of eggs	of honey and wax	p. 520, t 45 of all domestic animals sold or slaughtered	(My figures) all livestock products (β)	(My figures) all farm products (α+β)
	1909	1909	1909	1909	1909	1909	1909	1909	1909
The North	3,120	477	23	129	205	3	1,258	2,095	5,215
The South	1,922	114	6	61	75	2	414	672	2,594
The West	445	57	36	12	26	1	161	293	738
The U.S.A.	5,487	648	65	202	306	6	1,833	3,060	8,547

The same data ($ mill.) but for 1899

		(2)					?
The North	1,812	346	18	90	103	3	data
The South	989	97	4	40	32	2	not
The West	198	29	23	6	9	1	com-
The U.S.A	2,999	472	45	136	144	6	parable (p. 520)

p. 560, t. 24.

Average expenditures per acre improved land in farms for

	% of farms reporting expenditure for labour	labour		fertilisers		% of increase in expenditure for labour
		1909	1899	1909	1899	
The North	55.1	1.26	0.82	0.13	0.09	+ 70.8
The South	36.6	1.07	0.69	0.50	0.23	+ 87.1
The West	52.5	3.25	2.07	0.06	0.04	+119.0
The U.S.A.	45.9	1.36	0.86	0.24	0.13	82.3 p.t.o.*

Note: (1) The original gives Σ = 656. But this is wrong. Exclud

* See pp. 482-83.— Ed.

(p. 43, t. 8) Average value of farm property per acre of land in farms ($ and %)

All farm property			Land			Buildings			Implements and machinery			Livestock		
1910	1900	%+	1910	1900	%+	1910	1900	%+	1910	1900	%+	1910	1900	%+
66.46	37.77	76.0	46.26	24.48	89.0	10.93	6.98	56.6	2.07	1.35	53.3	7.20	4.96	45.2
25.31	11.79	114.7	16.72	7.08	136.2	4.03	1.98	103.5	0.83	0.50	66.0	3.74	2.24	67.0
40.93	18.28	123.9	30.86	12.01	157.0	3.40	1.79	89.9	1.04	0.56	85.7	5.63	3.92	43.6
46.64	24.37	91.4	32.40	15.57	108.1	7.20	4.24	69.8	1.44	0.89	61.8	5.60	3.67	52.6

p. 540, t. 10

Percentage of value of all crops (1909)

value of all crops %	crops with acreage reported	cereals	hay and forage	tobacco and cotton	vegetables	fruits and nuts	Σ of foregoing
100	93.7	62.6	18.8	0.9	7.5	3.3	93.1
100	92.8	29.3	5.1	46.8	7.5	2.6	91.3
100	82.2	33.1	31.7	0.0	8.5	15.5	88.8
100	92.5	48.6	15.0	16.9	7.6	4.0	92.1

(p. 513, t. 12)

Percentage of improved farmland (1909)

100	67.8	46.2	18.8	0.1	1.5	0.1	66.7
100	63.3	32.1	5.7	21.9	1.5	0.1	61.3
100	51.4	24.1	24.2	0.0	1.4	0.1	49.8
100	65.1	40.0	15.7	7.0	1.5	0.1	63.7

ing (N.B.) home consumption—(2) Including home consumption

	(p. 97, t. 1) Farm tenure. Number of farms ('000)			(p. 99, t. 3) Average acreage per farm			Average improved acreage per farm		
	1910	1900	%+	1910	1900	%+	1910	1900	+%
The *United States*									
All classes	6,361	5,737	10.9	138.1	146.2	—5.5	75.2	72.2	4.2
Farms operated by	3,949	3,653	8.1	151.6	152.2	—0.4	78.5	76.2	3.0
Owners { owning entire farm	3,355	3,202	4.8	138.6	134.7	2.9	69.7	69.2	0.7
leasing additional land	594	451	31.6	225.0	276.4	—18.6	128.1	125.7	1.9
Managers	58	59	—1.7	924.7	1,481.2	—37.6	211.9	184.6	14.8
Tenants	2,354	2,025	16.3	96.2	96.3	—0.1	66.4	61.9	7.3
Ten- { share tenants	1,528	1,273	20.0	93.2	92.4	0.9	69.1	65.0	6.3
ants { cash tenants	826	752	9.9	101.7	102.9	—1.2	61.3	56.7	8.1

📌 (p. 105, t. 7) % distribution of farms (Σ of vertical columns = 100)

p. 106, t. 9   Average

	The United States		The North		The South		The West		The North (α)		(β)	
	1910	1900	1910	1900	1910	1900	1910	1900	1910	1900	1910	1900
Owners	62.1	63.7	72.4	72.6	49.9	52.3	83.8	80.3	139.8	133.0	93.2	88.1
Managers	0.9	1.0	1.2	1.1	0.5	0.7	2.2	3.1	301.7	340.9	163.5	152.0
Tenants	37.0	35.3	26.5	26.2	49.6	47.0	14.0	16.6	144.9	124.5	115.0	96.1

	(p. 102, t. 6) Number of farms ('000)				% of farms				(p. 141, t. 27) The U.S.A.	Number of farms ('000) reporting domestic animals	
	1910	1900	1890	1880	1910	1900	1890	1880		1910	1900
Owners and managers	4,007	3,712	3,270	2,984	63.0	64.7	71.6	74.4			
Tenants	2,354	2,025	1,295	1,025	37.0	35.3	28.4	25.6	Total	6,035	5,498
{ share	1,528	1,273	840	702	24.0	22.2	18.4	17.5	Owners	3,794	3,535
{ cash	826	752	455	323	13.0	13.1	10.0	8.0	Managers	52	54
Σ=	6,361	5,737	4,565	4,009	100.0	100.0	100.0	100.0	Tenants	2,189	1,909

---

* This % was later pencilled in by Lenin. A separate sheet Institute of Marxism-Leninism under the C.P.S.U. Central Com-

(p. 115, t. 19) Number of farms ('000) and % + (-).

	The North			The South			The West		
	1910	1900	%+	1910	1900	+%	1910	1900	%+
Total	2,891	2,874	$0._6$	3,097	2,620	$18._2$	373	243	$53._7$
Owners	2,091	2,088	$+0._1$	1,544	1,370		312	195	
{ Owners	1,749	1,794	$-2._5$	1,329	1,237	$7._5$	276	171	$61._9$
{ Part owners	342	294	$16._5$	215	133	$61._3$	36	24	$49._8$
Managers	34	33	$2._9$	16	19	$-13._2$	8	8	$7._3$
Tenants	766	753		1,537	1,231		53	40	
{ Share tenants	483	479	$0._6$	1,021	772	$32._2$	25	21	$14._7$
{ Cash tenants	283	274	$3._3$	516	459	$12._3$	28	19	$47._7$

acreage per farm (α) all land (β) improved land

The South				The West			
(α)		(β)		(α)		(β)	
1910	1900	1910	1900	1910	1900	1910	1900
$149._3$	$162._8$	$56._4$	$55._4$	$241._5$	$282._8$	$84._5$	$94._5$
$1,514._7$	$2,734._1$	$198._6$	$169._4$	$2,323._2$	$3,303._9$	$439._1$	$363._2$
$64._5$	$71._2$	$39._3$	$38._1$	$313._1$	$337._4$	$151._5$	$148._3$

% of farms with livestock to all farms — my calculation		(p. 145, t. 28) Farms with horses ('000)		% of farms with horses (my calculation)		(My calculation from Divisions, p. 145, t. 28) Number of farms with horses ('000)					
						The North		The South		The West	
1910	1900	1910	1900	1910	1900	1910	1900	1910	1900	1910	1900
$94._9$—$95._8$		4,693	4,531	$73._8$	$79._0$	$.2,600$	2,620	1,771	1,694	320	217
$96._1$—$96._7$		3,216	3,107	$81._5$	$85._0$	$..1,873$	1,901	1,075	1,032	267	175
$89._6$—$91._7$		46	48	$79._3$	$81._3$	$...\,29$	28	11	14	7	6
$92._9$—$94._2$		1,431	1,376	$60._7$	$67._9$	$..\,698$	691	685	648	46	36

% of farms with horses (my calculation) *	The North		The South		The West	
	1910	1900	1910	1900	1910	1900
Total	$89._9$ %	$91._1$ %	$57._1$ %	$64._6$ % / $75._2$	$85._8$ %	$89._3$ %
owners	$89._6$	$91._0$	$69._6$	$-5._6$ / $52._6$	$85._6$	$89._8$
managers						
tenants	$91._1$	$91._8$	$44._6$	$—8._1$	$86._8$	$90._0$

containing these calculations is at the Central Party Archives of the mittee.— *Ed.*

(p. 158, t. 1)	Mortgaged farms		
	1910	1900	1890
Number of farms *owned*.............	3,948.722	3,638,403	3,142,746
Number of farms mortgaged.	1,327,439	1,127,749	886,957
%	33.$_6$	31.$_0$	28.$_2$

% of mortgaged	The North	41.$_8$	40.$_7$	40.$_3$
farms	The South	23.$_5$	17.$_3$	5.$_7$
p. 160	The West	28.$_4$	21.$_7$	23.$_1$

	1910		1890
Number of mortgaged farms	1,006,511		886,957
Value of land and buildings	6,330	$ mill	3,055
Total debt................................	1,726	" "	1,086
% of debt to value	27.$_3$%		35.$_5$%

? With reference to this increase in the proportion of farms mortgaged, it should be borne in mind that the fact of mortgage debt is not necessarily an indication of lack of prosperity. There can be no question that American farmers generally were more prosperous in 1910 than at the two preceding censuses. The percentage of mortgaged farms is said to be highest in the most prosperous states, such as Iowa and Wisconsin. In some cases a farm is mortgaged out of need, in others for improvements, etc. (p. 158).

N.B. The breaking-up of certain plantations into small farms—farms owned by their operators but mortgaged for part of the purchase price—probably also has had something to do with the increase in the proportion of farms mortgaged in the South (p. 159).

The number of farms owned by *Negroes* (coloured people in general, but these are mostly Negroes)=920,883 (=14.5%)(1910), including, only 17,884 in the North, and 12,858, in the West. In the *South*, there are 890,141, including owners — 218,467, tenants, 670,474, managers, 1,200.

Thus, in the South, the Whites have more owners than tenants, and the Negroes, vice versa.

In 1900, the Negroes had 767,764 farms. (including 740,670 in the *South*). Consequently, the number of Negro farms increased by +19.6%, and White farms, by +9.5%.

The total farm acreage increased in White farms by +4.4% and in Negro farms, +11.7%.
Improved land in farms increased: White, +15.2%, Negro, +19.5%.
Value of all farm property increased: White, +99.6%, Negro, +134.0%.

Farmers:					Average farm acreage			
The South	White		Negro		White		Negro	
	1910	1900	1910	1900	1910	1900	1910	1900
Total	100	100	100	100	141.3	172.1	47.9	52.1
Owners	60.1	63.0	24.5	25.2	162.1	177.2	71.8	71.6
Managers	0.7	0.9	0.1	0.2	1,612.1	2,962.8	291.5	269.0
Tenants	39.2	36.1	75.3	74.6	83.8	92.5	39.6	44.9

In the *South*, the number of White *share-tenants* increased from 492,000 to 637,000 (+29.5%), and Negro, from 281,000 to 384,000 (+37.0%).

Quantity and value of livestock on White and Negro farms.
Total farms in the U.S.A. (p. 248).

		Number	Value $
Dairy cows	White	19,655,747	683,996,175
	Negro	969,685	22,240,132
Horses	White	16,780,511	1,903,612,666
	Negro	649,907	54,942,151
Mules	White	3,133,740	413,530,751
	Negro	653,576	84,451,579

Concerning the role, importance and place of *tenants* vis-à-vis *o w n e r s*:

Tenant farmers reported a much larger proportion of the value of land than of the value of buildings, implements & machinery, or livestock. This is largely due to the fact that tenant farmers in general are less well-to-do than farm owners and are less able to furnish their farms with expensive equipment (pp. 100-01). The average for the United States (1910) shows: the value of owners' land = 66.$_8$% of all property, and that of "tenants" = 74.$_9$% (p. 101, Table 5).

Concerning the owners of farms leased, the authors (p. 102) refer to the inquiry during the 1900 Census, when the *names* of owners of tenant farms were studied. They say there was no concentration or "absentee landlordism". The owners of leased farms are for the most part former tenants "who have either retired altogether, gone into other business, or taken up farms in newer sections of the country".

"In the South the conditions have at all times been somewhat different from those in the North, and many of the tenant farms are parts of plantations of considerable size which date from before the Civil War." In the South, "the system of operation by tenants—chiefly coloured tenants—has succeeded the system of operation by slave labour" (102).*

‖N.B.

‖N.B.

Concerning rent:

The development of the tenant system is most conspicuous in the South, where the large plantations formerly operated by slave labour have in many cases been broken up into small parcels or tracts and leased to tenants. As more fully explained in Chapter I, these plantations are in

---

* See present edition, Vol. 22, p. 26.— *Ed.*

N.B. | many cases still operated substantially as agricultural units, the tenants being subjected to a degree of supervision more or less similar to that which hired farm labourers are subjected to in the North" (p. 104).

N.B. | "A very low proportion of tenant farms is ... shown for the Mountain and Pacific divisions, where it is doubtless attributable mainly to the fact that those divisions have been only recently settled and that many of the farmers in them are homesteaders who have obtained their land from the Government" (p. 104). | N.B.

The whole Chapter II ("Farm tenure") does not contain any analysis of the causes of the *growth* (respective decrease) in the *number of owners* of land. These authors are bourgeois scum: they gloss over the most important thing (expropriation of the small farmers)!!

Growth of rural population (1900-10)	$+11._2\%$	
" number of farms ....⌐	$+10._9\%$	(less)
" " owners	$+ 8._1\%$	(still less)

An obvious increase in expropriation!!

But the increase is even more evident if we take the *North*, the *South* and the *West*.

The total number of farms has gone up from 5,737,372 to 6,361,502, i.e., by *624,130* (p. 114, Table 18), i.e., by $10._9$ per cent. But in the *North* the increase is only $0._6\%$ ($+16,545$ farms!!). This is stagnation. Moreover, there was also an absolute *reduction* in the number of farms in three out of the four divisions of the North, namely, New England, Middle Atlantic and East. In North Central, there was an *absolute drop in the number of farms* (by *32*,000). **Only** in West North Central was there an increase by *49*,000 (hence, in $\Sigma = +16,500$). But West North Central includes states like the two Dakotas, Nebraska and Kansas, where homesteading is still extensive (see *Statistical Abstract*, p. *28*).

In general, the number of owners in the entire North:

1900 — 2,088,000
1910 — 2,091,000

+3,000 = $0._1$%!!!

	The entire North owners:	part owners:
1900	1,794,216	293,612
1910	1,749,267	342,167
	−44,949	+48,555

Thus, there was a reduction in the number of owners!! The number of *part* owners went up!!

And this same North had 60% of all the improved land in the United States (1910)!!

In this North, the acreage of improved land increased by $10._9$%, from 261 million to 290 million acres!!

In the *West*, the growth in the number of farms and the number of owners is understandable: the country is being settled, and there is a growing number of *homesteads* (see *Statistical Abstract*, p. *28* and the above quotation from p. *104*, p. *3* of these extracts).*

And the *South*?? Share tenants (*mostly* Negroes) there mainly (1) account for the growth in the number of farms. This means greater exploitation of the Negroes. Then (2), there is a growing number of *owners*. Why?? Apparently it is due to the parcellisation of the *plantations*. P. 265 (Table 8) shows that the acreage in the ·1,000-and->-acre farms in the United States fell by 30,702,109 acres ($-15._5$%), including +2,321,975 in the North, and −1,206,872 in the West. Nearly the whole falls to the *South—31,817,212* ($-27._3$%). And this same South accounts, out of the total increase in the number

---

* See p. 451.—*Ed.*

of farms (+624,130), for +477,156*) (i.e., the bulk, about
³/₄), with a growing number of small farms:

under	20 acres	+115,192
20-49	”	+191,793
50-99	”	+111,690

$$\Sigma = 418,675$$

The essence is the disintegration of the slave-holding
plantations!!

The *South* (number of farms)	
White farmers	coloured
1910 2,207,406	890,141
1900 1,879,721	740,670

with the Whites having more owners than tenants, and
the coloured *vice versa*.

---

*) 1910: 3,097,547
   1900: 2,620,391

   +477,156

	(p. 257, t. 1) Number of farms		(My abbreviation) idem ('000)		(p. 309, t. 18) Number of farms with horses	
	1910	1900	1910	1900	1910	1900
Total	6,361,502	5,737,372	6,361	5,738	4,692,814	4,530,628
Under 20 acres	839,166+	673,870	839	674	408,601+	373,269
20-49	1,414,376+	1,257,496	1,415	1,258	811,538—	834,241
50-99	1,438,069+	1,366,038	1,438	1,366	1,116,415—	1,123,750
100-174	1,516,286+	1,422,262	1,516	1,422	1,302,086+	1,260,090
175-499	978,175+	868,020	978	868	890,451+	798,760
500-999	125,295+	102,526	125	103	116,556+	96,087
1,000 and over	50,135+	47,160	50	47	47,167+	44,431

(p. 257, t. 1)	Increase in number of farms (1900-1910)		(p. 257, t. 1) All land in farms (acres)			
	increase	+%	1910	1900	increase	%
Total	624,130	10.9	878,798,325	838,591,774	40,206,551	4.8
Under 20 acres	165,296	24.5	8,793,820	7,180,839	1,612,981	22.5
20-49	156,880	12.5	45,378,449	41,536,128	3,842,321	9.3
50-99	72,031	5.3	103,120,868	98,591,699	4,529,169	4.6
100-174	94,024	6.6	205,480,585	192,680,321	12,800,264	6.6
175-499	110,155	12.7	265,289,069	232,954,515	32,334,554	13.9
500-999	22,769	22.2	83,653,487	67,864,116	15,789,371	23.3
1,000 and over	2,975	6.3	167,082,047	197,784,156	—30,702,109	—15.5

*) On the question of horse ownership, it should be noted
not make up for the decrease in farms with horses. This
The *South* showed the *greatest growth* — 1900:1,155,000; 1910:
growth in the number of farms reporting mules fails to make

(My abbreviation)*)

(p. 257, t. 2)

idem ('000)		% of farms with horses		Number of farms % of total		All land in farms		Improved land in farms		% of improved land in farms	
1910	1900	1910	1900	1910	1900	1910	1900	1910	1900	1910	1900
4,693	4,531	73.8	79.0	100	100	100	100	100	100	54.4	49.4
409	373	48.9	52.4	13.2+11.7		1.0+ 0.9		1.7+ 1.6		90.9	89.7
812	834	57.4	66.3	22.2+21.9		5.2+ 5.0		7.6- 8.0		80.6	79.4
1,116	1,124	77.6	82.2	23.6-23.8		11.7-11.8		14.9-16.2		69.0	68.3
1,302	1,260	86.5	88.6	23.8-24.8		23.4+23.0		26.9-28.6		62.7	61.4
890	799	91.0	92.0	15.4+15.1		30.2+27.8		33.8+32.7		61.0	58.2
117	96	93.2	93.7	2.0+1.8		9.5+ 8.1		8.5+ 7.1		48.8	43.4
47	45	94.1	94.2	0.8=0.8		19.0-23.6		6.5+ 5.9		18.7	12.3

(ibidem)

Improved land in farms (acres)				% increase		Increase or decrease of share	
1910	1900	increase	%	Number of farms	Improved land	Improved land	Number of farms
478,451,750	414,498,487	63,953,263	15.4				
7,991,543	6,440,447	1,551,096	24.1	24.5	24.1-	+	+
36,596,032	33,000,734	3,595,298	10.9	12.5	10.9-	-	+
71,155,246	67,344,759	3,810,487	5.7	5.3	5.7+	-	-
128,853,538	118,390,708	10,462,830	8.8	6.6	8.8+	-	-
161,775,502	135,530,043	26,245,459	19.4	12.7	19.4+	+	+
40,817,118	29,474,642	11,342,476	38.5	22.2	38.5+	+	+
31,262,771	24,317,154	6,945,617	28.6	6.3	28.6+	+	+

that the growth in the number of farms reporting mules does
growth=1900:1,480,652 (=25.8%); 1910:1,869,005 (=29.4%).
1,478,000, i.e., 1900−44.1%; 1910−47.7%. There, too, the
up for the increase in the number of horseless farms.

The authors give *no* valid reasons for their grouping. "Government land has for the most part been sold approximately that amount" (p. 257).

N.B. "As judged by improved acreage, which is probably less than 20 acres) are becoming of relatively less impor- This is the normal result of the fact that the very large the country, where agriculture is developing most rapidly" a relatively *greater* growth of the *share* of the big farms

	The North Per cent of total						% of improved land in farms		The Per cent Number of farms	
	Number of farms		All land in farms		Improved land					
	1910	1900	1910	1900	1910	1900	1910	1900	1910	1900
Σ	100.0	100.0	100.0	100.0	100.0	100.0	70.1	68.3	100.0	100.0
<20	9.5+	8.7	0.6	0.6	0.8	0.8	86.1	86.3	16.2	14.7
20-49	13.9-	16.0	3.3	4.2	3.6	4.7	76.2	76.2	30.9	29.2
50-99	24.2-	26.3	12.5	14.6	13.5	16.0	75.3	74.6	22.4	22.3
100-174	29.5+	29.0	28.1-	29.7	29.3-	31.6	73.2	72.6	18.1	19.8
175-499	20.2+	18.0	38.1	36.0	39.8	37.3	73.1	70.5	10.4	11.6
500-999	2.2+	1.6	10.3	7.9	9.0	6.6	60.8	56.9	1.3	1.6
1,000 &>	0.5+	0.4	6.9	6.9	4.1	3.1	41.1	30.5	0.7	0.9

	(ctd) The West		Increase from 1900 to 1910: (absolute						The	
	% of improved land in farms		The North							
			Number of farms		All land in farms		Improved land in farms		Number of farms	
	1910	1900	absolute	%	absolute	%	absolute	%	absolute	%
Σ	34.2	29.0	16.5	0.6	30,725	8.0	28,573	10.9	477.2	18.2
<20	87.3	85.0	25.1	10.0	116	4.8	95	4.5	115.2	29.9
20-49	73.9	71.4	-57.9	-12.6	-2,295	-14.2	-1,743	-14.2	191.8	25.1
50-99	62.2	57.4	-55.2	-7.3	-4,072	-7.3	-2,708	-6.5	111.7	19.2
100-174	37.1	38.5	18.1	+2.2	2,503	2.2	2.435	2.9	42.7	8.2
175-499	43.4	46.7	65.9	12.7	19,720	14.3	17,966	18.5	18.6	6.1
500-999	46.6	44.1	18.5	40.4	12,430	40.9	8.756	50.6	-0.8	-2.0
1,000 &>	22.9	17.2	2.1	16.4	2,322	8.8	3.773	47.0	-2.0	-8.8

N.B. only:
or otherwise disposed of in quarter sections of *160* acres or   N.B.

the best standard, the smaller farms (excepting those of
tance and the large farms of relatively greater importance.
farms are found for the most part in the newer sections of   N.B.
(p. 258). This last explanation is wrong, for we find
in such *old* divisions as New England and Middle Atlantic.

South

All land in farms		Improved land		% of improved land in farms	
1910	1900	1910	1900	1910	1900
100.0	100.0	100.0	100.0	42.5	34.8
1.6	1.2	3.5	3.2	93.3	91.9
8.4	6.7	16.4	15.8	83.1	82.0
13.6	11.2	20.0	19.4	62.7	60.2
20.8	+18.9	25.3	+25.2	51.6	46.4
24.0	22.2	24.4	24.9	43.2	39.1
7.6	7.5	5.5	6.1	30.9	28.1
23.9	32.2	4.8	5.4	8.5	5.9

The West — Per cent of total

Number of farms		All land in farms		% of improved land in farms	
1910	1900	1910	1900	1910	1900
100.0	100.0	100.0	100.0	100.0	100.0
16.7	15.5	0.5	0.4	1.2	1.0
15.3	14.0	1.6	-1.2	3.6	2.9
11.8	11.7	2.9	2.2	5.3	4.4
27.5	-28.6	14.0	+11.3	15.2	+15.0
19.5	19.4	20.2	15.6	25.7	25.2
5.3	6.1	12.4	11.0	16.9	16.7
3.9	4.8	48.3	58.4	32.3	34.8

figures=1,000 farms or acres)

South

All land in farms		Improved land in farms	
absolute	%	absolute	%
-7,583	-2.1	24,583	19.5
1,301	29.5	1,278	31.5
5,406	22.2	4,772	23.9
7.497	18.5	5.731	23.5
5,351	7.8	6,345	20.0
4.796	6.0	5,369	17.1
-118	-0.4	712	9.3
-31,817	-27.3	375	5.5

The West

Number of farms		All land in farms		Improved land in farms	
absolute	%	absolute	%	absolute	%
130.4	53.7	17,065	18.2	10,797	39.8
24.9	66.5	195	58.8	178	63.3
23.0	67.5	731	66.8	566	72.5
15.5	54.8	1,104	52.5	787	65.2
33.2	47.8	4,945	46.8	1,683	41.4
25.7	54.5	.7,818	53.5	2,911	42.6
5.1	34.5	3,478	33.8	1,874	41.3
2.9	25.3	-1,207	-2.2	2,797	29.6

Three main groups clearly stand out (see + and − for **the United States**): small farms (under 49 acres), medium (50-174) and large (175 and >). (These limits are also indicated by the "official" allotment ["homestead"]=160 acres). Taking these three groups, we obtain the following basic %% results:

| | | % of total | | | | Increase (or—) 1900-10 | |
| | | 1910 | | 1900 | | | |
		Number of farms	Improved land	Number of farms	Improved land	% of farms	% of improved land
The United States	small	35.4	9.3	33.6	9.6	+	−
	medium (50-174)	46.4	41.8	48.6	44.8	−	−
	large	18.2	48.8	17.7	45.7	+	+
The North	small	23.4	4.4	24.7	5.5	−	−
	medium	53.7	42.8	55.3	47.6	−	−
	large	22.9	52.9	20.0	47.0	+	+
The South	small	47.1	19.9	43.9	19.0	+	+
	medium	40.5	45.3	42.1	44.6	−	+
	large	12.4	34.7	14.1	36.4	−	−
The West	small	32.0	4.8	29.5	3.9	+	+
	medium	39.3	20.5	40.3	19.4	−	+
	large	28.7	74.9	30.3	76.7	−	−

| | | % of total | | | | 1900-10 Increase (+) or decrease (−) | |
| | | 1910 | | 1900 | | | |
		Number of farms	Improved land	Number of farms	Improved land	% of farms	% of improved land
The United States	small	58.0	24.2	57.4	25.8	+	−
	medium (100-174)	23.8	26.9	24.8	28.6	−	−
	large	18.2	48.8	17.7	45.7	+	+
The North	small	47.6	17.9	51.0	21.5	−	+
	medium	29.5	29.3	29.0	31.6	+	+
	large	22.9	52.9	20.0	47.0	+	−
The South	small	69.5	39.9	66.2	38.4	+	−
	medium	18.1	25.3	19.8	25.2	−	−
	large	12.4	34.7	14.1	36.4	−	+
The West	small	43.8	10.1	41.2	8.3	+	+
	medium	27.5	15.2	28.6	15.0	−	+
	large	28.7	74.9	30.3	76.7	−	−

The distinctive features of the three sections stand out clearly:

The North: 1) The highest development of capitalism. 2) Stagnation in the number of farms. 3) Reduction in the number and share of medium farms. 4) Growth in the number and share of large (and very small, but to a less degree). 5) Weak latifundia (>1,000 : $0._5\%$ of the farms and $6._9\%$ of the land).

The South: 1) The lowest development of capitalism. 2) The greatest development of share-tenancy ($49._6\%$ are tenant farms). 3) Vast latifundia (>1,000 acres: $0._7\%$ of the farms and $23._9\%$ of the land; in the North $0._5\%$ of the farms and $6._9\%$ of the land). 4) Disintegration of these latifundia of the former slave-owners (1900-10: — 32 million acres — $27._3\%$). 5) The highest % of small farms (43-47%). Summary: from slave-owning latifundia to small commercial agriculture.

The West: 1) Tremendous increase in the number of farms: $+53._7\%$!! Homesteads and small commercial agriculture!! 2) Vast. % of land in large farms (76-75%). 3) Very large latifundia (>1,000:$3._9\%$ of the farms and $48._3\%$ of the land). 4) The lowest % of tenant-farmers and a *r e d u c t i o n* of it.

| N.B. (on the question of "acreage statistics") | % of improved land in the <20 acre farms =73-96% by divisions, and in the >1,000 acre farms $6._2$-$43._4\%$ by divisions. The contrast between these two sets of percentages is the natural result of the fact that small farms throughout the country usually specialise in cropping, whereas large farms, which in some sections also specialise mainly in cropping, in other sections almost exclusively go in for stock raising (p. 264). |

In the South there is a "process of breaking up great plantations into small farms, chiefly operated by tenants" (p. 264).

The great development of small fruit and other farms on the Pacific coast, due, in part at least, to irrigation projects organised in recent years, is reflected in the increase in small farms of less than 50 acres in the Pacific division (p. 264).*

Concerning the commercial character of stock raising, it is interesting to note the % of farms selling *livestock*, and the % of stock sold and slaughtered

	Value of all domestic animals sold or slaughtered on farms in 1909 ($ mill.)		Cattle (excluding calves)	Calves	Swine	Cattle (excluding calves)	Calves	Swine
			(% of all farms selling stock)			Ratio (%) between number of domestic animals sold or slaughtered and number on hand:		
The United States	1,833	100.0	32.0%	23.0%	28.9%	40.7%	100.9%	90.9%
The North	1,258	68.6%	42.4%	34.5%	44.9%	42.9%	124.3%	97.5%
The South	414	22.6%	23.3%	13.3%	15.9%	40.7%	68.2%	77.6%
The West	161	8.8%	23.9%	13.5%	13.2%	33.4%	61.8%	87.9%
New England	30.4	1.7%	34.7%	34.6%	16.4%	43.6	320.8	126.8
Middle Atlantic	89.6	4.9%	36.2	48.6	23.0	28.6	241.2	123.5

---

* See present edition, Vol. 22, p. 51.—*Ed.*

(p. 349, t. 14) (My abbreviation of table)

Number of farms reporting

	cattle 1910	cattle 1900	dairy cows 1910	dairy cows 1900
The United States	5,284,916	4,730,480	5,140,869	4,513,895
The North	2,582,462	2,568,255	2,546,115	2,503,655
The South	2,426,302	1,972,548	2,334,605	1,835,841
The West	276,152	189,677	260,149	174,399

Per cent of farms reporting

	cattle 1910	cattle 1900	dairy cows 1910	dairy cows 1900	(Horses) 1910	(Horses) 1900	(Mules) 1910	(Mules) 1900
The United States	83.1	82.4	80.8	78.7	73.8	79.0	29.4	25.8
The North	89.3	89.4	88.1	87.1	90.0	91.2	12.4	10.7
The South	78.3	75.3	75.4	70.1	57.2	64.6	47.7	44.1
The West	74.0	78.1	69.7	71.8	85.8	89.2	8.5	7.9

Average number per farm reporting

	cattle 1910	cattle 1900	dairy cows 1910	dairy cows 1900	(Horses) 1910	(Horses) 1900	(Mules) 1910	(Mules) 1900	
The United States	11.7	14.3	4.0	3.8	4.2	4.0	2.3	2.2	+0.2
The North	12.8	14.4	5.3	4.8	4.9	4.4	2.9	2.6	+0.5
The South	8.0	11.3	2.4	2.3	2.6	2.7	2.1	2.0	+0.1
The West	33.6	44.6	5.2	5.0	7.6	10.5	4.5	6.3	+0.2

(p. 367, t. 26)

	Horses 1910	Horses 1900	Mules 1910	Mules 1900
The United States	4,692,814	4,530,628	1,869,005	1,480,652
The North	2,600,709	2,620,082	359,024	306,573
The South	1,771,659	1,693,878	1,478,382	1,154,810
The West	320,446	216,668	31,599	19,269

(p. 387, t. 36)

	Swine (all swine) 1910	Swine (all swine) 1900	(all swine) % 1910	(all swine) % 1900	(all swine) avg 1910	(all swine) avg 1900
The United States	4,351,751	4,335,363	75.6	68.4	13.4	14.5
The North	1,971,059	2,193,438	76.3	68.2	19.2	19.5
The South	2,230,841	2,023,508	77.2	72.0	8.3	9.2
The West	149,851	118,417	48.7	40.1	12.2	12.3

These data show the North concentrating livestock ownership against the South and the West. Data on average per farm: dairy cows: North—4.8 and 5.3; horses—4.4 and 4.9; mules: 2.6 and 2.9; swine—19.5 and 19.2 (the smallest reduction).

> The figures for the divisions show that this applies wholly only to East North Central and West North Central. In New England, the average number of cows *declined*, but that of horses remained *the same* in New England and Middle Atlantic.

(p. 309, t. 18)

(My calculation)

	Farms reporting dairy cows (ibid. '000)				1910	1900		Farms reporting horses	% of farms reporting horses See p. 5*
	1910	1900	1910	1900					
The United States	5,140,869	4,513,895	5,141+	4,514	80.8	78.7 +2.1		+36,000	−3.5
<20	443,331	334,361	444+	334	52.9	49.5 +3.4	+110,000	−22,000	−8.9
20-49	1,006,877	829,033	1,007+	829	71.2	65.9 +5.3	+178,000	− 8,000	−4.6
50-99	1,260,346	1,150,172	1,260+	1,150	87.1	84.1 +3.0	110,000	+42,000	−2.1
100-174	1,361,251	1,264,680	1,361+	1,265	89.8	88.9 +0.9	+ 96,000	+91,000	−1.0
175-499	913,991	803,667	914+	804	93.5	92.6 +0.9	+110,000	+21,000	−0.5
500-999	112,167	92,670	112+	93	89.6	90.3 −0.7	+ 19,000		
1,000 and>	42,906	39,312	43+	39	86.0	82.9 +3.1	+ 4,000	+ 2,000	−0.1

* See pp. 454-55.—*Ed.*

(p. 271, t. 12) Number of farms

	The North 1910	The North 1900	The South 1910	The South 1900	The West 1910	The West 1900
Σ	2,890,618+	2,874,073	3,097,547+	2,620,391	373,337+	242,908
<20	276,042+	250,904	500,614+	385,422	62,510+	37,544
20-49	401,332-	459,264	955,907+	764,114	57,137+	34,118
50-99	699,417-	754,621	694,737+	583,047	43,915+	28,370
100-174	852,051+	833,963	561,544+	518,836	102,691+	69,463
175-499	582,778+	516,910	322,612+	303,986	72,778+	47,124
500-999	64,313+	45,795	41,183-	42,015	19,799+	14,716
1,000 & >	14,685+	12,616	20,950-	22,971	14,500	11,573

(My calculation for the divisions)

Farms reporting domestic animals

	The North 1910	The North 1900	The South 1910	The South 1900	The West 1910	The West 1900	
Σ	2,769,135	2,766,215	2,923,891	2,503,219	341,757	228,983	6,034,783
<20	226,816	216,345	405,764	327,690	52,386	32,200	684,966
20-49	374,099	431,353	900,990	728,509	53,112	31,941	1,328,201
-99	679,498	729,586	681,654	569,986	41,595	27,043	1,402,747
-174	833,045	819,122	554,235	511,269	91,144	65,585	1,478,424
-499	577,839	511,980	319,794	301,383	69,720	46,273	967,353
-999	63,354	55,391	40,775	41,647	19,498	14,556	123,627
1,000 & >	14,484	12,438	20,679	22,735	14,302	11,385	49,465

(My calculation for the divisions)

Value of all domestic animals

	The North 1910	The North 1900	The South 1910	The South 1900	The West 1910	The West 1900	
Σ	2,863.7	1,835.3	1,284.3	782.4	611.9	361.4	ΣΣ 4,760 mill.
<20	49.5+	35.6	58.5+	33.3	41.9+	31.0	
-49	138.6+	100.3	194.5+	91.2	27.9+	11.3	
-99	441.1+	293.0	239.6+	115.1	33.3+	14.2	
-174	881.9+	548.5	293.5+	155.3	94.6+	55.8	
-499	1,059.5+	633.0	280.2	157.3	127.7+	65.2	
-999	190.0+	122.1	72.0+	46.8	77.1+	43.2	
1,000 & >	103.2+	102.7	146.0-	183.4	209.2+	140.8	

Farms reporting horses

	The North		The South		The West		% of farms reporting horses The North		
	1910	1900	1910	1900	1910	1900	1910	1900	1900 ±
Σ	2,600,709—	2,620,082	1,771,659+	1,693,878	320,446+	216,668	89_9	91_4	-1_5
<20	180,119+	176,851	183,375+	168,012	45,107+	28,406	65_2	70_5	-5_3
20-49	330,346—	387,672	431,805+	416,991	49,387+	29,578	82_3	84_4	-2_1
50-99	641,509—	696,599	435,226+	401,520	39,680+	25,631	91_7	92_3	-0_6
100-174	805,125+	797,766	411,207+	399,859	85,754+	62,465	94_5	95_6	-1_1
175-499	567,012+	504,209	256,142+	249,479	67,297+	45,072	97_3	97_5	-0_2
500-999	62,329+	44,810	35,055—	36,941	19,172+	14,336	96_9	98_0	-1_1
1,000 &>	14,269+	12,175	18,849—	21,076	14,049+	11,180	97_0	96_5	$+0_5$

Farms reporting dairy cows

	The North		The South		The West		% The North		
	1910	1900	1910	1900	1910	1900	1910	1900	±
Σ	2,546,115+	2,503,655	2,334,605+	1835,841	260,149+	174,399	88_8	87_7	1_7
<20	166,143+	151,359	245,526+	164,950	31,662+	18,052	60_2	60_3	-0_1
20-49	324,302—	361,715	641,207+	443,786	41,368+	23,532	80_8	78_7	$+2_1$
50-99	635,791—	672,516	590,109+	455,892	34,446+	21,764	90_9	89_1	$+1_8$
100-174	790,434+	774,299	504,825+	440,942	65,992+	49,439	93_5	92_8	$+0_7$
175-499	558,017+	490,228	298,761+	274,032	57,213+	39,407	95_7	94_8	$+0_9$
500-999	58,100+	42,579	37,048—	37,437	17,019+	12,654	90_3	93_1	-2_8
1,000 &>	13,328+	10,959	17,129—	18,802	12,449+	9,551	90_8	86_9	$+3_9$

Number of mature horses

	The North		The South		The West	
	1910	1900	1910	1900	1910	1900
Σ	11,316,712	9,826,344	4,073,946	3,888,382	2,039,760	1,791,240
<20	280,688		242,330		136,011	
20-49	719,887		654,711		142,956	
50-99	1,944,522		823,210		151,830	
100-174	3,521,068		1,043,386		427,684	
175-499	3,871,018		871,197		518,337	
500-999	689,898		185,274		263,827	
1,000 & >	289,631		253,838		399,115	

For 1900 there are data only on *all* horses (for 1910 these data are *not* available).

Number of dairy cows

	The North		The South		The West	
	1910	1900	1910	1900	1910	1900
Σ	13,596,483+	11,986,550	5,688,368+	4,282,555	1,340,581+	866,528
<20	278,221−	289,135	376,500+	262,187	71,223+	49,274
20-49	824,089−	848,854	1,089,372+	716,853	128,297+	66,612
50-99	2,670,595+	2,453,724	1,254,360+	898,269	154,263+	82,035
100-174	4,756,705+	4,147,973	1,418,157+	1,114,074	300,130+	280,275
175-499	4,469,057+	3,761,844	1,194,299+	950,115	362,757+	153,261
500-999	477,560+	383,171	221,737+	193,677	158,655+	111,629
1,000 &>	120,256+	101,849	133,943−	147,380	165,256+	123,442

Farms reporting mules

	The North		The South		The West	
	1910	1900	1910	1900	1910	1900
Σ	359,024	306,573	1,478,382	1,154,810	31,599	19,269
<20	5,693	6,743	102,402	77,900	1,442	1,333
20-49	26,405	28,900	435,559	311,829	2,277	1,236
50-99	66,539	63,078	370,582	276,723	2,628	1,290
100-174	119,581	101,259	320,772	263,195	8,019	4,071
175-499	121,574	92,258	206,335	182,037	9,472	50,084
500-999	14,906	10,795	28,584	27,739	3,796	2,799
1,000 & >	4,326	3,540	14,148	15,387	3,965	3,456

(p. 270, t. II) Average value per farm ($)

		All farm property		Land		Buildings		Implements and machinery		Livestock	
		1910	1900	1910	1900	1910	1900	1910	1900	1910	1900
The North	Σ	9,507	5,030	6,618	3,260	1,564	930	296	180	1,029	660
	< 20	2,849	1,875	1,334	919	1,213	728	98	71	205	157
	20-49	3,464	2,118	1,961	1,212	992	579	138	92	374	235
	50-99	5,772	3,455	3,602	2,128	1,279	773	223	146	667	408
	100-174	9,713	5,416	6,696	3,538	1,622	994	318	203	1,077	682
	175-499	17,928	9,342	13,369	6,451	2,209	1,349	484	290	1,867	1,253
	500-999	27,458	15.196	21,172	10.275	2,558	1.792	733	434	2,996	2,694
	1,000 & >	52,969	28,805	40,631	17,481	4,068	2,528	1,198	643	7,072	8,153
The South	Σ	2,897	1,629	1,913	978	461	274	95	69	428	309
	< 20	838	483	450	240	237	132	27	20	124	92
	20-49	1,217	673	734	393	230	125	42	29	212	126
	50-99	2,237	1,171	1,390	692	407	218	81	52	359	208
	100-174	3,692	1,818	2,415	1.099	608	328	128	78	541	313
	175-499	6,742	3,414	4,608	2,138	1,023	608	219	132	893	536
	500-999	14,430	6,908	10,423	4,431	1,780	1,056	453	285	1,775	1,136
	1,000 & >	47,348	26,807	36,390	15,660	2,897	1,930	1,065	1,211	6,996	8,006
The West	Σ	12,155	7,059	9,162	4,639	1,009	690	310	218	1,673	1,512
	< 20	5,025	2,953	3,342	1,523	867	507	108	79	710	844
	20-49	7,359	3,578	5,727	2,544	912	560	202	123	518	351
	50-99	9,404	4,358	7,386	3,101	967	570	263	162	789	524
	100-174	7,205	3,763	5,375	2,343	665	445	221	153	944	823
	175-499	14,111	7,667	10,844	5,184	1,082	790	398	282	1,788	1,412
	500-999	27,662	14,601	21,205	10,006	1,749	1,176	722	456	3,986	2,963
	1,000 & >	74,186	44,972	55,110	29,443	3,206	2,402	1,384	915	14,486	12,212
The United States	Σ	6,444	3,563	4,476	2,276	994	620	199	131	774	536
	< 20	1,812	1,139	956	564	605	375	56	42	195	158
	20-49	2,103	1,280	1,284	750	474	303	76	55	270	172
	50-99	4,175	2,499	2,649	1,536	848	532	156	106	522	325
	100-174	7,313	4,022	5,021	2,590	1,182	724	241	155	869	554
	175-499	13,955	7,175	10,291	4,872	1,734	1,059	390	234	1,540	1,012
	500-999	23,208	11,714	17,644	7,842	2,174	1,402	639	376	2,751	2,094
	1,000 &>	56,757	31,799	43,047	19,530	3,330	2.206	1,196	987	9,185	9,077

Average value per acre ($)

All farm property		Land		Buildings		Implements and machinery		Livestock	
1910	1900	1910	1900	1910	1900	1910	1900	1910	1900
66.46	37.77	46.26	24.48	10.93	6.98	2.07	1.35	7.20	4.96
308.84	193.56	144.55	94.82	131.44	75.19	10.59	7.35	22.26	16.19
100.67	60.41	56.98	34.57	28.83	16.52	4.01	2.62	10.85	6.69
77.96	46.66	48.63	28.74	17.27	10.43	3.01	1.97	9.01	5.51
71.26	39.75	49.13	25.96	11.90	7.29	2.33	1.49	7.90	5.00
66.25	35.00	49.40	24.17	8.16	5.05	1.79	1.08	6.90	4.69
41.24	22.90	31.79	15.48	3.84	2.70	1.10	0.65	4.50	4.06
27.14	13.80	20.82	8.37	2.08	1.21	0.61	0.31	3.62	3.90
25.31	11.79	16.72	7.08	4.03	1.98	0.83	0.50	3.74	2.24
73.36	42.16	39.37	20.91	20.77	11.51	2.35	1.72	10.87	8.02
39.18	21.12	23.58	12.33	7.39	3.91	1.35	0.91	6.81	3.97
32.30	16.80	20.07	9.94	5.88	3.13	1.17	0.74	5.18	2.99
28.08	13.78	18.37	8.32	4.63	2.49	0.97	0.59	4.12	2.37
25.55	12.92	17.46	8.09	3.88	2.30	0.83	0.50	3.38	2.03
21.96	10.68	15.86	6.85	2.71	1.63	0.69	0.44	2.70	1.76
11.69	5.28	8.99	3.08	0.72	0.38	0.26	0.24	1.73	1.58
40.93	18.28	30.86	12.01	3.40	1.79	1.04	0.56	5.63	3.92
595.50	333.61	395.87	172.03	102.66	57.31	12.85	8.89	84.12	95.38
230.42	111.59	179.32	79.35	28.55	17.46	6.33	3.82	16.22	10.96
128.79	58.80	101.15	41.85	13.24	7.69	3.60	2.18	10.81	7.07
47.67	24.71	35.56	15.39	4.40	2.92	1.46	1.00	6.24	5.41
45.77	24.71	35.17	16.71	3.51	2.54	1.29	0.91	5.80	4.55
39.79	20.89	30.50	14.81	2.52	1.68	1.04	0.65	5.73	4.24
20.08	9.50	14.92	6.22	0.87	0.51	0.37	0.19	3.92	2.58
46.64	24.37	32.40	15.57	7.20	4.24	1.44	0.89	5.60	3.67
172.89	106.90	91.22	52.92	57.73	35.19	5.37	3.96	18.57	14.83
65.55	38.74	40.00	22.72	14.77	9.16	2.36	1.65	8.42	5.21
58.22	34.62	36.94	21.28	11.83	7.37	2.17	1.47	7.28	4.51
53.97	29.69	37.05	19.11	8.72	5.35	1.78	1.14	6.42	4.09
51.45	26.74	37.95	18.15	6.39	3.95	1.44	0.87	5.68	3.76
34.76	17.70	26.43	11.85	3.26	2.12	0.96	0.57	4.12	3.16
17.03	7.58	12.92	4.66	1.00	0.53	0.36	0.24	2.76	2.16

Note:

"...In the Mountain and Pacific divisions farms of 100 to 174 acres show a lower average value of buildings per farm than those of 50 to 99 acres. This condition is probably due to the fact that the farms of 100 to 174 acres in these divisions consist in considerable part of homesteads recently taken up by settlers who have not had time, or perhaps have not accumulated means, to construct expensive buildings" (p. 271).

Homesteads in the West

"...The high averages (value of all farm property—for *small* farms) in these two divisions [Mountain and Pacific] are partly due to the presence of numerous small and highly cultivated fruit and vegetable farms, many of which are irrigated" (p. 272)

Small farms in the West....

On the question of *crop yields*:

	Average yield per acre (bushels)						Milk produced (gallons) average per cow (p. 486, t. 14)		(p. 485) Dairy cows (1909) average per farm
	Corn[1] (p. 584, t. 15)		Wheat[2] (p. 593)		Oats[3] (p. 603)				
	1909	1899	1909	1899	1909	1899	1909	1899	
United States	25.9	28.1	15.4	12.5	28.6	31.9	362	424	3.8
New England	45.2	39.4	23.5	18.0	32.9	35.9	476	548	5.8
Middle Atlantic	32.2	34.0	18.6	14.9	25.5	30.9	496	514	6.1
East North Central	38.6	38.3	17.2	12.9	33.3	37.4	410	487	4.0
West " "	27.7	31.4	14.8	12.2	27.5	32.0	325	371	4.9
South Atlantic	15.3	14.1	11.9	9.5	15.5	11.7	286	356	2.1
East South Central	18.6	18.4	11.7	9.0	13.4	11.1	288	395	1.9
West " "	15.7	21.9	11.0	11.9	21.4	25.8	232	290	3.1
Mountain	15.8	16.5	23.1	19.2	34.9	30.4	339	334	4.7
Pacific	24.0	25.2	17.7	15.6	35.3	31.4	475	470	5.1

[1] *corn.* 1909: 20.6% of all *improved* land.
[2] *9.3%* " " " " " "
[3] *7.3%* " " " " " "

In the *North*, we must *consider separately* (α) New England+Middle Atlantic and (β) *East and West* North Centrals

α—31-41% (value of all crops)=hay and forage

β—14-16%

Mostly sown grasses (from hay and forage) ‖ α—crops are mostly higher
The *part* of wild, meadow, etc. grasses is *considerable* ‖ β—crops are mostly lower

α—17-21% (idem) vegetables
β—4-7%

α labour and fertilisers (per acre) are high
β labour and fertilisers (per acre) are low

α—Almost *no* homesteads ‖ High population density. ‖ Buy feed for livestock.
β—Homesteads *exist* ‖ Low population density. ‖ Sell feed for livestock.

Summing up the *original* (not the final!!) entries for homesteads over the 10 years (1901-10), (*Statistical Abstract*, p. 28), we obtain:

The West......55.3 mill. acres $\begin{cases} \text{Pacific—}13.4 \\ \text{Mountain—}41.9 \end{cases}$

Homesteads The North ...55.2 ,, ,, (incl. *West North Central* 54.3)
The South ...20.0 ,, ,, (incl. **West South Central** 17.3)
$\Sigma = 130.5$

Thus, the *West* is a *solid* homestead area.
In the *North*—*one* division (West North Central) is a homestead area.
In the *South*—also *one* (West South Central) is a homestead area.

All farms = 1,182,099 . . 89,923,619 acres
plantations
or farms = 437,978 . . 28,296,815 "

| 325 counties |

11 southern states: Alabama, Arkansas, Florida, Georgia, Louisiana, Mississippi, North & South Carolina, Tennessee, Texas & Virginia.

Chapter XII. Plantations in the South

Tenant plantations of ((1910))

All tenant plantations	All classes	5 to 9 tenants	10 to 19 tenants	20 to 49 tenants	50 tenants and over	Census Year	Average acreage per farm		Average improved acres per farm	
							The South	The North	The South	The North
Plantations	39,073	26,562	9,160	2,939	412	1910	114.4	143.0	48.6	100.3
Landlord farms	39,073	26,562	9,160	2,939	412	1900	138.2	133.2	48.1	90.9
Tenant farms	398,905	168,089	118,862	82,404	29,550	1890	139.7	123.7	58.8	87.8
Average acreage	724.2	495.0	953.2	1,688.0	3,535.3	1880	153.4	114.9	56.2	76.6
" improved acreage	405.3	273.8	528.2	974.9	2,084.1	1870	214.2	117.0	69.2	69.2
Average acreage landlord farms { all land	330.9	227.3	438.4	785.5	1,374.6	1860	335.4	126.4	101.3	68.3
{ improved land	86.6	65.2	106.8	187.9	293.4	1850	332.1	127.1	101.1	65.4
Average acreage tenant farms { all land	38.5	42.3	39.7	32.2	30.1					
{ improved land	31.2	33.0	32.5	28.1	25.0					
Acreage of all land	28,296,815	13,147,956	8,731,179	4,961,152	1,456,528					
landlord farms	12,929,417	6,038,777	4,015,807	2,308,518	566,315					
tenant farms	15,367,398	7,109,179	4,715,372	2,652,634	890,213					
% in tenant farms	54.3	54.1	54.0	53.5	61.1					

"As a matter of fact ... a large proportion of the tenants in the South actually occupied a very different economic position from that usually occupied by tenants in other parts of the country. The plantation as a unit for general purposes of administration has not disappeared, and in many cases the tenants on plantations are subjected to quite as complete supervision by the owner, general lessee, or manager, as that to which the hired labourers are subjected on large farms in the North and West" (p. 877).

Chapter XI. *Irrigation.*

Arid region: 1,440,822 farms. $1,161,385,600$ acres, $388._6$ million acres of land in farms, $173._4$ million acres of improved land. $307._9$ million dollars.= cost of irrigation enterprises ($15._{92}$ per acre).

158,713 farms irrigated (13._7 million acres irrigated).

Average yield per acre (1909)

	on irrigated land	on unirrigated land	±%
corn (bushels)	23._7	25._9	— 8._5
oats	36._8	28._5	+29._1
wheat	25._6	15._3	+67._3%
barley	29._1	22._3	+30._5%
alfalfa	2._94 tons	2._14	+37._4%

Taking into account the fact that Mr. Himmer (*Zavety*, 1913, No. 6) makes a downright lying assertion about the 1910 Census, to the effect that in the United States of America "there are no areas where colonisation is no longer continuing, or where large-scale capitalist agriculture is not disintegrating and is not being replaced by family-labour farms" (p. 60) * —let us dwell on the
2 divisions: New England
and Middle Atlantic. Colonisation = 0. (No homesteads).

---

* See present edition, Vol. 22, pp. 37-38 —*Ed.*

The capitalist character of agriculture:

		1909	1899	%
Expenditure for labour (per improved acre)	New England	4.$_{76}$	2.$_{55}$	+86%
	Middle Atlantic	2.$_{66}$	1.$_{64}$	+62%
	Pacific	3.$_{47}$	1.$_{92}$	+80%
	Mountain	2.$_{95}$	2.$_{42}$	+22%
	Average for the United States	1.$_{36}$	0.$_{86}$	+58%

Thus, the capitalist character is **most pronounced** and is developing **most strongly!!!**

Himmer was "confused" over the fact that not only was the average farm acreage in these divisions declining in general (U.S.A. 146.$_2$—138.$_1$; New England 107.$_1$—104.$_4$; Middle Atlantic 92.$_4$—92.$_2$), but that there was also a decrease in the quantity of improved land (U.S.A. +72.$_2$+75.$_2$; New England 42.$_4$—38.$_4$; Middle Atlantic 63.$_4$—62.$_6$)!!!

Besides, in terms of improved acreage, New England farms are *the smallest*!!

The silly ass has failed to see the difference between small acreages and the capitalist character of agriculture.

		1909	1899	
Expenditure *for fertilisers* (per improved acre)	New England	1.$_{30}$	0.$_{53}$	+145%
	Middle Atlantic	0.$_{62}$	0.$_{37}$	+ 78%
	South Atlantic	1.$_{23}$	0.$_{49}$	+151%
	Average for the United States	0.$_{24}$	0.$_{13}$	+83%

Let us note that most fertiliser is used on land under *cotton* (the South!) (see 1900 Statistics). Cotton: 18.$_7$% of the farms; 22.$_5$% of the expenditure for fertilisers

cf. p. 1 of extracts (1910) (p. 560) *

N.B. || % of farms hiring labour

New England	66.$_0$%
Middle Atlantic.......	65.$_8$%
East North Central..	52.$_7$
West " "	51.$_0$
Mountain	46.$_8$%
Pacific	58.$_0$%

|| N.B.

* See p. 444.—*Ed.*

Increase (or decrease) 1900-10

New England	Number of farms	%	All land in farms (acres) Amount	%	Improved land in farms (acres) Amount	%	Percentage of increase (1899-1909) in the value of all farm property	implements and machinery
Total	—3,086	—1.6	—834,068	—4.1	—879,499	—10.8	35.6	39.0
<20	6,286	22.4	41,273	14.9	30,984	15.5	60.9	48.9
20-49	17	0.1	—33,243	—2.9	—28,500	—4.7	31.4	30.3
50-99	—3,457	—7.0	—250,313	—7.2	—142,270	—9.1	27.5	31.2
100-174	—4,020	—8.4	—466,663	—7.7	—309,499	—12.3	30.3	38.5
175-499	—1,999	—6.7	—459,948	—6.1	—421,081	—15.3	33.0	44.6
500-999	6	0.3	36,311	2.8	—46,022	—12.8	53.7	53.7
1,000 and >	81	16.3	298,515	36.2	36,889	26.8	102.7	60.5
Middle Atlantic:								
Total	—17,239	—3.5	—1,669,034	—3.7	—1,465,317	—4.8	28.1	44.1
<20	5,754	7.7	29,704	4.1	15,550	2.5	45.8	42.9
20-49	—5,955	—7.1	—225,471	—8.0	—210,859	—9.5	28.3	37.0
50-99	—11,639	—8.2	—772,300	—7.6	—623,012	—8.1	23.8	39.9
100-174	—5,745	—4.4	—746,852	—4.5	—605,047	—5.1	24.9	43.8
175-499	495	1.0	169,095	1.4	—59,567	—0.8	29.4	54.7
500-999	—59	—3.1	—27,161	—2.3	17,990	3.8	31.5	50.8
1,000 and >	—90	—16.1	—96,049	—8.0	—372	—0.2	74.4	65.2

These figures are a clear indication that the small *farms* are being displaced by the large.

In both divisions, *all* the medium groups (20-499) have been *losing* (%).

The gains were registered by (1) the smallest (<20)

(2) the large (*500-999* and *1,000* and >).

In percentage and absolute terms (quantity of *improved* land), the *large* farms gained **more** than the small!!
[The small farms (under 20 acres) here are very frequently out-and-out capitalist farms] because they have the maximum % of land under vegetables and a minimum under *cereals*.

The % increase in agricultural implements and machinery (=constant capital in its most important form, which is directly indicative of technical progress) is at a *maximum* in the *large* farms, at a minimum in the *medium* farms, with the large ones doing *better* than the smallest!!!

(p. 266, t. 9)

Percentage distribution of total value

United States	All farm property		Implements and machinery	
	1910	1900	1910	1900
Total	100.0	100.0	100.0	100.0
(α) < 20	3.7 −	3.8	3.7 −	3.8
(β) 20- 49	7.3 −	7.9	8.5 −	9.1
(γ) 50- 99	14.6 −	16.7	17.7 −	19.3
(δ) 100-174	27.1 −	28.0	28.9 −	29.3
(ε) 175-499	33.3 +	30.5	30.2 +	27.1
(ζ) 500-999	7.1 +	5.9	6.3 +	5.1
(η) 1,000 and >	6.9 −	7.3	4.7 −	6.2
New England:				
Total	100.0	100.0	100.0	100.0
	12.0 +	10.1	7.8 +	7.3
	13.3 −	13.7	11.5 −	12.2
	20.0 −	21.2	20.8 −	22.0
	24.2 −	25.1	27.9 −	28.0
	24.4 −	24.8	27.3 +	26.2
	3.9 +	3.4	3.3 +	2.9
	2.4 +	1.6	1.5 +	1.3
Middle Atlantic :				
Total	100.0	100.0	100.0	100.0
	8.9 +	7.8	6.5 =	6.5
	11.3 =	11.3	10.6 −	11.1
	24.6 −	25.5	27.2 −	28.0
	31.9 −	32.7	34.5 =	34.5
	20.3 +	20.1	19.4 +	18.1
	1.8 =	1.8	1.3 =	1.3
	1.2 +	0.8	0.6 +	0.5

United States	All farm property		Implements and machinery	
	1910	1900	1910	1900
The North: Total	$100._0$	$100._0$	$100._0$	$100._0$
small $\{$	$2._9-$	$3._3$	$3._1-$	$3._5$
	$5._1-$	$6._7$	$6._5-$	$8._2$
	$14._7-$	$18._0$	$18._1-$	$21._3$
medium	$30._1-$	$31._2$	$31._7-$	$32._7$
large $\{$	$38._6+$	$33._4$	$32._9+$	$29._0$
	$6._4+$	$4._8$	$5._5+$	$3._8$
	$2._8+$	$2._5$	$2._1+$	$1._6$
The South: Total	$100._0$	$100._0$	$100._0$	$100._0$
small $\{$	$4._7+$	$4._4$	$4._6+$	$4._2$
	$13._0+$	$12._0$	$13._7+$	$12._4$
	$17._3+$	$16._0$	$19._2+$	$16._7$
medium	$23._1+$	$22._1$	$24._4+$	$22._4$
large $\{$	$24._2-$	$24._3$	$24._1+$	$22._3$
	$6._6-$	$6._8$	$6._4-$	$6._7$
	$11._4-$	$14._4$	$7._6-$	$15._5$
The West: Total	$100._0$	$100._0$	$100._0$	$100._0$
small $\{$	$6._9+$	$6._5$	$5._9+$	$5._6$
	$9._3+$	$7._1$	$10._0+$	$7._9$
	$9._1+$	$7._2$	$10._0+$	$8._7$
medium	$16._3+$	$15._2$	$19._6-$	$20._0$
large $\{$	$22._6+$	$21._1$	$25._0-$	$25._1$
	$12._1-$	$12._5$	$12._3-$	$12._7$
	$23._7-$	$30._4$	$17._3-$	$20._0$

Conclusions:

(1) Two old divisions (New England + Middle Atlantic). Maximum growth of the *big* farms. Erosion of the medium. Lesser growth of the smallest.

(2) The North (capitalism). Growth of *large* farms at the expense of the *small*.

(3) The South (transition from slavery to capitalism). Growth of *small* farms at the expense of *the large*. (*N.B.*: The role of the largest is *a b o v e* average.)

(4) The West (new lands. Maximum of homesteads). Growth of *small* at the expense of the *large*. (*N.B.*: The role of the largest and the large is **above** average.)

(5) Summary. $\Sigma\Sigma$ (The United States): *Displacement of all the small* and *all the medium ones*. Displacement of the *l a t i f u n d i a* (1,000 and $>$). Growth of *big capitalist* farms (*175-500*; *500-1,000*).

The United

It is interesting to compare the data on the %%

Number of farms			A) Quantity of improved land		B)) (Value) all farm property		C)) (Value) land	
			%% of acreage					
1910	1900		1910	1900	1910	1900	1910	1900
+13.2	11.7	+smallest (<20)	1.7	1.6	− 3.7	3.8	− 2.8	2.9
+22.3	21.5	−small and	7.6	8.0	− 7.3	7.9	− 6.4	7.2
−22.6	23.8	−medium	14.9	16.2	−14.6	16.2	−13.4	16.1
−23.8	24.8	—	26.9	28.6	−27.1	28.0	−26.7	28.2
+15.4	15.1	+large and	33.8	32.7	+33.3	30.5	+35.4	32.2
+2.0	1.8	+latifundia	8.5	7.1	+ 7.1	5.9	+ 7.8	6.2
=0.8	0.8	+(latifundia)	6.5	5.9	−6.9	7.3	+ 7.6	7.1

(− 3.7   3.8
(−49.0   52.6
(+40.4   36.4
− 6.9   7.3

This is remarkable!

There is an increase in the *value* of land!! (both in the large farms and the latifundia).

Only in two divisions is there *no* decline of the *latifundia* (1,000 ·and>), namely, the oldest and capitalist divisions, New England and Middle Atlantic! In these two divisions, the role of the latifundia has *increased in all respects* (including even livestock!!) (Middle Atlantic=0.6—0.6 livestock, New England, 1.5—1.4 livestock).

The exception (N.B.) is the maximum destruction of latifundia in *West South Central* = 21.3—41.9, and in *the West*=33.6—38.5, i.e., just where the latifundia are *outsized*!!

Added

All the added value to all farm property =+$ 20,551 *million*.

		$ mill.	
Of this smallest		+ 753	
small and		+1,365	4,708 —
medium		+2,590	
		+5,368	5,368 —
large and		+7,422	
latifundia		+1,707	10,475 —
		+1,346	
			Σ=20,551

In these 10 years, the *industrial workers* (1900: 4.7 million, 1910—6.6 · million) (+40.4%) increased their wages by $ *1,419* million (+70.6%).

States:
distribution of various elements in the farms

(Value) buildings		(Value) implements and machinery		(Value) livestock		(Value) all farm property		All land	
1910	1900	1910	1900	1910	1900	1910	1900	1910	1900
+ 8.0	7.1	− 3.7	3.8	− 3.3	3.5	− 3.7	3.8	+ 1.0	0.9
−10.6	10.7	− 8.5	9.1	+ 7.8	7.0	− 7.3	7.9	+ 5.2	5.0
−19.3	20.4	−17.7	19.3	+15.2	14.5	−14.6	16.7	−11.7	11.8
−28.3	29.6	−28.9	29.3	+26.8	25.6	−27.1	28.0	+23.4	23.0
+26.8	25.9	+30.2	27.1	+30.6	28.5	+33.3	30.8	+30.2	27.8
+ 4.3	4.6	+ 6.3	5.1	= 7.0	7.0	+ 7.1	5.9	+ 9.5	8.1
− 2.6	2.9	− 4.7	6.2	− 9.3	13.9	− 6.9	7.3	−19.0	23.6

livestock	livestock ± %
26.3—25	
+1.3	−0.2
26.8—25.8	+0.8
+1.2	+0.7
46.9—49.4	+1.2 *
−2.5	−4.6

value:

% of farms	mill. farms	idem (1900)
58.0	3.7	(3.3)
23.8	1.5	(1.4)
18.2	1.1	(1.0)
100.0	6.3	(5.7)

* Lenin left out the next group of 175 to 499; +2.1.—Ed.

Some economic elements (resp. classes) in the U.S.A.,

		1900	1910+	+%
Capitalists in industry:	Number of enterprises ('000)	$207._5$	$268._5+$	$61+29._4\%$
Urban population +34.$_8$%	Number of wage workers ('000)	4,713	6,615+	$1,902+40._4\%$
Agriculture:	Number of farms ('000)	5,737	6,361+	$624+10._9\%$
Rural population +11.$_2$%	Number of hired labourers (cf. p. 1 and over)*.		$82._3\%:70._6\%=x:40._4\%$ $x=47._1\%$	
Production of all cereals (mill. bushels)		4,439	4,513+	$74+1._7\%$

Industry:

Value of products
(number of enterprises ('000) and %
of total)

Should be 190*4* instead of 1900

	production:	1900	1910	$\div$ + %
	(< \$20,000) s m a l l	144	180	$+36+25\%$
		$66._6\%+$	$67._2\%$	
	(\$20,000-\$100,000) m e d i u m	48	57	$+\ 9+18._7\%$
		$22._2\%-$	$21._3\%$	
	(\$100,000 and >) l a r g e	24	31	$+\ 7+29._1\%$
		$11._2\%+$	$11._4\%$	
	Total	216 100%	268 100%	$+\ 52+24._2\%$

Agriculture:

Number of farms ('000) and % of total

	1900	1910	
(under 99 acres) s m a l l	3,297	3,691	$+394+11._9\%$
	$57._4\%$	$+58._0\%$	
	1,422	1,516	$+\ 94+\ 6._6\%$
(100-174) m e d i u m	$24._8\%$	$-23._8\%$	
	1,018	1,154	$+136+13._3\%$
(175 and >) l a r g e	$17._7\%$	$+18._2\%$	
	Total	5,737 100%	6,361 100%	$+624+10._9\%$

---

* See pp. 482-83.—*Ed.*

according to the 12th (1900) and 13th (1910) censuses

	1900	1910 +	+	%			1900	1910	+	%
Their capital ($ mill.)	8,975	8,428 +9,453	+105.3%			Value of products ($ mill.)	11,406	20,672 +9,266	+81% *	
Their wages ($ mill.)	2,008	3,427 +1,419	+70.6%							
Value of their property ($ mill.)	20,440	40,991 +20,551	+100.5%							
Their wages ($ mill.)	357	652+	295+	82.3%						
Their value ($ mill.)	1,483	2,665+	1,182+	79.8%						

	1900	1910+	+	%
Value of products ($ mill.)	927	1,127+	200+	21.5%
	6.3%	5.5%		
	2,129	2,544+	415+	19.5%
	14.4%—	12.3%		
	11,737	17,000+	5,263+	44.8%
	79.3%+	82.5%		
	14,793	20,671+	5,878+	39.7%
	100%	100%		
Value of their property ($ mill.)	5,790	10,499+	4,709+	81.3%
	28.3%—	25.6%		
	5.721	11,089+	5,368+	93.8%
	28.0—	27.1%		
	8.929	19,403+	10,474+	117.3
	43.7%**+	47.3%		
	20.440	40,991+	20,551+	100.5%
	100%	100%		

---

* In the Fourth Russian edition of Lenin's *Collected Works* this figure has been corrected to 81.2% (see present edition, Vol. 22, p. 94).—*Ed.*

** In the Fourth Russian edition of Lenin's *Collected Works* this figure has been corrected to 43.6% (Ibid., Vol. 22, p. 98).—*Ed.*

Three types:
1) The North
2) The South
3) The West

For a characteristic of the population

Per cent distribution by class of

(Abstract of the Census, p. 92)

		total population	White native	White foreign-born	Negro
United States	rural	53.7	55.8	27.8	72.6
	urban	46.3	44.2	72.2	27.4
New England	rural	16.7	20.4	7.6	8.2
	urban	83.3	79.6	92.4	91.8
Middle Atlantic	rural	29.0	33.7	16.1	18.8
	urban	71.0	66.3	83.9	81.2
East North Central	rural	47.3	51.6	28.6	23.4
	urban	52.7	48.4	71.4	76.6
West North Central	rural	66.7	68.4	60.8	32.3
	urban	33.3	31.6	39.2	67.7
South Atlantic	rural	74.6	74.4	34.0	77.9
	urban	25.4	25.6	66.0	22.1
East South Central	rural	81.3	82.2	33.3	80.8
	urban	18.7	17.8	66.7	19.2
West South Central	rural	77.7	78.4	60.8	78.0
	urban	22.3	21.6	39.2	22.0
Mountain	rural	64.0	64.0	60.3	28.0
	urban	36.0	36.0	39.7	72.0
Pacific	rural	43.2	44.2	38.7	16.6
	urban	56.8	55.8	61.3	83.4

*) Total of two vertical figures = 100

within the U.S.A. (1910)

> **N.B.   N.B.**
> The Negroes are in flight *from the South (mostly to the cities)*. The North is giving up its population to the *West*. The foreign-born avoid the *South*.

community:*) % of all population		[ibidem p. 175] % of population (1910)			Gain or loss (1910) from interstate migration	
Foreign-born	Negro	Born in division of residence	born in other divisions	foreign-born	White persons	Negro persons
14.5	10.7	72.6	12.3	14.7	—	—
27.7	1.0	66.2	5.5	27.9	− 226,219	+ 20,310
25.0	2.2	69.7	4.9	25.1	−1,120,678	+186,384
16.8	1.6	73.4	9.3	16.8	−1,496,074	+119,649
13.9	2.1	65.4	20.2	13.9	+ 472,566	+ 40,497
2.4	33.7	92.6	4.7	2.5	− 507,454	−392,827
1.0	31.5	91.5	7.3	1.0	− 974,165	−200,876
4.0	22.6	72.3	23.3	4.0	+1,434,780	+194,658
16.6	0.8	41.8	40.2	17.2	+ 856,683	+ 13,229
20.5	0.7	35.8	40.3	22.8	+1,560,561	+ 18,976

Volume IV. Occupation Statistics
Table 15, p. 54

Number of persons 10 years of age and over engaged in

Both sexes	1910	1900	1890	1880	Overstatement in the number of women (×)
Agricultural pursuits	12,567,925	10,381,765	9,148,448	7,713,875	12,567,925
Agricultural labourers	6,088,414	4,410,877	3,586,583	3,323,876	_ 468,100
Dairymen and dairywomen	35,014	10,875	17,895	8,948	12,099,825 ⌐ 10,381,765
Farmers, planters and overseers	5,981,522	5,674,875	5,281,557	4,229,051	116%
Gardeners, florists, nurserymen, etc.	143,462	61,788	72,601	56,032	+16%
Lumbermen and raftsmen	127,154	72,020	65,866	30,651	
Stock raisers, herders and drovers	122,189	84,988	70,729	44,075	
Woodchoppers	27,567	36,075	33,697	12,731	
Turpentine farmers and labourers	28,967	24,735	19,520	7,450	
Other agricultural pursuits	13,636	5,532		1,061	
Apiarists	2,145	1,339	1,773	1,016	

	1910	1900	
Agricultural labourers	6,088,414	4,410,877	$\boxed{6{,}088 \div 4{,}410 = 137\%}$
Male	4,566,281	3,747,668 →	$4{,}566{,}281 \div 3{,}747{,}668 = 121.8\% = +21.8\%$
(X) Female	1,522,133	663,209	$100 - 21.8 = 78.2$
(p. 27)+(1910−1900)=129.5% (1900—1890:÷23.3%; **page. 26**).			
(α) Female farm labourers working on the *home farm*	1,176,585 [+166.8%]	441,055	
(β) Female farm labourers working *out*	337,522 [+53.4%]	220,048	
idem *male* (α) (home farm)	−2,133,949	?	
(p. 91) (β) (working out)	−2,299,444	?	
	(Σ=4,433,393)		

Total number of *hired* labourers in agriculture:

	1910	1900	
Female (working out)	337,522	220,048	
Male (” ”)	2,299,444	1,798,165	**(roughly=78.2% of 1910 figure)**
	Σ=2,566,966 *	2,018,213	see p. **2 over****

---

* The total is with Lenin's correction, see p. 485.—*Ed.*
** See p. 485.—*Ed.*

16*

Industrial statistics show

	wage workers	wages
1899	4.7 mill.	$ 2,008 mill.
1909	6.6 ”	$ 3,427 ”
	+40.4%	+70.6%

Consequently, the increase in the **number** of *hired labourers* in *agriculture* could be estimated:

		Increase in number of farms	Increase in rural population
The North	40%	+ 0.6%	+ 3.9%
The South	50%	+18.2%	+14.8%
The West	66%	+53.7%	+49.7%
	48%	+10.9%	+11.2%

(×) Concerning the number of women gainfully employed* in agriculture (1910), the author (p. 27) believes their number to be *overstated* and **estimates** these figures as the more *probable*: (p. 28)
total number of women engaged in agriculture: *1,338,950* instead of *1,807,050* (i.e.— 468,100),
and total number of women engaged in *all* branches of the economy, *7,607,672*, instead of *8,075,772* (—468,100).

My addition: referring this entire overstatement, only to those working on the home farms, we have:
$1,176,585 — 468,100 = 708,485 \div 441,055 = \textbf{166\%} + 66\%$

---

* See p. 483.—*Ed.*

Thus, according to the Occupation Statistics (see p. **1 over**) *

	1910	*1900+*		
Total persons occupied in agriculture ...	12,099,825	10,381,765+16%		
		** see No. 1 (below)		
Farmers	5,981,522	5,674,875+ 5%	5,981,522	5,674,875
Hired labourers	2,566,966	2,018,213+27%	2,566,966	105.4 / 2,018,213
(see p. *1 over*)		* see No. 2 (below)		127

I must say, on the whole, that American Occupation Statistics are not worth a damn, for they say absolutely nothing about the "status of person in industry" (and make no distinction between the owner, the home-farm worker and the hired labourer).

That is why their scientific value is almost **nil**. ‖N.B.‖

N.B.

Then they say nothing at all about collateral employment.

My totals are from p. *235* of the *Statistical Abstract*.

No. 1: +16%, whereas the *rural population=* +11%. Why? Clearly, because of the increased number of *women* employed.

No. 2: Σ expenditure for *labour*+48%. Why? Clearly, because *poor farmers* are also hired (collateral employment).

---

* See pp. 482-83.—*Ed.*
** See p. 482.—*Ed.*

Occupation Statistics

Per cent distribution:

Total persons employed (10 years of age and >)

	Total persons occupied	Agriculture, forestry and animal husbandry	Extraction of minerals	Manufacturing and mechanical industry	Transportation	Trade	Public service	Professional service	Domestic and personal service	Clerical occupation
United States	38,167,336	33.2	2.5	27.9	6.9	9.5	1.2	4.4	9.9	4.6
New England	2,914,680	10.4	0.3	49.1	6.5	10.6	1.7	4.8	10.7	5.9
Middle Atlantic ...	8,208,885	10.0	4.2	40.6	8.0	12.0	1.4	4.9	11.8	7.1
East North Central	7,257,953	25.6	2.6	33.2	7.6	10.6	1.1	4.8	9.2	5.3
West North Central	4,449,043	41.2	1.8	20.0	7.8	10.4	1.1	5.2	8.5	3.9
South Atlantic....	5,187,729	51.4	1.8	18.6	5.0	6.1	1.0	3.0	10.5	2.6
East South Central	3,599,695	63.2	1.9	12.4	4.0	5.3	0.6	2.6	8.4	1.7
West South Central	3,507,081	60.1	0.7	12.6	5.2	7.0	0.8	3.3	8.1	2.1
Mountain	1,107,937	32.4	9.4	19.5	10.3	8.7	1.7	5.2	9.1	3.6
Pacific	1,934,333	22.6	2.4	27.2	10.3	12.6	2.0	6.0	11.3	5.5

Written between
May 5 (18), 1914 and
December 29, 1915
(January 11, 1916)

First published in 1932
in *Lenin Miscellany XIX*

Printed from the original

NOTES
AND
INDEXES

NOTES

[1] This work was written in parts: the first nine chapters, from June to September 1901, and the last three, in the autumn of 1907. In the Fourth Russian edition of Lenin's *Collected Works*, it appeared in Vol. 5 (chapters I-IX) and in Vol. 13 (chapters X-XII); in the Fifth edition of the *Collected Works*, the whole of it is in Vol. 5. The present volume contains the preparatory material: plans for and the contents of the work, critical remarks on the writings of bourgeois economists and revisionists, and elaboration and analysis of agricultural statistics.

The four variants of the plan in this volume reflect Lenin's elaboration of the structure and content of "The Agrarian Question and the 'Critics of Marx'". Lenin's primary aim is to expose the general theoretical views of the "critics", the "law of diminishing returns" as scientifically unsound and the theory of rent connected with it, together with the Malthusian conclusions from both. He then outlines a detailed critical analysis of bourgeois and revisionist writings on the key problems of agrarian theory and agrarian relations (concentration of production in agriculture, machinery in agriculture, etc.), and exposure of the "critics'" tenuous and scientifically dishonest methods of inquiry and use of factual material. Lenin makes a special analysis of the statistical data and results of monographic descriptions of agrarian relations in France, Germany and other countries for an examination of the actual processes in agriculture, the capitalist system in contemporary agriculture and a critique of bourgeois and revisionist writings.

The variants of the plan show the successive extension of the range of questions and their content, and Lenin's changes in the order of the various points. Lenin repeatedly returned to the fourth variant, the most elaborate and complete. There, the Roman numerals of the eleven sections of the plan are in pencil, as are also the additional notes to point 12: "the journal *Nachalo* (*The Beginning*) I, pp. 7 and 13" and to point 21: "Latifundia. (Cf. Hertz 15; Bulgakov II, 126, 190, 363)". In point 12, beginning with "No. 4, 141" and to the end of the paragraph and in the note to this point (12) on the right, "Engels on Belgium, No. 10, 234", and also in the note to point 18, beginning with the words: "Bulgakov II, 289" and to the end of the paragraph, the words are lightly crossed in pencil.   p. 29

[2] For extracts and critical remarks on the books *Bäuerliche Zustände in Deutschland*, Berichte, veröffentlicht vom Verein für Sozialpolitik. Bd. 1-3. Leipzig, 1883 (*The Condition of the*

Peasants in Germany. Published by the Social Policy Association. Vols. 1, 2, 3) see *Lenin Miscellany XIX*, pp. 166-80. Lenin used this material in his work, "The Agrarian Question and the 'Critics of Marx'" (see present edition, Vol. 5, pp. 180-81. and Vol. 13, pp. 182-94).   p. 29

[3] Lenin's remarks on Baudrillart's book, *Les populations agricoles de la France. La Normandie (passé et présent)* (*The Agricultural Population of France. Normandy, Past and Present*), Paris, 1880. See *Lenin Miscellany XXXII*, pp. 82-105. For Lenin's remarks on Baudrillart's book, *Les populations agricoles de la France. 3'e série. Les populations du Midi*, Paris, 1893 (*The Agricultural Population of France*, Part III. *The Population of the South*) see this volume pp. 258-59.   p. 29

[4] A reference to the distorted translation and wrong interpretation of quotations from Frederick Engels's *The Peasant Question in France and Germany* in the Socialist-Revolutionary newspaper *Revolutsionnaya Rossiya* (*Revolutionary Russia*). See *Lenin Miscellany XIX*, pp. 287-93.   p. 29

[5] Lenin's remarks on the book by Hugo Böttger, *Die Sozialdemokratie auf dem Lande*, Leipzig, 1900 (*Social-Democrats in the Countryside*). See *Lenin Miscellany XIX*, pp. 304-06.   p. 29

[6] *Iskra* No. 3, April 1901, carried Lenin's article "The Workers' Party and the Peasantry", which was an outline of the agrarian programme of the R.S.D.L.P. (see present edition, Vol. 4, pp. 420-28).   p. 29

[7] For Lenin's critique of P. Maslov's anti-Marxist view of the theory of rent see present edition, Vol. 5, footnote on page 127.
                                                               p. 30

[8] A reference to the book by P. Mack, *Der Aufschwung unseres Landwirtschaftsbetriebes durch Verbilligung der Produktionskosten. Eine Untersuchung über den Dienst, den Maschinentechnik und Elektrizität der Landwirtschaft bieten*, Königsberg, 1900 (*Boosting Our Agricultural Production by Reducing the Costs of Production. An Inquiry into the Services Rendered to Agriculture by Machinery and Electricity*).   p. 30

[9] A reference to Kautsky's article, "Die Elektrizität in der Landwirtschaft." *Die Neue Zeit*, Stuttgart, 1900-1901, XIX. Jahrgang. Band I, No. 18, S. 565-72 ("Electricity in Agriculture", *New Times*, Stuttgart, 1900-1901, XIXth year of publication, Vol. 1, No. 18, pp. 565-72).   p. 30

[10] In 1900, *Russkoye Bogatstvo* (*Russian Wealth*), a journal of the liberal Narodniks, carried a series of articles by V. Chernov under the general title "Types of Capitalist and Agrarian

Evolution". Lenin gave a critique of Chernov's views in "The Agrarian Question and the 'Critics of Marx'". Here and below Lenin notes the issues and pages of the journal with Chernov's statements.   p. 30

[11] Ireland was regarded as the example of a country of large landed estates and small ("starvation") leaseholdings, where tremendous wealth existed side by side with dire poverty and recurring famines, a land from which masses of ruined farmers were in flight. Bulgakov tried to cover up the poverty and the dying-out of the Irish farmers with Malthusian arguments about a "surplus" population and "shortage" of land, whereas the real reason lay in the monopoly of the landed estates and the fierce exploitation of the small farmers.   p. 30

[12] In their preface to the 1882 Russian edition of the *Manifesto of the Communist Party*, Marx and Engels say this about landed property in the United States: "Step by step the small and middle landownership of the farmers, the basis of the whole political constitution, is succumbing to the competition of giant farms" (Marx and Engels, *Selected Works* in three volumes, Vol. 1, Moscow, 1962, p. 23).   p. 31

[13] See *Lenin Miscellany XIX*, p. 159.   p. 31

[14] Lenin's remarks on Georges Blondel's book, *Études sur les populations rurales de l'Allemagne et la crise agraire* (*Studies of the Rural Population in Germany and the Agrarian Crisis*), Paris, 1897. See *Lenin Miscellany XXXI*, pp. 84-86.   p. 31

[15] See *Lenin Miscellany XIX*, pp. 166-80.   p. 31

[16] *2a3b*—a pseudonym of P. N. Lepeshinsky.   p. 32

[17] Lenin gave a critique of Bulgakov's, "A Contribution to the Question of the Capitalist Evolution of Agriculture" which appeared in the journal of the Legal Marxists, *Nachalo*, Nos. 1-2 for 1899, in his works "Capitalism in Agriculture" (present edition, Vol. 4, pp. 105-59) and "The Agrarian Question and the 'Critics of Marx'" (ibid., Vol. 5, pp. 103-222, and Vol. 13, pp. 169-216).   p. 33

[18] *Rentengüter*—estates set up in Prussia and Poznan under laws passed by the Prussian Landtag on April 26, 1886, June 27, 1890 and July 7, 1891, for the purpose of settling German peasants in the eastern provinces of Germany. The establishment of these estates was designed to strengthen German and weaken Polish influence in these provinces and to assure the big landowners of cheap labour. This involved the break-up of large landed estates (sometimes bought from Polish landowners) into small and medium tracts title to which was transferred to German peasants upon the payment of the capital amount or the annual rent. When

a settler bought the land by paying the annual rent, he was
restricted in his disposal of it: he was not free, without
government permission, to divide the estate, sell it in parcels,
etc.   p. 35

[19] This is an outline of the contents of the second part of Lenin's
"The Agrarian Question and the 'Critics of Marx'" which was
first published in *Obrazovaniye* (*Education*), No. 2 in February
1906. The pagination of the manuscript by chapters warrants the
assumption that it dates to the period when Lenin was preparing
the manuscript for publication in the journal.   p. 39

[20] The two remarks at the bottom of the manuscript enclosed in
rectangles are a reckoning of the time it took to read this part of
the manuscript. The first remark relates to Chapter V and the
first part of Chapter VI, and is the result of Lenin's trial in rapid
silent reading on the basis of which he drew the conclusion (in
the second remark) that it would take "about 2 hours" to read the
whole manuscript.   p. 39

[21] This material is preparatory for Lenin's lectures on "Marxist
Views of the Agrarian Question in Europe and Russia" which he
gave at the Higher Russian School of Social Sciences in Paris on
February 10-13 (23-26), 1903. The school was founded in 1901 by
a group of liberal professors who had been expelled by the tsarist
government from higher schools in Russia (M. M. Kovalevsky,
Y. S. Gambarov and E. V. de Roberti); assistance was given to
the school by I. I. Mechnikov, Elisée Reclus, G. Tard and others.
It operated legally. The student body consisted mainly of young
revolutionary Russian émigrés in Paris and Russian students.
Lenin was invited to lecture on the agrarian question at the
insistence of *Iskra*'s Paris group with the support of the
Social-Democratic section of the students. Lenin gave four
lectures on February 10, 11, 12 and 13 (23, 24, 25 and 26), 1903
and these were a great success.

In preparing for his lectures, Lenin studied many sources on
the agrarian question and made numerous extracts from the
works of Marx and Engels, the resolutions of the International,
and from books and articles by Russian and foreign authors
(P. P. Maslov, V. P. Vorontsov, David, Nossig, Böttger, Stumpfe,
etc.); he also compiled tables on the basis of Bavarian, Prussian,
Württemberg, Dutch and other agricultural inquiries, and made a
special translation of Engels's article, "The Peasant Question in
France and Germany" (see *Lenin Miscellany XIX*, pp. 295-300).
Lenin drew up a programme for his lectures and mailed it to the
school beforehand, and wrote two variants of the plan.   p. 40

[22] See Karl Marx, *Capital*, Vol. III, Moscow, 1966, p. 812, and also
Lenin, *Collected Works*, Vol. 3, pp. 155-56.   p. 40

[23] See Engels, "The Peasant Question in France and Germany" (Marx and Engels, *Selected Works* in three volumes, Vol. 2, Moscow, 1962, pp. 426-27). p. 40

[24] The first four chapters of Lenin's "The Agrarian Question and the 'Critics of Marx'" were published in *Zarya* (*Dawn*), a Marxist scientific and political journal (published legally at Stuttgart in 1901 and 1902 by the *Iskra* Editorial Board). They appeared in No. 2-3 in December 1901, under the title "The 'Critics' on the Agrarian Question. First Essay". p. 40

[25] See present edition, Vol. 5, pp. 215-22 and the extract "On the Question of the Co-operatives" from the German agricultural statistics in *Lenin Miscellany XIX*, p. 302. p. 41

[26] For Lenin's remarks with an analysis of the data from the Bavarian and Württemberg inquiries see *Lenin Miscellany XXXII*, pp. 50-80, and 155-60. p. 41

[27] A reference to the following articles by Marx and Engels: "Die Gesetzenwurf über die Aufhebung der Feudallasten" ("The Bill on the Abolition of Feudal Services") and "Die Polendebatte in Frankfurt" ("Debates on the Polish Question in Frankfort") (see Marx/Engels, *Werke*, Bd. 5, Berlin, 1959, S. 278-83, 331-35 and 341-46). For extracts from these articles see *Lenin Miscellany XIX*, p. 303. p. 41

[28] A reference to an article by Marx and Engels entitled "Zirkular gegen Kriege" ("Circular Against Kriege"), section two "Oekonomie des *Volks-Tribunen* und seine Stellung zum Jungen Amerika" ("The Political Economy of *Volks-Tribun* and Its Attitude to Young America") (see Marx/Engels, *Werke*, Band 4, Berlin, 1959, S. 8-11). p. 41

[29] For extracts from the resolutions of congresses of the International see *Lenin Miscellany XIX*, pp. 303-04. p. 41

[30] A reference to the 1874 second section of Engels's Prefatory Note to his work "The Peasant War in Germany" (see Marx and Engels, *Selected Works* in three volumes, Vol. 1, Moscow, 1962, pp. 648-54). p. 41

[31] A reference to the debates at the German Social-Democratic Parteitag in Breslau in October 1895. p. 41

[32] Lenin's remarks on P. Maslov's book, *Conditions of Agricultural Development in Russia*, see *Lenin Miscellany XIX*, pp. 307-09; see also Lenin's letter to Plekhanov (present edition, Vol. 34, pp. 150-51). p. 42

[33] "Essay II" means chapters V to IX of Lenin's "The Agrarian Question and the 'Critics of Marx'", published in *Obrazovaniye*, No. 2, February 1906 (see present edition, Vol. 5, pp. 159-222). p. 42

[34] Lenin calculated the rent on a page of the manuscript containing the entry: "Essay II (agrarian statistics)".   p. 43

[35] See Karl Marx, *Capital*, Vol. III, Moscow, 1966, p. 812. p. 45

[36] A reference to Karl Kautsky's book *Die Agrarfrage* (*The Agrarian Question*).   p. 45

[37] See Karl Marx, *Capital*, Vol. III, Moscow, 1966, p. 798.
                                                               p. 45

[38] See Karl Marx, *Capital*, Vol. III, Moscow, 1966, pp. 748-72, Chapter XXXXV, "Absolute Ground-Rent".   p. 46

[39] See Karl Marx, *Capital*, Vol. III, Moscow, 1966, pp. 670-71.
                                                               p. 47

[40] For the extract with Marx's comment on R. Jones (*Capital*, Vol. III, Moscow, 1966, pp. 780-81) see *Lenin Miscellany XIX*, pp. 309-10, and also Lenin's *The Agrarian Programme of Social-Democracy in the First Russian Revolution, 1905-1907* (present edition, Vol. 13, pp. 305-06).   p. 47

[41] N.—on.—N. F. Danielson.   p. 49

[42] A reference to P. A. Vikhlyaev's "Sketches of Russian Agricultural Reality", St. Petersburg, 1901.   p. 50

[43] Lenin's lecture on "The Agrarian Programme of the Socialist-Revolutionaries and of the Social-Democrats" was read in Paris on March 3, 1903, after the lectures on the agrarian question at the Higher Russian School of Social Sciences. The rules of the school did not allow Lenin to draw any conclusions concerning the programme and tactics of the Party in his lectures, and so he formulated them in a special lecture given outside the school, for members of the Russian colony. His lecture was discussed for four days, from March 3 to 6. Among his opponents were Nevzorov (Y. M. Steklov) from the *Borba* group, B. N. Krichevsky from *Rabocheye Dyelo*, Vladimirov (V. M. Chernov) from the Narodniks, N. Chaikovsky and O. Minor from the Socialist-Revolutionaries, and V. Cherkezov from the anarchists.
    The present volume contains two variants of the outline of the lecture, the plans and the outlines of the concluding speech and the resumé of the lecture. For Lenin's records of the speeches of his opponents and extracts from various sources and writings see *Lenin Miscellany XIX*.
    The volume and content of the lecture outlines warrant the assumption that he also intended to use them as the plan for a pamphlet against the Socialist-Revolutionaries. Of his intention to write such a pamphlet Lenin told Plekhanov in a letter of January 28, 1903 (see *Lenin Miscellany IV*, p. 208).   p. 53

[44] *Socialist-Revolutionaries* (S.R.s)—a petty-bourgeois party in Russia, founded in late 1901-early 1902 as a result of the merger of

various Narodnik groups and circles (the Union of Socialist-Revolutionaries, the Socialist-Revolutionary Party, etc.). The newspaper *Revolutsionnaya Rossiya* (*Revolutionary Russia*) (1900-05), and the journal *Vestnik Russkoi Revolutsii* (*Herald of the Russian Revolution*) (1901-05) and later the newspaper *Znamya Truda* (*Banner of Labour*) (1907-14) were its official organs. The views of the S.R.s were a mixture of Narodnik and revisionist ideas; the S.R.s tried, said Lenin, to "patch up the rents in the Narodnik ideas with bits of fashionable opportunist 'criticism' of Marxism" (see present edition, Vol. 9, p. 310). The S.R.s failed to see the class distinctions between the proletariat and the peasantry, glossed over the class stratification and contradictions within the peasantry, and denied the proletariat's leading role in the revolution. Their tactics of individual terrorism, which they claimed to be the main means of fighting the autocracy, did a great deal of harm to the revolutionary movement and made it more difficult to organise the masses for the revolutionary struggle.

The agrarian programme of the S.R.s called for abolition of private property in land and for egalitarian tenure by communes, and also development of all types of co-operatives. This programme, which the S.R.s claimed would "socialise" the land, had nothing socialist about it, because, as Lenin proved, the elimination of private property in land alone would not do away with the domination of capital and mass poverty. The real and historically progressive content of their programme was the struggle to abolish the landed estates, a demand which was an objective reflection of the interests and aspirations of the peasants during the bourgeois-democratic revolution.

The Bolshevik Party exposed the S.R.s' attempts to masquerade as socialists, waged a persistent struggle against the S.R.s for influence among the peasants and showed the harm their tactics of individual terrorism were inflicting on the working-class movement. At the same time, the Bolsheviks were prepared on definite terms to enter into temporary agreements with the S.R.s to fight against tsarism.

Because the peasantry consisted of diverse class elements, the S.R. Party ultimately failed to achieve ideological and political stability and suffered from organisational confusion, constantly vacillating between the liberal bourgeoisie and the proletariat. As early as the years of the first Russian revolution, its Right wing split off from the Party to form the legal Trudovik Popular Socialist Party (Popular Socialists), which held views close to those of the Cadets, while its Left wing took shape as a semi-anarchist League of "Maximalists". During the period of the Stolypin reaction, the S.R. Party was plunged into total ideological and organisational disarray. During the years of the First World War, most S.R.s adopted social-chauvinist attitudes.

After the victory of the February 1917 bourgeois democratic revolution, the S.R.s joined the Mensheviks as the mainstay of the counter-revolutionary bourgeois-landowner Provisional Government, and their leaders (Kerensky, Avksentyev and Chernov) were members of the government. The S.R. Party refused to support the peasant demand for eliminating the landed estates and came out in favour of preserving them. S.R. Ministers of the Provisional Government dispatched punitive expeditions against peasants seizing landed estates.

At the end of November 1917, the Left wing of the S.R.s formed an independent Left S.R. Party. In an effort to retain their influence among the peasant masses, the Left S.R.s gave nominal recognition to the Soviet power and entered into an agreement with the Bolsheviks, but soon began to fight against the Soviet Government.

During the years of the foreign military intervention and the Civil War, the S.R.s engaged in counter-revolutionary subversive activity and gave active support to the interventionists and whiteguards, taking part in counter-revolutionary plots, and organising terrorist acts against the leaders of the Soviet state and the Communist Party. After the Civil War, the S.R.s continued their hostile activity against the Soviet state at home and among the whiteguard émigrés abroad.   p. 53

[45] *Narodism*—a petty-bourgeois trend in the Russian revolutionary movement which emerged in the 1860s and 1870s. The Narodniks worked to overthrow the autocracy and hand the landed estates over to the peasants.

At the same time, they denied that capitalist relations were naturally developing in Russia and so believed the peasantry, and not the proletariat, to be the chief revolutionary force; they regarded the village commune as the embryo of socialism. Their tactics—individual acts of terrorism—could not and did not bring them success; they failed equally in their efforts to revolutionise the peasantry by spreading the ideas of utopian socialism.

In the 1880s-1890s, the Narodniks were prepared to accept the tsarist regime; they expressed the interests of the kulaks and fought Marxism tooth and claw.   p. 53

[46] Here and below the references are to A. Rudin's pamphlet, *On the Peasant Question*, 1903. Lenin wrote Plekhanov on January 28, 1903: "Have you seen the pamphlet by Rudin (a Socialist-Revolutionary, *On the Peasant Question)?* What brazen swindlers! I am *itching* to do something about this Rudin and No. 15 on socialisation!... It has occurred to me to write an article against Rudin and have a special publication of articles against the Socialist-Revolutionaries together with 'Revolutionary Adventurism'" (*Lenin Miscellany IV,* p. 208).   p. 53

[47] A quotation from the appeal "From the Peasant Union of the Socialist-Revolutionary Party to All Workers of Revolutionary Socialism in Russia", which was carried by *Revolutsionnaya Rossiya* No. 8, p. 8.

Revolutsionnaya Rossiya (*Revolutionary Russia*)—an illegal paper of the S.R.s, published in Russia from the end of 1900 by the Union of Socialist-Revolutionaries (No. 1, dated 1900, actually appeared in January 1901). From January 1902 to December 1905, the paper was published abroad (in Geneva) as the official organ of the S.R. Party.

In his outlines of the lecture on "The Agrarian Programme of the Socialist-Revolutionaries and of the Social-Democrats", Lenin gave a critique of the article "The Peasant Movement" and the appeal which appeared in *Revolutsionnaya Rossiya* No. 8, and also of a series of articles in Nos. 11-15 under the general title of "Programme Questions".   p. 53

[48] Lenin's remarks on the pamphlet, *To All the Russian Peasantry from the Peasant Union of the Socialist-Revolutionary Party*, 1902. See *Lenin Miscellany XIX*, pp. 315-16.   p. 56

[49] A reference to A.S. Martynov's pamphlet, *The Workers and the Revolution*, published by the Union of Russian Social-Democrats, Geneva, 1902.   p. 56

[50] See quotation from A.N. Engelhardt's book *From the Countryside* in *Lenin Miscellany XIX*, p. 310.   p. 56

[51] For a summary of these data see *Lenin Miscellany XIX*, p. 313, and for a commentary on them, the resumé of the lecture (this volume, p. 67).   p. 56

[52] For the quotation from V.V. (V.P. Vorontsov) see *Lenin Miscellany XIX*, pp. 311-12; Lenin gave a part of this quotation and a comment on it in his article "Reply to Criticism of Our Draft Programme" (see present edition, Vol. 6, p. 451).
                                                     p. 57

[53] Lenin's remarks on the book *Les syndicats agricoles et leur oeuvre* par le comte de Rocquigny (Count de Rocquigny. *Agricultural Syndicates and Their Activity*). See *Lenin Miscellany XXXII*, pp. 24-49.   p. 57

[54] There is a mistake in the name of the source. It should be *Russkiye Vedomosti* (*Russian Recorder*), to whose editorial V. Chernov referred in the discussion of Lenin's lecture on March 4, 1903. See *Lenin Miscellany XIX*, p. 270 and p. 282 (point 12).   p. 66

[55] On February 4, 1903, *Russkiye Vedomosti* reported on a conference of landlords and tenants held in Dublin in December 1902. The conference produced a report stating the general terms on which, it believed, the land could be bought out from the landlords with the help of the Treasury.   p. 64

[56] These figures characterise the different class sections of the peasantry owning horses, and mean that 1.5 million farms of the

peasant bourgeoisie had 6.5 million horses of the total of 14
million on the peasant farms; 2 million middle-peasant farms had
4 million horses; 6.5 million semi-proletarian and proletarian
farms (that is, the farms of the peasant poor) had 3.5 million
horses. For details see present edition, Vol. 6, p. 383, and *Lenin
Miscellany XIX*, p. 343.   p. 68

[57] These are two variants of the plan for an article or a lecture on
"The Peasantry and Social-Democracy". There is no record of
Lenin having done either.

Lenin's notes on his study of the authors referred to in these
plans are published in this volume, and also in *Lenin Miscellanies
XIX, XXXI* and *XXXII*.   p. 69

[58] The summary and critical remarks on S. Bulgakov's book,
Capitalism and Agriculture, were set down by Lenin in a
notebook which he entitled, "Agrarian Material. Russian (and
Foreign) Writings on the Agrarian Question". This preparatory
material was extensively used in his work "The Agrarian
Question and the 'Critics of Marx'", in which he gave a
comprehensive critique of Bulgakov's views.   p. 73

[59] See Karl Marx, *Capital*, Vol. III, Moscow, 1966, p. 745.
                                                                 p. 73

[60] These figures mean that 55 farmers owned agricultural machines
in 1855 and 236, in 1861, and that the number of those using
machinery was 1,205. In 1871, the two categories were counted
together and gave a total of 2,160, and in 1881, 4,222.
                                                                 p. 76

[61] In 1892, the British Parliament passed the *Small Holdings Act* in
an attempt to keep the farmers in the countryside and revive the
yeomanry, the small peasants ruined in the 18th and the early
19th centuries who had been a source of cheap labour for the big
capitalist farms. The Act was not extensively applied and was of
small practical importance.   p. 77

[62] *Instleute*, Instmann—agricultural labourers in Germany signing
long-term contracts and living in their own dwellings on land
owned by big landowners. In addition to cash, they also received
a part of the crop from a specified plot of land (half-tenancy).
                                                                 p. 78

[63] *Middleman*—a type of kulak acting between landlords and
tenants in Ireland. They leased tracts of land from landlords
(from 20 to 150 acres and over), split them up into small parcels
(from 1 to 5 acres) and leased them by the year to small tenants
on harsh terms.   p. 84

[64] *P.S.*—author of the article "Die neuere russische Gesetzgebung
über den Gemeindebesitz" ("The Latest Russian Communal
Legislation") in *Archiv für soziale Gesetzgebung und Statistik*
(*Archives of Social Legislation and Statistics*), 7. Band, Berlin,
1894, S, 626-52.   p. 97

[65] Lenin used this material in his work "The Agrarian Question and the 'Critics of Marx'" (see present edition, Vol. 5, pp. 140-44).
                                                                        p. 107

[66] See Karl Marx, *Capital*, Vol. I. Moscow, 1965, pp. 335 and 348.
                                                                        p. 108

[67] Lenin gave a critical analysis of the data from M. Hecht's book, *Drei Dörfer der badischen Hard (Three Villages in the Hard of Baden)*, Leipzig, 1895, in Chapter V of "The Agrarian Question and the 'Critics of Marx'"—"'The Prosperity of Advanced, Modern Small Farms.' The Baden Example" (see present edition, Vol. 5, pp. 159-67).   p. 116

[68] In the first line of this note, Lenin indicates a discrepancy in Hecht's data concerning the size of area under grain in Friedrichsthal. On p. 28 the author says that the area under grain was 143 Morgen=51.48 ha, but on p. 21, the figure is said to be 18 per cent of the total area under crop, which gives 46.44 ha. The second line of the note is a rough recalculation of 678 Morgen (the area under grain for Blankenloch on p. 28 of Hecht's book) into hectares.   p. 122

[69] The first column of figures (dividend) shows the total area of land (in ha) for each village separately: Friedrichsthal, Blankenloch and Hagsfeld; the second column (divisor) shows the average quantity of land (in ha) per family for each village; the third column gives the rough number of families in each village.
                                                                        p. 122

[70] Lenin gave a part of his critical analysis of H. Auhagen's article "Ueber Gross- und Kleinbetrieb in der Landwirtschaft" ("On Large- and Small-Scale Production in Agriculture") in Chapter VI of "The Agrarian Question and the 'Critics of Marx'", entitled "The Productivity of a Small and a Big Farm. An Example from East Prussia" (see present edition, Vol. 5, pp. 168-69).
                                                                        p. 126

[71] The source analysed by Lenin contains a mistake: the figure should be 1,806.58 instead of 806.58. Lenin corrected it in "The Agrarian Question and the 'Critics of Marx'" (see present edition, Vol. 5, p. 168); there should be a corresponding change in the figure 1,965.08 and the percentages.   p. 131

[72] While working on "The Agrarian Question and the 'Critics of Marx'", Lenin made use of material from an article by the German economist K. Klawki, "Ueber Konkurrenzfähigkeit des landwirtschaftlichen Kleinbetriebes" ("The Competitive Capacity of Small-Scale Production in Agriculture") which appeared in Thiel's *Landwirtschaftliche Jahrbücher (Agricultural Yearbooks)*, Bd. XXVIII, Berlin, 1899.
      Klawki's article gives a description of 12 typical German farms (four each of the large, medium and small) operating in similar conditions. Lenin made a thorough examination of and

critically reworked the data given in the article, which was a
detailed inquiry but did not provide the necessary generalisations
and correct conclusions. The data from Klawki's article were
used by Lenin mainly in Chapter VI, "The Productivity of a
Small and a Big Farm. An Example from East Prussia" (present
edition, Vol. 5, pp. 167-81). Lenin showed the groundlessness of
Bulgakov's attempts to use Klawki's article to back up the
bourgeois theory that small farms were superior to large farms.
The scientific treatment of the data given in Klawki's inquiries,
says Lenin, confirms the technical superiority of big farms and
shows that the small farmer is overworked and underfed, being
gradually degraded to day labourer or farm-hand on the large
farm; Lenin shows that as the number of small farms grows there
is a spread of poverty and proletarisation among the peasantry.

Lenin's conclusions, drawn after a thorough examination and
reworking of the data in Klawki's article, are borne out by the
mass data on peasant farms in Germany. In contrast to Klawki,
who failed to go into the substance of economic processes and
ignored the comparative analysis of different groups of farms
(basing his conclusions on indiscriminate averages), Lenin gave a
profound Marxist analysis of the development of peasant farms
under capitalism and brought out their various types. On the
strength of these data, Lenin drew up a summarised table (see
present edition, Vol. 5, p. 170).

As a result of his careful verification and scientific tabulation
of the data in Klawki's article, Lenin showed that the latter was
wrong in calculating the comparative incomes on large and small
farms. Lenin said the unscientific methods used by Klawki to
show the superiority of the small farms were, in their main
features, practised by all bourgeois and petty-bourgeois economists. That is why an examination of all these methods, as
exemplified by Klawki's inquiry, is of great interest. Lenin took
the concrete statistical data with which Klawki operated to
expose the false methods used in the processing and employment
of statistical data, and also the completely unfounded conclusions drawn by bourgeois and petty-bourgeois economists
concerning the laws governing agricultural development under
capitalism.

p. 138

[73] *Landwirtschaftliche benutzte Fläche*—cultivated farmland. In his
preparatory material, Lenin uses the term in most cases without
translating it into the Russian, and includes in it farmland in the
strict sense of the term (that is, land under crops, meadows and
best pastures) and also orchards, vegetable gardens and vineyards. In some cases, Lenin translates this term as "farmland"
(see p. 192). On p. 358, Lenin indicates that the German source
substituted the term "Ueberhaupt landwirtschaftliche Fläche" for
"landwirtschaftliche benutzte Fläche" to designate the same data.

In his work *New Data on the Laws Governing the
Development of Capitalism in Agriculture*. Part One. *Capitalism*

and Agriculture in the United States of America, Lenin wrote: "In grouping farms by acreage, American statisticians take total acreage and not just the improved area, which would, of course, be the more correct method, and is the one employed by German statisticians" (see present edition, Vol. 22, p. 49).   p. 144

[74] *Scharwerker*—an able-bodied member of the family or a non-member living in the household of the agricultural labourer and bound by the contract between the head of the household and the landowner to work on the landowner's estate but paid by the head of the family.   p. 148

[75] *Deputant*—a labourer who is paid a permanent annual cash wage and in addition gets specified payments in kind as part of his wage—a plot of land and a dwelling on the landowner's estate.
            p.155

[76] *Deputant's land*—land made available by the landowner to an agricultural labourer under contract in part payment of his wages in kind.   p. 158

[77] The manuscript is a notebook bearing this title on the cover in a coloured pencil. The extracts must have been made at the same time as those from Klawki's article (see pp. 138-59), because at the end of the extracts from Klawki's article there is a note saying "Cf. *Brase's* article, especially pp. 292 and 297-98."
            p. 160

[78] Data from A. Sòuchon's book, *La proprieté paysanne (Peasant Property)*, was to be used in "The Agrarian Question and the 'Critics of Marx'" and in the lectures on "Marxist Views of the Agrarian Question in Europe and Russia", which Lenin gave in Paris on February 23-26, 1903 and also for his work "The Peasantry and Social-Democracy" (see pp. 29, 41, 49, 70).
            p. 170

[79] Souchon's reference (text and footnote 1 on p. 24 of his book) to *Ministère de l'agriculture française. Enquête de 1892,* p. 247 à 249 *(The French Ministry of Agriculture, 1892 Inquiry).*   p. 170

[80] *The Allotments Act* was adopted on September 16, 1887, with the view of allotting small parcels of land to labourers. Souchon says the following: "The application of the Allotments Act in essence consists in giving the labourers tiny plots to enable them to eke out their earnings with some meagre agricultural resources, and at best to have one cow or a few sheep" (p. 151).   p. 172

[81] Lenin intended to use the material on F. Maurice's book, *L'agriculture et la question sociale. La France agricole et agraire (Agriculture and the Social Question. Agricultural and Agrarian France),* Paris, 1892 in his work "The Agrarian Question and the 'Critics of Marx'". See plans for this work on pp. 29, 31, 35, 36.
            p. 173

[82] Lenin read the book by A. von Chłapowo-Chłapowski, *Die belgische Landwirtschaft im 19. Jahrhundert. Münchener volkswirtschaftliche Studien.* Herausgegeben von L. Brentano und W. Lotz. Stuttgart, 1900 (*Agriculture in Belgium in the 19th Century. Munich Economic Studies*), when preparing "The Agrarian Question and the 'Critics of Marx'". This is indicated by his mention of the book in the preliminary plans for his work (see pp. 29, 32, 36). Lenin also intended to use this material in his lectures on the agrarian question in Paris (see p. 49).

p. 178

[83] The present volume contains a part of Lenin's remarks on the Baden Inquiry.

The extracts from the Baden Inquiry are preparatory material for Chapter VII, "The Inquiry into Peasant Farming in Baden", in "The Agrarian Question and the 'Critics of Marx'" in which extensive use of the data is made for an analysis and characteristic of the class stratification of the peasantry under capitalism.

Lenin said the materials of the Baden Inquiry made it possible to distinguish and bring out different groups of peasants. However, the authors failed to give any scientific grouping of peasant farms; instead of comparing the various groups of farms, they compared whole communities. This method of using indiscriminate averages, thereby glossing over the class distinctions within the peasantry, was used by the "critics of Marx" in the agrarian question.

Lenin gave a scientific characteristic of the class structure of the German countryside and for that purpose used the summarised data of the Baden Inquiry. He brought out three typical economic groups: the large-, the middle- and the small-peasant farms, and to do this he processed and analysed statistical data relating to 31 large, 21 medium and 18 small farms.

For the three typical groups of peasant farms, Lenin determined the average size of landholding, the average size of family and employment of hired labour, and also the results of economic operations in the form of net profit. In working out the data on landholdings and net profit, Lenin gave two calculation variants: for all the 70 farms, and for the group minus the 10 farms in the three communities which had exceptionally large holdings. This method of bringing out typical phenomena, with a simultaneous verification of conclusions on the data for the whole aggregate of phenomena, is of great importance for statistical methods.

As a result of his economic analysis, Lenin showed that the big-peasant farms using hired labour, permanent and casual, and obtaining the highest net profit per farm, were entrepreneurial and capitalist. Meanwhile, the small-peasant farms were hardly managing to make ends meet. On the strength of the scientifically processed data of the Baden Inquiry on the quantity of the key products consumed by the groups of peasant farms, Lenin showed that the small peasant was cutting back his consumption which was well below that of the middle and the big peasant. If the small peasant spent as much on cash products as the middle peasant did, he would run up a great debt and the middle peasant would also incur a debt if he spent as much as the big one. According to this, Lenin drew the conclusion that the "'net profit', not only of the small peasant, but also of the middle peasant is a *pure fiction*" (see present edition, Vol. 5, p. 185). In this way, Lenin exposed the false method used by the "critics of Marx" to understate the plight of the small peasants, their malnutrition and ruin.

On the strength of his analysis of the Baden Inquiry, Lenin concluded that the main features of the peasant economy in Germany were similar to those in Russia, and that the process of capitalist development was leading to the formation of a minority of capitalist farms operating with hired labour, and forcing the majority of peasants increasingly to seek subsidiary employment, that is, to become wage workers. "The differentiation of the peasantry," Lenin wrote, "reveals the *profoundest* contradictions of capitalism in the very process of their *inception* and their further development. A complete evaluation of these contradictions inevitably leads to the recognition of the small peasantry's blind alley and hopeless position (hopeless, outside the revolutionary struggle of the proletariat against the entire capitalist system)" (see present edition, Vol. 5, p. 190). In this way, Lenin showed the economic basis for the common interests of the working class and the small peasantry, and the need for their alliance in the struggle against capitalism.

The material Lenin obtained as a result of his work on the Baden Inquiry, apart from its great political and economic importance, was also of major methodological importance for an understanding of the methods Lenin used to process and apply statistical data in Marxist economic analysis (for instance, the use of scientifically tabulated statistical groupings of peasant farms, determination and use on their basis of differentiated averages for income, consumption, etc., by class groups of peasants). Lenin's methods for processing statistical data are a valuable contribution to the methodology of Marxist statistics.   p. 180

[84] The extracts of data on 70 budgets mentioned here are a big table entitled "Summary of Data on 70 budgets from the Baden Inquiry", which included the statistical data from the Baden Inquiry processed by Lenin. These extracts made in a notebook are at the Central Party Archives of the Institute of Marxism-Leninism under the C.P.S.U. Central Committee. When tabulating these data for large-, middle- and small-peasant farms, Lenin determined the average landholdings, size of family, and current receipts and outlays (showing the major items) and calculated the surplus or deficit by comparing the receipts and outlays. In addition, the table contains the indicators on labour (such as the expenditure of labour per hectare, hired labour, showing day

labour separately), and also data on subsidiary earnings, etc. For
an analysis of these data see present edition, Vol. 5, pp. 182-88.
                                                              p. 181

[85] The text of chapters VII and IX (as first published in the journal
Obrazovaniye No. 2, 1906) of "The Agrarian Question and the
'Critics of Marx'" shows that in that work Lenin intended to
examine French agricultural statistics and to give a critical
analysis of the works of French economists. Judging by a note in
Chapter IX (see present edition, Vol. 5, p. 215), he made a
special study of the state of wine-growing in France. It is
possible, therefore, that he used E. Seignouret's book, *Essais
d'économie sociale et agricole (Essays on Social and Agricultural
Economics)*, to prepare his work "The Agrarian Question and the
'Critics of Marx'" in June-September 1901.   p. 186

[86] Lenin's notebook entitled "From German Agrarian Statistics"
contains remarks on and extracts from *Statistik des Deutschen
Reichs*, Neue Folge, Bd. 112. *Die Landwirtschaft im Deutschen
Reich nach der landwirtschaftlichen Betriebszählung vom
14.VI.1895*, Berlin, 1898 (*Statistics of the German Reich*, New
Series, Vol. 112. *Agriculture in the German Reich According to
the Agricultural Census of June 14, 1895*). It shows how Lenin
processed the data of the two agricultural censuses in Germany
(1882 and 1895), which he used to prepare "The Agrarian
Question and the 'Critics of Marx'" (mainly chapters VIII and
IX). The notebook dates to the first period of Lenin's writing of
this work (1900-01). It contains some later extracts made by
Lenin from the German agricultural census of 1907 in *Statistik
des Deutschen Reichs*, Band 212, Teil 1a.— *Berufs- und Betriebszählung vom 12. Juni 1907. Landwirtschaftliche Betriebsstatistik*, Berlin, 1909 and Band 212, Teil 2a, 1910 (*Statistics of
the German Reich*, Vol. 212, part 1a.— Census of Occupations
and Enterprises of June 12, 1907. *Statistics of Agricultural
Enterprises*, Berlin, 1909, and Vol. 212, part 2a, 1910). Lenin
made these additions in 1910 for a work on German agriculture.
    Lenin used the German agricultural statistics to show that the
"critics" of Marx's economic doctrine were wrong when they
said that in the West large farms were being supplanted by the
middle- and small-peasant farms.
    Having reworked the German agrarian statistics, Lenin
showed two processes of proletarisation of the peasantry: first,
more and more peasants were being deprived of their land, which
meant that farmers were being transformed into landless labourers; second, the peasants were increasingly dependent on
subsidiary earnings, that is, there was a growing integration of
agriculture and industry, which marked the first stage of
proletarisation.
    Lenin's treatment of German agrarian statistics sets a model
for the scientific analysis and processing of statistical data. Lenin
did not stop at grouping farms under one head (say, area), but

went on to classify them under several heads, such as number of agricultural machines, area under special crops, etc., and used combined groupings, e.g., dividing each group (say, acreage) into subgroups by quantity of cattle and other characteristics. Lenin found that he had to rework and verify the statistical data he made use of; he reworked a number of tables (such as that characterising the concentration of commercial gardening, etc.), widening the intervals between the groups of farms to find the more typical, and at the same time bringing out the latifundia connected with industries (sugar refining, wine-making, etc.). Lenin calculated the percentages showing, for instance, the share of separate groups of farms, determined the absolute averages showing the use of the major types of agricultural machines per 100 farms in each group of farms (grouped by acreage), etc.

p. 189

[87] Lenin summarised these data on land concentration in wine-growing on the basis of the preceding table. The left column of figures denotes the grouping of farms, the right column, the corresponding grouping of land for these farms. The first pair of figures relates to vineyards under 20 ares; the second, to vineyards of 20 to 50 ares; the third, to vineyards of 50 ares-5 hectares and over.

p. 192

[88] Lenin examines the data on the number of cows on various farms in 1895 to characterise the concentration of cattle on the large farms. The total number of farms and the total number of cows on all farms of all three groups are given in the manuscript at the top of the table (for lack of space below).

p. 213

[89] Fragmentary notes on separate sheets.

In addition, the Central Party Archives of the Institute of Marxism-Leninism under the C.P.S.U. Central Committee have unpublished preparatory material relating to French agricultural statistics, which contains summaries and extracts from various sources. Among them are, above all, the collections *Statistique agricole de la France. Résultats généraux de l'enquête décennale de 1892 (Agricultural Statistics of France. General Results of the 1892 Decennial Inquiry). Statistique générale de la France. Résultats statistiques du Dénombrement de 1896 (General Statistics of France. Statistical Results of the 1896 Census)* and also the results of censuses for other years. Lenin also made many statistical extracts with explanations and critical remarks on the following books: K. Kautsky, *Die Agrarfrage (The Agrarian Question)*; S. Bulgakov, *Capitalism and Agriculture*, Vol. II; F. Maurice. *L'agriculture et la question sociale. La France agricole et agraire (Agriculture and the Social Question. Agricultural and Agrarian France)*; A. Souchon, *La propriété paysanne. Étude d'économie rurale (Peasant Property. An Essay on Agricultural Economy)*; N. Kudrin, *The Peasant Question in France; The Bulletin of the Labour Bureau* for 1901, etc.

Most of the extracts from French statistics are summarised data, in particular, groupings of farms by acreage for various years. Lenin notes as a positive aspect of the French statistics the separate classification of the "active" (that is, the gainfully employed) population, and makes extensive extracts of data by categories within the "active" population. Lenin takes the same data from the above-mentioned book by Maurice and makes a comparison of similar statistical data taken from various sources; he characterises these sources and draws conclusions on the annual changes in the numerical strength and share of each group (category) of the "active" population.

This material from French agricultural statistics, reworked and summarised by Lenin, added up to a comprehensive picture of various aspects of farming among different class groups of peasant farms, confirming the Marxist propositions concerning the superiority of large farms and the growth of their role, and the proletarisation of the small peasants.   p. 218

[90] This summarised table was compiled by Lenin on the strength of the statistics of the countries concerned for the corresponding years. The separate data on Germany, Britain and the United States were taken from the *Statistik des Deutschen Reichs*, Band 112; some of the data on France, from the same source, and others, from the *Statistique agricole de la France. Résultats généraux de l'enquête décennale de 1892*. Tableaux; the data on Belgium, from the *Statistique de la Belgique. Agriculture. Recensement général de 1880* (*Statistics of Belgium. Agriculture. General Census of 1880*) and from *Annuaire statistique de la Belgique 1896* (*The Statistical Yearbook of Belgium for 1896*); the data for Denmark, from *Die Neue Zeit*, XIX. Jahrgang 1900-1901, Band II, p. 623, G. Bang's article, "Die landwirtschaftliche Entwicklung Dänemarks" ("Agricultural Development of Denmark").   p. 224

[91] Lenin gave the name of Dutch agricultural inquiry of 1890 to "Uitkomsten van het Onderzoek naar den Toestand van den Landbouw in Nederland" ("The Results of the Inquiry into the State of Agriculture in the Netherlands") published in four volumes at the Hague in 1890. The results of this inquiry into 95 communities differed from similar inquiries in other countries in failing to provide full data, and, as Lenin remarked, failing to give summaries for all communities. But Lenin managed to extract interesting data from this source to characterise various groups of farms (typical communities) and also groups of farms (within separate communities) classified by area, the number of labourers and farm-hands, the number of horses and other characteristics. These data showed the capitalist nature of Dutch farming.   p. 227

[92] Lenin intended to give a critique of E. Stumpfe's views on large- and small-scale production in agriculture in a number of

his works (see this volume, pp. 42, 49, 70), in view of the fact that many of the "critics of Marx" referred to Stumpfe's works. p. 231

[93] G. Fischer's work, *Die sociale Bedeutung der Maschinen in der Landwirtschaft* (*The Social Importance of Machinery in Agriculture*) was studied by Lenin before Stumpfe's article, "Ueber die Konkurrenzfähigkeit des kleinen und mittleren Grundbesitzes gegenüber dem Grossgrundbesitze" ("On the Competitiveness of Small and Medium Land Holdings as Compared with Large Land Holdings"). In his extracts from this article, Lenin mentions Fischer's work as having been studied by him (see p. 238). p. 248

[94] Lenin's remark at the end of the text "No wonder its pages remain uncut (at the British Museum)" warrants the assumption that Lenin studied Turot's book during his stay in London, where *Iskra* was then being published, that is, not earlier than April 1902. In London, Lenin made a study of the agrarian question in connection with the working out of the Party's agrarian programme; before giving his lectures and talk in Paris (in February-March 1903), he studied the French agricultural economy. Turot's book is also mentioned in Lenin's notes on the book by E. Lecouteux (see *Lenin Miscellany XXXII*, p. 381). p. 257

[95] Lenin first mentioned Baudrillart in his extracts from Hertz's book *The Agrarian Questions in Relation to Socialism* (June-September 1901). In his plans for "The Agrarian Question and the 'Critics of Marx'" Lenin refers to Baudrillart from mention of him by Hertz and Bulgakov. In the outlines of his lectures on "Marxist Views of the Agrarian Question in Europe and Russia" (1903, before February 10 (23)), Lenin refers to Baudrillart's works as having been studied by him earlier. This volume contains Lenin's remarks on one book by H. Baudrillart, *Les populations agricoles de la France*. 3-me sèrie. *Les populations du Midi* (*The Agricultural Population of France*. Part 3. *The Population of the South*), Paris 1893. For extracts from and critical remarks on another of Baudrillart's books, *Les populations agricoles de la France*. *La Normandie* (*The Agricultural Population of France*. *Normandy*), Paris 1880 see *Lenin Miscellany XXXII*, pp. 82-105. Both take up the greater part of a notebook which Lenin entitled "*Baudrillart*+Backhaus". p. 258

[96] The full name of the book is Comte de Rocquigny, *Les syndicats agricoles et leur oeuvre* (*Agricultural Syndicates and Their Activity*), Paris, 1900. For extracts with Lenin's critical remarks on this book see *Lenin Miscellany XXXII*, pp. 24-49. p. 261

[97] A reference to Élie Coulet's book, *Le mouvement syndical et coopératif dans l'agriculture française. La fédération agricole.*

(The Syndicalist and Co-operative Movement in French Agriculture. The Agricultural Federation). Montpellier, 1898. See p. 260.
                                                                            p. 261

[98] Rouanet, quoting Deschanel's speech in the Chamber of Deputies extolling the activity of the agricultural syndicates in favour of the labourers, said: "That is how Mr. Deschanel writes the history of agricultural syndicates to the applause of members of these syndicates who thrilled with delight when they suddenly learned of the excellent things they had done."   p. 262

[99] In his lectures, "Marxist Views of the Agrarian Question in Europe and Russia", and in his talks in Paris, Lenin mentions Nossig as one of "many writers who sympathise with the criticism of the Marxist theory rather than with this theory itself". He adds; "Their own data speak against them" (see present edition, Vol. 6, p. 347). Notes on the manuscript indicate that Lenin repeatedly returned to it. Thus, some words are retraced in blue pencil, apparently to make for easier reading; the translation of some words is given in plain pencil in brackets.
                                                                            p. 263

[100] Lenin read E. David's book, *Socialismus und Landwirtschaft* (*Socialism and Agriculture*) soon after it was published. In a letter to G. V. Plekhanov on March 15, 1903, Lenin wrote: "I had already ordered David's book and am now reading it. Terribly watery, poor and trite" (present edition, Vol. 34, p. 150). In an article entitled "Les beaux esprits se rencontrent (Which May Be Interpreted Roughly as: Birds of a Feather Flock Together)" (which was published in *Iskra* No. 38, April 15, 1903) Lenin criticised the main propositions of David's book (see present edition, Vol. 6, pp. 433-35). Lenin gave a full-scale critique of David's book—"the principal work of revisionism on the agrarian question"—in Chapter X of "The Agrarian Question and the 'Critics of Marx'" (present edition, Vol. 13, pp. 171-82).
   The nature of Lenin's underlinings shows that he returned to his remarks and brought out some places in blue and red pencils; in a second reading, he underlined in red pencil all the sources mentioned in the manuscript.   p. 265

[101] A reference to Engels's article "The Peasant Question in France and Germany" (see Marx and Engels, *Selected Works*, Vol. II, Moscow, 1962, pp. 420-40).   p. 265

[102] Empty talk and unbridled flights of fancy, after a character in Gogol's *Dead Souls*, the landowner Manilov.   p. 271

[103] A reference to the work of V. V. (V. P. Vorontsov), *Progressive Trends in Peasant Farming*, St. Petersburg, 1892, pp. 70-84 (see present edition, Vol. 3, pp. 274-75).   p. 275

[104] A reference to Drechsler's data which he published as the results of two agricultural inquiries, in 1875 and 1884. Lenin is referring to two works on this question: 1) "Die bäuerlichen Zustände in einigen Teilen der Provinz Hannover" in *Schriften des Vereins für Sozialpolitik.* XXIV. 1883; 2) "Die Verteilung des Grundbesitzes und der Viehhaltung im Bezirke des landwirtschaftlichen Kreisvereins Göttingen" in *Landwirtschaftliche Jahrbücher* herausgegeben von Dr. H. Thiel. XV. Band. Berlin, 1886 [1) "The Condition of Peasants in Some Parts of the Province of Hannover" in the *Works of the Social Policy Association*; 2) "Distribution of Land Property and Cattle in the Area of the Göttingen District Agricultural Society", in the *Agricultural Yearbooks* published by Dr. H. Thiel]. Lenin gave a critical analysis of the data from both works in Chapter XI of "The Agrarian Question and the 'Critics of Marx'" (see present edition, Vol. 13, pp. 182-94).   p. 281

[105] The notes and extracts from *Hand and Machine Labor* (*Thirteenth Annual Report of the Commissioner of Labor*, 1898, Vols. I and II), which first appeared in the Fourth Russian edition of Lenin's *Collected Works*, were made in a notebook containing extracts from books on economics, statistics and philosophy, and also from newspapers dated October 19 and 21, 1904. Lenin must have made these extracts at the Geneva Library in the autumn of 1904.

The following reference is noted on the second page of the manuscript: "See examples on separate sheet." The examples taken from both volumes of the book, *Hand and Machine Labor,* and noted down by Lenin on a separate sheet are given on pp. 284-86 of this volume.   p. 282

[106] Lenin first mentions the work of Leo Huschke, *Landwirtschaftliche Reinertrags-Berechnungen bei Klein-, Mittel- und Grossbetrieb dargelegt an typischen Beispielen Mittelthüringens* (*Calculation of Net Income in Agricultural Production on Small, Medium and Large Farms from Typical Examples in Central Thüringia*) in two of his plans: "The Peasantry and Social-Democracy" (see p. 70). Lenin used some of the material published here in a footnote to Chapter VI, "The Productivity of a Small and a Big Farm. An Example from East Prussia", in the 1908 edition of "The Agrarian Question and the 'Critics of Marx'" (see present edition, Vol. 5, p. 179). He said he hoped "to return to Herr Huschke's interesting book" (ibid.).   p. 287

[107] This is a notebook on the cover of which is written: "German Agrarian Statistics (1907)" and on top of that, in coloured pencil:
"1) German agrarian statistics,
"2) Russian agrarian statistics,
"3) Statistics on *strikes* in Russia + Hungarian agrarian statistics."

Lenin's study of the German agricultural census of 1907 relates to the period from 1910 (before September) to 1913 (after June).

Lenin attached special importance to an analysis of German agrarian statistics in studying the laws governing the development of capitalism in agriculture and in exposing bourgeois apologetics in the agrarian question. "Germany belongs to the leading and most rapidly developing capitalist countries. Her censuses of agricultural enterprises are possibly on a higher level than anywhere else in Europe. It is understandable therefore why German and Russian writers displayed such interest in the results of the latest census of 1907 (the first and the second censuses were taken in 1882 and in 1895). Bourgeois economists and revisionists sing out in chorus that Marxism—for the hundredth and thousandth time!—has been refuted by the data of the census" (see *Lenin Miscellany XXV*, p. 127). That is why Lenin believed that it was necessary to make a detailed analysis of the German census of 1907.

The material of German agrarian statistics was taken mainly from the three volumes of the collection *Statistik des Deutschen Reichs*. Neue Folge. Band 112. *Die Landwirtschaft im Deutschen Reich nach der landwirtschaftlichen Betriebszählung vom 14. Juni 1895*, Berlin, 1898; *Statistik des Deutschen Reichs*. Band 202. *Berufs- und Betriebszählung vom 12. Juni 1907, Berufsstatistik*, Berlin, 1909; *Statistik des Deutschen Reichs*. Band 212. *Berufs- und Betriebszählung vom 12. Juni 1907, Landwirtschaftliche Betriebsstatistik* (Teil 1a; 1b; 2a), Berlin, 1909-10 [*Statistics of the German Reich*, New Series, Vol. 112. *Agriculture in the German Reich According to the Agricultural Census of June 14, 1895*; *Statistics of the German Reich*, Vol. 202, *Census of Occupations and Enterprises of June 12, 1907*; *Occupation Statistics*; *Statistics of the German Reich*, Vol. 212. *Census of Occupations and Enterprises of June 12, 1907. Statistics of Agricultural Enterprises* (Part 1a; 1b; 2a)].

This statistical material, like that which follows, was partially used by Lenin in the writing of his article "The Capitalist System of Modern Agriculture" (see present edition, Vol. 16, pp. 423-46). Lenin also planned to use the material of German agrarian statistics in another article on German agriculture.

The material of German agrarian statistics contains numerous extracts from tables, parts of tables and separate statistical data not only from the above-mentioned collection, *Statistics of the German Reich*, but also from articles by Zahn, Schmelzle and others. Some data on fertilisers were taken from French sources.

The material of German agrarian statistics which Lenin processed and systematised illustrated various forms of capitalist development in agriculture.

On the strength of the extensive statistical data on the agricultural population contained in German agrarian statistics, Lenin studied the proletarisation of the peasantry. The data on the use of machinery, the percentage of farms with draught cattle, and the composition of the draught animals, the growth of agricultural industries, dairy farming, etc., showed the development of large-scale capitalist production.

Special interest attaches to Lenin's explanations to the table (taken from the results of the 1907 Census in Volume 202 of the *Statistics of the German Reich*) which classifies the population by main occupation of the gainfully employed (see pp. 342-45, 370). The principle of classifying the rural population of Germany, according to the data for 1882 and 1895, into three main groups (I, II and III) was described and substantiated by Lenin in his work "The Agrarian Question and the 'Critics of Marx'" (present edition, Vol. 5, pp. 217-22) which is indicated on p. 346 ("Distribution (in thousands) adopted in *The Agrarian Question*, p. 244").

For technical reasons, some tables from German statistics in this volume are given in parts. p. 297

[108] The data under the heads bracketed in the table were used by Lenin to calculate the number of hired labourers. See the last column of the table (p. 323). p. 320

[109] A reference to the article by Fr. Zahn, "Deutschlands wirtschaftliche Entwicklung unter besonderer Berücksichtigung der Volkszählung 1905 sowie Berufs- und Betriebszählung 1907" ("The Economic Development of Germany with Special Account of the 1905 Census of Population and the 1907 Census of Occupations and Enterprises") published in *Annalen des Deutschen Reichs* (*Annals of the German Reich*) No. 7 for July and No. 8 for August 1910. p. 324

[110] A reference to Schmelzle's article, "Die ländliche Grundbesitzverteilung, ihr Einfluss auf die Leistungsfähigkeit der Landwirtschaft und ihre Entwicklung" ("Distribution of Rural Land Holdings, Its Influence on the Productivity and Development of Agriculture") published in *Annalen des Deutschen Reichs* No. 6 for June 1913. p. 335

[111] The two following tables giving the data for 1882 and 1895 are taken from Chapter IX of "The Agrarian Question and the 'Critics of Marx'" published in the collection *The Agrarian Question*. Part I, St. Petersburg, 1908 (see present edition, Vol. 5, pp. 218-20). In the first table, Lenin made a correction of two misprints in the collection: he switched the designation of the categories "c 2)" and "c 3)". p. 346

[112] Lenin gives the data from *Statistik des Deutschen Reichs*. Band 211. *Berufs- und Betriebszählung vom 12. Juni 1907. Berufsstatistik*. Abteilung X. "Die berufliche und soziale Gliederung des deutschen Volkes". Berlin, 1913 (*Statistics of the German Reich*. Vol. 211. *Census of Occupations and Enterprises of June 12, 1907. Occupation Statistics*. Section X. "Occupational and Social Classification of the German People"). p. 355

[113] A notebook, entitled *Austrian Agricultural Statistics*, containing the first document under the same title and in it pages 4 and 5 of the original (see pp. 388-95). p. 369

[114] This plan reflects the three stages of Lenin's work on the material based on his study of the data of the 1907 German agricultural census and collected in his notebook, *German Agrarian Statistics* (see pp. 297-371).

The first stage was the compilation of a general plan for the processing of these data under 13 heads (0-12). The second stage was the drawing up of the plan and the writing of the first article, "The Capitalist System of Modern Agriculture", in which Lenin dealt with the first five (0-4) points of the general plan (see present edition, Vol. 16, pp. 423-46). The other points remained for another article. The third stage was the drafting of the plan for another article consisting of the five points or topics. This article was never written.

The time it took Lenin to work on the plan as a whole is determined by the time it took him to collect the material on German agrarian statistics on the basis of the 1907 Census, that is, from 1910 to 1913.   p. 372

[115] This and the following marking in the margin on the left, opposite the various points of the general plan, signify the numeration and size of the chapters of Lenin's article "The Capitalist System of Modern Agriculture" (article I) (present edition, Vol. 16, pp. 423-46), which was written on the basis of this plan. The Roman numerals (from I to VII) designate the chapters of the article, the Arabic numerals (from 1 to 87), boxed and in round brackets, the pages of the manuscript of the article. The left column of figures in the numeration of the points in the general plan, added in blue pencil, coincides with the numeration of the chapters of the article.   p. 372

[116] Material on Hungarian agrarian statistics, which Lenin used in part in his article, "The Capitalist System of Modern Agriculture" (see present edition, Vol. 16, pp. 443-45), was published in *Lenin Miscellany XXXI*, pp. 274-97.   p. 373

[117] The reference to 1895 means a comparison with the data of the German agricultural census of 1895.   p. 373

[118] See Note 104.   p. 373

[119] A list of statistical tables given by Lenin in "The Capitalist System of Modern Agriculture" (article one), with an indication of the manuscript pages containing the tables (see present edition, Vol. 16, pp. 433, 438, 440, 444, 445, 446). Tables 4, 5, 6, 7 and 8 are on pages of the manuscript which have not been found.
                                    p. 375

[120] Extracts of data from Danish statistics date approximately to 1911, a fact established from the date of the latest of the Danish statistical publications quoted here by Lenin, *The Statistical Tables* for the 1909 Census.

Lenin took down the data to show the concentration of capital and production in Danish agriculture. He tabulated all the farms into four big groups (under 3.3 ha—proletarian and semi-proletarian farms; 3.3 to 9.9 ha—small peasants; 9.9 to 29.7 ha—big peasants and peasant bourgeoisie; and over 29.7 ha—capitalist agriculture) to show the distinction between the economic types of farms. The two lower groups (63.4 per cent of all farms) had, in 1909, 11.7 per cent of the land and 17.2 per cent of the big horned cattle; and the two higher groups (36.6 per cent of all farms) had 88.2 per cent of the land and 82.8 per cent of all horned cattle. This revealed the typical capitalist stratification of farms and the concentration on the entrepreneurial farms of almost 90 per cent of the land and more than 80 per cent of the big horned cattle. Lenin makes special mention of the increase in the number of large farms from 1898 to 1909. In that period, the total number of farms increased by 1.7 per cent, while farms with 15-49 head of big horned cattle went up by 35 per cent, and those with 50 and more head, by 46.3 per cent. Lenin used the data on the comparative quantities of horned cattle in Denmark, Germany and Russia per 1,000 population, per 1,000 hectares, and per square kilometre to show the high level of livestock farming in Denmark. p. 376

[121] The extracts from Austrian agricultural statistics apparently date to the period from 1910 to 1912, for Volume 28 of *Oesterreichisches statistisches Handbuch* (*The Austrian Statistical Handbook*) mentioned by Lenin in the beginning was issued in 1910, and Volume 29, mentioned in a later addition on the same page of the manuscript, was published not earlier than November 1911 (the Preface to the volume was dated October 1911).

The materials on Austrian agricultural statistics contain mainly data characterising area, personnel in agricultural and forest enterprises, the use of agricultural machinery and the maintenance of draught animals. The characteristic of agricultural and forest enterprises in respect of the area of cultivated land and the use of agricultural machinery is given as a statistical grouping in the form of a combined table reflecting the interconnection between the two. The second half of the table (see p. 385) was compiled by Lenin from a number of tables in the said collection with the view to further dividing up the medium group of farms (2-100 ha) into 5 subgroups by area.

The grouping of agricultural and forest enterprises by productive area (see pp. 388-95) classifies the enterprises with regard to hired labour; Lenin obtained the statistical data on strictly family farms and on farms with persons not belonging to the family by reworking the data of Table 6 from the collection *Oesterreichische Statistik*. The material on Austrian statistics illustrated the development of capitalism in agriculture and was apparently intended by Lenin for use in later works on the agrarian question. p. 383

[122] Schmelzle's article, "Die ländliche Grundbesitzverteilung, ihr Einfluss auf die Leistungsfähigkeit der Landwirtschaft und ihre Entwicklung" ("Distribution of Rural Land Holdings, Its Influence on the Productivity and Development of Agriculture"), was published in *Annalen des Deutschen Reichs für Gesetzgebung, Verwaltung und Volkswirtschaft* No. 6. This issue was published on June 10, 1913, so that Lenin could not have read the article before July 1913. p. 397

[123] A reference to the work of H. Quante, "Grundkapital und Betriebskapital". *Landwirtschaftliche Jahrbücher* von H. Thiel. XXXIV. Band, Heft 6. Berlin, 1905. S. 925-72 ("Land Capital and Production Capital". H. Thiel's *Agricultural Yearbooks*). p. 397

[124] A reference to Dr. K. Vogeley's work, *Landwirtschaftliche Betriebsverhältnisse Rheinhessens. Arbeiten der Deutschen Landwirtschafts-Gesellschaft.* Heft 133 (*Production Relations in the Agriculture of the Rhine-Hesse. Transactions of the German Agricultural Society,* Part 133). p. 397

[125] A quotation from Schmelzle of Dr. A. Burg's work, *Beiträge zur Kenntnis des landwirtschaftlichen Betriebs im Vogelsberg. Arbeiten der Deutschen Landwirtschafts-Gesellschaft.* Heft 123 (*A Contribution to the Study of Agricultural Production in Vogelsberg. Transactions of the German Agricultural Society,* Part 123). p. 398

[126] The extracts from E. Laur's book date approximately to 1913, since they were made by Lenin between two entries dating to 1913. Lenin made use of the statistical data from 1886 to 1906, which enabled him to give a comprehensive characteristic of tendencies in the development of Swiss agriculture in that period. Together with other material, these data were apparently intended by Lenin for a continuation of his work, *New Data on the Laws Governing the Development of Capitalism in Agriculture.* p. 402

[127] The manuscript of Lenin's remarks on E. Jordi's book, *The Electric Motor in Agriculture,* is among extracts from newspapers and journals for September 1914, in a notebook entitled "Engels, Savoy, etc., Certain Other Things, and Extracts on War". p. 406

[128] The documents published below are preparatory material for Lenin's *New Data on the Laws Governing the Development of Capitalism in Agriculture. Part One. Capitalism and Agriculture in the United States of America.* This material consists of two parts: the first contains diverse variants of the plan for this work, and the second, statistical material from the American censuses taken in 1900 and 1910. "Remarks on American Agricultural Statistics" is an introduction to this statistical material (see pp. 416-20).

Lenin wrote the variants of the plan on the back of sheets containing his article, in German, "Der Opportunismus und der Zusammenbruch der zweiten Internationale" ("Opportunism and the Collapse of the Second International") (see present edition, Vol. 22, pp. 108-20). The sheets are not numbered, so that the variants of the plan are arranged as they approximate the final plan given in the contents of the published book. Apart from complete variants of the plan, there are fragments of it on the same sheets.

"Remarks on American Agricultural Statistics" contain important methodological propositions on the study of types of farms and comparative characteristics of farm groupings under three heads: area, principal source of income, and gross cash income. Lenin emphasises the importance of grouping farms under the last two heads, and shows the limits of application and the shortcomings of the grouping by area alone, for it glosses over the displacement of small-scale production (lumping together a minority of growing farms with a mass of backward farms going to seed). In Lenin's grouping of farms by income, the land factor is subordinate to capital. The specific feature of Lenin's methodology in this case was the grouping (in a combined table) by two factors, which resulted in a comparison of the statistical data on farm area within the limits of one type of farm. Lenin believed the insufficient use of combined tables to be a flaw in American statistics, which failed to use combined tables showing type of farms (they gave 7-10 groups of farms, which Lenin reduced to three main groups, corresponding to three types of farm). On the 1900 Census Lenin wrote: "...Here too, no classification gives all the essential characteristics of the type and size of farm" (present edition, Vol. 22, p. 61).

The second part of the preparatory material—"American Agrarian Statistics"—consists of the statistical data of the two American censuses taken in 1900 and 1910 processed by Lenin. They are: Census Reports. Volume V. Twelfth Census of the United States, taken in the year 1900. Agriculture. Part 1. Washington, 1902, and Thirteenth Census of the United States, taken in the year 1910. Volume V. Agriculture. 1909 and 1910. Washington, 1914. On the back of the first three pages of extracts from the Thirteenth Census of 1910, there are extracts from Volume IV of the same census (Statistics of Occupations). In addition, there are some data drawn from the Statistical Abstract of the United States. Washington, 1912.

Lenin starts by giving a list of the extracts from the 1900 Census. The extracts from the Twelfth Census of 1900 take up 12 numbered pages (with certain phrases or words given in bold type or underlined); and those from the Thirteenth Census of 1910, 16 pages. In addition, there are several separate sheets with various calculations made by Lenin (e.g., the percentage of farms reporting horses in 1900-10). The results of these calculations are given in Lenin's New Data on the Laws Governing the

Development of Capitalism in Agriculture (see present edition, Vol. 22, pp. 91-92).

Of the greatest value in Lenin's study and demonstration of capitalist development in general, and the displacement of small-scale by large-scale production in industry and agriculture, in particular, was the material of the Twelfth Census of 1900, which yielded the three different methods of grouping farms (by principal source of income, by acreage, and by value of the farm product—gross cash income). But here, as was noted above, none of the groupings is fully applied in respect of all the essential characteristics of the type and size of farm. In the results of the 1910 Census, Lenin pointed out, even the traditional grouping of farms by acreage was not given in full. Lenin filled these gaps: he drew up a comprehensive (summary) table giving a comparison of the three groupings. In his analysis, Lenin showed that grouping by acreage (a method favoured by bourgeois statisticians) was limited and insufficient, and proved the need to modify the methods of inquiry, grouping, etc., in accordance with the forms of capitalist penetration into agriculture.

As has been said, the material of the Thirteenth Census of 1910 was poorer in content, so that Lenin was unable to make the same groupings, analyse them and draw the relevant conclusions. He made use of the absolute and part of relative data of the 1910 Census for a comparison. On pp. 442-45 of this volume, apart from data on agriculture, he gives data on population in the three main divisions of the United States: the industrial North, the former slave-holding South, and the homestead West; for these three main divisions, Lenin wrote out data characterising the commercial character of livestock farming, notably, the concentration of livestock owned in the North. Lenin arrives at a general conclusion for the country as a whole that small and medium farms are being supplanted, and that large capitalist farms are growing. Further, on pp. 478-79 there are statistical data which Lenin used to refute the assertions of bourgeois economists that the law of the large-scale production supplanting the small-scale does not apply to agriculture. These data served as the basis for § 15 ("A Comparative Picture of Evolution in Industry and Agriculture") of Lenin's *New Data on the Laws Governing the Development of Capitalism in Agriculture.* He arrives at the conclusion that "there is a remarkable similarity in the laws of evolution" in industry and agriculture.

Lenin began to work on the American 1900 statistics in Paris (in 1912), but did not finish working on this volume. In a letter to Isaac A. Hourwich, Washington, from Cracow on February 27, 1914, Lenin wrote: "When I made a study of American agricultural statistics (Vol. V. *Agriculture—Census of 1900*) in Paris, I found a great deal of interesting matter. Now, in Cracow, I am unable to obtain these publications" (see present edition,

Vol. 36, p. 271). In a letter from Poronin to N. N. Nakoryakov in New York on May 18, 1914, he said he had received Volume V of the 1900 Census and asked for Volume V of the Thirteenth Census of 1910 (see present edition, Vol. 35, p. 140).

New Data on the Laws Governing the Development of Capitalism in Agriculture. Part One. *Capitalism and Agriculture in the United States of America* (see present edition, Vol. 22, pp. 13-102) was apparently completed in 1915, and in January 1916 sent from Berne to Maxim Gorky for Parus Publishers. In a letter he sent at the same time, Lenin wrote: "I have tried in as popular a form as possible to set forth new data about America which, I am convinced, are particularly suitable for the popularising of Marxism and substantiating it by means of facts.... I should like to continue, and subsequently also to publish, a second part—about Germany" (see present edition, Vol. 35, p. 212). The book was first published in 1917 by Zhizn i Znaniye Publishers.

p. 408

INDEX OF SOURCES

A

Annalen des Deutschen Reichs für Gesetzgebung, Verwaltung und Volkswirtschaft, München-Berlin. 1910, N 6, S. 401-441; N 7, S. 481-518; N 8, S. 561-598; 1911, N 3-4, S. 161-248.—324-25, 326-27, 340-41, 353-54, 355.
—1913, N 6, S. 401-434.—335, 397-401.

Annuaire statistique de la Belgique. Vingt-septième année.—1896. T. 27. Bruxelles, J.-B. Stevens, 1897. X, 383, XII p.; 4 carte. (Ministère de l'Intérieur et de l'Instruction Publique).—224.

Arbeiten der Deutschen Landwirtschafts-Gesellschaft. Hft. 118. Betriebsverhältnisse der deutschen Landwirtschaft. Stück I. Verfasser: P. Teicke, W. Ebersbach, E. Langenbeck. Berlin, 1906. XXVI, 225 S.; 22 Tab.—398.

Arbeiten der Deutschen Landwirtschafts-Gesellschaft. Hft. 123. Betriebsverhältnisse der deutschen Landwirtschaft. Stück II. Verfasser: H. Aussel, A. Burg. Berlin, 1906. [1], 171 S.; 6 Tab.—398.

Arbeiten der Deutschen Landwirtschafts-Gesellschaft. Hft. 130. Betriebsverhältnisse der deutschen Landwirtschaft. Stück III. Verfasser: P. Gutknecht. Berlin, 1907. 215 S., 5 Tab.—398.

Arbeiten der Deutschen Landwirtschafts-Gesellschaft. Hft. 133. Betriebsverhältnisse der deutschen Landwirtschaft. Stück IV. Verfasser: G. Stenkhoff, R. Franz, K. Vogeley, Berlin, P. Parey, 1907. 139, 117 S.; 15 Tab.—397, 398.

Arbeiten der Deutschen Landwirtschafts-Gesellschaft. Hft. 218. Betriebsverhältnisse der deutschen Landwirtschaft. Stück XXI. Verfasser: O. Sprenger. Berlin, 1912. 80 S.; 2 Tab.—398, 400.

Archiv für soziale Gesetzgebung und Statistik, Berlin, 1894, Bd. VII, S. 626-652.—97.
—1900, Bd. XV, S. 406-418.—30, 31, 33, 107-10, 254.

Auhagen, H. "Über Groß- und Kleinbetrieb in der Landwirtschaft."—In: *Landwirtschaftliche Jahrbücher,* Berlin, 1896, Bd. XXV, S. 1-55.—31, 34, 39, 42, 49, 69, 70, 101, 104, 106, 126-37, 252, 267, 268, 269, 271, 281.

Aus dem literarischen Nachlaß von K. Marx, F. Engels und F. Lassalle. Hrsg. von F. Mehring. Bd. III. Stuttgart, Dietz, 1902, VI, 491 S.—41, 50, 56, 57, 60.

Avenel, G. Histoire économique de la propriété, des salaires, des denrées et de tous les prix en général depuis l'an 1200 jusque'en l'an 1800. T. I. Paris, Imprimerie nationale, 1894. XXVII, 726 p.—81.

B

Backhaus, A. Agrarstatistische Untersuchungen über den preußischen Osten im Vergleich zum Westen. Berlin, P. Parey, 1898. 303 S. (Berichte des landwirtschaftlichen Instituts der Universität Königsberg i. Pr. III).— 108.

— "Die Arbeitsteilung in der Landwirtschaft."— In: *Jahrbücher für Nationalökonomie und Statistik*, Jena, 1894, Folge 3, Bd. 8, S. 321-374.— 75.

Bang, G. "Die landwirtschaftliche Entwicklung Dänemarks."— In: *Die Neue Zeit*, Stuttgart, 1900-1901, Jg. XIX, Bd. II, N 45, S. 585-590; N 46, S. 622-631.— 225, 277, 280.

Baudrillart, H. Les populations agricoles de la France. La Normandie (passé et présent). Enquête faite au nom de l'Académie des sciences morales et politiques. Paris, Hachette et Cie, 1880. XII, 428 p.— 29, 30, 31, 35, 41, 49, 70, 97, 100, 258, 259.

— *Les populations agricoles de la France.* [2-ème série]. Maine, Anjou, Touraine, Poitou, Flandre, Artois, Picardie, Ile-de-France. Passé et présent. Paris, Guillaumin et Cie, 1888. XII, 643 p.— 29, 30, 31, 35, 41, 49, 70, 97, 100, 258, 259.

— *Les populations agricoles de la France.* 3-e série. Les populations du Midi (Méditerranée, Alpes, Pyrénées, Massif Central), Provence, Comté de Nice, Comtat Venaissin, Roussillon, Comté de Foix Languedoc passé et présent. Paris, Guillaumin et Cie, 1893. VI, 655 p.— 29, 30, 31, 35, 41, 49, 70, 97, 100, 258, 259.

Bäuerliche Zustände in Deutschland. Berichte, veröffentlicht vom Verein für Sozialpolitik. Bd. 1-3. Leipzig, Duncker u. Humblot, 1883. 3. Bd. (Schriften des Vereins für Sozialpolitik. XXII-XXIV).— 29, 30, 39, 41, 42, 49, 101, 246.

— Bd. I. X, 320 S.— 31, 34, 39, 84, 114, 115.

— Bd. 2. VIII, 344 S.— 31, 34, 39, 84.

— Bd. 3. VI, 381 S.; 2 Tab.— 281, 373; 374.

Bensing, F. Der Einfluß der landwirtschaftlichen Maschinen auf Volks- und Privatwirtschaft. Breslau, 1897. IX, 205 S.— 88-95. 108, 238, 249, 250, 270, 271.

Bernstein, E. Die Voraussetzungen des Sozialismus und die Aufgaben der Sozialdemokratie. Stuttgart, Dietz, 1899. X, 188 S.— 266.

Blondel, G. Études sur les populations rurales de l'Allemagne et la crise agraire. Avec neuf cartes et plans. Paris, L. Larose et Forcel, 1897. XII, 522 p.; 9 carte.— 31, 34.

Böttger, H. Die Sozialdemokratie auf dem Lande. Ein Beitrag zur deutschen Agrarpolitik. Leipzig, E. Diederichs, 1900. 155 S.— 29, 30, 32, 37, 41, 51, 57, 60, 64, 65.

Brase-Linderode. "Untersuchungen über den Einfluß der Verschuldung ländlicher Besitztümer auf deren Bewirtschaftung".— In: *Landwirtschaftliche Jahrbücher*, Berlin, 1899. Bd. XXVIII, S. 253-310.— 159, 160-68.

Brentano, L. Agrarpolitik. Ein Lehrbuch. I. Teil: Theoretische Einleitung in die Agrarpolitik. Stuttgart. J. G. Cotta, 1897. 145, VI S.— 32, 75.

Brinkmann, F. Die Grundlagen der englischen Landwirtschaft und die Entwicklung ihrer Produktion seit dem Auftreten der internationalen Konkurrenz. Hannover, M. und H. Schaper, 1909. 128 S.—398.
Buchenberger, A. Agrarwesen und Agrarpolitik. Bd. I-II. Leipzig, C. F. Winter, 1892-1893. 2 Bd. (Lehr- und Handbuch der politischen Ökonomie. Hauptabteilung III. Teil II).—69, 70.

C

Census reports. Vol. 5. Twelfth Census of the United States, taken in the year 1900. Agriculture. P. I. Washington, United States Census Office, 1902. CCXXXVI, 767 p.; 18 plates.—408, 414, 421-41, 478-79.
Chłapowo-Chłapowski, A. Die belgische Landwirtschaft im 19. Jahrhundert. Stuttgart, J. G. Cotta, 1900. X, 184 S. (Münchener volkswirtschaftliche Studien. 37. Stück).—29, 32, 36, 41, 49, 178-79.
Conrad, J. "Agrarstatistik."—In: Handwörterbuch der Staatswissenschaften. 3. gänzlich umgearb. Aufl. Bd. I. Jena, G. Fischer, 1909, S. 237-255.—362-363.
— Die Stellung der landwirtschaftlichen Zölle in den 1903 zu schliessenden Handelsverträgen. Beiträge zur neuesten Handelspolitik Deutschlands, herausgegeben vom Verein für Sozialpolitik. Leipzig, 1900. 155 S.—266.
Coulet, E. Le mouvement syndical et coopératif dans l'agriculture française. La fédération agricole. Montpellier-Paris, Masson et Cie, 1898. VI, 230 p.—260, 261.

D

[*Danielson, N.*] Die Volkswirtschaft in Rußland nach der Bauern-Emancipation. Autorisierte Übersetzung aus dem Russischen von G. Polonsky. T. I-II. München, 1899. 2 T. Author: Nicolai—on.— 97, 105.
[*Danmarks Statistik*]. Statistisk Tabelvaerk, Aeldste Raekke, 5 Haefte... 1838. Udgivet af det Statistiske Bureau. Kobenhavn, [1840].—376.
— Statistisk Tabelvaerk, 3-de Raekke, 3-e Bind, indeholdende Tabeller over Kreaturholdet i Kongeriget Danmark og Hertugdömmet Slesvig den 15de Juli 1861 og i Hertugdömmet Holsteen og Hertugdömmet Lauenborg den 15de Februar 1862. Udgivet af det Statistiske Bureau. Kobenhavn, Bogtrykkeri, 1864. XXXII, 100 S.—376.
— Statistisk Tabelvaerk, 3-de Raekke, 10 Bind, indeholdende Tabeller over Kreaturholdet i Kongeriget Danmark den 16de Juli 1866. Udgivet af det Statistiske Bureau. Kobenhavn, Bogtrykkeri, 1868. XI, 135 S.—376.
— Statistisk Tabelvaerk, 3-de Raekke, 24 Bind, indeholdende Oversigter over Kreaturholdet i Kongeriget Danmark den 15de Juli 1871. Udgivet af det Statistiske Bureau. Kobenhavn, Bogtrykkeri, 1873. XI, 133 S.—376

— *Statistisk Tabelvaerk, 4-de Raekke, Litra C, N 1.* Kreaturholdet den 17de Juli 1876. Udgivet af det Statistiske Bureau. København, Bogtrykkeri, 1878. XXI, 136 S.—376.

[*Danmarks Statistik*]. *Statistisk Tabelvaerk, 4-e Raekke, Litra C, N 3.* Kreaturholdet den 15de Juli 1881. Udgivet af det Statistiske Bureau. København, Bogtrykkeri, 1882. XXVIII, 135 S.—376.

— *Statistisk Tabelvaerk, 4-de Raekke, Litra C, N 6.* Kreaturholdet den 16de Juli 1888. Udgivet af det Statistiske Bureau. København, Bogtrykkeri, 1889. LXIV, 151 S.—376, 377, 378-79, 380, 381, 382.

— *Statistisk Tabelvaerk, 4-de Raekke, Litra C, N 8.* Kreaturholdet den 15de Juli 1893. Udgivet af det Statistiske Bureau. København, Bogtrykkeri, 1894. LXIII, 163 S.—376, 377, 378-79.

— *Statistisk Tabelvaerk, 5-e Raekke, Litra C, N 2.* Kreaturholdet den 15de Juli 1898. Udgivet af Statens Statistiske Bureau. København, Bogtrykkeri, 1901. 52, 144 S.—376, 377, 378-79.

— *Statistisk Tabelvaerk, 5-e Raekke, Litra C, N 5.* Kreaturholdet i Danmark den 15de Juli 1909. Udgivet af Statens Statistiske Bureau. Kobenhavn, Bogtrykkeri, 1911. 51, 174 S.—376, 377, 378-81.

— *Statistiske Meddelelser, 4-de Raekke, 5-e Bind, 4-de Haefte.* Kreaturtaellingen i Danmark den 15de Juli 1898. Udgevet af Statens Statistiske Bureau. København, Bogtrykkeri, 1899. 15 S.—376, 377, 378-79.

— *Statistiske Meddelelser, 4-de Raekke, 16-de Bind, 6-e Haefte.* Kreaturholdet i Danmark den 15de Juli 1903. Udgivet af Statens Statistiske Bureau. København, Bogtrykkeri, 1904. 3, 60 S.—376, 377, 378-79.

David, E. "Bäuerliche Barbaren."—In: *Sozialistische Monatshefte,* Berlin, 1899, N 2. S. 62-71.—31, 34, 100, 111-15, 265.

— *Sozialismus und Landwirtschaft.* Bd. I. Die Betriebsfrage. Berlin, Verl. der Sozialistischen Monatshefte, 1903. 703 S.—41, 44, 48, 69, 70, 191, 238, 265-80, 281.

— "Zur Beweisführung unserer Agrarier."—In: *Die Neue Zeit,* Stuttgart, 1894-1895, Jg. XIII, Bd. II, N 36, S. 293-303.—240.

Déherain, P.-P. Les plantes de grande culture. Blé, pommes de terre, betteraves fourragères et betteraves de distillerie, betteraves à sucre. Paris, Carré et Naud, 1898. XVIII, 236 S.—264.

Delbrück, M. "Die deutsche Landwirtschaft an der Jahrhundertswende."—In: *Preußische Jahrbücher,* Berlin, 1900, Bd. 99, S. 193-205.—109-10.

Die Deutsche Volkswirtschaft am Schlusse des 19. Jahrhunderts. Auf Grund der Ergebnisse der Berufs- und Gewerbezählung von 1895 und nach anderen Quellen bearbeitet im Kaiserlichen Statistischen Amt. Berlin, Puttkammer u. Mühlbrecht, 1900. VII, 209 S.—195, 212-13.

Drechsler, H. "Die bäuerlichen Zustände in einigen Teilen der Provinz Hannover."—In: *Bäuerliche Zustände in Deutschland.* Berichte, veröffentlicht vom Verein für Sozialpolitik. Bd. 3. Leipzig, Duncker u. Humblot, 1883, S. 59-112, 2 Tab. (Schriften des Vereins für Sozialpolitik. XXIV).—281, 373, 374.

— "Die Verteilung des Grundbesitzes und der Viehhaltung im Bezirke des landwirtschaftlichen Kreisvereins Göttingen." — In: *Landwirtschaftliche Jahrbücher,* Berlin, 1886, Bd. XV, S. 753-811. — 281, 373, 374.

Dühring, E. Kursus der National- und Sozialökonomie einschließlich der Hauptpunkte der Finanzpolitik. Berlin, T. Grieben, 1873. XII, 563 S. — 82.

E

Engels, F. "Die Bauernfrage in Frankreich und Deutschland." — In: *Die Neue Zeit,* Stuttgart, 1894-1895, Jg. XIII, Bd. I, N 10, S. 292-306. — 29, 30, 32, 36, 40, 41, 45, 51, 57, 60, 64, 65, 70, 106, 265.

— *Vorbemerkung.* [zu: Der Deutsche Bauernkrieg]. 1. Juli 1874. — In: F. Engels. *Der Deutsche Bauernkrieg.* Leipzig, 1875, S. 3-19. — 41, 265.

— *Zur Wohnungsfrage.* S.-Abdr. aus dem "Volksstaat" von 1872. Zweite, durchges. Aufl. Hottingen-Zürich 1887. 72 S. (Sozialdemokratische Bibliothek. XIII). — 34.

Ergebnisse der Erhebungen über die Lage der bäuerlichen Landwirtschaft in den Gemeinden Willsbach OA Weinsberg, Öschelbronn OA Herrenberg, Oberkollwangen OA Calw, Wiesenbach OA Gerabronn, Ingerkingen OA Biberach und Christazhofen OA Wangen des Königreichs Würtemberg 1884-1885. Stuttgart, W. Kohlhammer, 1886. 392 S. — 41, 42, 49.

Ergebnisse der Erhebungen über die Lage der Landwirtschaft im Großherzogtum Baden 1883. [Karlsruhe, Braun], 1883]. 185 S.; 8 Taf. (In: *Erhebungen über die Lage der Landwirtschaft im Großherzogtum Baden 1883, veranstaltet durch das Großherzogliche Ministerium des Innern.* Bd. 4). — 29, 30, 31, 32, 34, 35, 38, 39, 41, 42, 49, 70, 180-85.

Erhebungen über die Lage der Landwirtschaft im Großherzogtum Baden 1883, veranstaltet durch das Großherzogliche Ministerium des Innern. Bd. 1-3. Karlsruhe, Braun, 1883. 3 Bd. — 29, 30, 31, 32, 34, 35, 38, 39, 41, 42, 49, 70, 181-82.

"Ermittelungen über die allgemeine Lage der Landwirtschaft in Preußen." Aufgenommen im Jahre 1888-89. I und II T. — In: *Landwirtschaftliche Jahrbücher,* Berlin, 1890-1891, Bd. XVIII, Ergänzungsband 3; Bd. XIX, Ergänzungsband 4. — 70.

F

Fischer, G. Die soziale Bedeutung der Maschinen in der Landwirtschaft. Leipzig, Duncker u. Humblot, 1902. 1, 66 S. (Staats- und sozialwissenschaftliche Forschungen. Bd. XX, Hft. 5). — 238, 248-55, 270, 271, 280.

Fritsch, J. Les Engrais. T. I-II. Paris, L. Laveur, S. a. 2 t. (L'agriculture au XXe siècle.) — 348-49.

Frost, G. "Feld- und Waldbahnen." — In: *Technische Rundschau,* Berlin, 1899, N 43. — 109.

G

Garola, C.-V. Engrais. Paris, 1903.—348-49.

Grabmayr, K. Die Agrarreform im Tiroler Landtag. Meran, F. W. Ellmenreich, 1896. 157 S.—169.

— *Schuldnot und Agrarreform.* Eine agrarpolitische Skizze mit besonderer Berücksichtigung Tirols. Meran, F. W. Ellmenreich, 1894. XII, 211 S.—168-69.

Grandeau. Annalles de la Station agronomique de l'Est.—263, 264.

Grohmann. H. "Die Niederländische Landwirtschaft im Jahre 1890."—In: *Landwirtschaftliche Jahrbücher,* Berlin, 1893, Bd. XXII, S. 741-799.—226-27.

Grunenberg, A. Die Landarbeiter in den Provinzen Schleswig-Holstein und Hannover östlich der Weser, sowie in dem Gebiete des Fürstentums Lübeck und der freien Städte Lübeck, Hamburg und Bremen. Tübingen, H. Laupp, 1899. X, 212 S. (Die Landarbeiter in den evangelischen Gebieten Norddeutschlands. In Einzeldarstellungen nach den Erhebungen des Evangelisch-Sozialen Kongresses hrsg. von M. Weber. 2. Hft.).—253.

H

Haggard, R. Rural England. Being an account of agricultural and social researches carried out in the year 1901-1902. Vol. I-II. London, N. York and Bombay, Longmans, Green and Co., 1902. 2 vol.—70.

Hainisch, M. Die Zukunft der Deutsch-Österreicher. Eine statistis-chvolkswirtschaftliche Studie, Wien, F. Deuticke, 1892. VIII, 165 S.—168.

Hand and Machine Labor. Vol. I-II. Washington, Government Printing Office, 1899. 1604 pp. 2 vol. (Thirteenth Annual Report of the Commissioner of Labor. 1898.)—270, 282-86.

Handwörterbuch der Staatswissenschaften. 3. gänzlich umgearb. Aufl. Bd. I. Jena, G. Fischer, 1909, S. 237-255.—362-63.

Hasbach, W. Die englischen Landarbeiter in den letzten hundert Jahren und die Einhegungen. Leipzig, Duncker u. Humblot, 1894. XII, 410 S. (Schriften des Vereins für Sozialpolitik. LIX).—76, 77.

Hecht, M. Die Badische Landwirtschaft am Anfang des XX. Jahrhunderts. Mit 6 Taf. u. 12 Karten. Karlsruhe, Braun, 1903. X, 262 S. (Volkswirtschaftliche Abhandlungen der Badischen Hochschulen. VII. Bd. I. Ergänzungsband).—399.

— *Drei Dörfer der badischen Hard.* Eine wirtschaftliche und soziale Studie. Leipzig, Wilhelm, 1895. 94 S.—29, 30, 31, 34, 38, 39, 41, 42, 49, 70, 101, 104, 111, 115, 116-25, 276, 279.

Herkner, H. Die Arbeiterfrage. 2. völlig umgearb. und stark verm. Aufl. Berlin, 1897. XVI, 608 S.—251.

Hertz, F. O. Die agrarischen Fragen im Verhältnis zum Sozialismus. Mit einer Vorrede von Ed. Bernstein. Wien, 1899. VII, 141 S.—29, 31, 32, 33, 34, 35, 36, 40, 41, 48, 76, 84, 87, 96-104, 266.

Holmes, G. K. "Progress of Agriculture in the United States."—In: *Yearbook of the United States Department of Agriculture.* 1899. Washington, 1900, pp. 307-334.—254.

Holtz, T. Die agrarischen Aufgaben der Gegenwart. 2. unveränderte Aufl. Jena, G. Fischer, 1895, VIII, 190 S.—69, 70.

—*Handbuch der landwirtschaftlichen Betriebslehre.* 2. umgearb. Aufl. Berlin, Verl. für Landwirtschaft, Gartenbau und Forstwesen, 1896. VIII, 638 S.—69, 70.

—*Die ländliche Arbeiterklasse und der preußische Staat.* Jena, G. Fischer, 1893. VI, 300 S.—251.

—*Vorlesungen über Agrarwesen und Agrarpolitik.* Jena, G. Fischer, 1899. VI, 294 S.—80.

Hubach, C. "Ein Beitrag zur Statistik der Verschuldung des ländlichen Grundbesitzes in Nieder-Hessen."—In: *Landwirtschaftliche Jahrbücher,* Berlin, 1894, Bd. XXIII, S. 1035-1043.—70.

Huschke, L. Landwirtschaftliche Reinertrags-Berechnungen bei Klein-, Mittel- und Großbetrieb dargelegt an typischen Beispielen Mittelthüringens. Jena, G. Fischer, 1902. VI, 184 S. (Abhandlungen des staatswissenschaftlichen Seminars zu Jena. Bd. 1. Hft. 4.)—70, 287-93.

J

Jahrbuch der deutschen Landwirtschafts-Gesellschaft, Berlin, 1899, Bd. 14, S. 141-145.—109.

Jahrbuch für Gesetzgebung, Verwaltung und Volkswirtschaft im Deutschen Reich, Leipzig, 1899, 23. Jg., Hft. 4, S. 283-346.—248.

Jahrbücher für Nationalökonomie und Statistik, Jena, 1894, Folge 3, Bd. 8, S. 321-374.—75.

Jordi, E. Der Elektromotor in der Landwirtschaft, Bern, 1910.—406-07.

K

Kautsky, K. Die Agrarfrage. Eine Übersicht über die Tendenzen der modernen Landwirtschaft und die Agrarpolitik der Sozialdemokratie. Stuttgart, Dietz, 1899. VIII, 451 S.—31, 34, 37, 40, 44, 45, 46, 48, 101, 102, 112-13, 115, 128, 248, 266, 276.

—"Die Elektrizität in der Landwirtschaft."—In: *Die Neue Zeit,* Stuttgart, 1900-1901, Jg. XIX, Bd. I, N 18, S. 565-572.—30, 31, 34, 254.

—*Das Erfurter Programm in seinem grundsätzlichen Teil.* Stuttgart, Dietz, 1892. VIII, 262 S.—65.

—*Die soziale Revolution.* I. Sozialreform und soziale Revolution. Berlin, Exp. der Buchh. "Vorwärts", 1902. 64 S.—42, 70.

—*Die soziale Revolution.* II. Am Tage nach der sozialen Revolution. Berlin, Exp. der Buchh. "Vorwärts", 1902. 48 S.—42, 70.

—"Tolstoi und Brentano."—In: *Die Neue Zeit,* Stuttgart, 1900-1901, Jg. XIX, Bd. II, N 27, S. 20-28.—32.

—"Sozialismus und Landwirtschaft."—In: *Die Neue Zeit,* Stuttgart, 1902-1903, Jg. 21, Bd. I, N 22, S. 677-688; N 23, S. 731-735; N 24, S. 745-758; N 25, S. 781-797; N 26, S. 804-819.—64, 65.

— "Zwei Kritiker meiner *Agrarfrage*." — In: *Die Neue Zeit*, Stuttgart, 1899-1900, Jg. XVIII. Bd. I, N 10, S. 292-300; N 11, S. 338-346; N 12, S. 363-368; N 14, S. 428-463; N 15, S. 470-477. — 34.

Keup, E. und Mührer, R. Die volkswirtschaftliche Bedeutung von Groß- und Kleinbetrieb in der Landwirtschaft. Mit einer Einleitung von Dr. O. Auhagen. Berlin, 1913. XXXI, 414 S. — 398.

Klawki, K. "Über Konkurrenzfähigkeit des landwirtschaftlichen Kleinbetriebes." — In: *Landwirtschaftliche Jahrbücher*, Berlin, 1899, Bd. XXVIII. S. 363-484. — 29, 30, 31, 34, 38, 39, 41, 42, 49, 69, 70, 138-59, 251.

L

"Die Landfrage auf den Kongressen der Internationale." Eine Reminiszenz. — In: *Die Neue Zeit*, Stuttgart, 1894-1895, Jg. XIII, Bd. I, N 12, S. 357-364. — 41.

Die Landwirtschaft in Bayern. Nach der Betriebszählung vom 12. Juni 1907. Hft. 81 der Beiträge zur Statistik des Königreichs Bayern. Hrsg. vom K. Statistischen Landesamt. München, Lindauer, 1910. [3], 215, 225 S.; 3 Kart. — 400.

Die landwirtschaftliche Enquête im Großherzogtum Hessen. Veranstaltet vom Großherzogtums Ministerium des Innern und der Justiz in den Jahren 1884, 1885 und 1886. Bd. I-II. — 70.

Landwirtschaftliche Jahrbücher, Berlin, 1886, Bd. XV, S. 753-811. — 281, 373, 374.

— 1887, Bd. XVI, S. 481-530. — 108.

— 1890, Bd. XVIII, Ergänzungsband 3. XIX, 648 S. — 70.

— 1891, Bd. XIX, Ergänzungsband 4. 579 S. — 70.

— 1893, Bd. XXII, S. 741-799. — 226-27.

— 1894, Bd. XXIII, S. 1035-1043. — 70.

— 1896, Bd. XXV, S. 1-113. — 31, 34, 39, 41, 42, 49, 69, 70, 100, 101, 105, 106, 126-37, 231-39, 251, 267, 268, 271, 275, 281, 397.

— 1899, Bd. XXVIII, S. 253-310, 363-484. — 29, 30, 31, 34, 38, 39, 41, 42, 49, 69, 70, 138-59, 160-68, 251.

— 1905, Bd. XXXIV, S. 925-972. — 397, 399.

Landwirtschaftliche Statistik der Länder der ungarischen Krone. Bd. IV-V. Budapest, 1900. 2 Bd. — 373, 374.

Lange, F. A. J. St. Mill's Ansichten über die soziale Frage und die angebliche Umwälzung Sozialwissenschaft durch Carey. Duisburg, Falk und Lange, 1866. VIII, 256 S. — 82.

Laur, E. Grundlagen und Methoden der Bewertung, Buchhaltung und Kalkulation in der Landwirtschaft. Berlin, 1911. — 399.

— *Statistische Notizen über die Entwicklung der schweizerischen Landwirtschaft in den letzten 25 Jahren.* Brugg, 1907. — 402-05.

Lecouteux, E. L'agriculture à grands rendements. Paris, 1892. 363 p. (Bibliothèque agricole). — 70.

— *Cours d'économie rurale.* T. 1-2. Paris, 1872-1879. 2 t. — 70.

Losch, H. "Die Veränderungen im wirtschaftlichen und gesellschaftlichen Aufbau der Bevölkerung Würtembergs nach den Ergebnisse der Berufs- und Betriebszählung vom 12. Juni 1907." — In: *Würtembergische Jahrbücher Statistik und Landeskunde*, Stuttgart, 1911, Hft. 1, S. 94-190. — 399.

M

Mack, P. Der Aufschwung unseres Landwirtschaftsbetriebes durch Verbilligung der Produktionskosten. Eine Untersuchung über den Dienst, den Maschinentechnik und Elektrizität der Landwirtschaft bieten. Königsberg, 1900. 56 S.—30, 31, 33, 109.

Malthus, T. R. An Essay on the Principle of Population or a View of Its Past and Present Effects on Human Happiness. London, Ward, Lock and Co., [1890]. XLII, 614 p.—82.

Martiny, B. Prüfung der "Thistle"-Melkmaschine. Aus Veranlassung der deutschen Landwirtschafts-Gesellschaft ausgeführt. Berlin, Unger, 1899. 117, 83 S. (Arbeiten der deutschen Landwirtschafts-Gesellschaft. Hft. 37).—109.

Marx, K. Das Kapital. Kritik der politischen Ökonomie. Bd. I. Buch I: Der Produktionsprozeß des Kapitals. Hamburg, O. Meissner, 1867. XII, 784 S.—267, 268.

— *Das Kapital.* Kritik der politischen Ökonomie. Bd. I. Buch I: Der Produktionsprozeß des Kapitals. 3. verm. Aufl. Hamburg, O. Meissner, 1883. XXIII, 808 S.—108.

— *Das Kapital.* Kritik der politischen Ökonomie. Bd. III, T. 2. Buch III: Der Gesammtprozeß der kapitalistischen Produktion. Kap. XXIX bis LII. Hrsg. von F. Engels. Hamburg, Meissner, 1894. IV, 422 S.—30, 34, 40, 45, 46, 47, 70, 73, 275, 278.

Maurice, F. L'agriculture et la question sociale. La France agricole et agraire. Paris, Savine, 1892. 380 p.—29, 31, 35, 36, 99, 173-77.

Mill, J. St. Principles of Political Economy with Some of Their Applications to Social Philosophy. 4 Ed. Vol. 1. London, J. W. Parker and son, 1857, XVI, 606 pp.—278.

Mitteilungen der deutschen Landwirtschafts-Gesellschaft, Berlin, 1899, Jg. 14, Stück 17, 25. September, S. 201-274.—108.

N

Die Neue Zeit, Stuttgart, 1894-1895, Jg. XIII, Bd. I, N 10, S. 292-306.—29, 30, 32, 36, 40, 41, 45, 51, 57, 60, 64, 65, 70, 106, 265.

— 1894-1895, Jg. XIII, Bd. I, N 12, S. 357-364.—41.

— 1894-1895, Jg. XIII, Bd. II, N 36, S. 293-303.—240.

— 1899-1900, Jg. XVIII, Bd. I, N 10, S. 292-300; N 11, S. 338-346; N 12, S. 363-368; N 14, S. 428-463; N 15, S. 470-477.—34.

— 1900-1901, Jg. XIX, Bd. I, N 18, S. 565-572.—30, 31, 34, 254.

— 1900-1901, Jg. XIX, Bd. II, N 45, S. 585-590; N 46, S. 622-631.—225, 277, 280.

— 1900-1901, Jg. XIX, Bd. II, N 27, S. 20-28.—32.

— 1902-1903, Jg. 21, Bd. 1, N 22, S. 677-688; N 23, S. 731-735; N 24, S. 745-758; N 25, S. 781-797; N 26, S. 804-819.—64, 65.

Neuere Erfahrungen auf dem Gebiete des landwirtschaftlichen Betriebswesens. Neunzehn Vorträge gehalten auf dem von der Deutschen Landwirtschafts-Gesellschaft veranstalteten VII. Lehrgange für Wanderlehrer zu Eisenach vom 31. März bis 6.

April 1910, Berlin, 1910. XI, 460 S. (Arbeiten der Deutschen Landwirtschafts-Gesellschaft. Heft 167).—399.
Nicolai—*on*—see Danielson.
Nossig, A. Revision des Sozialismus, Bd. 2. Das System des Sozialismus. (Die moderne Agrarfrage). Berlin-Bern, 1902. VII, 587 S.—40, 48, 263-64.

O

Österreichische Statistik hrsg. von der K. K. Statistischen Zentral-kommission. Bd. LXXXIII. Hft. I. Ergebnisse der land-wirtschaftlichen Betriebszählung vom 3. Juni 1902 in den im Reichsräte vertretenen Königreichen und Ländern. I. Hft. Analitische Bearbeitung. Summarische Daten für das Reich, die Verwaltungsgebiete und Ländern, nebst Anhang, enthaltend Über-sichten nach natürlichen Gebieten. Bearb. von dem Bureau der K. K. Statistischen Zentralkommission. Wien, 1909. [4], XLV, 65 S.—369, 383, 384-85, 393-95, 396.
Österreichisches statistisches Handbuch für die im Reichsrate ver-tretenen Königreiche und Länder. 27. Jg. 1908. Hrsg. von der K. K. Statistischen Zentralkommission. Wien, 1909. IV, 506 S.—383, 386-87.
Österreichisches statistisches Handbuch für die im Reichsrate ver-tretenen Königreiche und Länder. 28. Jg. 1909. Hrsg. von der K. K. Statistischen Zentralkommission. Wien, 1910. IV, 510 S.—383, 386, 388-92, 396.
Österreichisches statistisches Handbuch für die im Reichsrate ver-tretenen Königreiche und Länder. 29. Jg. 1910. Hrsg. von der K. K. Statistischen Zentralkommission. Wien, 1911. IV, 484 S.; 3 Diagr.—383.

P

P. S. "Die neuere russische Gesetzgebung über den Gemein-debesitz."—In: *Archiv für soziale Gesetzgebung und Statistik,* Berlin, 1894, Bd. VII, S. 626-652.—97.
Petersilie, A. "Schichtung und Aufbau der Landwirtschaft in Preußen und seinen Provinzen, nach den Betriebszählungen von 1882, 1895 und 1907."—In: *Zeitschrift des Königlich Preußischen Statistischen Landesamts,* Berlin, 1913, 53. Jg:, S. 67-108.—399.
Preußische Jahrbücher, Berlin, 1900, Bd. 99, S. 193-205.—110.
Pringsheim, O. "Landwirtschaftliche Manufaktur und elektrische Landwirtschaft."—In: *Archiv für soziale Gesetzgebung und Statis-tik,* Berlin, 1900, .Bd. XV, S. 406-418.—30, 31, 33, 107-10, 254.
Protokoll über die Verhandlungen des Parteitages der Sozialdemok-ratischen Partei Deutschlands. Abgehalten zu Breslau vom 6. bis 12. Oktober 1895. Berlin, Exp. der Buchh. "Vorwärts", 1895. 223 S.—41, 69.
Protokoll über die Verhandlungen des Parteitages der Sozialdemok-ratischen Partei Deutschlands. Abgehalten zu Hannover vom 9. bis 14. Oktober 1899. Berlin, Exp. der Buchh. "Vorwärts", 1899. 304 S.—65.

Q

Quante, H. "Grundkapital und Betriebskapital."—In: *Landwirtschaftliche Jahrbücher,* Berlin. 1905. Bd. XXXIV, S. 925-972.—397, 399.

R

La Revue Socialiste, Paris, 1899, T. XXIX. janvier-juin, p. 219-237.—260, 261-62.
Ricardo, D. On the Principles of Political Economy and Taxation. Third edition. London, Murray, 1821. XII, 538 pp.—40, 47.
Rocquigny, R. Les syndicats agricoles et leur oeuvre. Paris, A. Colin et Cie, 1900. VIII, 412 p.; 1 carte. (Bibliothèque du Musée Social).—57, 63, 69, 70, 262.
Rouanet, G. "Revue économique. Du danger et de l'avenir des syndicats agricoles."—In: *La Revue Socialiste.* Paris, 1899, T. XXIX. janvier-juin, p. 219-237.—260, 261-62.
Rümker, K. "Benkendorf und seine Nebengüter." Skizze eines landwirtschaftlichen Musterbetriebes der Provinz Sachsen.—In: *Landwirtschaftliche Jahrbücher.* Berlin. 1887. Bd. XVI, S. 481-530.—108.

S

Schmelzle, H. "Grundsätzliches zur Fleischteuerung."—In: *Wochenblatt des landwirtschaftlichen Vereins in Bayern,* München, 1912, N 47 [und folgende].—401.
—"Die ländliche Grundbesitzverteilung, ihr Einfluß auf die Leistungsfähigkeit der Landwirtschaft und ihre Entwicklung."—In: *Annalen des Deutschen Reichs für Gesetzgebung, Verwaltung und Volkswirtschaft,* München-Berlin, 1913, N 6, S. 401-434.—335, 397-401.
Seignouret, M. E. Essais d'économie sociale et agricole. Beaugency, J. Laffray, 1897. VII, 300 p.—186-88.
Sering, M. Die Agrarfrage und der Sozialismus. [Review of the book:] Kautsky, K. *Die Agrarfrage.* Eine Übersicht über die Tendenzen der modernen Landwirtschaft und die Agrarpolitik der Sozialdemokratie. Stuttgart, 1899, Dietz Nachf., VII u. 451 S.—In: *Jahrbuch für Gesetzgebung, Verwaltung und Volkswirtschaft im Deutschen Reich,* Leipzig, 1899, 23. Jg., Hft. 4, 283-346.—248.
—Die Bodenbesitzverteilung und die Sicherung des Kleingrundbesitzes.—In: Verhandlungen der am 20. und 21. März 1893 in Berlin abgehaltenen Generalversammlung des Vereins für Sozialpolitik über die ländliche Arbeiterfrage und über die Bodenbesitzverteilung und die Sicherung des Kleingrundbesitzes. Leipzig, Duncker u. Humblot, 1893, S. 135-150. (Schriften des Vereins für Sozialpolitik. Bd. LVIII).—398.
—Die innere Kolonisation im östlichen Deutschland. Leipzig, Duncker u. Humblot, 1893. IX, 330 S. (Schriften des Vereins für Sozialpolitik. Bd. LVI).—239, 266, 268.
Seufferheld, A. Die Anwendung der Elektrizität im land-

wirtschaftlichen Betriebe, aus eigener Erfahrung mitgeteilt. Stuttgart, Ulmer, 1899. 42 S.— 109.

Sinell. "Über den augenblicklichen Umfang der Verwendung von Elektrizität in der Landwirtschaft."— In: *Jahrbuch der deutschen Landwirtschafts-Gesellschaft,* Berlin, 1899, Bd. 14, S. 141-145, in section: Die Winterversammlung 1899 zu Berlin.— 109.

Sismondi, S. Études sur l'économie politique. T. I. Paris, C. Treuttel et Würtz, 1837. XI, 470 p.— 265.

Sociale Rundschau, Wien.— 169.

Souchon, A. La propriété paysanne. Étude d'économie rurale. Paris, Larose et Forcel, 1899. VIII, 257 p.— 29, 30, 35, 41, 49, 70, 81, 99, 170-72, 220.

Sozialistische Monatshefte, Berlin, 1889, N 2, S. 62-71.— 31, 34, 100, 111-15, 265.

Statistik des Deutschen Reichs, Neue Folge, Bd. 112. Die Landwirtschaft im Deutschen Reich. Nach der landwirtschaftlichen Betriebszählung vom 14. Juni 1895. Bearbeitet im Kaiserlichen Statistischen Amt. Berlin, Puttkammer u. Mühlbrecht. 1898. VIII, 70, 500 S.— 29, 30, 31, 32, 35, 38, 39, 41, 42, 70, 189-217, 224-25, 267, 299, 318-19, 332-38, 341, 358, 359, 360-61, 362, 363, 373, 374.

Statistik des Deutschen Reichs, Bd. 202. Berufs- und Betriebszählung vom 12. Juni 1907. Berufsstatistik. Hrsg. vom Kaiserlichen Statistischen Amte. Abteilung I. Einführung. Die Reichsbevölkerung nach Haupt- und Nebenberuf. Berlin, Puttkammer u. Mühlbrecht, 1909. [5], 240, 134 S.— 298, 342-45, 370-71.

Statistik des Deutschen Reichs, Bd. 211. Berufs- und Betriebszählung vom 12. Juni 1907. Berufsstatistik. Abteilung X. Die berufliche und soziale Gliederung des deutschen Volkes. Bearbeitet im Kaiserlichen Statistischen Amte. Berlin, Puttkammer u. Mühlbrecht, 1913. [6], 325, 270 S.— 298, 355.

Statistik des Deutschen Reichs, Bd. 212. Berufs- und Betriebszählung vom 12. Juni 1907. Landwirtschaftliche Betriebsstatistik. Hrsg. vom Kaiserlichen Statistischen Amte. Teil 1 a, 1 b, 2 a. Berlin, [1909-1910]. 3 T.— 297-375.

Teil 1 a, [1], 14, 366 S.— 190, 297, 298, 300-01, 367.

Teil 1 b, S. 367-681.— 297, 298, 302-09, 324-27, 328-29, 347, 356, 366.

Teil 2 a, [6], 380 S.— 189, 194-95, 196-97, 198, 203, 205, 211, 297, 298, 299, 310-23, 334, 335, 336, 337, 338, 367, 368.

Statistische Monatsschrift, Wien, 1901, Jg. 27, Nr. 1.— 169.

Statistisches Jahrbuch für das Deutsche Reich. Hrsg. vom Kaiserlichen Statistischen Amte. 31. Jg. 1910. Berlin, Puttkammer u. Mühlbrecht, 1910. XXXII, 410, 67 S., 2 Diagr.— 298.

Statistique agricole de la France. Résultats généraux de l'enquête décennale de 1892. Paris, 1897, pp. 451, 365.— 29, 30, 31, 35, 170, 218-23, 224.

Statistique de la Belgique. Agriculture. Recensement général de 1880.— 224.

Stumpfe, E. Der kleine Grundbesitz und die Getreidepreise. Leipzig, Duncker u. Humblot, 1897. 130 S. (Staats- und sozialwissenschaftliche Beiträge. Bd. III. Hft. 2).— 42, 49, 240-47.

— "Über die Konkurrenzfähigkeit des kleinen und mittleren Grundbesitzes gegenüber dem Großgrundbesitze." — In: *Landwirtschaftliche Jahrbücher*, Berlin, 1896, Bd. XXV, S. 57-113. — 41, 70, 101, 231-39, 251, 268, 269, 275, 397.

T

Technische Rundschau, Berlin, 1899, N 43. — 109.
Thiel's Landwirtschaftliche Jahrbücher — see *Landwirtschaftliche Jahrbücher.*
Thirteenth Census of the United States, taken in the year 1910. Vol. IV-V. Washington, Government Printing Office, 1913-1914. 2 V. (Department of Commerce. Bureau of the Census).
—Vol. IV. Population. 1910. Occupation Statistics. 1914. 615 pp. — 482-86.
—Vol. V. Agriculture. 1909-1910. General Report and Analysis. 1913. 927 pp. — 442-81.
— Vol. V. Abstract of the Census. 1914. — 451, 469, 485.
Tourdonnet, de. Étude sur le métayage en France. — 258.
Turgot, A. R. J. Oeuvres. Nouv. éd. classée par ordre de matières avec les notes de Dupont de Nemours augm. de lettres inéd., des questions sur le commerce, et d'observations et de notes nouv. par E. Daire et H. Dussard et precédée d'une notice sur la vie et les ouvrages de Turgot par E. Daire. T. I. Paris, Guillaumin, 1894. CXVIII, 675 p. — 278.
Turot, P. L'enquête agricole de 1866-1870. Résumée. Paris, 1877. XV, 504 p. — 257.

U

Uitkomsten van het Onderzoek naar den Toestand van den Landbouw in Nederland, ingesteld door de Landbouwcommissie, benoemd bij Koninklik besluit vom 18. Sept. 1886. [4 banden]. Gravenhage, 1890. — 226-30.
Untersuchung der wirtschaftlichen Verhältnisse in 24 Gemeinden des Königreichs Bayern, München, R. Oldenbourg, 1895. XXXII, 575 S. — 41, 42, 49, 70, 88, 246.
Untersuchungen betreffend die Rentabilität der schweizerischen Landwirtschaft im Erntejahr 1909/10. Bericht des schweizerischen Bauernsekretariats an das schweizerische Landwirtschafts-Departement. Bern, 1911. — 398, 401.

V

Vandervelde, É. Le collectivisme et l'évolution industrielle. Paris, Société nouvelle de librairie et d'édition, 1900. 285 p. (Bibliothèque socialiste. N 2-4). — 29, 32, 36.
Verhandlungen der am 20. und 21. März 1893 in Berlin abgehaltenen Generalversammlung des Vereins für Sozialpolitik über die ländliche

*Arbeiterfrage und über die Bodenbesitzverteilung und die Sicherung
des Kleingrundbesitzes.* Leipzig, Duncker u. Humblot, 1893 S.
135-150. (Schriften des Vereins für Sozialpolitik. Bd, LVIII).—
398.
Vogeley-Alsfeld, K. "Landwirtschaftliche Betriebsverhältnisse
Rheinhessens mit besonderer Berücksichtigung des Wein-
bauers."—In: *Arbeiten der Deutschen Landwirtschafts-
Gesellschaft,* Hft. 133. Betriebsverhältnisse der deutschen Landwirtschaft. Stück IV. Verfasser: G. Stenkhoff, R. Franz, K.
Vogeley, Berlin, P. Parey, 1907, S. 1-117.—397.

W

Wagner, A. *Grundlegung der politischen Ökonomie.* 3. Aufl. Teil I.
Grundlagen der Volkswirtschaft. Halbband 1-2. Leipzig, C. F.
Winter, 1892-1893. 2 Büch. (Lehr- und Handbuch der politischen
Ökonomie.)—101.
Weber, M.—see Grunenberg, A.
*Werner und Albert. Der Betrieb der deutschen Landwirtschaft am
Schluß des XIX. Jahrhunderts.* Berlin, 1900. 96 S. (Arbeiten der
Deutschen Landwirtschafts-Gesellschaft. Hft. 51).—398.
West, E. *The Application of Capital to Land 1815.* London,
Underwood, 1815. 54 pp. (A Reprint of Economic Tracts).—47.
Würtembergische Jahrbücher für Statistik und Landeskunde, Stutt-
gart, 1911, Hft. 1, S. 94-190.—399.
Wochenblatt des Landwirtschaftlichen Vereins in Bayern, München,
1912, N 47 [und folgende].—401.
Wolff. Les Engrais. Paris, 1887.—348-49.

Y

Yearbook of the United States. Department of Agriculture. 1899.
Washington, 1900, pp. 307-334.—254.

Z

Zahn, F. "Deutschlands wirtschaftliche Entwicklung unter besonderer Berücksichtigung der Volkszählung 1905 sowie der Berufs-
und Betriebszählung 1907".—In: *Annalen des Deutschen Reichs für
Gesetzgebung, Verwaltung und Volkswirtschaft,* München-Berlin,
1910, N 6, S. 401-441; N 7, S. 481-518; N 8, S. 561-598; 1911, N
3-4, S. 161-248.—324-25, 326-27, 340, 341, 353, 354, 355.
Zeitschrift des Königlich Preußischen Statistischen Landesamts.
Berlin, 1913, 53. Jg., S. 67-108.—399.

3

Заветы, Спб., 1903, № 6, стр. 39-62,—408, 410, 471-72.
Заря, Stuttgart, 1901, № 1, апрель, стр. V.—54.
— 1901, № 2 - 3, 1 декабря, стр. 259 - 302.—40, 47, 48.

И

Искра, [Мюнхен], 1901, № 3, апрель, стр. 1-2.—29, 30, 32, 37.

К

«К читателям».— *Заря,* Stuttgart, 1901, № 1, апрель, стр. V.—54.
Каблуков, Н. Об условиях развития крестьянского хозяйства в
    России. (Очерки по экономии сельского хозяйства). М.,
    «Книжное дело», 1899. VIII, 309 стр.—34, 65.
Карышев, Н. Крестьянские вненадельные аренды. Дерпт, Г. Лак-
    ман, 1892. XIX, 402 стр., XVI стр. прилож., 15 карт, 5
    диагр.—65.
«Ко всему русскому крестьянству от Крестьянского союза
    партии социалистов-революционеров». Б. м., тип. партии
    социалистов-революционеров, 1902, 32 стр.—56, 58, 62, 63.
«Крестьянское движение».— *Революционная Россия,* [Женева],
    1902, № 8, 25 июня, стр. 1-5.—54, 55, 56, 57, 58, 60.

Л

Ленин, Н.— см. *Ленин, В. И.*
[*Ленин, В. И.*] *Аграрный вопрос.* Ч. 1. Спб., 1908, 264 стр. Перед
    загл. авт.: Вл. Ильин.—346.
[*Ленин, В. И.*] «Аграрный вопрос и «критики Маркса»».— В кн.:
    [Ленин, В. И.] *Аграрный вопрос,* Ч. 1. Спб., 1908, стр. 164-
    263. Перед загл. авт.: Вл. Ильин.—346.
— «Аграрный вопрос и «критики Маркса»». [Гл. V-IX.—
    Образование, Спб., 1906, № 2, стр. 175-226. Подпись:
    Н. Ленин.— 42, 44, 45, 49.
— «Гг. «критики» в аграрном вопросе».— *Заря,* Stuttgart, 1901, №
    2-3, декабрь, стр. 259-302. Подпись: Н. Ленин.—40, 47, 48.
— «Рабочая партия и крестьянство».— *Искра,* [Мюнхен], 1901,
    № 3, апрель, стр. 1-2.—29, 30, 32, 37.
— *Развитие капитализма в России.* Процесс образования вну-
    треннего рынка для крупной промышленности. Спб.,
    М. И. Водовозова, 1899. IX, IV, 480 стр.; 2 л. диагр.; VIII стр.
    табл. Перед загл. авт.: Владимир Ильин.— 45, 46, 47, 48, 51, 52,
    55, 64, 65, 70, 109.

М

Мануилов, А. Аренда земли в Ирландии. М., Л. Ф. Пантелеев,
    1895. [1], 319 стр.—84.

Скворцов, А. Влияние парового транспорта на сельское хозяйство. Исследование в области экономики земледелия. Варшава, М. Земкевич, 1890. VIII, VI, 703 стр.—74.

— *Основания политической экономии.* Спб., О. Н. Попова, 1898. IX, 432 стр.—74.

Социал-Демократ, Женева, 1892, кн. 4, стр. 65-101.—64, 66, 67.

Струве, П. Б. Критические заметки к вопросу об экономическом развитии России. Вып. 1. Спб., И. Н. Скороходов, 1894. X, 292 стр.—82.

Ч

Чернов, В. «К вопросу о капиталистической и аграрной эволюции.»—*Русское Богатство,* Спб., 1900, № 11, стр. 232-248.—34.

— «Крестьянин и рабочий, как категории хозяйственного строя.»—В кн.: *На славном посту (1860-1900).* Литературный сборник, посвященный Н. К. Михайловскому. Ч. II. [Спб.], Н. Н. Клобуков, [1900], стр. 157—197.—34, 36, 96.

— *Типы капиталистической и аграрной эволюции.*—*Русское Богатство,* Спб., 1900, № 4, стр. 127-157; № 5, стр. 29-48; № 6, стр. 203-232; № 7, стр. 153-169; № 8, стр. 201-239; № 10, стр. 212-258.—30, 31, 32, 34, 36, 37, 48, 99, 105.

Ш

[*Шишко, Л. Э.*] *Беседы о земле.* Изд. 2-ое, пересмотренное, партии социалистов-революционеров и Аграрно-социалистической лиги. Б. м., 1902, 16 стр. (Народно-революционная б-ка. № 4).—63.

Э

Энгельгардт, А. Н. Из деревни. 11 писем. 1872-1882. Спб., М. М. Стасюлевич, 1885. 563 стр.—56, 62.

Энгельс, Ф. Крестьянский вопрос во Франции и Германии. 15-22 ноября 1894 г.—106.

— «*Предисловие к Крестьянской войне в Германии*». 1 июля 1874 г.—41.

NAME INDEX